The Bequest of John T. Ward

Uncovering A Hidden Legacy in Black
American History, Exploring Stories of
Antebellum Resistance

SHANNA WARD

PALLADIUM PUBLISHING LLC

© 2025 Shanna Ward
Published by Palladium Publishing LLC
infor@bequest1820project.com
To learn more about the author, visit
www.bequest1820project.com

ISBN: 979-8-9899755-1-8 (hardcover)
ISBN: 979-8-9899755-0-1 (softcover)
ISBN: 979-8-9899755-2-5 (E-book)

Cover design by Shanna Ward
Edited and formatted by Andrea Leeth
FIRST EDITION
Printed in the United States of America
All Rights Reserved

CONTENTS

ACKNOWLEDGMENTS

The word "bequest" typically means a gift left behind—land, property, wealth entrusted to the next generation.

But in the shadow of slavery, that word bore a crueler meaning. A bequest could be a mother. A child. A human life … passed down like livestock, stripped of dignity, and rendered into ink and numbers in a white man's will.

And yet, this is a different kind of bequest.

This is not a transfer of chains—but of fire, of names once nearly forgotten, now spoken aloud with reverence.

It is our inheritance of truth, resistance, and unbreakable lineage.

I dedicate this work, this offering, to the ancestors.

To those whose backs bore the weight of empires.

To those who dreamed of freedom in tongues they were forbidden to speak.

To those who died nameless in ledgers but live again in these pages.

I dedicate The Bequest: 1820 Project to my family—both here and watching from beyond.

To my mother, Jeanie Ward—your spirit walks with me. Even in death, you lead me. Your grace has been my compass, your voice my shelter.

To my father, James E. Ward—affectionately known as "Che"—
Thank you for the fire in your voice, the truth in your lessons, and the
legacy of resistance you planted in my soul. You didn't just teach me
history—you taught me *who we are*. You made justice a birthright,
not a choice. Because of you, I walk with purpose. I speak with
courage. And I fight, knowing the blood in my veins remembers.

To my children, Kahlil and Aaliyah—you are my heartbeat, my
reason, my revolution. Everything I do is to leave you a name, not
just a number. A truth, not just a myth

To my brother, Sharif Ward, and his family for their strong
support, with special acknowledgment to my nephew Mehki, the
youngest to carry the Ward name.

To my aunt, Jacqueline Tshaka—your wisdom sharpens me, your
fire of encouragement keeps me brave. You taught me how to walk
with both grief and glory.

To my best friend and rock, Nikko Washington—you reminded
me who I was when I forgot. You reminded me: I've never stood
alone. To my early believers—Me-Ann Ingram, Leslie Eaves, Kevin
Muhamad, George Shanklin and John Bryant—you caught the
vision before I could even name it. When I doubted myself, your
faith and financial support for this project held the line.

To the Ward family—every branch, every root:

This is ours. A testament. A resurrection. A record they couldn't
erase.

To the late Daisy Ward, who first gathered the fragments of our
story with love and foresight. She left us the beginnings of a legacy—I
now pass that torch forward.

This book is more than history.

It is a bridge back to what was stolen.

It is a reclaiming of what was silenced.

It is a love letter to the past and a beacon for what comes next.

To every child who will one day ask, "Where did we come from?"—may this book whisper back …

You come from fire, you were born from those who were meant to be extinguished but instead became light, heat, and force.

You come from those who survived the auction block and still managed to build legacies.

You come from the bequest they could not destroy.

This work would not have been possible without the generous support, guidance, and expertise of so many individuals and institutions who helped breathe life into history's forgotten corners.

To the dedicated archivists, librarians, and staff at the Columbus Downtown Metropolitan Library, the Ohio History Center, and the Phyllis Hamner Local History and Genealogy Room at the Lawrence County Public Library—thank you for safeguarding the records that tell our story. Your careful stewardship of our collective memory provided the backbone for this book.

To the tireless team at the Harvard Library, Faculty of Arts and Sciences—your assistance in navigating historical records and legal archives during the height of COVID added critical depth and clarity when access was most limited. I am deeply grateful.

To Kristi Farrow, author of the Finding Josie blog, your early research was a spark. Unknowingly, you were my first breadcrumb, pointing me toward a truth it would take years to fully uncover.

To Rita Fuller of Columbus Black History Tours—your storytelling, your walking tours, and your unwavering commitment to making local Black history in Columbus, Ohio, visible and alive were deeply inspiring. Thank you for honoring the legacies beneath our feet.

To Angela Capers, for your diligent and loving work on the Ward Family, your attention to detail helped shape the foundation of this historical journey. When I doubted, your faith held the line.

And to every family historian, courthouse clerk, cemetery record keeper, and unnamed archivist who helped along the way, your unseen labor is sacred. This book stands on the shoulders of your quiet diligence.

From dusty files to digital scans, from oral histories to fragile photographs—you helped resurrect a lineage of courage, complexity, and resilience.

I am forever grateful.

With humility and honor,
—Shanna Ward

PREFACE

History is not just a record of what happened; it is an inheritance. It is a bequest, passed down from one generation to the next, shaping our present and demanding accountability—*The Bequest of John T. Ward*. It is more than just the life story of a man; it is an exploration of a legacy—one of resistance, survival, and the relentless pursuit of freedom.

John T. Ward was born into a world that saw him as property. Like so many others, he was entered into ledgers and wills, passed down not as a son or a brother, but as an asset to be inherited. When his enslaver died, Ward was manumitted, but freedom was never as simple as a signature on a document. Manumission often came with restrictions—freed Black individuals were required to leave their home states, prove their self-sufficiency, or face re-enslavement under oppressive laws. He and his family were thrust into a world where systemic racism, legal restrictions, and racial terror sought to keep them in bondage—if not in chains, then through poverty, exile, and exclusion.

His journey is one of transformation, from enslaved child to conductor on the Underground Railroad, from a man fighting for his own survival to a leader fighting for the liberation of others. His story, long overshadowed by the grander narratives of abolition, deserves to be told—not just as an individual triumph, but as a testament to the endurance of Black resistance.

This book traces Ward's ancestry back to his enslaved grandparents, who endured the horrors of the plantation system, to his mother, Hannah, a woman whose defiance against brutality became the foundation of his own strength. It follows his escape from Virginia's tightening grip on freed Black people, leading him to Ohio—a state that promised freedom but harbored its own hostilities. It details his dangerous work guiding fugitive slaves to freedom, his near-miraculous escape from bounty hunters, and the network of Black abolitionists who risked their lives for a cause greater than themselves.

The fight for freedom was not just physical; it was economic, political, and deeply personal. Ward's story does not end with abolition. He became a successful businessman, proving that self-sufficiency was a radical act in a world that sought to keep Black Americans economically powerless. His entrepreneurial success was not just a means of survival but a continuation of his fight, providing resources to sustain the Underground Railroad and uplift his community.

Through meticulous research—letters, census records, oral histories, and historical documents—this book reconstructs a narrative that history has too often neglected. It highlights the role of Black activists, entrepreneurs, and abolitionists who defied the odds, challenging a system that sought to erase them.

But this book is more than a biography; it is a call to action.

Hope remains strong in me for past, present, and future generations that this story is shared nationwide. What my grandfather lived through—what he endured, witnessed, and overcame—is potent enough to make the world better and to fight injustice wherever it appears. If you have ever felt touched by some incredible force knowing that nothing in the physical world touched you, you know what it means to have reached the spirit world. Our ancestors' DNA is in us. For every fugitive slave that has been subject to stop and frisk on the road to freedom to those who threw themselves overboard, choosing death over slavery, we acknowledge that they live on in us.

John T. Ward's story forces us to confront uncomfortable truths about America's past. It reveals the ways in which the struggle for Black freedom did not end with the Civil War but continues today in the fight for economic justice, reparations, and the dismantling of systemic racism. Ward's life was shaped by the brutal realities of slavery, but his legacy is one of resilience, faith, and the belief that no system of oppression is unbreakable.

This is the story of a man who refused to be erased.

This is the story of a family who refused to be forgotten.

This is the story of Black resistance.

This is the story of America's reckoning.

This is *The Untold Story of John T. Ward.*

CHAPTER 1

The Click

Every great dream begins with a dreamer. Always remember, you have within you the strength, the patience, and the passion to reach for the stars and change the world.

-Harriet Tubman

I t was a hot afternoon in 2021, during the height of the COVID-19 pandemic, the kind of day that pressed against your skin like a weighted blanket. The birds had retreated into the trees for shade, and the streets were eerily quiet, free of the usual traffic. I was out on the deck, sipping a glass of lemonade sweetened with a dollop of honey. The heat made me feel lazy, and I welcomed the stillness, letting my short frame sprawl across the cushions of the outdoor bench. It was my day to rest, and nothing was going to stop me.

In the hush of the afternoon, the second hand on my pocket watch ticked louder than usual. It was a 14k gold heirloom from Elgin, over a century old, passed down from my grandfather. I'd often twirl it between my fingers when my mind was racing too fast, and I needed to slow it down. With each gentle swing of the hand, my eyelids got heavier, like I was being rocked to sleep by a hypnotist's pendulum. Every soft tick tugged me deeper, pulling me toward unconsciousness, the sound crooning me into rest.

The ticking got louder, suddenly snapping me awake. I took another sip of my lemonade to shake off the haze. More alert now, I noticed two men coming down the sidewalk—one pushing some kind of wheeled contraption, the other glancing at it every now and then while scribbling into a small notebook. As the device passed in front of my house, it let out a series of sharp clicks. One of the men gave me a good-natured wave, and I returned it with a sleepy smile.

I recognized the machine was a freeman rodometer. The "freedmen," as folks called them, were out surveying the neighborhood—digging trenches and measuring distances to expand the road. Every time they completed a section, that machine would click to mark their progress. Watching them move ahead under that heavy sun, I felt a little pang of sympathy. But then again, work was never easy. I knew that better than most.

Maybe it was the heat—or maybe it was the freeman logo stamped on that rodometer—but something in that moment pulled my mind back in time. I saw, in my mind's eye, my ancestors' bare backs bent under the punishing sun, their beautiful Black skin glistening with sweat as they toiled in fields of cotton, vegetables, and sugar cane. The rodometer's click turned in my imagination into the clatter of tools, of calloused hands hammering against hardship. And there I sat, in the comfort of rest, a glass of lemonade in hand to soothe my throat—grateful to God for a mercy they never knew.

Like so many times before, I caught myself daydreaming about my great-grandfather and the kind of life he must've lived as a freedman in the era of slavery. I grew up knowing I came from the stock of a freedman, but I often wondered—how? I also learned that my great-great-great-grandfather, John T. Ward, had been a conductor on the Underground Railroad—but to what extent? I knew he'd served in the Civil War, but why did he fight for this country … or did he? Could he truly defend a nation that once claimed ownership of his body, his people?

Though I'd heard countless stories growing up—passed down through my father and grandparents—there was still so much I didn't know. So much I still needed to understand.

I twirled what little ice was left in my glass. The lemonade was gone, and the condensation had started to dry up in the late-afternoon heat. I should have gotten up and went about my day, but the pull of my heritage kept me anchored to that seat, lost in thought.

Before I knew it, the sun had dipped low, and porch lights blinked on up and down the block. I should've gotten up too—but instead, I let the breeze wash over me as the heat of the day finally eased. The crickets—quiet for so long during the stillness of the pandemic—had returned, their song rising with the coming dark. The sky deepened to indigo, then black, revealing a quiet scatter of stars.

I leaned back into the bench, letting my body sink further into stillness. My eyelids grew heavy again, and I gave myself a few more moments of rest. I tried to count the stars, but I kept coming back to one: Polaris.

How many of our ancestors had looked up at that same star—the North Star—shining in the very same twilight sky, centuries ago? What passed through their minds as they labored under that same brutal sun, their backs bent, their spirits worn thin? Did they wonder about the ones who would come after them? Did they imagine descendants like me—free, resting beneath this same sky, a glass of lemonade in hand?

Or were their thoughts chained to the pain of the present? To the loved ones stolen in the night by the Fugitive Slave Act? To those who ran and never came back? Did they believe freedom was real—or just a cruel rumor, passed from one desperate heart to another?

As I drifted toward sleep, those questions lingered. I thought of my great-great-great-grandfather, waiting on the other side of danger, helping others escape bondage. I imagined his quiet brilliance—how he built wealth not for himself, but to lift others up and to finance freedom.

What must it have been like … to be hunted through the darkness of the forest, dogs barking, boots pounding the earth, gunshots cracking through the trees? I could almost hear the cruel shouts of the slave catchers: "Come back! Get back here, nigger!" The words tore through my mind like jagged glass.

Dark and troubling images flashed before my eyes. But I didn't have to imagine my ancestor's terror or the weight of his choices because as sleep pulled me under, I knew he was coming to visit me. He always came to me in dreams, and I had learned not to fear him.

This time, I felt his voice before I heard it. It moved through me, blending with the chorus of generations past—my ancestors, whispering through blood and memory, urging me to listen, remember, and tell their stories again. And with them came a feeling—familiar but heavy—like being hunted, not by men or dogs this time, but by something deeper, something spiritual.

It wasn't quite fear, but something close to it—a powerful awareness that things were shifting, and there would be no going back. This wasn't just change; it was transformation. And maybe the hardest part was letting go of who I had been, without yet knowing who I was becoming.

A heaviness settled in my chest, like I was carrying a weight I couldn't name. I felt off-balance, like standing at the edge of something vast and unseen. When I pictured myself, it wasn't the me I used to know. Something inside was unraveling, shedding, and making room for something new. The old routines, the familiar comfort of who I had always been, were slipping away. And though it was disorienting, some part of me understood; it had to happen.

The dreams came like storms—ancestral memories, flashes of lives not mine and yet somehow still mine—tearing through the seams of my spirit.

They didn't arrive gently.

They hit in sharp, vivid bursts, memories that felt foreign and familiar all at once. They weren't just mine; they carried the weight of something bigger, something collective, passed down like an heirloom and stitched into the soul.

They came with such intensity, unraveling the fabric of my psyche. The transition was violent and disorienting. But with each passing day, the weight became a little more bearable. Bit by bit, it felt less like something I was drowning beneath, and more like something I was meant to carry.

Still, the fear lingered.

"You are being hunted," his voice had warned, and I believed it. I could feel it. A dark presence, always just behind me, staying close to my heels. There was something in the air, in the space between my breaths, like being pulled into a storm I couldn't escape.

That prickling unease returned—like eyes on the back of my neck—something unseen, just beyond the veil, watching, waiting. The air felt thick, charged, like the moment right before lightning cracked the sky.

And just as panic rose in my chest, his voice returned, calmer this time, steady and grounding.

"You are not alone. This is part of your growth, a preparation for the next stage. It is a test. But not one you must face without guidance."

I took a deep breath and let that truth settle inside me. I didn't need to have all the answers. I didn't have to understand everything right now. The fear would come and go, but it wouldn't break me. I was moving forward, ready or not. And somehow, deep in my bones, I knew I wasn't walking this path alone.

There were millions who had come before me, and they were walking beside me now.

And, in that moment, I understood.

This wasn't about survival. It was about transformation.

The sun had set, and a frigid winter night settled in, freezing the landscape by the minute. The wind was sharp and biting, gnawing at every inch of exposed skin. Darkness had swallowed the last of the light, leaving only shadows to mark the path ahead.

***

It was the second week of February 1856. Under normal circumstances, running point on an escort might be routine. But not tonight, not with this cargo.

In his care were nine of the infamous seventeen fugitive slaves whose escape had made headlines across Ohio. Every county was buzzing with their names, and every bounty hunter from Cincinnati to Columbus was on the hunt. Helping them meant risking everything. If John T. Ward was caught, the consequences would be dire—not just for him, but for everyone in the network.

The last six clicks of the rodometer had gripped him with a quiet dread. The metallic sound, usually a steady rhythm of progress, now felt too loud, too exposed. It rattled his nerves. Even his own shadow, stretched long beneath the moonlight, made him flinch. He knew they were out there—lurking in the dark, waiting.

John T. carried a dagger tucked close to his body and a hidden pistol stowed beneath the wagon seat, his heartbeat in his throat. He swallowed hard, pushing down the unease rising like smoke in his chest. The mission had to continue—six clicks away. His hand trembled slightly as he adjusted the reins. Were those dogs in the distance or just the wind cutting through the trees? He was six clicks shy of the twelve-mile mark—six clicks from Clintonville, six clicks from safety.

The horses' hooves struck the frozen earth like the beat of an African djembe drum, steady and urgent. Their names were Freedom and Liberty, and they lived up to both. John T.'s heartbeat synced with their gallop, then stuttered every time the pace slowed, thrown off by any sudden noise and every shifting shadow.

Tonight would be long.

The wagon he drove was no ordinary cart; it was a borrowed Conestoga, rigged with a false bottom, lent by a fellow conductor in the network. A handmade rodometer clicked softly beside the wheel, its count marking each mile like a drumbeat of hope. Every click brought them one step closer to freedom. The wagon bed was layered with hay, shielding his precious cargo from curious eyes and cruel intentions.

**

Before each journey, John T. ran his hands through the manes of his horses. It was a quiet ritual, a sacred gesture of trust. They responded with a soft neigh, as if offering their own silent vow. Liberty and Freedom were rested, well-fed, and ready. His wife, Catherine, had packed fresh rye and Indian bread for the road, along with a few heavy quilts. She kissed his cheek before he left, unaware of how dangerous this night might become.

Earlier that day, while working his job as a janitor at Columbus City Hall, John T. overheard murmurs among the townsfolk. Word was spreading; a local law enforcement squad—thinly veiled as apologists—had been stationed for over a week near a neighborhood known as "Nigger Hollow," just south of the Franklin County Courthouse. It was a place where many freed Black families had settled. Most folks had no idea that the quiet janitor sweeping floors and polishing brass railings was the same man working behind the scenes to protect those families from the very men hunting them.

Normally, John T. would never run a mission like this alone. He relied on a network of trusted allies. But tonight, the risk was too high, and the window too narrow. The bounty hunters were close. The slaveholder was relentless. And the fugitives were depending on him.

His uneasiness came not only from the danger, but from the last-minute shift in plans. There was unfinished business waiting for him in Hamilton County. But for now, his hands—and his wagon—were full.

John T. reached National Pike and spotted the group—men and women waiting at a discreet meeting spot off Friend Street, arranged quietly days earlier. They'd never spoken to him before tonight. Their eyes were wary, unsure if they could trust this stranger to guide them toward the unknown.

But when John T. whispered the secret code, their shoulders eased. The tension lifted—a little—and in that moment, trust formed. No one said much. They knew better. Silence was their shield.

With a few subtle nods, they loaded the wagon. The women went in first, along with the bundles of food and quilts. Then the men climbed in, burying themselves beneath the hay. Every move was calculated, careful, and quiet.

John T. gestured to the rodometer mounted near the front wheel and leaned in close. "Twelve clicks," he whispered. "Just twelve more." He had found that showing the device—letting them see the distance toward freedom—calmed their nerves, making the journey feel real, doable.

But then he caught a glimpse of them—for a moment before they disappeared beneath the hay—and it shook him.

Their faces were ash-pale, lips cracked and bleeding from the brutal winter air. Frostbite began to bloom on their hands, and their feet were blistered raw—a clear sign they'd come far from the warmer South, most likely traveling on foot for miles. John T. knew without asking that they'd crossed the frozen Ohio River barely a week ago.

He could see it in their posture, in the way they barely held themselves upright. They were rail-thin, worn down by starvation. It was written on their bodies—evidence of a master who fed them just enough to keep them alive and working, nothing more.

Had they not seized horses and sleighs during their escape from the Kentucky plantation, they would have frozen crossing the river. Many who tried had perished in that same icy stretch, their names forgotten beneath the currents or swallowed by cracks in the ice. The Ohio River had become both a bridge and a grave.

The group's disappearance had made statewide news in the past few days—their names and descriptions repeated like a chant across Ohio. The local papers spread the story like wildfire, feeding a frenzy of speculation. Now, every bounty hunter in the region was likely on their trail—each one eager to claim the reward for nine missing fugitives.

Though the women trusted John T. with their lives, he could see the cost of that trust etched across their faces. They looked distraught—eyes red, swollen, and wet, like they hadn't stopped crying since the moment they fled the plantation. Grief clung to them. John T. could feel it radiating from their bodies like cold. They weren't just afraid for themselves; they were terrified for the ones left behind: friends, sisters, parents, children, all still in Cincinnati. They clung to each other now, whispering desperate prayers that their escape hadn't condemned their loved ones to punishment—or worse.

Looking at them, these weary souls with nothing left but hope, John T. couldn't help but think of Peggy, beloved Peggy, adored by her family. He heard the faint click of the rodometer and let the sound pull him into memory. He thought of the day Peggy's group split off after crossing the frozen river—and the tragedy that followed.

John T. and his teammates had read about it in the newspapers, but no headline could ever capture the full horror of what happened next.

Seventeen enslaved people escaped that night. The nine fugitives John T. now carried were part of the Marshall family, once held on the Marshall plantation. The other eight—Peggy Garner, her husband Robert, their four children, and Robert's parents—had belonged to the Maplewood Plantation in Kentucky.

Peggy was pregnant when they fled.

After parting ways with the Marshalls, Peggy and her family made their way to Hamilton County, Ohio, searching for an old family friend named Kite. Unable to continue on foot, especially with Peggy nearing the end of her pregnancy, they decided to take refuge with him in a small wooden cabin on the edge of town.

But the journey to Kite's door proved to be their fatal misstep. In asking around the neighborhood, knocking on doors, stopping strangers, they drew attention. Folks would later say that was what sealed their fate.

Soon after they arrived, the slave owner tracked them to the cabin. He brought with him a county marshal, deputies, and a warrant. They were there to retrieve what the law still called "property."

Unaware of the danger closing in, Kite had gone to seek help from Levi Coffin, the famed Quaker abolitionist known throughout Hamilton County for aiding fugitives. He hoped Coffin could arrange a safe house or secure transport farther north. But by the time Kite returned, it was too late.

The law had arrived.

Robert and his father reacted instantly. Seeing the master step into Kite's cabin, armed and flanked by deputies, they knew there would be no mercy. Robert drew a stolen pistol and fired, striking a deputy.

Peggy rushed to her children, panic rising in her chest. She knew what the death of a deputy would bring—swift, brutal retaliation. Their capture was now certain.

In that moment of despair, Peggy made an unthinkable decision. She grabbed her two-year-old daughter, Mary, and slit her throat with a knife. She could not bear the thought of her child being dragged back into bondage. The cabin erupted in chaos—screams, cries, and confusion, as Peggy, driven by desperation, tried to end the lives of her other children as well. She wounded them, but they survived. Then she turned the blade on herself.

She failed.

When word of what happened spread, abolitionists across the country were shaken. The story stunned even the most seasoned conductors of the Underground Railroad. But for Peggy, it had never been about defiance; it had been about mercy. About protecting her children from a future filled with chains.

The rodometer clicked again.

John T. listened to the steady rhythm of the horses' gallop and let the sound carry him into memory—into the countless stories he'd heard over a lifetime, stories of slaves, mothers, and choices no human being should ever have to make.

Many, like Peggy, chose death over the horrors of bondage. Time and again, families took their own lives—and their children's—believing it was more merciful than a lifetime in chains. John T. had heard such stories since childhood. One in particular haunted him: a family that leapt from a slave ship into the sea, clutching their children in their arms. They had chosen the ocean's depths over the plantation's cruelty.

Peggy Garner's story was no different, only more recent, more personal. Her family had endured horrific abuse. Of her four children, three were visibly of mixed race—mulatto, as the era cruelly labeled them. Peggy's body had not only been enslaved—it had been violated.

Children born from the union of a Black woman and a white man were often labeled "mulatto," and their lighter skin could sometimes offer small privileges within the twisted hierarchy of slavery. Some could pass for white, at least for a moment. But even the slightest trace of African ancestry—a coil in the hair, a hue in the skin, a shape in the nose—was enough to condemn them to the same brutal fate.

John T. Ward identified himself as a Black man, fully embracing both his heritage and the struggles that came with it. But identity, in the world he lived in, wasn't just a matter of personal truth; it was determined by others. He had no say in how he was recorded on census forms or legal documents. What white census takers saw—what they chose to see—dictated how he was labeled.

In the brutal calculus of slavery, racial mixing often influenced one's fate. Light-skinned enslaved people were sometimes pulled into the house to serve as cooks, maids, or wet nurses—not out of compassion, but as part of a larger strategy. By granting small privileges to those of mixed ancestry, slaveholders deepened divisions within the Black community, breeding mistrust and redirecting loyalty away from kin and toward the oppressor.

Only Thomas, the eldest, was fully Black. It was painfully clear that Peggy had been raped repeatedly by her enslaver; he was the father of her three youngest children. The pattern was undeniable. Every time the slave owner's wife gave birth, Peggy delivered a child the following year. It was as if Peggy had become the man's surrogate whenever his wife was unavailable.

Her body was not her own.

Even after childbirth, her suffering continued. Peggy was forced to wet-nurse the slave owner's children before she could feed her own. Her babies cried from hunger while she gave her strength to the oppressor's house.

She had thought about ending it many times before. Thought about taking her children's lives to spare them the hell she had known. But she never found the strength. Not until that day. Not until their capture was certain and she saw no other way.

On that day, Peggy made her final choice. She slit her daughter Mary's throat—not out of hatred or madness, but out of mercy. She saved her child from a life in chains.

Peggy knew exactly how her enslaver viewed Mary and the others. They weren't children to him; they were property, assets, and extensions of his ownership. Her act wasn't just defiance; it was theft. She had stolen what he believed was his.

And yet, some in town whispered that the man wept over Mary's body, that he cradled the child's lifeless form in his arms and tried to

carry her away, only to be stopped by a deputy who insisted it was
part of a crime scene.

No one would ever know if his grief was real, or if it was simply
the sorrow of a man mourning the loss of his investment.

Another click echoed from the wagon, and John T.'s mind slipped
back—ten years into the past.

It was a gift from his mother, wrapped in a weathered leather
pouch stamped with stars and a crescent moon. Inside was a
rodometer, a curious device with a rotating wheel and a tiny meter
to measure distance. To John T., it seemed sophisticated—almost
magical. The wheel turned with each rotation of the earth beneath it,
tallying the miles traveled like a silent witness to every journey.

He was fascinated. But instead of using it as intended, John T.
turned it into something symbolic. He built a replica that didn't

display numbers. It clicked only to mark each completed mile—no count, just sound. He preferred it that way. The number lived in his head, but the click was what mattered. Each one was a reminder.

The device always reminded him of her.

His mother had worked for an elderly Quaker widower on the outskirts of Clinton County. He was poor and couldn't afford to pay her for her labor, so he gave her the rodometer instead—something he'd once used on long western journeys to navigate uncharted land. It had been his compass. Now it was John T.'s talisman.

With every click of the homemade replica, John T. felt himself drawing close not just to a physical destination, but to the center of his memory. He thought of his mother, of who he was, and of where he came from.

If asked, he told people he was a free Black man from a small town outside Richmond, Virginia. And in the technical sense, that was true. But the deeper truth was harder to say aloud: John T. Ward was a child of slavery, a child of rape, a man born into a lineage scarred by violation. And still, he rode forward, carrying the burden with dignity.

John T. Ward was born in 1820 on the Ward Plantation in Pittsylvania County, Virginia. His mother was just twenty years old at the time. She used to tell him about a strange phenomenon in the northern sky the night he was born—how it shimmered in a way she'd never seen before. She took it as a sign. He was her firstborn, and she believed he was meant for something greater.

After John T., she gave birth to four more children, including a set of twins. All of them shared the same father, the plantation's white owner. It was a truth too bitter for words, but one she never hid from her son.

When the Fugitive Slave Act passed in 1850, the law didn't just fail to protect the enslaved; it actively turned the world against them. The penalties for aiding escapees became severe, and fear spread through every Black household, free or not. John T.'s growing involvement with the Underground Railroad and other clandestine resistance efforts put his entire family at risk. His siblings, aunts, and uncles began to pull away. They feared guilt by association.

They tried to stop him, not just with warnings, but with manipulation. They told him horror stories and whispered threats. "If you keep this up, they'll send you to the Devil's Half Acre."

That place was infamous. A hellish prison compound in Richmond where enslaved people were broken in body and mind. Overseen by the brutal jailer Robert Lumpkin, it was a name spoken only in fear.

John T. knew the stories were real. He also knew the deeper truth, that some of the most vicious enforcers in those places were other slaves—men forced into the role of "slave breakers," used to discipline their own under threat of death. It was cruelty turned inward, a weapon of control.

Even as a free man, John T. was not free from scrutiny. His every move was watched. He had to carry himself with unimpeachable character, as if to prove he deserved his freedom, every day, in every interaction. And still, he chose to rebel.

John T. had honored his own journey to freedom by helping others walk theirs. This group of nine was no exception. Saving them wasn't just a mission, it was a calling.

They were now approximately two clicks away from their destination, but the horses were growing restless. After covering more than ten miles today, they snorted and shuffled with fatigue, their strength beginning to wane. But John T. couldn't afford a stop—not now. Tonight, Freedom and Liberty would have to be pushed to their limits.

They knew this route well. They knew when they would normally pause for rest. But tonight wasn't normal.

John T. had named them with purpose: Freedom—quick, eager, and sharp under pressure—and Liberty—steady, powerful, and enduring. Together, they embodied everything he fought for. Just watching them reminded John T. why he risked everything to defy the law and deliver his people to liberation.

They were a remarkable breed, with a keen sense of direction. Even without his guidance, they could make their way from Clintonville back to Truro Township without a single misstep. But John T. would never take that risk—not now. The path had become dangerous. Slave catchers were getting wise to the patterns. Too many conductors had passed this way. Too many eyes were watching.

That was why, from the very beginning, John T. made a change—a small shift in course to avoid suspicion, a few extra clicks to ensure the safety of those hidden beneath the hay.

The rodometer clicked for the twelfth time.

John T. exhaled a long-held breath, the sound nearly lost beneath the steady creak of the wagon wheels. They were almost there.

As the wagon pulled up to the safe house, a wave of emotion flooded him. In the window sat an empty vase—the sign he had been hoping for. This vase was more than decoration; it was a silent code used by the Underground Railroad. The number of silk flowers once placed inside would signal how many fugitives were currently being sheltered. An empty vase meant the house was clear. No flowers meant there was space. No flowers meant safety.

He smiled. Tonight, the vase was empty. But by sunrise, there would be nine silk flowers swaying in the morning light—each one a symbol of survival.

To John T., this would be another mission completed. Another passage made. Another "parcel" delivered. But for the people he carried, this night was a threshold, a beginning, and a new name for freedom. They were finally out of reach from the men who would claim them.

With the wagon secure and the house cloaked in silence, John bowed his head. He whispered a prayer—not just for those he helped tonight, but for strength to keep going, for protection on the road ahead, and for the courage to continue even when the path grows darker.

John T. Ward was more than a conductor. He was an emissary of freedom.

***

When my eyes opened, they were wet.

I sat up slowly, reaching to brush the dampness from my lashes. The dream lingered—heavy, vivid, and alive. My ancestors' resilience, their quiet courage, had stirred something in me once again. I thought of their unity, their empathy, their willingness to risk everything not only for themselves, but for each other.

Their story—their truth—mattered more now than ever.

I stretched, stood, and gathered my things. The night air had cooled my skin, but something deeper had been set ablaze. I stepped back inside, heart steady, mind clear.

It was time to put John T. Ward's story to paper.

CHAPTER 2

The Planted Wards of Virginia

"Every European who set foot on the shores of the Americas came as an invader, not a discoverer. What they brought was death, destruction, and deception."

-John Henrik Clarke

The salt spray lashed Captain John Ward's face like a whip—sharp, relentless, and familiar. It was 1619. The Atlantic crossing had nearly broken the enslaved on the boat, but now the sea had spit them out onto the ragged edge of a continent soaked in both promise and blood. Virginia. A land wild and wounded, where empire took root not with treaties, but with steel and scripture.

Ward stood tall at the prow, his boots striking the shore like a declaration—bold and final, as if to stake his place in history. Behind him shuffled fifty souls—indentured, desperate, and debt-bound. Some were family. Most were fodder. He didn't pay for their passage out of kindness; it was ambition. Each one represented acreage, raw, untouched earth that would soon bear his name.

Fifty heads. Fifty claims. Under the Virginia Company's Headright System, the crown rewarded men like Ward for bringing labor into the New World—fifty acres per person, fifty lives multiplied into 2,500 acres, plus fifty more for himself—2,550 acres of dominion: forests to clear, rivers to bend, and people to push out.

The land was his to shape, carve, and name.

But the price of that dominion would be paid in blood—Indigenous and African, enslaved and indentured. The plantation system was still in its infancy, but men like Ward were its midwives. They didn't come with mercy. They came with contracts, guns, and prayers twisted to fit profit.

He turned and looked over the line of ragged bodies behind him. They would build his vision—or be buried beneath it.

This wasn't just a voyage. It was an invasion.

And the land—2,550 acres of it—was his reward.

The creek that snaked past his claim would one day bear his name—Ward's Creek, its slow whisper a constant reminder that the earth remembers. No deed or crown seal could silence the memory of conquest.

Captain John Ward hadn't crossed the ocean to beg for favor. He arrived in April of 1619 aboard the *Sampson*, his eyes hardened by salt and time, his ambitions as sharp as the blade on his hip. He came with fifty souls, each one earning him land through their passage. He carved 1,200 acres from Virginia's raw edge like a challenge to God.

He built his plantation like a fortress—not just against the land, but against fear, against the Company, and against failure. Rough timbers, hammered in with sweat and stubbornness, rose from the soil like defiance. This wasn't some fine estate. This was a stronghold, a statement.

And still, it wasn't enough.

The suffocating heat of the Jamestown assembly chamber in July 1619 pressed down like judgment. Governor Yeardley stood at the helm of the first General Assembly, voice ceremonial, but underneath the formalities, unrest brewed. Men jockeyed for power—new arrivals and seasoned survivors. Alliances were brittle, loyalty bought with tobacco and favors. The Virginia Company's grip was slipping, and everyone in the room could smell it.

Ward's name was known. He wasn't a stranger to suspicion. His plantation's size, its location, his private deals—all stirred whispers. Some delegates from Martin's Brandon were barred from taking their seats due to questionable land claims. But Ward—cunning and careful—had built more than a house. He had built leverage.

The fish from his creek didn't just feed his table; they fed reputations and silenced critics. His success, forged in isolation, demanded recognition. His seat in the House of Burgesses, if not welcomed, was earned through grit. It was a blade pointed not only at his rivals but at the fragile authority of the Company itself.

He hadn't come to plead. He came to claim.

And the land—the wild, blood-soaked land—answered only to men like him.

Then came the massacre of 1622.

The screams—raw, primal—still clawed through his dreams like specters of unfinished death. The stench of burning cabins, charred flesh, and spilled blood clung to the colony like a second skin— impossible to wash away. In a single, coordinated strike, over three hundred colonists were slaughtered by the Powhatan Confederacy. The land rose up to reject its invaders. Bodies lay twisted in the red clay, and rivers ran thick with the cost of arrogance.

Captain Ward felt death's icy fingers wrap around his neck that day. Only a timely warning from a Native ally spared Jamestown from joining the list of ghost settlements. But safety came with a price. The Crown, watching from across the sea, seized the opportunity. The Virginia Company's charter was revoked—its failures too great, its ambitions too reckless. Power shifted. England took direct control, placing its hand firmly on the reins of the colony.

But not everything was erased.

From the ashes and scorched timbers, one thing remained: the House of Burgesses, the first breath of American self-governance. A stubborn seed of rebellion, buried deep in blood-soaked soil, still pulsed beneath the surface. It was fragile, yes—but it lived.

Ward, bloodied but breathing, stood as a witness to that legacy. He had looked annihilation in the eye and survived. And though history might reduce him to a name etched in yellowed paper or on a forgotten map, he knew the truth. He had stood at the cradle of a nation still in labor—still screaming its way into being.

Blood and sweat birthed the American idea. And if nothing else, his name—Ward—was sewn into its earliest, bloodiest fabric.

Across the Atlantic, the axe fell—King Charles I beheaded, his crown severed from his body in a single, history-shattering stroke. The sickening thud echoed across the ocean, reverberating through Virginia, shaking the young colony to its roots. England unraveled into chaos, Cromwell's Puritan iron rule rising from the wreckage of monarchy.

Into this world came Walter Chiles, arriving from Bristol in 1638—a man of ambition, calculation, and the cold certainty of entitlement. He built his empire through land grabs, trade, and human exploitation. His rise—from merchant to burgess to councilor—was paved with the labor of the enslaved and the spoils of colonized land.

When one of his ships was seized under the Navigation Acts, it hit his pride. But Chiles, ever the strategist, didn't panic; he pivoted. He adapted. He survived.

Because men like Chiles didn't lose power. They learned how to make it permanent.

The blow came from across the sea—England's Navigation Acts, a series of royal mandates born from greed, aimed at tightening the Crown's grip on colonial trade. All goods bound for the colonies had to pass through English ports. Any ship not flying an English flag was considered a threat.

What the Crown called regulation, men like Walter Chiles saw as economic suffocation.

Chiles had built his wealth on transatlantic trade—tobacco, timber, and the human cargo packed in his ship's holds. But in 1652, his prized vessel—*The Fame of Virginia*—was seized. It was taken under a cloud of legal excuses by Captain Thomas Husband of the *Hopeful Adventure*, a man Chiles considered nothing more than a pirate with paperwork. The loss struck not just at his money but at his power, status, and pride.

He took the fight to the House of Burgesses, where he had become one of the most powerful voices. But what he got in return wasn't justice, it was *The Leopoldus*, a substitute ship offered as compensation, a hollow gesture, an insult dressed up as a favor.

Chiles wasn't interested in hand-me-downs. He wanted dominance.

He rejected the Speaker's gavel—the highest political seat in the chamber—not from modesty, but from strategy. It was a calculated move, a refusal to play by England's rules. It was a statement: You can take my ship, but you can't take my will.

He understood what others were only beginning to see: the Crown didn't view the colonies as part of a greater kingdom. They saw them as farms, as factories, and as profit. And when profit was threatened, loyalty meant nothing.

Still, for all his maneuvering, Chiles couldn't outrun the cost of the empire he helped build.

His land—vast, green, and violently taken—rested on the broken backs of enslaved Africans and displaced Native people. He might've battled London, but on Virginia soil, he ruled like a king.

But the system he helped create?

It was beginning to crack.

His bloodline carried the fire forward. Henry Chiles, his grandson, served as vestryman of St. Peter's Parish from 1699 to 1706, overseeing land disputes, tax levies, and spiritual governance. In 1703, he was formally recognized as Captain Henry Chiles—not just a title, but a declaration. He walked land steeped in conquest and controversy, his footsteps falling where trees had bled and boundaries had been born in battle.

The roads he traveled—pine-strewn and unforgiving—wound through a world built on domination. Every property line was a quiet war, every procession a performance of control. Beneath the polished veneer of respectability, darker truths festered. The plantation order thrived on suffering—hidden in ledgers, cloaked in sermons, and rooted in the very soil they called sacred.

In 1748, the brutality of the colonial system stepped out of the shadows and into the courtroom. A man named Sampson, enslaved by a man named Woodson, stood accused of stealing a horse—a capital offense, a death sentence on four hooves. The charge wasn't just theft; it was framed as rebellion, a challenge to the social order.

The courtroom pulsed with tension as witnesses—white and Black, enslaved and free—took the stand. Some spoke out of fear, others, in quiet complicity. Sampson, bound in chains yet unbroken in spirit, spoke for himself. He pleaded innocent. His voice was steady in a space designed to silence him. Against the odds, the court spared his life—but not his body.

He was sentenced to thirty-nine lashes at the public whipping post, each strike a message, a warning etched into flesh. Then he was returned to slavery, as if his pain had only been a pause in his punishment.

That one case tore through the illusion of justice—exposing the raw contradictions of colonial law. A system where a man could testify, could plead, could be heard ... but never be free.

Even as Henry Chiles recited his vestryman's oath, pledging himself to God, morality, and the good of the community, the very system he helped uphold was crushing lives beneath it.

The Chiles family legacy—wealth, land, authority—was built on these blood-soaked foundations. Power not just rooted in acreage, but in the backs of the bound.

By 1705, Virginia's mask of civility had worn thin. The elite were still haunted by the memory of Bacon's Rebellion—when poor white people and enslaved Black people dared to unite, even briefly, against the ruling class. That unity shook them. It could never be allowed again.

Their answer came swift and cold: the Virginia Slave Codes of 1705, *an Act Concerning Servants and Slaves.* But these weren't just laws. They were blueprints—architectural instruments of terror, designed to divide, degrade, and dominate.

Blackness was made synonymous with permanent bondage. Whiteness became a legal shield. Solidarity was criminalized. And mercy? Erased.

Each statute in the forty-one-point Slave Code wielded violence in ink. A silent cruelty louder than gunfire. African and Indigenous people—stripped of Christian status—were condemned to perpetual slavery. Slavery became hereditary, binding generation to generation like a blood curse.

Fear became law.

A glance. A word. A pause too long near a white man—any of it could summon the whip.

The enslaved were hunted like animals. Runaways were tracked through swamps, their footprints studied like prey, their breathless flight turned into spectacle. Notices. Dogs. Shackles. Bounties. The tools of domination sharpened with every rebellion, every escape.

But the cruelty didn't stop at Black skin. It reached into the minds of poor whites—crafting a false sense of superiority to keep them from uniting. The divide between Black and white laborers was no accident. It was a strategy.

The Headright System, once a tool to settle land, became a weapon: land for whites, stolen from Native nations, secured by loyalty to a lie.

Racism became currency. Whiteness became property.

Black humanity was erased—reduced to ledger entries, auction blocks, and inventory. Pain was legalized. Compassion outlawed.

This wasn't a mistake. It wasn't a misunderstanding. It was design.

The Slave Codes of 1705 did more than govern. They burned white supremacy into the legal soul of Virginia. These weren't just policies. They were shackles—forged in hate, signed in ink, echoed from plantation whipping posts to the railcars of Jim Crow.

Even the so-called freedom granted to Native peoples in 1691 was hollow. Declared no longer enslaved, they were funneled into servitude by another name. Their land was stolen. Their sovereignty smothered. Their nations gasped under the weight of colonial dominion.

And still—from that poisoned soil, something stirred.

Resistance took root, not in open war but in whispers. In songs sung low under moonlight, in hands that passed stolen food to the hungry, and in eyes that never forgot. Rebellion festered—silent, steady, and unrelenting—waiting for its moment to burn.

***

The Ward family's saga is no neat genealogy. It is Virginia's baptism in blood. An inheritance of dominion and denial haunted by a past that refuses to sleep.

Antrim Parish Church, 1759.

Candlelight flickered against ancient oak pews, casting long, skeletal shadows across the sanctuary. Humidity crawled with beeswax and damp earth, pulsing with an undercurrent of tension.

Two men stepped forward, their boots striking the stone floor like drums of old judgment.

Major John Ward Sr.—his face hardened by sun and silence—carried the weight of land conquered and held. A man whose hands shaped soil and legacy with equal precision. At his side stood Charles Lynch, younger, colder, his eyes gleaming with quiet calculation, a predator in a powdered wig and polished boots.

Together, they were the rising powers of Halifax County: landowners, vestrymen and enforcers of order.

Their public civility masked a deeper hunger, control of land, labor, and lineage. Their names would come to echo across plantations and courtrooms, across rebellion and law. But in that quiet church, beneath stained glass and scripture, a darker liturgy was already being written.

The congregation sat still, bathed in the amber glow of candlelight. Wax pooled and dripped like slow blood down iron sconces, casting trembling shadows across the stone walls. The silence was tense—not reverent but charged—like the moment before a blade fell.

Becoming a vestryman was no mere civic honor. It was a consecration—a pledge to uphold a system carved from scripture and sustained by subjugation, a vow not just to God, but to the quiet machinery of colonial control.

John Ward rose. His voice—deep, deliberate—broke the hush like thunder behind a closed door.

"I, John Ward," he intoned, "do solemnly declare … that I will conform … to the best of my ability."

Each word hung in the air, heavy with solemnity, laced with hidden steel. His oath—offered to both the Almighty and the Crown—settled like a shroud over the room, holy on the surface, oppressive underneath.

He wasn't just pledging faith. He was affirming dominion.

Charles Lynch followed. His voice—clear, unwavering—carried a sharp edge, a cold spark of ambition. There was precision in every syllable. A quiet confidence that cloaked something darker. His eyes didn't just reflect belief—they carried a promise and a threat.

Something stirred behind them—Halifax's future, yes—but something greater. The air itself seemed to tighten.

Their destinies were now sealed—not just by oath, but by the land beneath their feet, soil soaked in blood and ripe with consequence.

The vestry was no humble office. It was a throne.

In colonial Virginia, the Church of England wasn't just spiritual authority. It was government, economy, and surveillance. The steeple didn't just point to heaven—it cast a long shadow over every soul below.

Vestrymen like Ward and Lynch wielded real power. They levied taxes, built roads, enforced morality, and distributed justice. Their decisions shaped the rhythms of daily life—and the fates of the poor, the orphaned, and the condemned.

But behind their righteous facades lay deeper truths.

Ward and Lynch controlled more than money. They bound orphaned children into apprenticeships—labor trades dressed up as charity. They passed judgment in parish courts where adultery, drunkenness, and Sabbath-breaking were punished with fines, lashings, and public shame. The line between piety and punishment blurred beneath their gavels.

Yet under Ward's own roof, something heretical stirred. Baptist meetings—quiet, illegal, and defiant—gathered in secret.

It wasn't compassion that allowed it. It was foresight.

He understood what others refused to see: empires don't fall from thunderclaps. They crumble from within.

He allowed the whispers because he understood the strength of controlled fracture. He bent—but never broke, not yet.

Because he knew the truth. The system that cannot bend ... will eventually burn.

Lynch, meanwhile, carved roads and obedience with equal zeal. His calloused hands had shaped the timber for churches—and the invisible scaffolding of social order. Every nail driven into the chapel frame mirrored a rule enforced, a boundary drawn, a life pressed into servitude. His labor wasn't just physical; it was ideological.

Together, Lynch and Ward's vestryman ship wasn't just collaboration—it was a blood pact. A ruthless covenant forged in scripture, sweat, and subjugation. Their leadership was anchored in coerced labor, their so-called stability purchased with human suffering. Their vision of community required obedience—and obedience was built on fear.

They governed not only land, but souls. They administered not just fields, but fates. Their roadmap to the future was a paradoxical gospel—equal parts piety and ambition, faith and force.

Their legacy wasn't a straight line. It was a twisted tapestry, woven with threads of tradition and terror, righteousness pulled tight with repression.

That night, under flickering candlelight and whispered prayers, ambition mingled like smoke. Charles Lynch stood beside Ward, their camaraderie polished but thin—a sheen of civility masking the fire beneath. He smiled, but behind his eyes burned hunger. Peace reigned—for now—but war brewed in the shadows.

And Lynch would welcome it.

That evening, they were twin wolves cloaked in sheep's robes, shepherding a frontier that needed taming—in their view—and submission, in truth. Together, they presided over a quiet empire, where justice was personal, and order came at the crack of a whip.

Their power wasn't ceremonial—it was gilded, brutal, and real.

The parish levies they controlled rippled through the countryside like chains, linking households to the authority of the church—and through it, to them. The rhythmic pounding of enslaved laborers raising the walls of Ward's church beat a solemn cadence—a gospel of pain and permanence. Faith built on broken backs.

The roads they commissioned stretched across Halifax like veins, pulsing with their influence. Wards Road, pushing south, wasn't just infrastructure—it was control laid in clay, mile by mile, nail by nail. It led not only through the land but into the heart of a power structure disguised as divine order.

The Ward plantation flourished—its beauty fed by suffering. Its fertile fields, so prized, owed their bounty to the bodies bent beneath the sun, to the unpaid and unfree. A phantom humidity gripped the air not just with the scent of crops, but with an unspoken dread. Even the sugar harvested from his estate tasted bitter on Ward's tongue—sweetness ripped from agony.

He, a supposed man of God, lived wrapped in contradiction. His hands delivered blessings, but his feet walked atop a festering wound—stitched with the names of the forgotten.

Colonial Virginia mirrored his soul: a place of righteousness and cruelty, of prayer and punishment—where virtue stood arm in arm with violence. And the land remembered.

The spring evening's oath—spoken low beneath the flickering candlelight of Antrim Parish—carried far beyond those ancient pews. It was more than ritual. It was consecration wrapped in quiet violence. In that moment of silence and sanctity, a poisoned legacy was born.

What was offered as civic virtue was, in truth, a mask. What passed for religious authority became a weapon—sharp, sanctified, and unrelenting.

Behind every whispered vow stood a system: rigid, ruthless, and meticulously designed to control.

These contradictions—piety and oppression, righteousness and cruelty—became the inheritance of the European Ward line, passed like heirlooms through generations—not in scripture alone, but in land deeds inked in blood. In roads paved by the enslaved. In the quiet consent of those who claimed godliness while enforcing chains.

Their legacy is not a monument of faith. It is a monument of labor stolen and lives broken. It does not endure in stone, but in the echoes of voices buried beneath it—the cries of the enslaved, calling from the red Virginia soil they once tilled, bled into, and were forgotten by.

The story of Ward and Lynch is not just history. It is infrastructure. The architecture of American power—etched into laws, churches, plantations, and courts.

It is the blueprint of the American contradiction: a nation born proclaiming freedom, while feeding on bondage.

And the silence that followed that oath in Antrim Parish? That was not peace. That was complicity.

The red clay of Virginia, thick and unyielding, clung to Major John Ward Sr.'s ragged boots like consequence. It stuck to him with every step—earth and inheritance fused—a physical reminder of the legacy he carried and the blood price paid for it. The rivers that snaked through Halifax County murmured of old sins and older roots. Locals spoke of Ward as a man carved from granite—solid, immovable, born of the very landscape he ruled.

But his rise to vestryman was no quiet ascent. It was a seismic rupture, cracking open the fault lines buried beneath generations of ambition, sacrifice, and unspoken truths.

In the quiet whispers of history—buried beneath the weight of centuries and myth—the Ward family's legacy unfurled: part triumph, part haunting. It began with Major John Ward, remembered as a man of stature and solemnity, a symbol of honor in a time when the lines between virtue and violence blurred.

His legacy was etched into the fabric of America's brutal birth.

Ward fathered five sons: Henry, Thomas, Jeremiah, Lt. John Ward Jr., and William—all fiercely devoted to the Revolutionary War. Each bore the weight of a cause that demanded more than loyalty; it demanded blood, land, and the illusion of liberty. They toiled under the banner of freedom, though the land they defended remained tied to the backs of the enslaved. That contradiction— noble in war, complicit at home—defined the American paradox.

Some say the Ward line flowed with Irish blood as old as Jamestown itself, a family whose roots ran deep into the Virginia soil they tilled—soil stained with sweat, conquest, and silence.

In the rolling hills of Pittsylvania County, they settled—after crossing the ocean, after crossing lines of allegiance and power. There, in the uncertainty of a shifting world, Lt. John Ward Jr. was born. The details of his birth remain blurred by time, scattered between legend and fragmented records. Some claim he was born in a tent at Lower Cove, New Brunswick, while his father guarded the rear of a regiment. Others assert that in 1745, he and his brother Captain William Ward were born in Westminster, Massachusetts, their first cries drowned out by the thunder of revolution rising around them.

The Ward story isn't just one of battlefields. It's also one of diplomacy, commerce, and uneasy alliances.

The events at Ward's Tavern offer a glimpse into the volatility of Revolutionary-era Virginia. There, Major John Ward Sr.'s son, Benjamin Ward, serving as commissary, provided provisions not only to American troops but also to the Catawba Indians—the People of the River—whose respect he earned through trade, diplomacy, and honor.

It was a fragile alliance forged out of necessity. Lt. John Ward Jr., like his father before him, allowed the Catawba onto his land, offering safe trading grounds and pathways to survival. Commissary goods flowed both ways—flour for corn, cloth for hides, powder for allegiance. These weren't just exchanges. They were acts of calculated trust, formed in the shadow of war and the looming uncertainty of who would win—and who would be remembered.

This family didn't just witness history; they moved within it, shaping its edges with both conviction and compromise.

Ward and his sons stood at the crossroads of empire and resistance. Their story is a mirror held up to the fractured soul of early America.

Not merely patriots, not merely planters, but architects of a legacy built on both revolution—and reckoning.

Major John Ward Sr.'s wife, Anne—descendant of the Chiles family—wore the weight of her lineage like iron jewelry. Beautiful and burdened, her presence carried the sharp edge of inheritance. Her gaze, storm-dark and unflinching, bore the gravity of a name whispered with both reverence and fear.

Chiles. A name that echoed through vestries and courtrooms, plantations and pews—a legacy forged in dominion and discipline.

Their plantation sprawled across the Virginia horizon like a sleeping beast—a titan of wealth and control, raised not only by calloused hands but on the very bones of the forgotten. It was not merely land. It was empire. A kingdom rooted in cold pragmatism, sustained by calculated cruelty, and sanctified beneath the thin veil of divine order. The whip cracked in the name of righteousness. The ledger balanced in the name of God.

And always, the name John Lynch hovered above the family—spectral and unavoidable. Founder of Lynchburg, great-great-uncle to their line, and younger brother of Charles Lynch—the man behind "Lynch's Law"—his legacy walked a knife's edge between myth and menace. His presence was both blessing and curse. His blood ran through their veins, just as his methods left stains on their history.

The Wards, the Chiles, the Lynches—three houses bound in a blood-knot of influence, war, and wealth. Tangled so tightly, no one could say where one ended and the next began. Together, they did more than accumulate power; they engineered Virginia's origin myth: its revolutions, its roads, its courts, and its cruelty.

They built not only fortunes—but lies. Myths designed to justify their place at the top of the world they shaped.

In Major John Ward's journals, the pages detail the soldiers he housed during the Revolution—their boots ringing on his polished floors in 1781, their swords resting beside pewter mugs as they plotted liberty. But those pages are silent—willfully so—about the enslaved men and women who moved like shadows around them.

Who cooked their meals, laundered their uniforms, cleaned their vomit, nursed their wounds, endured their tempers, endured their lust, endured their indifference?

Their service—unacknowledged. Their suffering—erased. Their dreams—stolen. Their children—sold.

The scent of fear clung to that house like humidity—woven into the cotton, soaked into the floorboards, hanging in the stillness between footsteps. It was a home dressed as heaven, built on a foundation of hell.

Brutality begat brutality, handed down like a family Bible—justified in sermons, and recorded in the names of sons.

Major John Ward Sr., like so many of his class, had been raised on the lie of virtue—a lie polished by legacy, lacquered in memory, sealed with the blood of the voiceless. He dined beside reverends. He quoted scripture. But in his veins flowed the same poison his ancestors drank—a moral order shaped by ownership, softened by ritual, sustained by violence.

And one day, his descendants would have to answer for it.

Because the soil remembers. Because bones beneath fields still speak. Because even the polished halls of memory cannot silence the truth forever.

The Revolution ended. But for the Ward family, the war never truly stopped.

Their land—earned through loyalty and violence—expanded into dominion. Their names, once whispered with liberty and sacrifice, became etched in deeds, titles, and vestry records—symbols of power preserved through generations. But as their estates grew, so did the quiet rot beneath them.

The very soil they claimed as legacy had been tilled by the hands of the enslaved. Their "freedom" was forged on the backs of those denied it.

The Ward name passed down like scripture. But with each generation, the gospel cracked.

By the early 1800s, Virginia had changed—but not enough. Slavery was no longer a "necessary evil." It was the spine of the Southern economy. And the plantation class—descendants of men like Major John Ward—clung to it with the same fervor they once reserved for liberty.

The contradiction sharpened. The myth of patriotism could no longer mask the reality of the whip.

From this fractured bloodline emerged John T. Ward—a man who carried the weight of both oppression and promise in his veins. Born into a country still wrestling with the definitions of freedom, manhood, and worth, he did not inherit a plantation. He inherited its shadow.

He would not build empires. He would dismantle them.

John T. Ward was no stranger to legacy. He had heard the stories—of valor, of founding fathers, of the Ward name carved into Virginia soil. But he had also seen the scars. He had walked roads named after his ancestors, knowing they were laid by the broken backs of men who looked like him.

Where his forefathers fought under banners of freedom while owning men, John T. chose a different banner—one sewn by resistance, secrecy, and moral clarity.

As a conductor on the Underground Railroad, he became the antithesis of the world that bore him.

He turned roads into escape routes. He turned silence into strategy. He turned his back on the inheritance of comfort—and walked into the fire of conscience.

For John T. Ward, the revolution was not over. It had simply changed hands.

He was the answer to a legacy gone rotten. The redemptive echo of all the voices buried beneath the land his family once claimed. He did not erase history—he rewrote its terms.

Because even bloodlines drenched in contradiction can still birth freedom. Even poisoned trees can drop righteous fruit.

CHAPTER 3

Birth of a Plantation

"When you make men slaves, you deprive them of half their virtue; you set them, in your own conduct, an example of fraud, rapine, and cruelty."

-Olaudah Equiano

They didn't stumble into it. They engineered it.

The Europeans birthed the plantation through conquest—bold, blood-soaked, and unrelenting.

It began with stolen land. Land seized through royal charters, treacherous treaties, and genocidal force. Forests were leveled. Rivers were redirected. Native villages were erased. It wasn't a settlement. It was erasure.

Next came the money. Aristocrats, investors, and merchants from across the Atlantic—distant men with powdered wigs and cold ledgers—bankrolled the project. They never set foot on the soil they claimed. They never heard the screams. But their coin paid for ships, chains, sugar mills, and human cargo.

The enslaved were the foundation. Africans—torn from their homes, shackled in darkness, sold beneath fluttering European flags—were forced to cross an ocean that swallowed names, gods, and freedom. They arrived on strange shores and were fed into the furnace of empire.

To make it grow, they turned brutality into policy.

They lashed backs until fields were fertile. They worked children until their bones bent like saplings. They raped, divided, renamed, and reduced people into property.

And they kept records of it all: every pound of tobacco, every body broken, and every profit margin exceeded.

The plantation thrived not by accident, but by design. It became a living machine, land devouring forests, labor devouring lives, and overseers devouring souls.

And when the soil grew tired, or the enslaved too old to labor, they bought more or bred them.

To protect it, they wrote laws—codes that made Blackness a crime and whiteness a weapon. They taught themselves lies— lies about inferiority, lies about destiny, lies about God's will.

They whispered those lies to their children, wrapped them in sermons, and used them to sleep through nights while blood soaked the roots of their fortune.

That is how they built it:

With land soaked in conquest.

With labor purchased in chains.

With power sustained by cruelty.

And with silence—the silence of generations who knew but looked away.

The plantation was never just a field. It was a system, a strategy, a slow, grinding war against the human spirit.

And some of its ghosts still walk among us.

The Ward Plantation clawed its way to renown—a monument to ambition, sculpted from sweat and suffering. Its rise owed much to diligent stewardship, yes—but its foundation was laid upon the broken backs of enslaved people. Their cries, unheard but unforgotten, echo silently through the centuries.

Major John Ward Sr., the ambitious vestryman who moved like a shadow beside Lynch, was its architect. He laid more than roads and buildings. He laid the bones of a culture steeped in oppression, a legacy that would fester through generations.

Virginia's hills, lush and deceptively beautiful, carried the scent of rich earth mingled with the bitter tang of blood. The Staunton, Dan, and Banister Rivers—lifelines of both survival and sorrow—snaked through valleys where the vibrant green of tobacco fields masked a brutal truth. Profit perfumed the scene, sweet and heavy, but beneath it lingered the unmistakable scent of bondage—the crop that made their fortune was built on the denied humanity of those who planted it.

The journey to the market was a trial—a slow, grinding march against distance and decay. Hogsheads—massive barrels swollen with tobacco—groaned with each mile. Wagons rattled. Boats creaked. Men groaned. River workers, sun-beaten and calloused, fought the currents of the James. Their struggle, their labor, was the unseen cost behind the planters' wealth.

At the heart of this colonial world ...

Major John Ward—ambitious, relentless—along with his wife Anne Chiles, daughter of respected vestryman Henry Chiles, built their empire near the mouth of the Otter River. The land came through inheritance after Henry's death. By the 1760s, the Ward Mansion stood tall—a three-story monument to power and greed. Its polished floors and hand-wrought nails mocked the enslaved hands that built it.

Major John Ward Sr. and Anne Ward had seven children, each born into a legacy of survival and ambition:

- Lieutenant John Ward Jr., unmarried, died guarding the ancestral home.
- William Ward, who married into the wealthy Adams family, claimed a future in Pittsylvania after serving in the Revolution.

- Agatha Ward, beautiful and tragic, married into the Calloway family—only one of her eight children survived.
- Anne Ward, twice married—to Christopher Lynch and Benjamin Dillard—wove her lineage through the veins of Virginia's elite.
- Henry Ward, long-lived and dutiful, bore the burden of continuity.
- Jeremiah Ward, drawn by the call of the frontier, went west to Texas.
- Thomas Ward, the youngest, helped shape the wilds of Ohio into new territory.

The earth held onto some of them, refusing to release their names from its clay.

Lieutenant John Jr.—stoic and silent—died unmarried, his life tethered to the home like a watchman guarding ghosts. William Ward, a Revolutionary War captain, carved his name into Pittsylvania's history. Major Henry Ward inherited land and influence, his presence casting a long, commanding shadow over the next generation.

Others wandered into the wild.

Agatha's life was marked by grief, with eight children, only one lived. Anne was a survivor—crafty, strategic—twisting fate through marriage. Jeremiah answered the call of open skies, seeking liberty deep in Texas. Thomas, a dreamer and laborer, helped build Ohio from untouched land.

By the 1760s, their mansion stood—its elegance concealing a brutal truth. Corner fireplaces warmed its polished rooms, but beyond the walls, cold winds tore across fields worked by enslaved hands. Every nail in the front door gleamed with pride yet whispered pain.

The Virginia earth, red and iron-rich, clung to John Ward's boots like memory. From the ridges of King William to the open fields of Amelia, the land bore his name, in deeds, won in battle. He was not merely born to this—he took it.

John Ward married Anne Chiles, granddaughter of Captain Paul Harrelson, a sea-faring man who once claimed a life in New Kent County. Her family name spoke of status and structure—while John, forged by wilderness and war, brought force. Together, they were the union of aristocracy and survival.

But their wealth was not built on virtue.

It was built on law—laws written to protect slavery. John, by then a major in the Bedford Militia, rode across his lands as if ordained— not by faith, but by force. The neat rows of tobacco were planted in pain. The smoke and clay that lingered weren't comforting, they were evidence. This was not simply a home. It was a dynasty. A plantation birthed in war, secured by marriage, and watered in blood.

Yet prosperity carried brutal truths.

Samuel Ward, enslaved by the family of Major John Ward, lived each day under the shadow of freedom's cruel jest. Every breath was a reminder that liberty—so loudly proclaimed by the nation—was not meant for him. The lineage of John T. Ward would one day trace back to Samuel, anchoring his name and bloodline deep in the grim soil of the plantation.

Lucy, Samuel's wife, bore his children—each birth a miracle and a sentence. Their futures hung perilously between the harsh certainty of bondage and the fragile hope of escape. They were born as property, their lives feeding the wealth of the European-descended Ward family—valued not for their dreams, but for their labor, their bodies, their obedience.

Samuel faced an agonizing choice: flee into the unknown, chasing a freedom that might never come—or stay, bound not just by chains, but by love. Loyalty to Lucy. To the children who called him Papa in whispers when the night was safe. To abandon them was to taste freedom alone. To stay was to remain enslaved in body, but not in spirit.

It was the kind of decision that tore a man in two.

Stories of defiance swirled through the quarters, none more haunting than that of Mark Codman. Samuel had heard the tale of 1755 since childhood, when he was just eight years old. Whispers of rebellion turned to horror as Codman's body swung grotesquely in a metal gibbet for twenty years. Codman's desperate act to reunite with his family had become legend.

Codman, violently ripped from his loved ones, watched helplessly as one of his children was sold like livestock. His story lived on in infamy, even referenced by Paul Revere in letters during his famous midnight ride. Codman's only crime? Trying to hold on to family in a world built to rip it apart.

In an act of rebellion, he torched his master's warehouses, hoping the loss would force his loved ones to be sold to a more merciful owner. But the plan failed. When the cruelty escalated—when their master blinded an elderly enslaved man—Codman and two women poisoned him. And though the poison worked, justice did not follow.

One woman was burned at the stake. The other was sold into the hell of the West Indies sugar fields. Codman was hanged, his body left to rot in a metal gibbet for two decades—his bones creaking in the wind as a warning to all who dared dream of freedom.

Samuel was eight when they took Codman down.

The psychological scars ran deep. Samuel weighed his options every day. Stay, and live in chains beside his family—or run, and risk losing them forever. The stability of the plantation was cruel and cold. But it offered the illusion of safety. Freedom promised dignity, but it came with death at its heels.

Major John Ward, returned from war, brought with him not just medals, but a vision. The Revolution hadn't ended slavery, it refined it. What was once brute force became doctrine. Chaos became strategy.

Samuel watched the plantation rise—its mansion the mind, its quarters the body, its fields the veins pulsing with enslaved labor. The laws passed in Richmond became its skeleton: no reading, no gathering, no movement without white approval. This wasn't slavery of old. It was engineered—systemic, psychological warfare.

They split the people: house slave versus field slave, light skin versus dark, man against woman, old against young. A strategy meant to divide so no one could dream together.

Samuel had seen beatings for speaking out of turn, girls taken into the mansion and never returning the same. Mothers who didn't cry—because the crying had been beaten out of them long ago.

The plantation taught you how to forget. Forget your name, your language, your people. You weren't born. You were bred.

And the worst part? They made you complicit, extra food for betrayal, a cloth coat for turning in a runaway. They made you fear solidarity more than you feared the lash.

Samuel went quiet, not because he agreed—but because silence was survival. He carried the names of his ancestors like sacred drums in his chest, but never dared speak them. He survived in body. His spirit stayed hungry.

Major Ward thought himself benevolent—quoting scripture, offering "guidance." But Samuel saw the truth in his eyes: the cold gleam of a man proud of a machine that ran on bones.

And Samuel … dreamed, but not of peace. His dreams burned. They were filled with fire, with blood, with voices rising.

He didn't yet know what he would do.

Only that if he stayed silent too long, whatever remained of him would vanish.

The plantation was built to crush him. But in every whispered prayer, in every shared look of defiance, in every hand that scratched a forbidden word into the dirt, Samuel saw something dangerous.

Memory. Unity. Rage.

The masters built systems to kill hope.

But Samuel had learned something they didn't count on:

Hope, once buried, doesn't die.

It germinates.

After Anne's passing, the scent of sorrow lingered like smoke around Major John Ward. He found solace in Sarah Clark Lynch—a widow forged from frontier steel and quiet grace, the daughter of the indomitable Christopher Clark. A Quaker woman of fierce conviction, Sarah paid dearly for love, cast out by her own for marrying beyond her faith. Her sacrifice—like her love—was defiant, deep, and unshakable.

Together, John and Sarah spent their final years in the mansion, its timbers groaning under the weight of their history—echoes and memories stitched into every beam. Beneath the estate's silent stones, their dust now mingled—Sarah departing in 1792, John in 1816. Though the mansion itself was eventually claimed by fire, consumed in the hungry blaze of time, the surviving outbuildings still stand weathered, defiant sentinels of a forgotten empire.

Their stones murmur to those who dare to listen. The wind through ancient trees carries their saga—a legacy carved into the earth, alive in the soil, etched into the marrow of a nation that remembers, even when it tries to forget.

In 1805, John Ward—a man whose ambition burned like the fires of his tavern kitchen—secured his license. The original structure was a meager shack, a whisper of the empire he craved. But his sons, John Jr. and Jeremiah—ravenous wolves in sheep's clothing, eager to inherit their father's ruthless hunger for power—would transform it. It became legend. Dubbed the "Waldorf Astoria of Pittsylvania County," it stood as a glittering oasis of indulgence rising from the dust.

The kitchen was a storm—a brutal ballet of heat, sweat, and frantic hands. The reek of woodsmoke mingled with the tang of curing meat from the smokehouse—a temple to gluttony that hung heavy in the air. Polished wood gleamed under gaslight in the carriage house, a seductive promise to weary travelers on the treacherous road between Lynchburg and Danville. The very air pulsed with life: the raucous laughter of revelers, the clinking of glasses like a morbid symphony, and hushed whispers exchanged over smoky drinks.

The sulfur springs, waters once thought to heal aching feet, added a layer of mystique, drawing a constant stream of souls into their intoxicating embrace. The aroma of fine wines, expensive tobacco, and unspoken desires clung to everything—a suffocating perfume of power.

For decades, Ward's Tavern stood as a brutal testament to their dominion, a stage where the Ward family's drama played out beneath a judging moon. Their reach extended far beyond its walls. Wards Road—a monument to Major John Ward's ambition and engineering—snaked like a venomous serpent from Ward's Ferry on the Staunton River to Lynch's Ferry on the James. It was more than a route; it was a chokehold on the region's economy.

By 1809, a chill wind whispered secrets through ancient oaks as Major John Ward—his ambition sharp and cold—dictated his final testament. Three thousand nine hundred fifty-eight acres stretched across Bedford, Campbell, Pittsylvania, and Amherst Counties—a land empire now to be divided by legacy. The parchment crackled beneath the weight of history. Etched upon it were a grand stone house in Lynchburg, its gray facade a silent monument to power; tracts of fertile soil steeped in tobacco and toil; holdings in Franklin, Patrick, and Montgomery—raw lands heavy with potential, and with ghosts. His kingdom fell to a brood of ambitious heirs. The will read like a ledger of legacy.

He named the following children in his will: William Ward, John Ward Jr., Henry Ward, Agatha Ward Calloway, Anne Ward Dillard. Tracts named Hoopers and Island—names heavy with ghosts. Each child received a piece of his soul, carved into Virginia's soil—a reflection of his possessiveness and a desperate hope that they would carry it forward.

A bond of sixty thousand dollars was posted with the execution of Major John Ward's will, an enormous sum for 1809. In probate law, a bond serves as a safeguard, a pledge of honesty, binding the executor to preserve the estate's wealth. The larger the fortune, the heavier the bond. In Ward's case, it was not mere paperwork; it was a declaration of empire. Adjusted for inflation, that sixty thousand dollars equals roughly $1.54 million in 2025. Yet even that modern figure cannot capture its true weight. In the early nineteenth century, wealth was measured not only in coin but in land, crops, and the lives forced to cultivate them. When viewed through the lens of labor value, Ward's estate—nearly 3,958 acres spanning Virginia's richest counties—would translate to tens or even hundreds of millions today. His prosperity was built on an economy sustained by the unpaid labor of enslaved people, whose toil turned soil into currency and bondage into generational wealth. The bond he posted was not only a legal formality—it was the quiet signature of a system where human lives were collateral for legacy.

Lieutenant John Jr.—a solitary sentinel—burned with quiet intensity, bright but untethered. William married into the Adams family, their wealth a gilded cage he later abandoned for the rugged promise of Pittsylvania. The Staunton River twisted through Ward lands like a capricious serpent, bearing witness to the family's rise. Its waters mirrored the storm of a nation's birth, and the iron will that drove them.

But foremost among them: Lieutenant John Ward Jr.

He inherited more than stone and soil. He inherited Samuel and Molly, another slave—and the hundreds like them—whose backs had been broken under the Southern sun to sustain the Ward dynasty.

Samuel stood out.

A man whose gaze held decades of quiet defiance. Once a trusted overseer, now a shadow somewhere between obedience and rebellion, he moved through the Ward estate like a ghost with weight—silent, watchful, dangerous.

Unspoken truths hung heavy. Between master and enslaved, silence screamed through the rustling leaves.

In 1810, a toll bridge rose near Ward's Ferry—a spine of stone and strategy. Ward's Toll Bridge, constructed by enslaved labor, later folded into Virginia's highway system. But its bones whispered of forced hands. It was more than infrastructure—it was an empire built from bondage. A monument not to genius, but to greed.

***

Samuel's lineage was rooted in that soil.

His children with Lucy bore names passed carefully through generations: Simon, Hannah, Samuel Jr., Mary, Joseph, and Rachel. By 1827, over two dozen of their descendants were accounted for among their enslaver's wealth. Their names—family—used as inventory.

Still, Samuel held his fractured family together through endurance. The plantation twisted love into a cage stronger than iron. The fear of losing one another outweighed the desire to flee. That was the cruelty of it—bondage not just of body, but of heart.

Samuel remained. But within him burned the memory of Mark Codman and countless others who dared dream. Could he condemn Mark for fighting fire with fire? Scripture clashed with survival. Was endurance holy, or was it just another death? Samuel prayed—but heaven stayed quiet.

Was God watching?

Did He care?

Samuel stood at the edge of the tobacco field, morning fog curling low like a ghost's breath across the soil. The iron tang of dew mixed with the bitter scent of tobacco—sharp, acrid, alive. His hands were already stained with the resin of harvest, though the sun had yet to rise above the ridgeline.

He couldn't remember a time when his hands were clean.

Behind him, the great house loomed like a tombstone—tall, gray, and watching without eyes. Major Ward had built it with pride. Lieutenant John Ward Jr. now paced its halls with ambition. And Samuel—he moved through both men's shadows, half-man, half-tool, always measured, always watched.

He had once been called "trusted."

The overseers gave him a hat.

The house gave him meat on Sundays.

The other enslaved men gave him distance.

But Samuel knew what he was.

A bridge. A buffer. A blade turned inward.

His job was to keep order, count quotas, and report trouble. And if needed, punish those who stepped out of line. But every lash he didn't deliver became a silent act of resistance. Every warning whispered instead of shouted; every moment bought before the overseer arrived was a piece of himself he tried to salvage from the system that owned him.

He hated the Wards.

And he feared them.

And somewhere, in the corner of his soul that still remembered what love used to feel like—he pitied them.

Because he had seen it all. The quiet cruelty behind the silverware. The madness behind the family Bible. The way Lt. John Ward Jr. looked at the land—not as inheritance, but as empire.

One day, Samuel thought, this machine would crack. It had to. Something built on so much blood couldn't stand forever.

Until then, he endured, not because he was weak, but because he was waiting.

Waiting for a sign.

Waiting for an opening.

Waiting for the fire to come.

And when it did—he wouldn't look away.

The Ward Plantation rose from greed and violence. It fell with a whimper. But its echoes remained, long after the final deed was signed.

And still—the legacy did not vanish.

Major John Ward's ghost hovered. His descendants carried on the weight of his choices. The mansion was gone, but the land remembered, its memory lived not in documents alone, but in the wind, the woods, the rustle of leaves, and the metallic taste of blood money that still hung in the air.

From those beginnings—blood-sealed and boundary-marked— the Ward Plantation was born.

Not in a moment, but over generations.

It started with a marriage, John Ward and Anne Chiles, a strategic union of muscle and money, frontier and coastal prestige. Their 3,200 acres along the Staunton River swelled to 20,000 across Bedford, Pittsylvania, and Appomattox. Land that had once been wild, now bent beneath the yoke of profit.

And with the land came the system.

To hold it, they built the machine.

Structured. Intentional. Merciless.

The Ward Plantation wasn't just raised with timber and mortar. It was constructed with a blueprint of Southern aristocracy. Enslaved people became currency. The law—slave codes passed down like sacred scrolls—guaranteed control. The Willie Lynch doctrine didn't need to be named—it was already alive in the bones of Virginia's ruling class.

Divide the enslaved. Reward betrayal. Shatter families. Replace identity with labor.

The Wards didn't just inherit the system. They perfected it.

Samuel Ward was born into this world.

He carried the name, but not the freedom. His body belonged to the land his ancestors helped clear. His life was inked into the ledger like livestock. Yet, something in him resisted.

He loved Lucy—his wife, his anchor. Their children, though born into chains, were his rebellion. Their laughter, fleeting and soft, was proof that humanity could survive inside the belly of empire.

The Ward Plantation stood as a monument to the contradiction of America: manicured rows masking brutal roots. The mansion's polished floors had been washed with sweat. Every acre was a graveyard of forgotten names.

But history remembers.

And as the Ward name passed down—Major John, then to his children, and their children—the land kept memory. It held the blood, the bones, and the truth.

Samuel's descendants would carry both the name and the burden.

One day, a boy named John T. Ward would rise—not as a master, but as a conductor. He would choose freedom over comfort, resistance over inheritance.

He would walk the Underground Railroad.

He would be the answer to the lie his bloodline once told.

Because even trees planted in poisoned soil can still bear righteous fruit.

CHAPTER 4

Bequeathed

"I can be changed by what happens to me,
But I refuse to be reduced by it."

-Maya Angelou

The clock's relentless tick—eleven p.m.—hammered against the strained silence of my office. My back ached, a dull pain echoing a deeper one in my soul. The plush office chair offered no comfort; even the softness of my pillows felt distant, almost mocking. But the silence was deceptive—a thin veil hiding the storm of John T. Ward's turbulent existence, a life whose depth I was only beginning to grasp.

What were his nights like? Not the gentle hum of my air-conditioned sanctuary, but the suffocating heat of a Virginia slave cabin. Bodies packed tight in cramped quarters, air thick with sweat and dread. The raw, bitter tang of fear mixed with the metallic taste of exhaustion—a twilight of despair that never lifted. His dreams, if he had any, were likely shattered fragments of terror, nightmares born from the day's brutality. The relentless cycle: sunup to sundown labor, followed by restless, uneasy sleep. A rhythm of survival wrapped in chains.

How did he endure?

The question clawed at my chest. Then, cutting through the quiet—like a whisper, like a scream—came his voice. A voice torn from the folds of time, John T. Ward, not just letters on some faded census page, but a living soul crying out for justice. A man who, in the face of unspeakable oppression, had the audacity to live, to fight, and to love.

The surface I'd barely scratched cracked wide open, revealing a chasm deeper than records and registries could ever hold. It wasn't just research anymore. It was personal. A fire lit in my chest—a desperate, burning need to tell his story.

Morning came, and with it, fury.

"You were not a commodity, John T.! You were a man! A person! My grandfather!" My voice rose with conviction. "I will not let your story vanish into obscurity."

That moment became more than a promise. It was a vow. A sacred oath against silence. The brittle ledgers and cold census reports reduced his existence to a fraction—shadows of lives counted not in years, but in lashes. Humans were marked as property. Lives boiled down to digits, tallied by men who felt nothing. That truth—unflinching, ugly—fueled my resolve. These stories needed to be told. Their humanity needed to be restored.

The weight of that legacy pressed against John T. from birth, the shadow of his name stretching far and wide. But in that darkness, a flicker of resilience remained—passed down like a secret, smoldering in his bones, waiting to burn.

The scent of dust and forgotten truths hung in the air. Maya Angelou's words clawed at my soul: "I may be sold tomorrow, but you know I was here." That echoed through me. John T. Ward—his name whispered through the corridors of time, not a footnote but a flame, not a statistic, but a man.

His story branded itself into my marrow. Every ancestor who came before him, every soul who dared to dream of freedom—they cried out through him.

This wasn't just research anymore.

It was an excavation.

Each fact I uncovered felt like pulling bones from sacred ground. The silence of my office became unbearable, broken only by the scribble of my pen as I tried to capture it all—the pain, the dignity, the fight.

John T. Ward's story became a battle cry.

A refusal to be erased.

All my life I'd heard the family tale—that John T. Ward was born free. But now I knew the truth. He was born into bondage. Born to be passed down like a possession. Born to be bequeathed.

But not broken.

And the silence surrounding that truth? It would not hold.

It would shatter.

Bequeathing wealth has long been the strategic legacy of the European Ward family—a tradition that continues to this day. For them, to "bequeath" something in a will wasn't just about passing things down. It was a power move, a calculated strategy, a way to lock in wealth, preserve dominance, and make sure influence stayed exactly where they wanted it … in the hands of blood.

When the European Wards of Virginia crafted a will, it wasn't out of sentiment—it was about control. They didn't just pass down land, money, and status; they built an empire, one generation at a time. And they made sure it couldn't be touched by outsiders. Every clause, every condition, every signature was designed to keep the family name heavy and untouchable.

Wealth, for them, wasn't meant to scatter. It was meant to consolidate. To grow stronger as it passed down. That's why they leaned on systems like primogeniture—giving the bulk of the estate to the eldest son—to keep landholdings intact. The younger sons? They didn't get left behind. They were strategically placed in the military, the church, or family-backed businesses. That way, they were still moving the family's agenda forward, just from a different angle.

Marriage was never just about love. For families like the Wards, it was a business deal. Daughters were married off to cousins, second cousins, even uncles if needed—all to keep the bloodline "pure" and the wealth untouched. Intermarriage wasn't taboo—it was tradition. And every union tightened the grip they had on land, labor, and legacy.

Owning land meant power. And they weren't about to give that up. Land wasn't sold. It was leased, traded among family, or locked away in trusts. Many wills had clear instructions: "This land is not to be sold outside the family." That's how they kept their grip strong and their influence woven deep into Virginia's political and economic fabric.

But what cuts the deepest—what hurts the most—is that enslaved people were part of that legacy, written into those wills right next to the livestock and the land. Human beings, treated like property, passed down to secure the future of someone else's family. When

a plantation owner died, enslaved families didn't just face grief—
they faced fear. Death often brought separation, sale, or worse, all
depending on the whims of the heirs.

This system didn't just create wealth. It created dynasties.
The Wards—and other families like them—used law, marriage,
economics, and human exploitation to make sure their name and
their money stayed relevant long after the ink on the will had dried.
And it worked. Many of America's wealthiest families today can trace
their advantage back to this very formula: wealth protected by blood,
sealed with legal power, and passed down without interruption.

So, when we talk about bequeathing, we're not just talking about
leaving a house to someone in the family. We're talking about a
system. One that was designed, on purpose, to keep the power in the
family name—and to keep everybody else out.

The Ward family's legacy, like so many others, wasn't built by
chance. It was built by design. And that design left scars that still
show up in the present—through the land they still own, the wealth
they still control, and the names they made sure would never be
forgotten.

"I give and bequeath to my beloved son William Ward all my
lands above the mouth of Old Woman's Creek adjoining Staunton
River which he has a patent for. Also his proportional part of all
personal estate during his natural life and after his death to descend

to his three children Robert, John Ward and Milly Ward, to be equally divided between them. Item. I give and bequeath unto my beloved son John Ward the two tracts of land I purchased of Col. Thomas Dillard containing by estimation 800 acres. Also my tract of land in Amherst on the North Side of James River near Lynch's Ferry, containing by estimation 1000 acres. Also my stone house and lot in Lynchburg. Also the Spring Tract of land he purchased of his brother William. Also a tract of land known by the name of the Talbot Place, containing 597 acres. Also a tract known by the name of the John Stone Place which I purchased of Edward Terrell. Also a tract I purchased of Frank Smith on sycamore Creek in Pittsylvania, containing 645 acres. Also a small tract of seventy-six acres adjoining it. Also my tract purchased of Davis known as Indian Camps. Also his proportional part of negroes and all personal estate, all to him and his heirs forever. Item. I give and bequeath to my beloved son Henry Ward all my land adjoining the Ferry on the South Side of Staunton River, also my lands adjoining my ferry and the place I now live on the North Side of Staunton River, on Otter river, on Cheese Creek and the branches except the tract given to my son John. Also the tract of land at the mouth of Old Woman's Creek which he has possession of, together with the mill and the mill tract. Also a tract of land on the South Side of Staunton River purchased of Henry Chiles, known by the name of Jack's Place. Also his proportional part of negroes and personal property, all to him and his heirs forever. Item. I lend to my beloved daughter, Agatha Calloway her proportional part of negroes and all personal property during her natural life, and after her death to descend to her three children, David Calloway, Henry Calloway & Margaret Calloway, to be divided as follows, one-half to Margaret and one-half to David and Henry G. Calloway. Item. I give and bequeath to my beloved daughter Anne Dillard five pounds, she having received her part already. Item. I give and bequeath unto my three grandchildren vix. Lynch Dillard, Lucinda Dillard, and John Dillard my tract of land on Sycamore Creek above Early's mill containing by estimation 840 acres to be equally divided between them, but they are to give their mother Anne Dillard the privilege of cultivating as much thereof as she may choose to cultivate, also one-fifth part of my negroes & personal estate to be equally divided between the above name Lynch, Lucinda & John Dillard, but my desire is that Lynch, Lucinda & John Dillard do give their bonds to their mother, Anne Dillard, before they receive their portions for twenty-five pounds a year during her natural life, to be laid out on her at the discretion of my executor. My further desire is that John Calloway and Henry Ward to have all my back lands on Smith River in Franklin, Patrick and Montgomery Counties, except the lands on Buck's Ford. I do constitute, ordain and appoint John Ward and Henry Ward Executors of this my last will & testament revoking all other wills by me heretofore made. Whereof I have her unto set my hand and fixed my seal this 23rd day of January one thousand eight hundred and nine."

John Ward (seal)

Beneath it all—the Virginia soil, the pageantry of inheritance—lingered the scent of iron-rich earth and blood, not always blood spilled in war, but bled slowly through the crushing weight of domination. Inheritance was not a peaceful transfer of tradition. It was a siege. A generational war fought with contracts and kinship, every century a battlefield, and the Wards—ruthless architects of their own supremacy.

Their wealth was no static fortune. It was a living force, monstrous and evolving, fed by fear and obedience. Its roots wrapped around every institution they touched. Primogeniture was no quaint tradition—it was a law etched in blood. The eldest son bore the family's legacy like a burdened crown, while younger sons were dispatched like assets—tools to secure the perimeter.

Marriage became commerce. Cousins wed cousins; love sacrificed to lineage. Daughters were bartered like currency, their futures traded to forge alliances and seal estates. Silk gowns swept across polished floors and champagne glasses clinked in candlelight, but beneath the grandeur, it was all machinery. Cold, calculated, efficient. Every move, every match, every child—part of the same engine of control.

Virginia's rich soil, saturated with sweat and tears, fueled the Ward empire. Land wasn't just property—it was dominion, the foundation of their influence. Wills were weapons—legal instruments wielded to ensure no outsider breached their bloodline. The ink itself reeked of greed, inscribing an endless hunger for control.

And then there were the enslaved—human beings reduced to inventory, listed alongside livestock and acres—disposable commodities in the relentless pursuit of wealth. Auction blocks rang with tragedy. Families shattered. Children torn from mothers. This was the horrific soundtrack to the Wards' prosperity. Silent terror permeated the air. Lives exchanged like currency, overseen by men who played god with blood-stained ledgers.

The scent of old money clung to the Virginia air like summer humidity. Portraits of generations past stared down from gilded frames, silent sentinels of a dynasty built not on merit but on calculated cruelty, legal cunning, and arranged marriages. They weren't stewards of innovation; they were architects of oppression, their legacy rooted in exploitation.

Their ambition reached across generations, gripping fortunes amassed through systemic dehumanization. The soil groaned beneath inherited privilege. Echoes of their machinations still reverberate in the corridors of modern power. Descendants continue to reap ill-gotten gains, sheltered behind walls built on stolen dreams and broken bodies. This wasn't just inheritance. It was institutionalized injustice, baked into the very foundation of America.

The courtroom reeked of old parchment and decaying wealth. Henry Ward, grim-faced, refused his inheritance—a fortune forged from sweat, soil, and suffering. Sixty thousand dollars in 1809 spoke of an estate vast, oppressive, and cursed. Around him, names—Robert A. Ward, young John Ward, Lynch Dillard, Charles L. Terrell, John Lynch Jr., Samuel Pannill, and James C. Moorman—stood like tombstones of complicity, their oaths binding them to uphold a legacy deeper than guilt itself.

Major John Ward's will, dated January 23, 1809, wasn't a tribute to faith, it was a blueprint for domination. His plantation stretched wide along the Staunton River, a monstrous green beast fed by the lives of the enslaved. His eldest son, William, inherited this kingdom for life, followed by Robert, John, and Milly—branches on a tree watered with generations of tears. His second son, John Ward, was granted over 3,100 acres—land acquired through connections to Colonel Thomas Dillard and Edward Terrell. He, too, inherited human beings—lives branded for labor, souls inked into legacy.

"For him and his heirs forever." The words hung like a curse.

Agatha Calloway received little—souls and property on loan, her inheritance a reminder of the limits placed on women in a patriarchal order. Anne Dillard was granted just five pounds, her previous gifts swallowed by greed. Her children—Lynch, Lucinda, and John—were better favored, the stipend to their mother masking deep imbalances of power.

Henry Ward, surrounded by the wealth of mills and fertile land near the Otter and Staunton rivers, refused the executor's role. A quiet protest. The sixty-thousand-dollar bond—a massive sum—was designed to protect the estate but amplified the rot beneath its surface. This wasn't stewardship. It was the management of a kingdom built on the backs of the enslaved.

The bond weighed heavy. The enslaved—now entries in an estate ledger—waited in terror. Their fates balanced on the stroke of a pen. This was not inheritance. It was a blood reckoning.

By conservative estimates, sixty thousand dollars in 1809 translates to tens of millions today—a grotesque monument to generational wealth stolen from the enslaved and wrung from the earth.

For the enslaved, a master's death wasn't mourning—it was catastrophe. Panic. The auction block loomed, its shadow long and merciless. Whispers filled the quarters. Who would be sold? Who would vanish? Children stifled sobs beneath trembling hands. The mansion was silent, but every creak of its floors shouted danger.

The Deep South called like death. Cotton replaced tobacco. Demand rose. People became inventory. The arithmetic of bondage turned lives into profits.

Major Ward's will wasn't just law. It was a sentence. It passed judgment without hearing. And for men like Samuel Ward—my ancestor—it was the chain that bound their futures.

Samuel, a man of quiet resistance, lived within contradiction, loyal out of necessity, wounded by dignity. He walked the line between survival and subversion. His every breath was a rebellion. His legacy—etched in blood and resolve—would live on.

By 1823, the earth groaned anew. Lt. John Ward Jr. inherited not only the land but the burden of debt—and a fragile boy, his nephew, John Ward. The plantation shifted from routine to dread. Samuel, now grayer and more broken, was forced to oversee new arrivals. Their eyes reflected his despair.

His nephew, John Ward—barely more than a child himself—strutted about like a miniature tyrant, wielding cruelty inherited from his uncle, masking insecurity with arrogance. John Ward Jr., a grotesque embodiment of privilege, compensated for his slow wit with chilling viciousness, reveling in the crack of his whip that echoed across the fields—a grim testament to his desperate need for dominance. Alongside his cousin, Lynch Dillard—whose name became a whispered curse—he oversaw a reign of terror stretched across acres of relentless suffering.

The Virginia sun beat mercilessly on Samuel's back, turning flesh to raw leather, while the nights offered only bitter cold, mocking the warmth he desperately craved.

The Ward name was carved into the land not by legacy, but by suffering. Wards Road—etched into the earth by the relentless hands of the enslaved—was no mere passage. It was a monument to endurance and despair, a path laid brick by brick with blood, sweat, and stolen dreams. It bore the weight of over 130 souls, their backs bent beneath the unrelenting sun, their hands raw from clearing land that was never theirs to claim. Among them was John T. Ward's grandmother—her eyes, dark wells of sorrow, held the weight of generations lost to the insatiable greed of men.

The land groaned under the assault of their labor, the rhythm of axes and shovels a desperate hymn of survival. They worked in the blistering heat of day and the bone-chilling grip of night, their breath mingling with the dust that clung to their skin, thick as a second flesh. Tobacco and hemp—crops they would never profit from—thrived under their forced hands, the fields drinking in their toil like a ravenous beast. But it was the road—the road that bore their suffering—that remained. A cruel irony. An unmarked graveyard of will and body, standing even now as an unspoken testament to what was taken.

Lt. John Ward Jr., a man of privilege and power, stood at a distance, his gaze hollow, indifferent. He was a grotesque silhouette against the Virginia sky, watching his empire expand on the backs of men and women who would never taste freedom. Their existence was currency. Their labor, a ledger of flesh and bone, tallying up his wealth with every splintered callus, every drop of blood absorbed into the red clay.

The road was their sentence. It led to the mill, where the thunderous roll of tobacco barrels became a deafening requiem for the enslaved. It led to the Staunton River, whose sluggish waters carried his riches across to Ward's Tavern—a place of laughter, of wealth, of men who raised their glasses in celebration, unmoved by the misery that paved their fortunes.

And still, the land remembers. The road, once dubbed "Mother's Road," was their final offering, their silent rebellion carved into history.

It stands not as a tribute to those who ruled over them, but as a scar—a wound that whispers the truth no gilded history book can erase.

For generations, their truths festered in dusty footnotes and behind bolted doors, their voices choked by the iron grip of silence. But tonight, that silence broke. Each keystroke struck against the darkness—a resurrection in motion. I dragged them, kicking and screaming, from the grave of history.

I wrestled with the monstrous duality of the Ward name: the whip-hand Wards whose legacy stained the nation, and the Wards who bore that whip across their backs, spirits scorched but not broken. The same name—a bitter irony running like poison through the bloodline.

This isn't a sterile history lesson. It's about fire—the incandescent, unyielding fire that refuses to die. The kind that burns in the hearts of the oppressed, fierce and beautiful in its resistance. That fire lived in John T., passed down not for survival alone, but for revolution.

As night bled into a bruised dawn, the cursor blinked—a mocking heartbeat in the silence. And I knew this was only the overture. Shadows still cloak untold stories, names remain unsaid, truths lie unclaimed.

But I will write.

I will not rest until every last one of them is free. Until their voices—finally unleashed—roar across the centuries.

***

The Ward plantation had long been a place of hard, brutal work, long days, and whispered secrets—its silence heavy with generational pain. But in the wake of Phil Branch's death, an enslaved man on the Ward plantation, a different kind of darkness settled across the land. The kind that wasn't just grief—it was a warning. Something had shifted. The atmosphere grew thicker, colder, unnervingly still, like the ground itself was bracing for something greater. Those who remained—enslaved and free alike—carried the weight of his absence like a shroud. The trial and torment of Phil's final days didn't just leave scars—they carved a new layer of grief into the very bones of that plantation.

His death, right at the edge of a new year, felt like an omen. A signal that the world they knew—this carefully constructed empire of cotton, blood, and silence—was beginning to unravel. It was as if the land itself had stopped breathing, holding its breath for what came next.

On New Year's Eve, the skies opened up in mourning, a cold rain falling in slow, solemn rhythm. But even in the quiet heartbreak, there was a kind of resolve stirring. "But the Lord said to me, 'My grace is sufficient for you, for my power is made perfect in weakness,'"—2 Corinthians 12:9. That scripture—whispered among those huddled in quarters, passed from trembling lips to weary hearts—wasn't just comfort. It was armor. The other enslaved people didn't know what was coming, but somehow, they sensed change.

December 26, 1824. The night was bitter. The wind didn't just sting—it cut. Lt. John Ward Jr.'s plantation, grand and greedy, stood cloaked in a silence, broken only by the occasional creak of frozen branches. That night, the world turned on itself.

Phill Branch was more than muscle—he was heart. His laughter cracked through the fields like sunshine after the storm. He moved with confidence that wasn't arrogance; it was survival. But to Hilliard Johnson, a free Black man clawing to hold onto his freedom in a world built to steal it, Phill's light was too bright. It reminded him of everything he was scared to lose—and maybe never really had. Phill's pride became a threat. And Hilliard, bitter and burning, couldn't take it.

"Swaggering … I'll teach you a lesson," Hilliard hissed, his words sharp as the night wind.

It wasn't supposed to happen, maybe not that night, maybe not at all. But when Hilliard, recently exiled from Mrs. Vaughan's plantation by the cruel overseer Dick, spotted Phill just beyond the fence, the simmering envy erupted. Words flew. Then fists. The sickening crack of bone against bone shattered the stillness of the cold night.

Phill, fierce and unyielding, refused to fall easily. But Hilliard, possessed by rage and fear, snatched a jagged rock from the frozen ground. It connected with Phill's head—hard. Blood spilled in a slow, crimson bloom.

Still, Phill didn't give in. Bob, a fellow enslaved man, drawn by the chaos, rushed toward the fight. "Phill!" he cried, rushing forward, breath misting in the icy air. His feet slipped on the frost as he reached his friend, but he was too late.

Hilliard, eyes wild, seized the moment. Casting a glance toward the fence, he tore a long oak rail from the structure—its solid weight promising another blow.

Bob's heart froze as the scene played out in slow motion. "No please, no!" he screamed. But the words were swallowed by the cold.

With a roar, Hilliard swung the rail high, bringing it down with such force that the wood splintered. The crack of oak against bone rang out like a death bell. Phill went limp. The light in his eyes faded. He collapsed beside the shattered rail, his blood seeping into the frozen dirt—a final testament to the violence that had taken him.

Phill would survive for five more days, fighting for every breath, until the final one slipped away on New Year's Eve.

The plantation fell into a suffocating hush.

But death, especially this kind, never ended with burial.

Phill's murder would mark the final chapter of the old order. What the enslaved didn't know, even the Wards hadn't yet realized, was that freedom was already on the horizon, hidden inside the next will, stamped on the back of an estate transfer, and written in ink but rooted in blood.

Before the chains could be broken, the ground had to quake. And Phill's death shook everything loose.

As the years turned, those who had known Phill carried his memory like a burning coal—grief etched into their souls. In time, they would come to understand: *My grace is sufficient for you, for my power is made perfect in weakness.* His death wasn't just an ending—it was the beginning of something breaking open.

The Trial

The courtroom air hung thick with the scent of fear and stale candle wax. It clung to the walls like a second skin. A heavy hush fell over the room—not silence, but weight. This wasn't just a trial. It was something *unthinkable*: enslaved men, battered by a merciless system, were now being allowed to speak, to testify.

The idea alone crackled through the room like lightning, rattling the bones of every man seated within. A system built on Black silence now had to face a voice it had tried for centuries to erase.

Then, from that hush, David—known to many as Davy, Samuel Ward's nephew and a witness to Phill's attack—stepped forward.

His eyes—hollow, bruised by things too terrible to name—looked out over the crowd. He didn't just carry trauma. He *wore* it. His heart pounded like a drum of war. His voice, raw and cracked from disuse, pushed its way into the room, soft at first—but rising, steady, undeniable.

What he spoke was truth, soaked in sorrow and flame, not just about Phill's final moments, but about a system that treated Black life like it was disposable. Whether enslaved or technically "free," men like Davy and Samuel knew they were never safe. Their bodies, their rights, their very existence hung in the balance every day.

The case of Hilliard Johnson—charged for Phill's murder—wasn't just about justice. It was about the lie of freedom itself.

Davy spoke of that December night: the wind that cut like razors, the shadows that stretched long over Mrs. Vaughan's land, and the phantom scent of blood in the air. He saw it all. Two figures locked in a brutal fight. One moving with desperate rage, raining down blow after blow until the other crumbled.

He had seen it, whether the court wanted to hear it or not.

And now … they had no choice.

The image burned itself into Davy's memory: the swift retreat of the assailant, the desperate scurry into the darkness. Then—the chilling brush of a hand on his arm. The suffocating proximity of Hilliard Johnson—a predator, momentarily unmasked. Hilliard, trying to melt into the shadows, was playing a desperate game of hide-and-seek with the grim reaper himself.

Then came the voice—Bob, another soul caught in the suffocating web of bondage. His words sliced through the night: "Hilliard, here is your hat." Ordinary words on the surface, but in that moment, they were chilling—an epitaph of guilt, a damning inscription etched into the very fabric of the dark.

Davy's testimony was no mere statement; it was a living indictment of slavery itself, a crack in silence. His words weighed heavier than any manacles. It wasn't just a description; it was a visceral reliving of fear, of violence, of truth. That he was enslaved didn't matter in that moment. His words had weight. The brutality of Phill's murder shattered even the rigid caste of the court. Justice, rare and reluctant, demanded a voice—even one the law was designed to silence.

His testimony painted Hilliard not just as a murderer, but as a coward drenched in guilt—a man twitching under the weight of his own fear. His attempt to disappear into the dark? Futile. The blood was already screaming from his hands.

Then came Samuel, who also witnessed Hillard attack Phill.

His words didn't just confirm what had happened; they exposed it. Hilliard, he said, had whispered to him, "Nearly dead," not a confession, but a breath of panic. A man who had crossed a line and knew it. No swagger, no bravado—just the quiet dread of someone standing at the edge of his own grave.

Samuel had warned him: "Nine more days and the noose would loosen." But Hilliard was already unraveling—rewriting what happened in his head, twisting fear into a story, into a lie that might buy him survival.

This wasn't just some fight over pride. This was survival, desperation, strategy. Hilliard, a free Black man in a country that devoured freedom like it was a threat, knew the ground beneath him was always shifting. One wrong move, and he would disappear—buried not in earth, but in silence.

Samuel's testimony was no mere recollection. It was a scream. A howl ripped from the throat of a man who had lived too long inside his own silence. In that courtroom—a grotesque theater where the law saw only bodies to be owned or punished—his voice cracked the marble.

He didn't speak to be heard. He spoke to *rupture*.

The courtroom reeked—of fear, of sweat, of centuries of truths never told. But for once, Samuel had the floor. And what he laid bare was undeniable. His testimony shattered the pretense. He painted the plantation as it was, a living nightmare, heat pressing like a boot on the neck, air thick with the taste of iron, shadows moving with whip and threat.

This was no metaphor. This was memory.

Freedom and bondage weren't ideas—they were blood in the soil. His memories came sharp and clear: Phill. Bob. Davy. Names once whispered in the dark now spoken aloud. Names that rose like ghosts in the courtroom. Each one a cry, not for mercy, but for *recognition*.

The courtroom flinched, but the truth did not.

The law—blind and brutal—didn't see men. It saw tools. It saw threats. Southern justice, diseased from root to branch, offered no salvation. Even the concept of an "election to freedom" was hollow, a cruel joke in a system built to grind dreams into dust.

Even the silence of the courtroom was complicit.

But the eyes of those testifying—wide, steady, unflinching—weren't pleading. They were indicting. Behind them echoed a thousand lashings. A thousand stolen dreams. A thousand nights of wondering who would be taken next. And for once, their voices rose—not in plea. But in judgment.

Hilliard, once a freeman, tasted the sour tang of justice—a cruel joke dressed in dignity. Manslaughter. The word hung like a guillotine blade, the verdict a death sentence in slow motion. The May 31st date seared into the mind of the eighteen-year-old—marked his descent into darkness, the cold, damp stone of the Virginia Penitentiary pressing against his skin.

But the ultimate cruelty came later.

March 3rd, 1826—a searing brand of finality. Sold. Shackled. Returned to the very chains he'd so briefly escaped.

The Ward plantation fell into a heart-stopping hush. The unspoken dread in the eyes of the enslaved was palpable—a chilling testament to the brutal fragility of freedom and the crushing weight of despair. Their dreams, delicate as butterfly wings, were once again crushed beneath the iron heel of a system not just built to enslave—but to erase.

Even the trees seemed to hold their breath.

The enslaved walked softer. Spoke less. The fear was back—coiled and waiting, a silent predator stalking every breath. Every whisper held weight. Every prayer felt like it might be their last.

And in that silence, history carved itself into memory—not just in words, but in scars.

Lieutenant John Ward Jr., his face carved with the deep lines of a life weathered by the decay of a crumbling empire, felt the Virginia soil groan beneath his boots—a land heavy with broken promises. Tobacco, once the golden chain of his fortune, now crumbled to dust in his hands. Its brittle leaves mirrored the hollowness in his chest, a bitter reminder that wealth, once sweet with power, had soured. Overproduction had flooded the market, turning his legacy into a burden. The fields of Sulphur Springs, once pulsing with the rhythmic thud of enslaved labor, now fell quiet. The beat was erratic. The silence, damning.

The ghosts of his ancestors, those who had built their fortunes on the backs of stolen lives—whispered through the rustling leaves, warning him. Shame and regret lingered in every corner. He knew the system was failing. The grotesque edifice of slavery, once thought eternal, was rotting from within. Yet the hunger for wealth never slept—it simply shifted. Southward. To Georgia, Alabama, Mississippi—lands where cotton reigned and bodies were currency.

The Deep South called with its monstrous promise: untold riches built on fresh chains and fresh suffering.

He heard them in his mind—chains clanking, families screaming, footsteps in the dust as thousands marched southward, torn from the only homes they'd ever known. Slave traders, dressed in fine coats and lined with rot, stalked his estate like wolves. Their eyes calculated; their lips mouthed silent prices. His own enslaved people—the hands that had built this place from the soil up—were next.

Sulphur Springs, once a symbol of power, now stood as a crumbling monument to hubris and ruin. The Ward family, for all its wealth, stared down the barrel of financial collapse. The cold, logical choice was to sell. Sell them all. Feed them into the insatiable maw of cotton country. Cut his losses. Reinvest. Survive.

But something inside him resisted.

The faces of John T.'s grandfather Samuel and the generations who came before haunted his sleep—stern, silent men staring from the shadows of memory. And amid the decay of legacy and the roar of desperation, something ancient and human sparked in him. Defiance. Guilt. Maybe grace.

As the sun bled crimson over the hills on a fateful evening in 1826, Lieutenant John Ward Jr. drew his final breath. And with it, he delivered a thunderclap into history: "It is my will that all my slaves now living be free."

He had made a decision. He would free them.

But could he?

The words had sounded simple in his mind, but the reality was anything but. Freedom was not something he could simply give. The law was a maze—twisted, impenetrable, designed not to grant liberty but to ensure its denial. No man could create a new species of property unknown to the law. His slaves were not people under

Virginia's statutes. They were property. Chattel. No different from the land beneath his feet or the livestock in his fields. And property could not negotiate. It could not choose. It could not demand justice.

This was the twisted knot of the law. It gave a master the power to enslave but shackled his ability to liberate. Even if he wrote their freedom into his will, it would mean nothing unless his executors had the courage to follow through. And who would risk it? Would they dare commit to the hazardous and irreversible step of assenting to the bequests of freedom?

The courts did not look kindly upon those who upset the natural order of things. To free a slave was not just an act of conscience, it was an act of rebellion. A man's wealth was his legacy, and Virginia had ensured that legacy remained within the bloodline. That was how the great families sustained themselves. It was why cousin married cousin. Why fortunes passed through carefully arranged unions. Why no dollar, no acre, no single slave ever slipped through the cracks.

And if he went against that?

If he freed them, what then?

Even the law itself had turned against the possibility of true manumission. In 1782, the law had shifted, allowing for manumission by will or deed. But the Act of 1806 ensured that no freed slave could remain in Virginia. What kind of freedom was that? To be cast into the unknown, stripped from the land they had built, forced to flee the only home they had ever known?

He could already hear the whispers. The judgment. The betrayal of his own kind.

Lt. Ward Jr. had clenched his fists. The chain was heavy in his grasp—the same one passed down through generations. It was more than iron; it was law. It was blood. It was history. He had inherited it, just as his father and grandfather had before him, and now it bound him to the weight of what had been lost beneath a sun that bled crimson over the hills.

Would he be the one to break it? Or, like those before him, would he let it tighten—until the bones beneath it shattered?

He'd made a decision. He would free them. The words, once whispered in the dark sanctuary of his conscience, now clawed at his throat—raw and ragged. But the simple act of freedom was a viper coiled tight around his heart.

The law, a labyrinth of suffocating legalisms, was not a shield for justice but a weapon forged to perpetuate slavery. His slaves, under Virginia's cruel statutes, weren't people; they were property—indistinguishable from the very ground beneath his feet, mere chattel to be bought, sold, and traded like livestock. They couldn't negotiate their own liberation. They couldn't even voice their despair. The law granted him the power to enslave, yet bound his hands when he sought to liberate.

His will, a flimsy hope, would be rendered meaningless if his executors lacked the courage to defy the entrenched order. Who among his peers—his blood kin—would risk everything to honor such a dangerous bequest? Who would dare to unravel the tight, suffocating weave of Virginia's social fabric?

To free them was not an act of charity, it was insurrection. Virginia's aristocracy, his own kind, clung to their wealth and power like drowning men to a raft. Their fortunes, built on stolen labor, were secured through carefully orchestrated marriages, a suffocating web of alliances designed to maintain the status quo. Every slave, every acre, every dollar was a brick in their fortress. And he, Lieutenant Ward, was about to tear it down.

***

John T. Ward was not born into ease or privilege. He was born into a country that saw his Blackness as a burden, his body as property, and his voice as a threat. But he was also born with a legacy etched into his very bones—a legacy that would not be silenced, even when the world conspired to crush it.

The fires of injustice may have tried to reduce him, but they only refined him.

From the shadows of the Fugitive Slave Act to the frontlines of the Underground Railroad, John T. moved like a man summoned by history—not merely to survive, but to serve. He was not content to outrun the weight of his time. He chose to carry it. To confront it. And in doing so, he did not just leave behind stories—he bequeathed strength.

He gave us blueprint and backbone. Dignity and defiance. He proved that while hardship may shape us, it does not get to define us.

John T.'s life echoes the truth Maya Angelou dared to declare: he was changed by what happened to him, but he refused to be diminished by it. Instead, he became a living inheritance—a man not born for comfort, but for consequence.

No more the stench of the auction block. No more the brutal stomp of boots driving forced marches south. Only silence—staggering, stunned silence. The kind that falls when freedom bursts through the door, unannounced, undeniable, and real.

The Ward family—Samuel, his face a worn map of grief and grit, and his kin—stood at the threshold of the impossible. The chains that once bound them, both metal and unseen, now lay shattered at their feet. The taste of freedom filled their mouths—sharp, metallic, bittersweet. Sulphur Springs, with its endless fields of toil and torment, began to dissolve like a fever dream. The nightmare had finally broken.

They were free.

But the scars ran deep. Slavery had carved its mark into flesh and spirit. And though the chains were gone, what lay ahead was no promised land—it was a vast, unknown wilderness. Freedom was not a finish line. It was a beginning. A dangerous, uncertain, holy threshold.

Here, in the dim sanctuary of my study—amid the scent of aged paper, the brittle crackle of ancestral documents beneath my fingertips—I feel them. I hear them. This is more than research. This is reconstruction. Resurrection. Rebellion. An act of fairness against silence and erasure.

Samuel's endurance, and the strength of those who bore history's heaviest chains, will not be forgotten. I will be their voice—a counterpoint to the quiet that once tried to bury them. Their struggles, their triumphs, their breath and blood and brilliance will be etched into the marrow of memory.

Because when the veils of deceit are finally torn away, the truth doesn't whisper—it roars.

Ward's Freedom Eve.

Lieutenant John T. Ward's will did more than emancipate—it ignited something eternal. It freed bodies, yes. But more than that, it freed spirits. It offered a future beyond the dust-choked fields of Sulphur Springs, beyond the lash and the ledger, beyond the lie.

Samuel and his family stepped into that first dawn no longer as property, but as people. As legacy. As proof that dignity is not given by law—it is born into us.

They faced a horizon still heavy with shadow but filled—at last—with possibility.

The chains were gone.

The journey had only just begun.

He was born to be bequeathed.

CHAPTER 5

The Ward Emancipation of 1827

"It is my will and desire that all my slaves now living, or which may be living at the time of my death, be free, and I do hereby bequeath to every one of them their freedom immediately upon my death in as full and unlimited a manner as the laws of Virginia will admit of."

-Former Slave Owner, Lt. John Ward

The level of disrespect is staggering. I stumbled across a blog post written by descendants of the European Ward family— so casual, so smug—and the tone? Disgustingly indifferent. A sickening erasure.

They talk about the European Ward family cemetery with pride: "Family Cemetery: The graveyard contains many descendants, including burials from recent years."

Then, as if it were a footnote—an afterthought shoved beneath their polished legacy: "Outside the Cemetery Walls: There are many more unmarked graves, likely of enslaved people."

Likely? *Likely?!* The audacity to reduce generations of brutalized Black bodies—souls stolen and buried nameless in the dirt—to a guess. The unmarked graves, rotting quietly just beyond their whitewashed walls, are nothing but a whisper in their narrative. No names. No markers. No dignity.

Much of Lt. John Ward Jr.'s estate was passed down to his great-grandson, Col. Henry Ward Adams, and Col. Adams's wife, Annie Pauline Floyd. Their precious estate, Monteflora—a name meant to conjure beauty and grandeur—is nothing but a facade built on blood. Behind its iron gates lies a brutal history: the so-called temporary slave quarters. *Temporary?* What kind of twisted euphemism is that? There was nothing temporary about the agony endured there. Human beings were caged like animals in a brick hut, stripped of freedom, stripped of identity, their pain echoing off the very stones.

Shackles—actual shackles—still remain, clinging to the earth like cursed artifacts. The blogger has the nerve to call this "historically significant," as if it were a museum exhibit. As if the suffering of my ancestors is a curiosity to be documented—not mourned.

Two thoughts fought inside me: Was this absence because of the Quakers' so-called aversion to grave markers—a sanctimonious lie? Or was it the simpler, crueler truth? That Black bodies weren't deemed worthy of even a name carved in stone.

LeCompte's blog—his digital eulogy to silence—echoed that same cold disregard. His 2010 post dared to mention Col. Henry

Ward Adams and Annie Pauline Floyd, heirs of Monteflora, as if they were custodians of honor.

Monteflora. The name roughly translates to "Flowery Mountain" or "Mountain of Flowers."

A name dripping with bitter irony. Flowery Mountain, my ass. Every syllable burns like a branding iron.

That place isn't a home. It's a graveyard in disguise.

It conjures an image of natural beauty and elevation—but in the context of a plantation, that name is a cruel joke. It romanticizes a place that witnessed generations of brutality, forced labor, and erasure. The elegance of the name masks the horror of its history.

And plantation owner John Ward's headstone? A replacement. A pale, emotionless slab that barely hints at the weight of the man's life. It mocks the original's absence. It mocks all our absences. And the irony? The generational wealth built from the enslavement of my family paid for that stone. Their stolen labor, their stolen lives—now etched into marble that dares to forget them.

And those unmarked graves outside the walls? They're not just forgotten. They were meant to be forgotten.

The brick hut still stands—a cage, its mortar soaked in sweat and fear. Shackles once bound flesh to those walls. Iron still clings to the taste of the wind.

Locust Hill.

Even the name grates against my soul. A plantation disguised as heritage. A legacy smothered in silence. Centuries of screams lie buried beneath the manicured lawnsand self-congratulatory blog posts.

And to the owner of the blog where this was posted, another European Ward descendant replied, "This is wonderful information."

Tell me again about your family cemetery. And I'll show you a field of ghosts—screaming for justice in a world that still dares to forget them.

***

A bleak breath from the past howled low between rows of Ward headstones—granite behemoths, gleaming cold and heartless beneath a gunmetal sky. Each one stood like a soldier of silence, a monument not to honor, but to theft—a legacy built brick by brick on stolen lives. They were perfectly aligned, like a phalanx of judgment, daring me to speak what they refused to admit.

Even when the world forgets, the soil does not. It remembers. And it keeps its secrets—buried deep beneath centuries of blood, silence, and sin.

Just beyond the meticulously trimmed shrubs, the lie unraveled. There, the contrast hit me like a fist to the chest: the slave graveyard. No marble. No dates. No sacred scripture etched in stone. Just rusted iron stakes, crooked and clawing skyward—skeletal fingers of the forgotten, reaching from the earth. A silent scream. A brutal reminder.

Not even a name. Not even that.

The comforting lie of "pious tradition" was nothing but a mask. The truth was sharper, uglier: the enslaved were deemed unworthy of being remembered. Not even in death were we allowed to exist.

But Samuel Ward—my great-great-great-great-great-grandfather—existed. He endured. He fought. He stood carved into this land like a monument to survival. Weathered by time, but unbroken. Shaped by torment, but not consumed by it. The chains he bore didn't always show—but they were there. Heavy. Haunting.

He knew every inch of this place. Every twisted root. Every sun-bleached stone. He may have watched his own mother lowered into that nameless dirt, her grave marked only by the wind's mourning. And he knew—he knew—that one day, this same earth would swallow him too.

But before that day came, he made a vow.

He would burn a path forward with his own blood if he had to. A path for his children. One where their names wouldn't vanish. Where their stories wouldn't be devoured by the silence that had already taken so many. His pain became fuel. His fear became fire.

And on the day of the funeral, that fire burned hot beneath his skin.

The sun had risen cruel and bright, mocking the coldness of the morning's grief. The mansion's grounds stretched wide and beautiful, groomed to perfection—but beneath the beauty lay blood, betrayal, bones. Samuel, his sister Molly, and her children—David and Nancy—summoned like spirits from the underworld, called to the grand mansion. They moved slowly, deliberately. They carried the weight of generations with every step, each footfall echoing in the silence that swallowed the air. Their faces were stone—tired, yes, but carved with defiance. With memory.

They didn't need to speak—silence carried everything they meant.

It screamed. It trembled with rage, with centuries of swallowed cries and buried names rising like a storm.

This land may have tried to forget them. But they were still here. And this time, they would not be silent.

Then Samuel stepped forward. His back was straight—a blade forged by survival. His chest rose with breath long denied. In his calloused hands, the crinkled parchment: Lt. John Ward's will, signed July 30th, 1826. His eyes scanned the words. And then—

His voice cracked the sky.

"WE ARE FREE!"

The word hit like a thunderclap. FREE—a hammer, a bullet, a battering ram breaking open centuries of bondage.

"By the hand of Lieutenant John Ward! And this land—the Cooks' Estate—is OURS!"

Two hundred and ninety-four acres of rich Virginia land—purchased by the European Ward family from the Cooks, land that in 2025 would be valued between $1.5 million and tens of millions—now theirs. On paper, yes. On principle? Unbelievable. Unfathomable. Yet it was written.

Molly, Samuel's sister. Nancy, her daughter. Davy, her son, the same young boy who had slept fireside in the master's room, quiet as a shadow, favored—whatever that meant. They were named. Granted extra acres, livestock, even three hundred dollars—a fortune in 1827, equivalent to over fifty thousand dollars today. But Davy knew better than to trust a signature soaked in power. He'd seen promises split like dry bone.

The paper felt weightless in Samuel's hand. But in the heart? It was heavier than chains.

Later, after the burial soil had been packed and the mourners drifted away, the sun soared higher—cheerful, indifferent. Inside that haunted house, where the scent of death still clung to the walls, Samuel returned to his family. The mist had lifted. The dew had vanished. But something hung in the air—not grief, not just yet. Something else.

He stood tall before them, his voice steady, his presence holy.

"By the hand of Lt. John Ward," he said, "we are emancipated. We have been left the Cooks' Estate. Acres of land. And twenty dollars for each of my children."

A pittance—a cruel joke, considering the wealth extracted from their stolen lives. Yet in Samuel's voice, it rang with something greater. Not gold. Not paper. But dignity restored.

Silence fell. Then—an eruption.

Shouts cracked the air. Hands reached skyward. Mouths dropped open in silent praise. Others wept—sobs deep and trembling, bodies collapsing to their knees, overcome. Three generations of stolen time, of crushed dreams and nameless graves, rose up like a storm, and in its roar came joy—raw, unfiltered, sacred.

They wept for what was lost. They screamed for what had come. And above all, they clung to the sound of their own voices—finally heard, finally human, finally free.

Even as the thunder of joy rolled through the air, a bitter chill crept in slow, sharp, and cruel because beneath the celebration, it was there. The will, a fragile scrap of parchment, thin as breath, loaded like a gun. It declared freedom but not without strings. Not without shackles hidden in ink.

Children under fifteen? They had to stay.

Stay? Stay on the same land that had stolen their families, their years, their names? Stay to serve until they turned twenty-one?

Even now—even in the hour of so-called liberation—the plantation's grip sank its claws into the youngest. Into John T. Ward himself. The promise of freedom was already poisoned.

Because those children—those teenagers—were the future. Years of labor still ahead. Calloused hands yet to form. Backs not yet broken. And by keeping them, the slaveholder ensured the estate would stay alive. Profitable. Productive. Controlled.

It wasn't mercy. It was calculated.

While the elders—too worn, too wise, too defiant—were released like burdens cast off at the finish line, the young were retained. Bought with time. Trapped in a slow bleed of freedom. Every word of the will was a power play from the grave, a final act of manipulation that dressed itself in righteousness and rotted underneath.

This wasn't freedom. It was a delay. A bargain. A performance.

Slaveholders—facing their own mortality—sometimes felt the pressure to "do the right thing." But they rarely let go without taking something first. And here it was: an estate still humming with productivity, still turning a profit, still fueled by Black bodies too young to fight back.

And so, the cruel reality sank in.

Yes—some were free. But not all. Not yet.

Even in death, the master's hand reached back from the grave—tightening, calculating, controlling—refusing to let go completely.

And for the children left behind? The celebration had ended. The wait had begun.

In the final pages of his will, Lieutenant John Ward revealed the warped logic of slaveholding paternalism. He expressed a personal wish regarding his "favorite" enslaved individuals—a cruel distinction in itself. He stated his desire that they be permitted to remain together, as if family unity were a gift only he could grant. He singled out Nancy, a girl forced into womanhood who had given birth to her first child at the age of twelve, and declared that she should be allowed to remain in Virginia with her children.

But that gesture of selective mercy stopped there. No such compassion was extended to Samuel Ward or the rest of the enslaved community bound to him. They were excluded from this conditional kindness, revealing a clear and calculated hierarchy among the people he held in bondage. Nancy and her children were human enough to be kept together. The others were not even acknowledged as worthy of that consideration.

This decision unfolded under the shadow of a legal system designed to preserve the very structure of slavery, even as it allowed for the appearance of grace. Whether a master could legally emancipate an enslaved person was once a matter of legal uncertainty. That question was settled by the Act of 1782, which permitted slaveholders to free enslaved people by will or deed. The law remained in effect but was deliberately crippled by the Act of 1806, which required that any enslaved person freed after that date must leave the state of Virginia.

Freedom was granted—but only at the price of exile. The law made it clear: Virginia had no place for free Black people. To be free was to be banished from the land they had labored on, lived on, and built.

Even this cruelly conditional freedom was bound by rigid legal doctrine. "No man," the law declared, "can create a new species of property unknown to the law." No master could grant an enslaved person partial freedom or elevate them to a civil status the state refused to recognize. A man could choose to treat a human being as chattel, or follow the prescribed legal process of manumission, but he could not invent rights for them outside those narrow parameters. The enslaved were denied all social and civil capacity—by law, they were nothing.

***

Lt. John Ward's will stands as a disturbing testament to the contradictions of white supremacist rule—a man playing god, deciding who among the enslaved deserved to stay, who would be named, who would be forgotten. He showed favor to Nancy yet cast aside Samuel Ward and countless others with chilling indifference. And though the law permitted the illusion of liberation, it was ultimately a system built to punish freedom, to protect whiteness, and to ensure that the status quo remained intact.

The will itself felt heavy in my hands—not just in weight, but in meaning. Even the photocopy carried a gravity that pierced the skin. The faded ink, the swift, slanted colonial cursive, the texture of aged paper—all of it whispered a legacy I could not escape. This wasn't just a document. It was a ledger of lives.

Seventy names. Meticulously listed. Seventy souls, freed on paper—but at what cost?

Molly and her children—Nancy and Davy—their names carved onto the page before those of Lt. John Ward's own bloodline. Not an act of justice, but a calculated insult. A message. A deliberate affront to his family, and perhaps to the world that made him. Robert Ward, his own brother, was disinherited, cast aside over an unpaid debt. A single line in the will that said more than any courtroom testimony ever could: the lieutenant forgave nothing. Not blood. Not bonds. Not betrayal.

And then the inventory. A cold catalog of human suffering, masquerading as order. The enslaved were described like merchandise, like beasts.

"Skin tone: dark. Complexion: light. bright. Hair: bushy. straight. long. Teeth: missing. rotted. Color mulatto. Black. yellow."

These were not words; they were instruments of surveillance. Cold. Clinical. Stripped of empathy. They did not acknowledge humanity; they codified control. Each description, from skin tone to scars, was more than inventory. It was a blueprint for bondage. A system so precise, so invasive, it could double as a script for a fugitive slave poster. If they ran, their height, complexion, broken teeth, and burns would be weaponized, their pain transformed into a wanted ad.

They weren't just recorded. They were tagged, tracked, and primed for recapture.

Each individual was weighed and measured—heights approximated, ages guessed, scars and burns documented with the same precision you'd find in a livestock auction. Deformities noted. Bones counted.

And there was Hannah—my ancestor, John T. Ward's mother. Her entry said broken teeth, visible scars. That was all. But I knew what that meant. I could see her in my mind—her pain, her endurance, her silence broken only by breath. Her body, a testament to survival, even as the will recorded her like a damaged good.

Even the children were not spared. A four-year-old girl, Amanda Ward, was listed as being "occasioned by the King's Evil"—an archaic diagnosis of scrofula. A disease caused by a bacterial infection, often linked to contaminated water, poor sanitation, and malnutrition. Scrofula thrived in the very conditions that defined enslaved life— crowded quarters, unclean environments, and systemic disregard. The mere mention of it was a quiet scream, proof of the world she had been born into—malnourished, unwashed, uncared for. That entry alone told you everything about how they were treated.

But perhaps most haunting of all—the names. Every enslaved person listed by first and last name. Many carried the surnames of their oppressors: Ward, Roberts, Calloway, Craddock, Lynch. Echoes of ownership masquerading as identity. Their lineage erased, replaced with the names of those who bought, bred, and broke them.

And it didn't end there. Certificate numbers, bureaucratic branding, were assigned to each of them in the Pittsylvania County register of free Negroes. Human beings reduced to paperwork, stamped and filed like cattle in a government ledger. It was slavery dressed in the clothing of civilization.

And if that sounds familiar—it should. They lined them up. They measured their bodies. They examined their teeth. They tracked their injuries. They compared their value. And then, they decided their worth.

Sounds a lot like the NFL combine, if you ask me. Same scrutiny. Same systems. Different chains.

Lieutenant John Ward's will is a study in contradiction—a mirror held up to a society caught in the violent, uneasy transition from slavery to manumission. It is not the document of a liberator. It is the careful, calculated script of a man granting freedom on his own terms, wielding control even as he loosened his grip. His offer of liberty came not as a gift, but as a bargain—conditional, incomplete, and shrouded in the cold logic of property law.

His enslavements were not freed outright. They were permitted to choose freedom, but only if they accepted it under the boundaries he imposed. If any individual rejected the terms—or the world outside those terms—they could select a new master, who would then purchase them at a price set by two men handpicked by the executors. This wasn't emancipation. It was a transfer of ownership masquerading as choice.

He even sought to dictate the fates of mothers and children. Enslaved women—whom he reduced to the term "females"—could, if they wished to keep their children with them, do so only under the stipulation that those children would be allowed to obtain freedom at age twenty-one. Childhood, once again, became a sentence to bondage—a calculated delay of justice. Family, once again, became a bargaining chip in a master's legacy.

At the center of this will is a chilling paradox: freedom offered from the hand of the enslaver, yet only in ways that preserved his control beyond the grave. Lt. John Ward's legal language asserted not only dominance but ownership of destiny. He treated the enslaved as if they could make a "choice"—yet the entire structure of the law declared them incapable of legal will, incapable of personhood.

Ward's nephews, Lynch Dillard and John Ward Jr., stood as executors of this grim inheritance. They were not just stewards of land and livestock—they were the keepers of a peculiar brand of justice, dressed in legal formality but soaked in paternalism, hierarchy, and white supremacist logic.

At its core, the will dared to ask: can a person be property and also possess the legal agency to choose freedom?

It is a question soaked in contradiction—a society that wanted to seem moral while remaining in control, that sought to legalize compassion without relinquishing power. Lt. Ward's will, like the system it served, offered freedom in a cage—and called it justice.

This was no mere victory. It was an exorcism.

They were the newly emancipated Ward family—once enslaved, now awakened. Three generations who had borne the crushing weight of Pittsylvania County's chains, now rising, breathless, not just with freedom—but with fire.

But freedom, it seemed, was a word the law spoke differently depending on who you were.

Lieutenant John Ward's nephews—those vultures cloaked in inheritance—circled the estate like carrion beasts. They were cold, calculating, eyes skimming over the survivors not as people, but as property. As liabilities. As obstacles. They oversaw the division of the estate with the same detachment they might show dividing cattle—never mind the fact that what they were dissecting had once been human souls.

They were left with wealth—millions, by today's measure. Lt. John Ward's fifty-thousand-dollar bond from 1827 now stood equal to $3,062,435 in 2025, a monument to generational wealth built on generational pain.

And yet, for the old, the weary, the broken, there was no share. Only a cruel ultimatum: leave with nothing or be transferred like livestock to another master. Their very existence reduced once more to a pawn in a rigged game of legacy.

But Samuel—oh, Samuel was not one to bend.

He had weathered the whip, buried his name in silence, and now he stood reborn. He would not be broken. He would not be bought. While others whispered doubt, he spoke destiny. At dawn, he would claim his land, his future, his blood-soaked birthright. He would build it from the ground up—bricks of resolve, mortar of sweat and joy, a house standing defiant against every lash that had once split his back.

But instead of dawn's promise, they were met with a chilling spectacle.

Wagons.

Sent by one of the lieutenant's brothers. A clear, brutal message: leave.

Pack your meager belongings, your hard-earned pride, and vanish. The same hands that wrote their freedom now delivered their exile. What had felt like the promised land—the fertile Cooks' Estate, purchased by the late Lt. Ward—was suddenly yanked away, like a dirty rug from beneath their feet.

***

Sixty years. That was how long Samuel had prayed for this. And now, even in emancipation, he could feel the phantom of the whip—still lashing at his heels. The betrayal hit like smoke in the lungs. He turned to see the pain carved into his daughter Hannah's face, the thought of leaving her young children behind a silent scream in her eyes. The fields he had dreamed of tilling were now blurred behind the fog of sorrow and deceit.

Ohio. That was what they were offered now. A cold, unfamiliar freedom, hundreds of miles from the soil that had known their blood. A hollow echo of liberty. Still, Hannah stood tall, her eyes lit with righteous fury. She pressed the will, brittle and yellowed, into Samuel's calloused hand. The paper was cold as a tombstone, but its message burned: they were free, but their children were not.

A lifetime of stolen labor, reduced to a single, merciless clause.

Freshly turned earth and betrayal filled the scene. The taste of freedom soured in his mouth.

Even Davy—the quiet one, once trusted to sleep near the master's hearth—was cast out in the chaos. Confused. Panicked. But not defeated. He swore he would not leave until a court heard his voice—until the ink of that will translated into the soil beneath his feet. He would petition. He would speak. He would fight.

Because the promise had been made. And they would not let the dead speak louder than the living.

Samuel had seen it before—in the eyes of other freedmen—that hollow, hunted look born not from chains, but from broken promises. It was the look of men freed on paper but shackled by history, men whose birthright was plundered under the guise of law, whose futures had been auctioned off by lies dressed in liberty.

Samuel knew their story. He was living it.

A story woven with fraudulent deeds, stolen land, and the howl of hate-fueled mobs. A nation that had sold its soul to contradiction—promising liberty with one hand while tightening shackles with the other. And all the while, the government sat as silent accomplice, watching from marble halls as the very soil under their feet was ripped away.

Now, as the wagon creaked beneath him, its wheels groaning like the bones of the old, every sound and sensation pressed into Samuel like the weight of history. His lungs rasped against the winter air. The wind tore through his threadbare coat like teeth. And behind him, looming tall and unrepentant, stood the Cooks' Estate—a monument not to triumph, but to dreams stolen in the light of day. It cast its shadow across the fading sun like a curse.

He felt them then—his ancestors, their screams silent but unrelenting, echoing through his bones. The weight of their labor. Their prayers. Their unmarked graves. He gripped the reins so hard his knuckles turned to stone.

Let them steal the land. Let them burn his hopes to ash. They would never steal his spirit.

The memory of his children's faces—their hopes flickering like candlelight in his mind—fueled his resolve. This was not just about acres. Not just about a deed or a name carved into parchment.

This was about legacy. About survival. About proving that centuries of brutality could not kill the fire that burned in the hearts of the enslaved—and now, the freed. They had taken his soil. But they would never take his fight.

He clenched his jaw as the cold bit into his skin. The journey north was not a departure. It was a pilgrimage. A march toward something stolen long ago: dignity, freedom, and a future of their own making.

Through sheer will and grueling negotiations, Samuel had done what so many could not—he kept his family together. But the price was steep. Thirty-eight souls—the Ward family—crammed into rickety wagons pulled by oxen or walked, step by blistering step, nearly four hundred miles from Pittsylvania, Virginia to Lawrence County, Ohio.

Seventy had been freed. But thirty-eight newly manumitted Wards made it out with all their children.

Thirty-eight souls, ripped from the land that birthed them. Joints jarring against rough-hewn wood, skin cracked from cold, muscles screaming with every mile of exile. And still, they moved forward—toward a bleak promise, a whisper of safety on the wind.

Lawrence County, Ohio. Not paradise. But a chance. A place to begin again.

And behind them, in the red clay of Virginia, they left not just chains—but a message etched in the dirt: We may be gone. But we are not erased.

The Ward family's emancipation brought to mind another explosive moment in history—1833, when John Randolph of Roanoke, an elite Southern senator and slaveholder, freed 518 enslaved people in a single stroke of the pen.

Randolph—unmarried, calculating, cloaked in aristocratic charm—spent his life defending slavery. But behind closed doors, he plotted its undoing. His will stunned the South: "I give and bequeath to all my slaves their freedom ... heartily, that I have never been the owner of one."

A grotesque lie. He owned a six-thousand-acre Virginia tobacco plantation. His remorse came too late.

Randolph funneled eight thousand dollars—a fortune then, worth over two hundred thousand dollars today, into land in Mercer County, Ohio, for his newly freed people. But Ohio didn't welcome them. Fueled by panic and hate, politicians posted armed white men at the riverbanks to intercept them. Their presence was legal under the Black Laws of 1807—a barbaric system that criminalized Black freedom.

Virginia's relationship with slavery was twisted. Quakers urged emancipation, and the 1782 manumission law allowed slaveholders to free people without government approval. But freedom came with conditions—freed slaves had to leave or face re-enslavement.

The social order was cracking. Wealthy planters feared rebellion. Poor white people competed with freed Black people for labor and turned that frustration into violence. The hatred was growing—loud, organized, and legal.

Randolph's move wasn't redemption. It was a carefully choreographed betrayal—a final performance from a man who fed on human misery, then claimed innocence.

And still, the echo of those 518 souls remained—freed, only to face rifles at the border.

Just like the Ward family.

Lt. John Ward's will freed his people—but even he seemed to know Virginia might not let them stay. His actions, like Randolph's, came with conditions, omissions, and consequences. Freedom was never simple. And in both stories, freedom came with a price—and a target.

Of the 136 enslaved people emancipated by Lt. John Ward's will, thirty-eight were Wards—bound not in chains, but by hope, loaded into wagons, and sent toward the uncertain promise of Lawrence County, Ohio.

But Molly and her children—David, Nancy, and Nancy's two little ones—stayed behind in Virginia. They weren't ready to surrender the land or the lives they'd known. They believed there was a chance—a legal path—to remain on the soil where their ancestors were buried. Petitions were filed. Pleas were written.

And yet, when their case was called, no court showed up. No judge. No justice. The petitions were silently rejected, as though their voices had never spoken.

Still, they refused to be erased.

When Nancy's plea to remain in Virginia was denied, she granted her brother, David Ward, power of attorney to fight on her behalf. Eventually, Nancy moved to Warren, Ohio, carrying with her not just her children, but the crushing weight of exile.

Back in Virginia, the climate for free Black people was turning dangerous. Whites feared rebellion. They whispered of revenge. And then they acted. Threats were made—stay and be deported to Africa. The American Colonization Society (ACS), born from the same fear that once fueled slave patrols, aimed to remove freed Black people from American soil entirely. Liberia was the destination. Erasure was the goal.

For families like John T. Ward's, remaining in Virginia wasn't just unwelcomed—it was perilous. If they stayed, they could be seized and sold down South, traded into the depths of the cotton empire, stripped again of everything they had just won.

The threat was real. Virginia still trembled from the memory of Gabriel's Rebellion in 1800—a planned uprising led by an enslaved man named Gabriel, alongside his brothers. They sought to storm Richmond, to challenge the very institution that had dehumanized them. But betrayal came first. For a promised reward, someone gave them up. Gabriel and twenty-five others were hanged. The betrayer? He never got the reward.

The rebellion failed—but its echo shook Virginia to its core. It wasn't the loss that mattered—it was the realization of what enslaved people could do if they united. That fear never left.

So, Virginia made its choice: deny the freedmen their right to stay.

And the North, for all its talk of freedom, recoiled too. Laws and bonds and backroom deals kept Black families from settling freely.

With doors closing from every direction, the Ward family faced two paths: return to slavery or leave everything behind.

They chose to leave.

Pittsylvania to Lawrence County. From red clay to cold hills. The journey was long, the weight was heavy, but the alternative was unthinkable.

An escort was arranged. A wagon master led them north, tracing the winding artery of the river like a lifeline, guiding them out of bondage and into the unknown. On April 14, 1827, the wheels of their exile creaked across the border into Ohio.

Eyewitnesses called them ragged. Dirty. Empty-handed.

No gold. No titles. No comfort.

Many arrived with only the clothes on their backs and the memories of chains still etched into their skin.

But what they did carry—was will.

A sacred hunger to live. To be more than property. To claim a life not borrowed, not permitted, but rightfully their own.

Freedom came without wealth, without land, without the protection of law. But it came. And it came with fire.

Though they crossed into freedom, it did not greet them with open arms.

Ohio was cold—both in weather and welcome. White officials, already aware of their arrival, published letters of outrage, questioning why so many freed slaves were entering the county. The tone was sharp. The message was clear: you are not wanted here.

Still, they endured.

At first, there was no place to even lay their heads. No shelter. No peace. But soon, they found footing—secured housing, complied with bond laws, and slowly began to build something out of nothing.

They turned to what they knew: the earth. Decades of forced labor had taught them how to survive in dirt, in dust, in pain. Now, free Black men and women farmed, worked the land, and even acquired small tracts for themselves. They built cabins with blistered hands and erected schools for their children—tiny sanctuaries where hope could take root.

But not all found farmland.

In Black Fork, many of the Ward freedmen labored in the iron furnaces, where smoke choked the lungs and heat blistered the skin. The conditions were brutal, dangerous, and dehumanizing, but it was paid work. And payment, however meager, meant survival.

***

The Ward family—its wealth rooted in the marrow of the enslaved—was slowly consumed by the very fire it had kindled. What began as a dynasty of land, labor, and blood unraveled into a cursed legacy, where ashes replaced opulence and ghosts crept through halls once gilded with ambition.

Lieutenant John Ward Jr.'s shadow loomed long over the crumbling estate, its grandeur reduced to rot. The unexplained blaze that devoured the mansion was no accident. It was retribution wrapped in flame—a pyre lit by history itself. The house had never been a home; it was a mausoleum built on cursed ground, bequeathed to a daughter who died before she ever breathed its air. A cruel joke by fate—or perhaps something older, something darker.

John Ward Jr., his nephew, followed soon into the grave, leaving behind not an inheritance but a trail of ashes and accusation. The mansion, the fortune, the name—it all decayed in his hands, collapsing under the weight of its sins. Their deaths were not isolated tragedies but echoes in a symphony of national failure—the soundtrack of a country splintering beneath the weight of its own hypocrisy.

And yet, the fire kept burning.

John Ward, son of William and Mildred Adams Ward and nephew of Lt. John Ward Jr., found fleeting joy in the arms of Tabitha Hubbard Walden. But happiness was never meant to last. A heavy fruit tree, toppled during a routine clearing, crushed him—a grotesque parody of abundance, a bounty turned weapon. His death was brutal and ironic, nature itself delivering a verdict on a blood-soaked legacy.

The Catawba people, longtime allies and laborers at the Ward family trading post, gathered for Henry's burial—Lt. John Ward Jr.'s brother. Their ceremony, older than the mountains, was raw and holy. They pressed their foreheads together until blood welled, held it up to the sun, and let it drip into the soil. Their grief was sacred. Their mourning was elemental. It laid bare the hollowness of the Ward empire—a kingdom built without soul.

Then came Gettysburg—July 3, 1863. The name still scorches the family tree.

Robert Adams Ward, son of John and Tabitha, fell on that cursed field, swallowed by a war his ancestors helped ignite. Gunpowder and blood soaked the ground, and the cries of the dying wrote new scars across the family's name.

Henry Chiles Ward, his brother, returned from the war haunted and hollow, trailing whispers of a homicide—a shadow that never lifted. He died unloved and alone, a man poisoned by violence, too broken to belong to anyone again.

Then came the short lives of Mildred Adams Ward Leftwich, born in 1806 and gone by 1829, and her brother George Edward Ward, dead at only sixteen. Their names, their deaths, were not accidents but symptoms of something festering at the root. Fallen petals, each one wilting under the chill of a family tree grown in poisoned soil.

Even the children seemed fated to die young.

Robert A. Ward and George Edward Ward—the sixth and seventh children—snatched by fate in cruel succession. Their ends weren't just personal losses; they were harbingers. Omens carved into headstones. A foreshadowing of the Ward legacy's final unraveling.

By 1849, a cold wind cut through the core of the Ward dynasty, mirroring the storm inside Robert Ward himself. A shadow of the ruthless men who came before him, Robert was crushed beneath the weight of the legacy they built—one forged in blood and bondage. The bitter taste of their stolen prosperity lingered in his mouth like poison.

His decision to sell the tavern tract to James Hoskins Stone felt like a betrayal, a surrender, a confession.

It was more than the end of an era. It was the collapse of an entire world.

The Ward family's reign, rooted in slavery, dissolved into quiet ruin. The very air around the plantation held the weight of what had been done there—each gust carrying the sound of chains, each creaking floorboard whispering old secrets.

Robert was not simply a villain. He was the twisted product of a system that could distort even the softest soul. His hollow eyes flickered with regret—small sparks of humanity trying to survive in the ruins of empire. But the stain was permanent, etched into the soil and burned into the bones of the land.

These are not side notes in history. These are keys. Clues. Cracks in the veneer.

And what they point to ... is buried deeper. In the paper trail. The whip's shadow falls across every line.

The Catawba later honored Ward's memory with a traditional ceremony, seeking assurance that his spirit had ascended to the "happy hunting grounds." This ritual involved the dramatic act of pressing their foreheads together until red plasma flowed, collecting it in hay straws, and holding it up to the sun. If light passed through the straw, it was seen as a favorable sign, offering them solace that Ward had reached a place of peace.

But the ceremony also spoke to a deeper truth: the Catawba's profound spiritual understanding of life and death, a sacred rhythm that stood in sharp contrast to the brutal, dehumanizing world the Wards had helped build. It was as if the spirits of the past had come to collect their due—to remind the living that no wealth built upon suffering could remain untouched.

CHAPTER 6

Paper Trail of Tears

*"America is more our country than it is the whites'—
we have enriched it with our blood and tears ... and
yet, they make us buy ourselves back from the chains
they forged."*

-David Walker (Walker's Appeal, 1829)

Years later, I found myself on a different kind of journey—this
time, tracing the hidden threads of history through the archives
of Lawrence County. I made what I assume would be a simple
phone call, expecting a routine answer. Instead, the librarian's voice
crackled with surprise: "We've never heard of such a thing ... bonds,"
she said. "There are no records of anything like that here."

I was looking for the security bonds my ancestors would've been required to produce—proof of their tenuous freedom. Her words hit like a closed door. Then came the exph8il: the Lawrence County courthouse had burned down. Twice. The flames didn't just destroy buildings, they erased generations of records, stories, and names.

When I contacted the Columbus Library, I got the same response: nothing. As if the past had been swallowed whole.

Even now, the deeper layers of Black history—buried beneath outdated laws, bureaucratic red tape, and strategic silence—remain elusive. Deliberately hidden. Designed to stay buried.

But I dug anyway.

I felt like an archaeologist brushing dust from an ancient script, listening for the whispers of a lost civilization. Old newspapers crackled beneath my fingers. Wills, indentures, and deeds stared back at me like puzzle pieces from another life. Meeting notes from local churches spoke in codenames, dates, secret gatherings scrawled in hurried, ink-stained hands. Some were barely legible, the handwriting frantic, as if written in fear or haste.

Even when I couldn't decipher every word, I felt their weight.

These documents were more than paper.

They were artifacts of resistance. Of faith. Of survival.

I copied what I could, organizing each page carefully into my binder. With every crinkled sheet, I felt a flicker of triumph. These paper trails—these fragile, overlooked relics—were a treasure trove of truth.

They were the receipts.

Proof that our land was stolen.

Proof that we were here.

***

The wind bit at his face as Drury Farrow dismounted, boots crunching against the frost-hardened ground. He adjusted his coat with one hand, the other resting instinctively near the breast pocket where his freedom papers lay folded—creased and worn from years of carrying proof that he had a right to exist.

The courthouse stood before him, tall and gleaming, its whitewashed columns glaring in the morning sun like a monument to hypocrisy. *Justice*, it promised. But Drury knew better. In eighteenth-century Virginia, justice had never looked kindly on a Black man—especially not one who dared to live free.

Born around 1748, Drury was among the small, fragile class of free Black people in colonial Virginia—men and women who had clawed their way out of bondage through manumission, military service, or, like him, by the rare chance of being born to a free mother. His status granted him liberties, yes, but they came laced with chains. Every breath of freedom he took was shadowed by laws designed to tighten around his throat.

He was no stranger to the scrutiny of the law. He had lived his entire life under the cold gaze of a system that saw him as a mistake—an aberration that needed to be managed, taxed, and controlled. Free Black men were required to register annually, submitting themselves to government oversight like livestock. They paid taxes not only on their land and labor, but on their own existence. They had no right to vote, to own certain property, or to hold office. And they were never allowed to forget that their liberty could be revoked with the stroke of a quill or the loss of a single sheet of paper.

A single lost document could mean prison. Or worse.

They called him "Drury Farrow the Free Negro." It wasn't just a name—it was a label. A brand. It trailed him through courtrooms and tax records, through land leases and whispered conversations. Every transaction, every accusation, every defensive gesture he made was recorded and filed—evidence that he was being watched. He had gained his freedom, but the weight of it pressed on him like an iron yoke.

And yet, he kept walking.

The wooden steps creaked beneath his feet as he approached the courthouse door, heart pounding. A free Black man had no real allies in there—not among the clerks, not among the magistrates, and certainly not among the white landowners who questioned why he wasn't in chains like the others.

But Drury had no choice. He was here to be counted—again. To prove that he was not a fugitive. Not a threat. Not a ghost of the system that tried to vanish him. He had to leave a paper trail so thick, so undeniable, that even history would have to acknowledge him.

He inhaled, squared his shoulders, and pushed open the door.

This was survival in America: not just staying alive, but being *legible*—on paper, in records, under oath. Drury Farrow's story was written not in speeches or rebellion, but in ledgers and signatures. And it is because of those fragile documents that we know his name today.

Tithable of Pittsylvania County, Virginia, 1767 was more than just a tax. It was surveillance. It was control. A way to draw invisible lines around lives and label them property.

In colonial Virginia, being "tithable" meant you were counted not as a citizen, but as a financial unit—an asset to be taxed, tracked, and tallied.

The 1767 Tithable list for Pittsylvania County bore silent witness to a system that saw no contradiction in taxing people as both property and producers. The term "tithable" referred to any person subject to the poll tax imposed by the General Assembly—used to fund the very civil government that institutionalized their exploitation.

Under the law passed in 1705 by the House of Burgesses, this included all free white males over sixteen, all enslaved Black Americans, and Indigenous and mixed-race (mulatto) women aged sixteen or older. Notably excluded were white women (unless they were heads of household) and children under sixteen, regardless of race.

The purpose was brutal efficiency. This tax wasn't just economic—it was racial and gendered classification codified into law. It was a system built to fund a colony through the backs of those it refused to see as equals.

And when the sheriffs started playing games—hiding names, underreporting for bribes—the government cracked down. In March 1660, the House of Burgesses passed a new law dividing each county into four precincts, each overseen by a commissioner. These commissioners were instructed to post public notices on the doors of local churches ahead of the June 10th deadline, warning landowners to submit their tithable.

But even that wasn't enough to stop the fraud. So, the government took it further. After the deadline, county clerks were required to *nail* the entire list of names—each tithable soul—to the courthouse door, where it would hang for a full day, exposed to the eyes of every neighbor and passerby.

It was a public reckoning—and a trap.

Anyone could accuse. Anyone who knew a master was hiding tithable could come forward. And if the accusation proved true, the informant would be rewarded—with the very human being the master tried to conceal.

This was the chilling backdrop behind the 1767 list taken by John Wimbush, Gentleman, for Pittsylvania County.

Among the names recorded under Captain John Ward's household were:

John Cleveland, Thomas Hardy, Peter Lee, Harry, Jack, Abram, Bess, Tom and Ben, Nant, Jack, Dick, Matt, Tom, John, Thomas and Nant.

Seventeen souls. Seventeen tithable men and women. And that was only the ones sixteen or older. The law made it plain: any others—children, too young to tax—weren't counted yet. They were still coming up, still waiting to be cataloged like livestock when they reached working age.

Captain Ward's presence on this list confirmed he held property in Pittsylvania County, though records later place his family in Campbell County. That suggests something broader—a plantation operation likely split across counties. His sons, possibly still minors or living elsewhere, may show up in Bedford or Campbell County tithable instead.

But make no mistake—this list wasn't just a roll call. It was a document of power, of ownership, and of resistance yet to come. These names, preserved in brittle ink, speak the quiet truth about how America's early economy was funded: by counting Black bodies like coin.

This was the legacy Drury Farrow was born into. This was the paper trail he could never outrun.

Every year, without fail, Drury Farrow's name appeared in the tax records. Not because he committed a crime—but because he existed.

In 1774, he was summoned to appear before the Cumberland County Court. The charge? Failing to list himself as tithable. A bureaucratic technicality—but one with sharp teeth: fines, imprisonment, or even forced labor. That year, Drury narrowly escaped punishment. Others weren't so lucky. For free Black men like him, survival hinged not just on land or livestock, but on meticulous compliance with laws designed to trap them.

The courthouse steps groaned beneath his boots as he approached the magistrate's office. Drury wasn't there to defend wrongdoing, at least not by any moral standard. He was there because the law demanded he prove he was still free. Every year, free Black men were required to register: proof of status, proof of identity, proof of submission. Without it, he could be reclassified in an instant—as a runaway, a drifter, a fugitive, a slave.

Freedom, for men like Drury, was never a birthright. It was a condition—revocable, taxable, and constantly questioned.

The weight of his presence in that courthouse echoed far beyond the room.

It traced back to a law passed nearly seventy years earlier—a venomous statute that infected every corner of his life.

In 1705, the Virginia General Assembly passed a sweeping series of laws that did more than regulate labor—they codified race-based slavery and hardwired white supremacy into the legal foundation of the colony. The statute coldly declared that "all Negro, mulatto, and Indian slaves within this dominion ... shall be held to be real estate."

With those words, human beings were legally transformed into property—no different than acres of tobacco or herds of cattle.

But that was only the beginning.

These weren't just property laws—they were death sentences in disguise. The act went even further:

"If any slave resist his master ... correcting such slave and shall happen to be killed in such correction ... the master shall be free of all punishment ... as if such accident never happened."

A life, snuffed out, could be erased with legal indifference. No accountability. No justice. No name carved into memory—just another "accident."

And yet, the violence of this law didn't stop at the enslaved. It reached the freed.

The 1705 Slave Codes ensured that even freedom came with shackles. The ruling class, afraid of uprisings from the poor—Black and white alike—constructed a new caste. They labeled the landless and laboring the "giddy multitude," a dangerous mix of the desperate and the dispossessed. That fear drove a brutal shift: Black servants who once had a pathway to freedom were replaced by enslaved Africans, whose bondage was permanent, inherited, and absolute.

The lines between indenture and enslavement—between labor and life sentence—were erased.

And for free Black people? The punishment wasn't chains—it was constant surveillance and systemic humiliation.

Even their tax burden told the story. Free Black, Indigenous, and mixed-race women sixteen and older were declared tithable—while white women, unless they were heads of household, were spared. The message was clear: Black freedom would be taxed at every turn.

Drury had to pay not only on his tools, animals, and land—but on his own breath. On his right to live, to labor, to be.

It was legalized economic warfare.

Yet amid this grim design, the law made strange exceptions. The Moors—likely due to political alliances, diplomatic leverage, or religious kinship with European powers, were exempt. Their immunity wasn't about race. It was about convenience. This selective exemption laid the truth bare: race was never just about skin. It was a category, a tool, manipulated to justify power.

Drury Farrow carried all this on his shoulders each time he stepped into that courthouse. His freedom wasn't honored—it was tolerated, and only as long as the paperwork held.

A missing document could mean his name disappeared from the tax books ... and reappeared on a slave roll.

So, every year, Drury signed his name.

He kept the papers close.

He watched the calendar, met the deadlines, and stamped his existence.

Because for him, freedom wasn't a dream, it was a document.

And every year, the system dared him to lose it.

The 1705 Slave Codes were not just laws—they were an architecture of oppression. Drafted with cold precision, they ensured that Blackness in Virginia was no longer just a marker of difference, but a legal sentence. These statutes made it clear: to be Black was to be bound. Freedom for African-descended people would never be a natural right—it would be taxed, surveilled, delayed, or denied. The ink may have dried over a century ago, but the ghosts of those laws walked silently through every courthouse and clerk's office. Their reach extended far beyond the paper they were printed on, shaping the very structure of power, race, and control in America.

And now, Drury Farrow stood in the heart of that machinery.

He stepped up to the registrar's desk, the floorboards groaning beneath his boots. The room smelled of dust and ink—thick, stagnant, the kind of air that clung to men like a warning. This was a place where existence had to be certified, where rights were recorded only to be restricted. Behind the desk sat a clerk, bored, detached—a man who had likely performed this ritual a thousand times. Names, dates, payments. No questions. No humanity. Just ink on a ledger.

Then came the moment Drury had braced for: the tax.

He had known it was coming. He'd known for months. Every spare coin from his labor, every extra harvest from his land—he had set it all aside, preparing for this moment not as a formality, but as a fight for legitimacy. Still, preparation didn't soften the blow. It didn't lighten the weight of knowing what this act really meant.

White men paid taxes on property, income, and wealth. But for free Black men like Drury, the tax was different. This wasn't a payment for what he owned. It was a toll for existing—a financial penalty for not being enslaved. A bill for breathing free air. Proof that even after freedom was gained, the system demanded its due. It was a reminder that his liberty was never guaranteed—it was leased, conditionally.

And it wasn't just the men.

Drury thought of his mother, his sisters, and the Black women in his community—strong, resourceful, burdened with the same impossible terms. Free Black and mixed-race women were taxed as tithable too, unlike their white counterparts. White womanhood came with a cloak of legal protection. But Black womanhood was seen as suspect, taxable, and subordinate. The law didn't view them as wives or daughters—it saw them as bodies to be counted and controlled. Their very presence was an inconvenience the government sought to regulate.

Drury's hand went to his pocket.

He pulled out the coins—cool, hard, and heavy with meaning. He placed them on the desk without a word, the metallic clink landing like a verdict. The clerk made his mark. Another year, another registration. Another page added to the paper trail that defined Drury's life.

This was not freedom. This was compliance. Survival. A form of quiet resistance lived out on ledgers and receipts. Free Black people like Drury were not simply living—they were being tracked, monitored, and contained. The law demanded their humility, their money, and their silence, ensuring that they never grew too confident, too wealthy, or too bold.

And still, Drury paid, not because he accepted the terms—but because he knew the cost of not paying was far greater.

Although Drury was officially discharged from service in 1778, alongside forty-two others—that wouldn't be the end of his entanglement with a government determined to burden him for the color of his skin. Long after his military duty ended, Drury's name continued to appear in tax records, etched across county lines from Albemarle to Powhatan, Goochland, and Campbell. Each entry served as a reminder that his so-called freedom came with a price.

Unlike white citizens, whose taxes were calculated based on land and property, free Black men like Drury faced a far more insidious form of economic targeting. These weren't just financial obligations, they were instruments of control. The state scrutinized their movements, tracked their assets, and imposed taxes not only to extract money but to suppress upward mobility. Drury's horses and cattle marked him as a man of modest success, but success for a free Black man was dangerous. Being listed as taxable wasn't just a bureaucratic note—it was a tactic. A warning. A way to keep free Black men tethered to a system designed to keep them under pressure, always watching, always collecting.

In 1785 and 1786, Drury rented a plantation in Powhatan County from Robert Pleasants, a prominent Quaker and vocal abolitionist known for legally securing the freedom of enslaved people. But even allies had limits. In August 1790, Pleasants sued Drury over an unpaid rent debt of £10—a sum equivalent to about $44.40 at the time, based on the value of silver. It wasn't just about the money. It was about power.

Drury didn't back down. In October of that year, he filed a countersuit in Goochland County's chancery court, asserting that he had already paid part of the debt. What followed was a legal clash that drew in multiple depositions, including a striking testimony from Samuel Red, a formerly enslaved man who had been freed by Pleasants himself. Red testified that Drury admitted he owed the debt—but also that he was trying to sell his livestock to make good on it. The case laid bare the fragile line that free Black men like Drury had to walk. He had land, animals, and rental agreements—but at any moment, his financial foundation could be challenged and shaken by a white landowner with legal power on his side.

By 1802, Drury was living in St. Ann's Parish, Albemarle County, where his name appeared once again on the tax rolls—this time beside his son Daniel. It wasn't enough that Drury paid taxes on his own possessions; as a free Black man, he was forced to pay taxes on his adult sons as well. The message from the state was clear: Black freedom, even when legally recognized, would carry a cost. It would be taxed, tracked, and punished. And for families like Drury's, simply existing meant bearing the crushing weight of a system engineered to remind them they were never truly free.

Over the next decade, Drury Farrow's footsteps carved a quiet trail through the Virginia backcountry—from Buckingham County to Campbell County—each move a calculation for survival in a world stacked against him. By 1813, census records show him with two free Black males and four other free persons of color in his household. These were likely his children or kin, each one trying to forge a future in a land where their freedom was seen not as a right—but as a threat.

Drury's life was the story of a free Black man wrestling for control over his own destiny in a society meticulously engineered to deny him that right. Though legally free, every corner of his existence was taxed, surveilled, and contested.

He was heavily taxed on his horses, cattle, and even his male family members; forced to register as a tithable, so the state could monitor his finances and movements like a man on parole; and sued for debts, stripped of protection under a legal system that bent in favor of white landowners.

This wasn't freedom. It was a balancing act on a knife's edge.

Picture him—Drury Farrow—riding alone on a weathered horse down a winding dirt road, the wheels of his mind turning with worry and calculation. The scent of damp soil mixed with the bitter perfume of drying tobacco leaves—a smell that hung over the Southern air like a curse and a memory. This was the land he had fought to carve his name into. A land that could—at any moment—erase him.

They called him the "Free Negro," but Drury knew better. Freedom, for a Black man in early nineteenth-century Virginia, was a brittle illusion—beautiful from a distance, but sharp-edged and dangerous up close.

He had earned his standing through grit—accumulating livestock, property, and a shred of status. Yet every achievement painted a target on his back. The law never let him forget that he wasn't supposed to thrive. He was an anomaly in a world that thrived on chains. Every tax notice, every court summons, every forced registration whispered the same message: you don't belong.

His legacy was not written in marble or cast in bronze, but in the soil he worked, the taxes he paid, the children he raised, and the silence he defied. Drury Farrow was never meant to leave a legacy—not by the standards of the system that sought to crush men like him. Yet, he did. His life stands as a searing testament to Black resilience, a quiet rebellion against a nation that demanded his obedience but denied his humanity.

Drury turned away from the courthouse, his steps slow and deliberate. The coins had left his hands. His debt was paid. He had done what the law required of him—again. But in his bones, he knew it would never be enough. It was never just about taxes or livestock. It was about control. About reminding him that his freedom was conditional. At any moment, the world could shift beneath his feet and drag him back into a shadow he never chose.

Still, he walked, not with rage, not with rebellion, but with the sheer defiance of endurance. He bought land. He built a life with his bare hands. He educated his children when the law said they should remain ignorant. And when the world tried to write him out, he made himself permanent.

For years, I traced bloodlines, peeling back pages of history. If the Irish Wards could follow their line back to the damn Mayflower, I knew I could trace mine. And when I reached the edge of the archive, the furthest branch on the tree, I found him—Drury, the "Free Negro." Catherine Moss Ward's grandfather. Yes, my great-great-great-grandmother. A woman truly born free.

He didn't carry a musket or lead a rebellion, but Drury fought with something deeper. He fought with survival, with presence. And through his quiet resistance, he carved the first steps of a legacy that would echo through generations.

His granddaughter, Catherine, would carry that fire. And the man she married—one with a sharp mind and an unshakable will—would take it even further. He would fight not just for his name, but for his people. Through political resistance, through organizing, through the Underground Railroad, he would pick up where Drury left off. His name was John T. Ward.

The 1705 Slave Codes tried to reduce free Black men to little more than entries in a tax ledger. But Drury Farrow refused to be a number. He was a man, a builder, a keeper of dignity, and a forerunner to a movement.

And that was a legacy no law could erase.

John T. Ward grew up to be a conductor on the Underground Railroad and a pioneer of Black economic power. He understood what too many had learned the hard way: freedom was never given. It had to be fought for, protected, and defended—daily.

If his ancestors had been stripped of their land, pushed out, erased from the record, John T. would make sure the next generation of Wards built something no one could take away, not with law, not with lies, and not with violence.

The past was prologue. The fight was never over.

For John T. Ward, the forced exile of his grandfather Samuel in 1827 wasn't just a family story, it was a defining moment. It shaped how he would fight for justice, resist, and walk through the world.

Unlike Davy, John T. Ward would never beg to stay. He would demand to be heard.

The truth of what happened in 1827 was undeniable: David and Nancy Ward stayed. Samuel Ward was exiled, and from that point forward, history split in two.

Where David asked for permission, John T. demanded recognition. Where David sought safety in silence, John T. rose with voice and conviction. He spoke truth in public forums. He fought on battlegrounds of justice. He wielded the pen like a weapon.

But now, through truth-telling, we trace those broken lines. We follow what was meant to be erased. We amplify the voices the law tried to silence. We remember. We restore.

Today, I bring those paths back together. I can track them. I can document them. I can tell the story they tried to bury. And that is why—I will not stop.

Now, imagine this: You walk away from nearly three hundred acres of fertile Virginia farmland—your inheritance, your bequest, what was bequeathed to you—knowing deep in your bones you may never lay eyes on it again. You cross state lines, not in triumph, but in quiet torment, leaving behind the sacred soil that fed your ancestors, cradled your history, and carried your name.

And when you arrive—free, but not welcome, your hard-won liberty is not met with promise, but with pointed fingers and laughter—not with opportunity, but with public humiliation. Freedom, you learn, is not the end of struggle. It's the beginning of a new kind of battle.

You survived slavery, but freedom has not made you free.

In Lawrence County, Ohio, you're not welcomed, you're watched. White officials don't recognize your dignity; they scoff at your clothes, whisper about your character, and question your very right to stand on the same ground. Before your feet even touched the soil, your presence was already a problem. Letters had been written. White residents demanding answers—why were so many freed slaves "flooding" the county?

Your freedom, hard-earned and holy, arrives not as a triumph, but as a threat. And they make sure you feel it. Every glare. Every question. Every closed door. You are not seen as a settler. You are not welcomed as a neighbor. You are seen as a threat.

The Ward family, newly emancipated and hopeful, stepped into this storm.

Back in Virginia, they had land, nearly three hundred acres—an inheritance worth close to two million dollars by today's standards. But to stay and claim it meant risking everything. Freedom, in the South, was fragile. One forged paper, one false accusation, one crooked judge could send a free man back into bondage.

And then came the deception. They were tricked, swindled out of the very land that had been promised. This wasn't a misunderstanding. It was a well-orchestrated betrayal—possibly at the hands of one of Lt. John Ward's own brothers or nephews, a man rumored to have paid the family's five-hundred-dollar bond to help them relocate to Ohio. Whether out of guilt, political calculation, or manipulation, the relocation was made to look like mercy.

But it was really a convenient removal.

In Ohio, freed Black families were subjected to a cruel legal hurdle: a five-hundred-dollar bond and two white witnesses—required to prove they would not become a burden to the state. The Ward family, newly freed but determined, met that burden. They placed a down payment and paid the bond in full within three weeks. They did everything that was asked of them—and still, the betrayal followed them.

Samuel Ward would spend the final years of his life fighting to reclaim what had been stolen.

He wrote letter after letter to claim the Cook Estate—the land that had been promised as part of their inheritance. What he received was silence, stonewalls, and delays. The land deeds conveniently lacked valid descriptions—a bureaucratic sleight of hand that erased their rights with the stroke of a pen. Then, a year later, came the devastating revelation: the land had been sold.

But by whom? And to whom? Under what authority? No one could—or would—answer.

Samuel continued to press for answers. He pored over documents. He pleaded for justice. But he died in 1830 with nothing returned to him. The Cook Estate was gone. His name, his fight, buried in silence.

And yet, he left behind something far more powerful than land: resistance.

The newly freed Ward family and others were sent to Poke Patch, Burlington, and Black Fork, small, tightly knit Black settlements hidden in the wooded hills of Lawrence County, Ohio. These enclaves, established as early as 1818, became fragile sanctuaries for the newly emancipated. Often built near Quaker communities, their quiet sympathy for fugitives offered only a threadbare shield against the ever-present threat of re-enslavement.

Forty miles from the Ohio River, these settlements provided a sliver of distance from danger—but never true safety. Even in Ohio, liberty was conditional. Slave patrols prowled the edges of these communities, armed with lies, ready to drag anyone they could falsely brand as "suspicious" back into bondage.

In this uncertain land, safety was forged in numbers. Black families gathered not only for fellowship—but for survival.

When the Ward family arrived, only fifteen free Black residents lived in Lawrence County. By 1829, that number had surged—and with it, tensions rose. White residents grumbled that no one was enforcing the bond law. The pressure grew.

Still, the Wards pressed forward.

Newly emancipated and determined, they didn't shrink. They placed their down payment. Paid their bond in full within three weeks. They joined a growing community of survivors—a place where their pain was understood and their resilience mirrored.

They found more than shelter. They found a spiritual home. A Black Baptist church had already been established, and by 1821, it had linked with an anti-slavery Baptist association near the Black Fork settlement. Where the law failed them, faith carried them. Where government looked away, fellowship held them up.

What they lost in land, they rebuilt in hope. What was stolen in Virginia, they planted again—in exile, in community, and in fire.

But let's be clear: A crime was committed. And it left a scar not only on the soul of one family, but on the conscience of a nation.

As my distant cousin Daisy Ward would later write in *The Perfect Law of Liberty*, this was not an isolated injustice. It was part of a calculated pattern—one that betrayed freedmen through red tape, silence, and state-sanctioned theft. A pattern that erased Black prosperity before it could take root.

"When they take it from us, they take more than just soil and trees; they take our legacy, our freedom, and our place in this world."

The Ward family was tricked out of their land, not by accident—but by design. It was orchestrated. It was deliberate. It was theft.

And still—they endured.

Their story is not only one of survival, but of defiance, not just of suffering, but of legacy. A legacy that says: You may try to erase us—but we will not disappear.

This is not just a chapter in a family's story. It is a reckoning.

It is history that demands to be remembered. And only by confronting the past can we build a future rooted in truth, justice, and liberty for all.

Their story is a monument—not just to resilience, but to truth. A reminder that liberty was never handed over. It had to be fought for, letter by letter, generation by generation, and scar by scar.

Through painstaking research, I was able to pinpoint the exact moment Samuel Ward and his family were exiled from Virginia—a forced removal hidden in plain sight, betrayed only by the cold ink of historical documents.

The *Ohio State Journal*, dated May 3, 1827, reports the Ward family's presence in Lawrence County, Ohio, as early as April 14, 1827. That date isn't just a line in a newspaper, it's a time-stamped indictment. It proves that Samuel was already gone—ripped from Virginia soil—before David Ward ever submitted his petition to the Virginia legislature. The removal happened first. The paperwork came later. It was all a calculated cover-up.

But the deception runs deeper.

According to Pittsylvania County deed records, Samuel Ward's land was "transferred" to David Ward on August 20, 1827. On paper, it looks routine. But we know better. Samuel was already in Ohio—

exiled. This wasn't a transaction. It was a theft recorded in real time; a legal lie meant to strip him of his bequest.

Even worse? The indenture has no land description. None. What kind of court allows the sale of property with no land boundaries, no coordinates, no detail? Who buys land with description unless they never intended to be questioned?

And on that same day, August 20, 1827, there are two different entries, claiming Samuel sold the same land to David Ward and Daniel Ward. How? A man can't sell the same land twice. Especially not when he's three hundred miles away in another state.

It's clear the court couldn't decide which lie to go with.

They weren't trying to document a transaction. They were scrambling to legitimize theft.

And they knew no one would stop them. Because Samuel was a freedman, and in 1827, freedmen had no voice in a courtroom controlled by white men who made the rules.

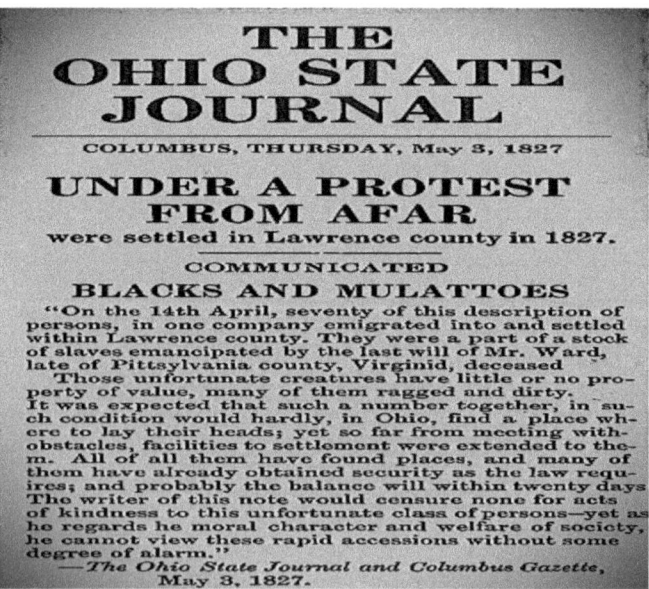

THE OHIO STATE JOURNAL

COLUMBUS, THURSDAY, May 3, 1827

UNDER A PROTEST FROM AFAR

were settled in Lawrence county in 1827.

COMMUNICATED

BLACKS AND MULATTOES

"On the 14th April, seventy of this description of persons, in one company emigrated into and settled within Lawrence county. They were a part of a stock of slaves emancipated by the last will of Mr. Ward, late of Pittsylvania county, Virginid, deceased

Those unfortunate creatures have little or no property of value, many of them ragged and dirty. It was expected that such a number together, in such condition would hardly, in Ohio, find a place where to lay their heads; yet so far from meeting with obstacles, facilities to settlement were extended to them. All of all them have found places, and many of them have already obtained security as the law requires; and probably the balance will within twenty days The writer of this note would censure none for acts of kindness to this unfortunate class of persons—yet as he regards the moral character and welfare of society, he cannot view these rapid accessions without some degree of alarm."

—*The Ohio State Journal and Columbus Gazette,* May 3, 1827.

Let's not forget what was at stake. Virginia law demanded twenty dollars for every enslaved person over fifteen years old. That means—without interest—Samuel's heirs are owed well over one hundred thousand dollars, possibly double depending on their ages at the time of his death. They didn't just steal land. They stole labor, legacy, and generational wealth, lied under oath to cover it up.

This wasn't just betrayal. It was a systemic crime.

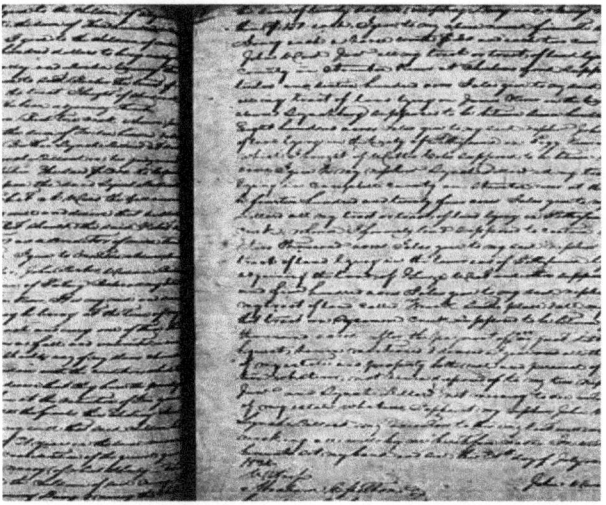

Facsimile of the Last Will and Testament of Lt. John Ward, dated 1826. This original handwritten document, composed in 19th-century cursive, outlines the bequest of land and the manumission of enslaved individuals, including the family of Samuel, Hannah Ward and John T. Ward. As customary in the antebellum South, enslaved people were listed alongside livestock and property, underscoring the dehumanizing legal norms of the era. This will serves as a foundational document in tracing the early history of John T. Ward and the Ward family legacy in Virginia and Ohio.

And while Samuel was being erased from Virginia records, Ohio told another story. Black settlements were thriving—building towns, churches, schools, and lives from scratch. That success fueled white resentment. The sight of Black prosperity enraged those who believed freedom was never meant for people like Samuel Ward.

Domestic white terrorism followed. Freedmen were harassed, hunted, and warned to stay close together. Children were taught not to wander off—not just for safety, but for survival.

Because just two years earlier, in 1825, Pennsylvania exposed a nightmare: bands of white kidnappers stealing Black children under ten years old, selling them south into slavery, and collecting blood money for every life stolen.

That's the world Samuel fled into.

And that's the system that ripped everything from him—and got away with it.

Until now.

Meanwhile, back in Virginia …

It was the winter of 1827, and David Ward stood alone against the law.

A free Black man in a state that wanted no such thing to exist. A man torn between the liberty he had earned and the soil where his soul was rooted. The letter he clutched in trembling hands—penned not in ink but in blood, sweat, and twenty-five years of sacrifice—was his last hope.

The Virginia General Assembly had passed its decree: *No free Black shall remain within state lines for more than twelve months.* Refuse, and you'd be stripped of your liberty—dragged back into slavery.

David Ward had been a slave once. Born into bondage on the plantation of John Ward the elder, he had served not just in the fields, but in the shadows of the man himself. Lt. John Ward Jr.—the wealthiest landholder in Pittsylvania County, unmarried, isolated, and riddled with disease—trusted no one but David.

And why wouldn't he?

For twenty-five years, David had slept by his master's side, night after night, never once leaving unless dispatched on errands. When sickness came—sudden, vicious, convulsive—David sprang into action, often saving the man's life before death could strike. He was nurse, steward, bodyguard, and caretaker rolled into one.

For two decades, David also managed the Ward Ordinary, the tavern that served travelers and locals alike. He took their bags. He poured their drinks. He tallied their bills and collected their coins. He kept the keys to the storeroom and the liquor. He managed accounts, supervised laborers, ran the plantations, and handled debts. He held, at times, John Ward's money—and his secrets.

No white man, no overseer, and no blood relative had ever held that trust.

But now, the state of Virginia had turned its back on him.

When John Ward died, he left David his freedom, a home, and the right to live in Pittsylvania County. It was more than a gesture—it was a testament. The final act of a dying man who understood the worth of the slave who had saved his life and built his legacy.

David had done everything by the book.

He had petitioned the County Court of Pittsylvania for permission to stay in Virginia, as required by law. Thirty judges presided over that court. Twenty-nine of them voted in David's favor.

Only one opposed him—not because David was unworthy, but because that judge had vowed never to approve any petition from a free Black person, regardless of circumstance. One man's ideology—one cold-hearted vote—had the power to destroy a life.

And so, with the clock ticking toward forced exile or re-enslavement, David turned to his final lifeline: the Virginia General Assembly.

The letter he wrote to them was not just a plea—it was a fight for survival.

"You have proclaimed by your laws that some of this almost outcast race may be permitted to remain amongst you," he wrote. *"You have conceded these favors to those distinguished for fidelity and attachment to the institutions of your country. I beg you—do not take away the humble pittance left to me for my old age. I beg you—do not drive me from my birthland, my home, my life."*

He warned them—what message would it send if a man like him, loyal, law-abiding, and faithful beyond reason, could be cast out like trash? What hope would remain for the enslaved? If virtue meant nothing, then why even try? David did not raise his voice. He did not threaten. He did not challenge the law with fury—but with facts, loyalty, and honor. He made his case not as a rebel, but as a son of Virginia—one who had given his youth, his strength, and nearly his life to the state's prosperity.

He asked for one thing: the right to remain in Pittsylvania County on the condition of good behavior. He backed his plea with witness statements, a copy of John Ward's will, and the county court's overwhelming support.

But on December 19th, 1827, the Assembly gave its response: Rejected. Just like that—rejected.

David Ward, once the most trusted man in the household of a Virginia patriarch, now faced the full cruelty of the law. He had twelve months to leave the state or risk being snatched back into chains. The same state whose laws once recognized his loyalty now threatened to turn him into a criminal for simply existing freely.

It was the price of Black freedom in America.

David Ward's petition is more than a letter. It is the very definition of resistance—not with weapons, but with truth, with honor, and with an unshakable belief in justice. This is not the story of a man who begged like a dog. This is the story of a man who stood tall in front of power, spoke plainly, and dared to ask: What is a man's worth if his freedom means nothing?

The year was 1827, and the courts were brimming with conflict. Meanwhile, the Staunton River raged below the shattered remains of what had once been a proud feat of engineering—a toll bridge built by Major John Ward, a calculated move to capitalize on the growing flow of commerce between Virginia's counties. But the bridge was no longer just a structure washed away by floodwaters. In the aftermath of a disaster, it became something else entirely: a symbol, a battlefield.

The broken timbers echoed with the clash of inheritance, power, and control.

This bridge, like so many structures in early Virginia, stood on the backs of the enslaved Ward families who built it—stone by stone, beam by beam. Their labor carved prosperity from the wilderness. And yet, what they built, white dominance sought to erase. The toll bridge's ruin marked more than the end of safe passage across the Staunton—it marked the unraveling of a legacy, a foreshadowing of legal battles to come, and a brutal reminder that Black labor built the foundations of Virginia's wealth, even as it was systematically excluded from its rewards.

The executor and nephew of the late Lt. John Ward Jr., John Ward, stood at the riverbank, watching the ruin. The bridge, constructed to support the bustling trade between counties, had become something far greater: a lifeline, a legacy. And now, it was ground zero in a bitter war—not just over property, but over inheritance, legitimacy, and control.

Years earlier, John Ward Sr. had entered into a lease agreement with John Lynch and Patsey Barbour. The contract was clear: the Ward family would retain access to the bridge and adjoining land. But when the tolls began—when they were barred from crossing their own father's bridge—it was no accident. It was a betrayal. A calculated move. And John Ward Jr. knew it.

This wasn't about a bridge. It was a warning. A declaration of how power truly operated in America.

The legal fight that followed—*John Ward Jr. vs. Patsey Barbour*— should have been simple. A contractual dispute. But in 1827, the law wasn't a shield for Black families. It was a blade. Instead of upholding the Ward family's clear rights, the court case dragged through a system built not to deliver justice but to maintain the racial hierarchy.

What they encountered wasn't a misunderstanding, it was a message: land ownership was never meant to secure Black freedom.

It was a lie fed to the hopeful, while white executors, speculators, and local officials twisted the legal system to stall, challenge, and ultimately strip Black families of what was rightfully theirs.

The Ward family had legal documents. They had paid bonds. They had earned their place. But the system made them fight for every inch—and lose it, inch by inch.

And here's the deeper truth: even white women like Patsey Barbour, though named in the will, were not safe from the system's appetite for control. In 1827, women had few rights under the law. Under the legal doctrine of *coverture*, a married woman had no legal identity apart from her husband. She couldn't own property, sign contracts, or sue in court. Only unmarried women (*feme sole*) retained any real legal power—but even that could vanish with a marriage license.

Patsey's claim to toll bridge rights was unusual—and precarious. Her exclusion revealed something deeper: property, power, and legal protection were never intended for anyone outside the white, landowning male class.

And yet, if even she—a white woman with documentation—could be denied land and economic rights, what chance did a Black family have?

Newly freed families like the Wards weren't just navigating gender bias. They were facing the full brutality of a racial caste system. The law wasn't just indifferent to their rights—it was weaponized against them.

Land was promised then stolen. Bonds were paid then ignored. Deeds were drafted but written in invisible ink.

The case of the toll bridge exposed it all: contracts meant nothing when white power felt threatened. Legal victories were illusions. The courts weren't arbiters—they were enforcers of a system built to deny

Black families access to generational wealth, economic independence, and political power.

Because in 1827, owning land wasn't just about legacy. It was a step toward voting, toward self-determination. And that made Black ownership dangerous in the eyes of those who built the system to exclude them.

Patsey Barbour's struggle was real. But it was a mirror—a chilling reflection of something far more severe: if she could be denied her rightful claim, Black families were never meant to survive the system at all.

David Ward was born into bondage, freed by law, but bound still by history. He did not raise his voice. He didn't need to. His very presence in the courtroom was thunder enough—a freed Black man, no longer property, daring to ask not for privilege, but for permanence. He sought no reparation, only the right to remain in the red clay that had soaked up his ancestors' sweat.

But his petition—so careful, so reasonable—cut deeper than any rebellion. It demanded the state reckon with a truth it had buried beneath tobacco fields and legal parchment: What, if anything, does Virginia owe to the hands that built her?

The Commonwealth, brittle and blistering under the weight of its contradictions, flinched. White lawmakers, still drunk on power and paralyzed by fear, whispered behind closed doors. A man like David—loyal and trusted even by the family who once enslaved him—had become a paradox too dangerous to ignore.

This was no ordinary plea. It was an indictment wrapped in humility, a spark inside dry timber. And everyone in the room knew that if David Ward was allowed to stay, others would come knocking. If he belonged here, what did that say about the system that said he never should?

Dr. John B. Rutledge of Campbell County, a respected physician, bore witness to this quiet storm. He had served for five years as the attending doctor to the late John Ward Sr.—a man chronically ill and prone to sudden, violent attacks of sickness. Rutledge's testimony was unflinching: without David and Nancy Ward's constant care, their master would have died years earlier. These weren't just house servants, they were healers, guardians, lifelines. Rutledge stood at Ward's bedside in his final moments and heard the dying man, with a voice ragged from age and illness, tell David and Nancy they had done more than he ever could have hoped. They had saved his life—again and again—and he prayed they would one day be rewarded. Rutledge confirmed that their petition to remain in Virginia was not only truthful but rooted in a sacred bond of trust between master and formerly enslaved, one that defied the norms of their time.

Captain James Adams, another voice of white authority, added his own powerful affirmation. A former justice of the Pittsylvania County Court, Adams had known David Ward for twelve years and lived just five miles from him. He had once handed $310—an enormous sum in 1819—directly to David when the elder Ward was away. He never questioned it. And weeks later, the books were balanced to the penny. Such trust, from a white man to a Black man in antebellum Virginia, was virtually unimaginable. Adams had seen David's petition and knew most of the claims to be fact. The only justice who voted against allowing David to stay, Adams revealed, didn't dispute the merits of the case—he simply refused to support any petition from a Black person, no matter how noble.

And then, astonishingly—scandalously—came the testimony of John Ward's own white family.

Robert A. Ward, a close relative excluded from the will, came forward—not to contest the estate, but to defend David and Nancy.

He had known them from birth and vouched for their character in terms that echoed reverence. They had achieved, he wrote, a "weight of character far beyond any slaves now or heretofore known by me." Robert A. Ward's support wasn't just rare—it was defiant. He had nothing to gain. And yet he stood on principle.

Even more shocking, Lynch Dillard and John Ward Jr.—the executors of the very will that emancipated David and Nancy—also stepped into the fray. Their account painted a picture that upended every plantation trope. John Ward Sr., they revealed, had never married, nor placed a white manager over his property. Instead, he entrusted his entire estate—his inn, his finances, his guests, his liquor, even his legal papers—to David and Nancy. They kept the storeroom keys. They ran the business. David negotiated debts, managed enslaved laborers across plantations, and was often the only one his master relied on for urgent, high-level decisions.

During John Ward Sr.'s long, painful decline, it was David and Nancy who administered his care—day in, day out. When the end came, John Sr. handed David his final will and testament, instructing him to guard it until death and then deliver it to the executors. He obeyed, faithfully, with a precision and loyalty that surpassed even blood ties.

And yet, it wasn't enough. The system David trusted would never love him back.

For a Black man in 1827 Virginia to receive such staggering endorsements—from physicians, judges, neighbors, and even the white heirs of his former master—was unprecedented. These testimonies should have sealed David's place in the community forever. But the law had already made its decision. David and Nancy's extraordinary virtue collided with a system designed to erase them.

By 1831, Virginia would pass laws officially expelling free Black people from the state. But the campaign to purge them began years earlier—in whispers and shadows. Even as David fought for his right to stay in the only home he had ever known, the tide was turning against men like him. His very presence—respected, capable, free— threatened the fragile power balance of white supremacy.

Davy stayed. He fought for himself. But not for the others?

A troubling silence hung over his extended Black family many of whom were cast out without protest. Among them was Samuel Ward, who fled to Ohio, never to return. The question gnaws at history's edge: Did David Ward only fight for himself and his sister?

This realization stirs something deep within me. How do we reconcile this? Was Davy simply pragmatic—recognizing that the system would never grant safety to all, so he fought only for what he could salvage? Or did he deliberately distance himself from the rest of the family, securing his own position while the others were cast away?

This uneasy contradiction in David's story evokes a haunting comparison: Stephen, the infamous house slave portrayed by Samuel L. Jackson in *Django Unchained*—a man whose loyalty to his white master became a weapon wielded against his own people.

Was David, too, a man who had internalized the plantation's twisted logic? Did he come to see himself as exceptional—set apart from the fate of other freedmen—because of his proximity to white power? His actions suggest a dangerous seduction: the belief that loyalty and usefulness to the master class could grant protection, even favor.

Like Stephen, David may have adopted the hierarchy that once held him in chains, positioning himself not alongside his kin, but above them. That dynamic—though it may have offered a fleeting sense of security—ultimately left him exposed and alone. His refusal, or inability, to align with the collective struggle of the Ward family underscores the high cost of individualism in the face of systemic oppression.

And it forces us to ask painful, necessary questions: Was freedom in 1827 reserved only for those who remained loyal to their white benefactors? Was there an unspoken rule that Black people could be free—but only if they didn't challenge the structure that once enslaved them?

"They have healed the wound of my people lightly, saying, 'Peace, peace,' when there is no peace."— Jeremiah 6:14

This verse pierces the illusion David clung to—the belief that excellence, loyalty, and quiet obedience could buy him true freedom within a system designed to reject him. It speaks to the false balm of surface-level acceptance—a fragile peace offered only to those who never dared to disrupt the order. Behind that illusion was a deeper truth: the wound had never healed. It had simply been ignored.

David, for all his integrity and unwavering service, remained bound to a structure that only celebrated Black excellence when it posed no threat. His reward was not liberation—but tolerance, conditional and brittle.

And when he left Pittsylvania County for the North, he left behind more than soil and memory—he walked away from the collective strength of his people. In choosing the path of individual survival, he abandoned the possibility of shared resistance. His decision to walk alone made him visible, respectable, even commendable—but deeply vulnerable.

In the end, for all his victories on paper, David was no freer than the relatives who had been driven out—just quieter, just more polite.

Though the land was gone, the fire remained. His descendants carried that resolve like a torch passed through generations. Because when the dominant society takes land from us, they're not just seizing soil and trees; they're stealing our legacy, our freedom, our place in this world.

The story of the Ward family is more than history—it's a war journal. A testament to survival. A grim reminder of the systems built to destroy Black wealth and erase Black presence.

This wasn't a one-time betrayal. It was a sanctioned campaign of theft—approved by government officials, enabled by courts, and met with silence by society.

And it didn't stop with Samuel Ward.

The Perfect Law of Liberty lays it bare: Freedmen's land was stolen through forged deeds, doctored records, and outright lies. Samuel Ward's signature was forged on a deed while he was already in Ohio—a man exiled, his name hijacked to finalize a theft. In one breath, Virginia's courts claimed the land had been sold under his name. In the next, they denied the land ever existed.

How does land get sold and vanish at the same time?

It doesn't. It's fraud. It's conspiracy. It's calculated erasure.

These weren't clerical errors. These were weapons. Part of a larger, insidious pattern, a blueprint for racial disenfranchisement designed to keep Black families landless, powerless, and economically trapped. Public records were manipulated. Legal loopholes twisted. Judges and clerks looked the other way or helped pave the path of theft.

And families like the Wards? They were left to fight ghosts in courthouses—battling forged signatures, deeds that never existed, and a justice system that decided long ago they didn't matter.

But the contradictions are not mistakes. They're openings, cracks in the wall. And through those cracks comes light.

Legal challenges. Public reckoning. Restoration.

We must expose every forged deed. We must call out every manipulated record. We must drag the truth out from under centuries of dust and denial

Because justice buried is justice denied.

John T. Ward inherited more than a name. He inherited a war. A war for land. A war for dignity. A war for existence inside a system built to erase Black futures and rewrite Black legacies.

That land was supposed to be a beginning, a foundation, and a foothold toward freedom.

But it was stripped from them—not with whips or chains, but with pen strokes and court stamps. Legal sabotage wrapped in bureaucracy. White executors, cloaked in red tape and powered by racial entitlement, blocked every claim the Wards tried to make. They stalled, they challenged, they lied until the land slipped away, piece by piece, generation by generation.

But the fight? It's not over. It never was. And this time, we know the playbook.

This wasn't just the Wards' story. It echoes across time, across coasts.

In the early 1900s, Charles and Willa Bruce built a sanctuary, Bruce's Beach in Manhattan Beach, California, a haven for Black families. Until the city seized it in 1924 under "eminent domain"—a lie wrapped in legalese. They claimed it was for a public park. But the land sat empty for decades. It wasn't about parks. It was about removing Black wealth from the shoreline.

It took nearly a century of activism before the land was returned to their descendants in 2022.

Further south on Hilton Head Island, Gullah families, descendants of freed slaves, have fought to keep their ancestral land. Passed down informally through generations, their property is labeled "heirs' property"—a legal gray zone. Developers prey on it. Courts exploit it. Through partition sales and loopholes, Black land is swallowed by the system once again.

Different names, different states, but the same blueprint—theft through legality, erasure through silence. And families, generation after generation, are forced to fight for what was already theirs.

But we're not silent anymore. And this time, we're coming with receipts. Yes, a paper trail.

In 1922, Ennis Ward went looking for answers—and refused to settle for silence.

A descendant of Samuel Ward, Ennis had grown up with whispers—stories passed down about land that had been promised, stolen, buried beneath lies and legal tricks.

But Ennis wasn't interested in folklore. He wanted the truth. And he was ready to hunt it down.

He reached out to John Thomas Hornaday, a formidable figure in Yellow Springs, Ohio—no stranger to battles against bureaucracy. Hornaday was a veteran pension agent with thirty-five years of trench work behind him, a man who knew how to navigate the tangled mess of government red tape that so often crushed Black families trying to claim what was theirs.

Hornaday had roots in purpose. He studied at Wilberforce College, then Antioch College from 1885 to 1888, before launching a real estate and notary public office by 1890. His reputation only grew when the U.S. Secretary of the Interior commissioned him to argue pension cases—a rare honor. He served as Justice of the Peace in Miami Township for two decades, was deeply active in Central Chapel AME Church for forty years, and held respect as a proud member of the Masonic Fountain Lodge.

He was not just a bureaucrat. He was a gatekeeper, an advocate, and a lifeline.

And during a time when Black veterans and their widows were routinely denied benefits, Hornaday stood in the breach. The pension system was a battlefield—rigged and rotten, weighed down by racism, buried in "lost files," and choked by requirements meant to exclude Black families. Most formerly enslaved people had no official birth records. That alone was enough for white officials to delay or deny their claims.

Meanwhile, white pension agents and attorneys ran a predatory side game—charging Black families outrageous fees, dragging out their cases, and too often pocketing the money while delivering nothing.

It was theft wrapped in paperwork.

And it didn't stop with pensions. Land theft was the next front—just as strategic, just as devastating. Black-owned land, bought or promised during Reconstruction, became the target of white developers, county clerks, and crooked lawyers. Entire Black families were pushed off their land through legal loopholes, backroom deals, forged documents, and "errors" no one corrected.

Ennis Ward wanted to know what happened to the Cook Estate—three hundred acres of promised land.

Hornaday responded with clarity, gravity, and something that felt like prophecy.

According to legal records reviewed by an attorney in the pension office, the Cook Estate—once sprawling, once full of promise—was worth thirty thousand dollars in 1922.

Thirty thousand dollars. That wasn't just wealth. That was stability for generations, a shield against poverty, a tool for power.

But the land was long gone—stolen, buried, and erased.

Hornaday made it plain; this wasn't just about acres and title deeds. This was a moral debt, a theft that echoed across time. He didn't know when justice would come—but he was sure of one thing: it would.

Because stolen land doesn't rest. It haunts. It lingers. And eventually, the truth demands to be paid in full.

This was never just about the Ward family. It was about every Black family that had land ripped out from under them. It was about every ancestor who died believing justice might find their descendants. It was about a system designed to erase Black legacy while protecting white wealth.

So, the question Hornaday left Ennis with still hangs in the air: When will justice be delivered?

Because justice delayed isn't just denied—it's devoured. And the clock is still ticking.

CHAPTER 7

Partus Sequitur Ventrem

"All children born in this country shall be held bonded or free only according to the condition of the mother."

-Virginia Act enacted in 1662

The first time I learned that a child's freedom was determined by their mother's status, it shattered everything I thought I knew about justice and inheritance. I was sitting in a classroom at my HBCU in the 1990s when my professor said, in a voice heavy with truth, "If your mother was free, you were free. If she was enslaved, so were you." That statement lodged itself deep within me. It sparked a relentless question that would follow me for years: How was John T. Ward—born in Richmond, Virginia, a place drowning in the horrors of slavery—granted the gift of freedom?

That question became a thread I couldn't stop pulling. My search for answers took me down painful historical paths where I came face-to-face with the brutal and unspoken realities of enslaved women's lives. Among the most haunting of these discoveries was a plantation death ledger. It was a sterile, chilling list of names and dates—a cold record of life lost. But it was what wasn't said that kept me up at night.

The entries for infant deaths stood out. Their brief descriptions, vague causes, and silent patterns told a different story—one of despair. There were too many, too consistent, and too quiet. I began to see what no one had written: these were not simply victims of disease or misfortune. They were acts of defiance. Some mothers, consumed by the unbearable knowledge of what life in chains would mean for their babies, chose the only form of freedom they could offer—release. Their silence screams through history, not because they didn't love their children, but because they loved them too much to let them suffer.

Resistance through suicide and collective refusal among enslaved Africans proves that the idea of "death over bondage" was never just poetic. It was a lived, often fatal, act of rebellion.

Long before Patrick Henry's famous cry—"Give me liberty, or give me death!"—echoed through colonial halls, African men, women, and children were already living that creed in the belly of slave ships and across the blood-soaked soil of plantations.

They leapt into oceans. They refused to eat. They chose death not from despair, but as a final, defiant declaration of dignity, a protest against a world that refused to acknowledge their humanity.

Their sacrifice was America's first, and most unacknowledged, declaration of liberty.

That realization shook me to my core. It forced me to confront what it truly means to choose between life and bondage. It reminded me of the words that echo through generations—Matshona Dhliwayo's quiet defiance:

"I would rather die free than live in bondage."

And Killmonger's haunting farewell in *Black Panther*:

"Bury me in the ocean with my ancestors who jumped from ships, because they knew death was better than bondage."

These are more than lines from art or memory—they are reverberations of a shared truth, the cries of those who understood freedom's price. They carry the ghostly cadence of enslaved women who lived without choices, only consequences. Yet even in their silence, they resisted.

Even my father instilled this truth in me from a young age: "It's better to die standing up than to live on your knees." That wasn't just advice—it was armor. A reminder that dignity must be protected, even at the cost of everything.

Because survival without soul isn't freedom, it's another kind of cage.

In that reckoning, I learned of the existence of "fancy girls." These were young, often light-skinned enslaved women sold not for labor, but for sexual exploitation. They were displayed at auctions with calculated cruelty—dressed in fine fabrics, bathed and perfumed like dolls—while white men appraised their bodies as property and pleasure. Their bodies were bought, violated, and passed along; their worth measured only in flesh. There was no romance, no illusion of power, just ownership and abuse. The trauma didn't end with the act; it lingered in the forced births, in the children left unacknowledged, unprotected, and unseen in the records. These women's wombs were weaponized, and their silence was legislated.

And yet, in the shadows of that violence, I return to Hannah—John T. Ward's mother. I think of her with deep reverence. She, too, lived in a world that brutalized Black women's bodies, that tried to define her worth by what could be taken from her. But she made a different choice. She chose life. She chose to carry and raise her children despite the trauma, despite the pain of conception, despite the weight of what the world would say—or never say—about them. Because of Hannah's courage, I am here. Because she chose to live and love in the face of all that horror, our legacy did not end. It began.

This truth doesn't simplify the past. It doesn't offer easy answers or cast judgment on the women who made different choices. It holds space for them too—for their pain, their resistance, and their unspeakable grief. But it also forces us to ask, what do we do with this inheritance? How do we honor women who turned their wombs into battlegrounds and sanctuaries?

In today's climate of fierce debates around reproductive rights, I think about women like Hannah—about the impossible choices they made with unimaginable stakes. Their decisions weren't just about survival. They were about faith—faith in a future beyond bondage, in children who might live to see a freer world.

This chapter is not just a reflection. It is a memorial and a mandate. A call to remember the women whose voices were never written down. A vow to carry their strength with us. And a prayer that we build a world where no woman—no mother—ever has to make such choices again.

Partus Sequitur Ventrem is Latin for "that which is born follows the womb." It was a law passed in Virginia in 1662 that defined the legal status of children born in America. The legislation, inspired by Roman law regarding chattel slavery and personal property, declared that children born to free women would inherit their mother's freedom, while children born to enslaved women would inherit their mother's bondage. This is how John T. was born into slavery, even though his biological father was a white man. However, the opposite was also true—if a white woman gave birth to a mixed-race child, that child would be born free.

With the widespread rape of enslaved Black American women by their slave masters, this law ensured that the illegitimate children born from sexual violence could not expect freedom. Furthermore, their biological fathers were not held accountable and bore no legal responsibility for their mulatto children. This led many slave masters to father children as a commodity—gaining either free labor or profit from their sale.

Stories of children conceived between enslavers and the women they enslaved were passed down as oral history, often cloaked in painful whispers and guarded gossip. The Ward family carried one such secret. In my research, I discovered family trees listing John T.'s father's name simply as "John."

It wasn't just young, unmarried women like Hannah—John T.'s mother—who were raped and impregnated on the plantation. That horror alone is unbearable. But it was also well known that even enslaved women who were married were not spared. Their vows meant nothing to the men who claimed ownership over their bodies.

There were no boundaries, no protections. Just the brutal truth that any Black woman—regardless of her age, status, or marriage—could be violated at any time. The plantation was not merely a site of forced labor. It was a hunting ground for power, domination, and generational trauma.

In my research, I discovered that my relatives had different ways of telling—or concealing—the Ward family's history. It often depended on who was doing the telling, how they viewed the past, and which parts they believed were important or safe enough to share. The stories varied based on perspective, emotional connection, or even survival. I also dug into public archives.

I consider myself fortunate. While gathering information for this book, I connected with relatives who offered a wide range of views on the same history. It reminded me how people can witness the same events but walk away with different truths—truths shaped by social conditioning, personal beliefs, and what they needed to believe to keep moving forward.

At the same time, those discoveries often came with a heavy weight. The deeper I dug, the more my heart ached—for my ancestors, and for the millions of other enslaved people who never lived to see justice or even basic human dignity.

One of the most painful truths was how enslaved Africans were treated—not as people, but as property to be transferred like livestock. They were given as family gifts on birthdays, included in marriage dowries, used to settle divorce cases, passed on through inheritance, mortgaged for loans, or sold to cover debts. I even came across records showing fraudulent transactions designed to avoid taxes.

There were endless reasons behind the buying, selling, and trading of Black bodies between slave-owning families. Slavery wasn't just tolerated; it was a normalized, essential part of the economy.

And still, in all those transactions, the humanity of the enslaved was erased in the most degrading ways.

Take John T. Ward, for example. He didn't know his birth date. There was no certificate, no official record to mark his arrival into the world. He was born to a Black mother and a white father he never knew. It's likely that his father was the "master" of the house or possibly the overseer—perhaps even John Ward, the nephew of Lieutenant John Ward Jr.

John T. Ward's mother, Hannah, was just eighteen years old when she first became pregnant, and only twenty when she gave birth to him. In the cruel machinery of American slavery, it was common for enslaved girls to be forced into motherhood as early as age thirteen— not through love, but through violence. Enslavers exploited their reproductive capacity to increase their human property and to produce wet nurses for their own wives.

Thankfully, Hannah's situation was slightly different. Her enslaver was unmarried, which may have delayed the inevitable. But even then, the violence and exploitation of Black girlhood were never far away. Within the same family line, Nancy Ward—John T.'s cousin and the daughter of David Ward—was only twelve years old when she became pregnant with her first child. As the niece of Samuel

Ward, her youth and vulnerability were preyed upon before she ever had a chance to grow.

This wasn't just a family tragedy—it was generational trauma. These were not isolated cases, but symptoms of a brutal system built on the backs, bodies, and wombs of Black girls and women. Hannah's strength in raising John T. amid that legacy is all the more remarkable. She carried him not only through childbirth—but through history.

Plantation owners often promised enslaved women freedom if they bore fifteen children. Girls like Hannah were groomed for this purpose. But rape on the plantation was never just about reproduction—it was about dominance. It was about power. White men used sexual violence to control Black women and to emasculate Black men. That abuse frequently began as soon as girls reached puberty, sometimes as young as thirteen.

The trauma they endured didn't end on the plantation. It lingers still, etched into memory, stitched into silence, and carried in the DNA of the Black American experience.

The term "Children of the Plantation" is a euphemism used to describe those with ancestry tracing back to slavery—children born to enslaved or freed Black women and fathered by white owners, their relatives, or overseers. Despite being their own blood, these children were considered property, treated no differently than any other slave on the plantation.

The "one-drop rule" ensured that mixed-race children could never assimilate into white society. Even those who could pass for white were still legally and socially classified as Black. Rarely, some white fathers provided for these children—offering education, opportunities, or even manumission. But those cases were the exception, not the rule.

In April 1778, Jane Robinson of Loudoun County, Virginia, became the first person granted emancipation under the 1765

Commonwealth legislation. Born to a white woman, Jane was a mulatto. Though the 1765 law didn't abolish slavery, it created a process for manumission—allowing owners to legally free enslaved people under certain conditions. It was a small crack in a brutal system, but a significant one.

In more than three years of research, I found only one document that showed a Black family formally recorded as a full biological unit—two parents and their children—during the 1700s. The most complex record I examined was a plantation ledger that tracked one enslaved man fathering children with three different women in the same household. That was the reality: fractured family trees, erased paternity, and a cruel economy that traded in flesh and blood.

In the case of the Ward family, John T.'s grandfather Samuel had children only with his wife, Lucy—another rare stability. Their daughter Hannah had both Black and mixed-race children, including John T., much like Peggy Garner. Yet no father is listed in the records in the Register of Free Negroes of Pittsylvania County, Virginia.

Critical Family Theory is a powerful framework for disturbing and dismantling the silence around stories like this. It allows us to interrogate the ways power operates through erasure—how slavery didn't just exploit bodies, but dismembered families, shredded histories, and silenced legacies. The distortion and absence of Black family narratives in historical archives is not accidental. It was designed.

Among the most violent erasures were the children of enslaved women fathered by white men. These children were often unnamed, unacknowledged, denied rights, and scrubbed from official records. Their births were hidden, their presence buried under shame, property ledgers, and systemic denial.

White men rarely admitted to fathering these children. Everyone knew, but no one said it aloud. Their silence protected a lie—the lie that Black women were unrapeable, that their children were just more property. On paper, slave marriages didn't exist. In practice, they were ripped apart regularly. Estimates suggest that over 20 percent of enslaved marriages were broken by the sale of one or both spouses. And even more common? The sale of children—babies torn from their mothers' arms, sold like cattle, and families split apart without warning or mercy.

More than one-third of enslaved children grew up without one or both parents—not just because of death, but because slavery was structured to destroy Black family bonds. Most enslaved families lived on separate plantations, unable to maintain any cohesive structure. But in the Ward family, Samuel and Lucy defied that norm. Against all odds, they remained together. Their love, their bond, was an act of resistance, a quiet revolution in the face of a system built to erase them.

During the Emancipation Proclamation era and the 1870 census, I found the largest compilation of documented Black marriage records. Every United States census since the first one in 1790 has included the question of racial identity. The classification of race has always fluctuated, especially for freedmen. When marshals on horseback conducted the first census, race was viewed as a fixed physical trait. But it was the census taker who made the final decision on how to record someone's race—often based on their own personal beliefs, assumptions, and perceptions of "Black blood," usually judged by skin tone alone.

In many cases, a mixed-race person—Black and Native, or White and Native—might be labeled as "mulatto." But that wasn't the case for John T. Ward. He must've known it was futile to think of himself as close to white, even though he was half white by blood. He would never be accepted by them. That fantasy was just another tool of division—on the plantation and beyond.

He knew white folks would often show favoritism toward lighter-skinned slaves over their darker-skinned brethren. But under the law, it didn't matter—slaves were still slaves. No matter the shade, they were still counted as property.

Some mixed-race folks didn't feel accepted by either side, too white to be Black, too Black to be white. But more often than not, the local and national Black leaders were mixed-race folks—like James Poindexter, Frederick Douglass, Charles Langston, and others who navigated that in-between space and used it to speak truth to power.

Still, it would've been foolhardy for mulattos like John T. to think of themselves as white or even "half-white" in any meaningful way. They were born and raised in bondage. Black in every legal and social sense. Nothing came easier for them. In fact, John T. may have had to work harder to prove his loyalty to the Black community, since some mulattos collaborated with white slave masters, earning reputations as betrayers or opportunists.

Many tried to pass for white, hoping to escape the crushing weight of racism, believing they could slip through the cracks of white society. But let's be real—enslaved people of all shades were still strung up from the same oak trees. The white man's rope didn't discriminate when it came time for punishment.

That said, a darker-skinned Black man was often scrutinized more severely, while someone like John T. may have gotten a pass for his lighter complexion—at least in some spaces. But knowing what I know of John T., I believe he would've been quicker to swing than to bow. I don't see him as docile toward the white men who enslaved him. If anything, I believe he would've fought harder—not just for himself, but for his darker-skinned brethren.

After all, didn't he carry the blood of the violent white man who enslaved him?

Black women of childbearing age were expected to produce as many offspring as possible. Refusing to bear children was seen as refusing to increase an enslaver's wealth—a direct challenge to the system. It was an act of resistance, a bold rejection of the slave owner's authority to make motherhood the defining role of an enslaved woman's life.

Our first story of such resistance takes place in Missouri in 1845, where an enslaved woman gave birth to her fifth child—a son named Stephen. Like Peggy Garner's act of killing her daughter, infanticide was an extreme form of maternal resistance. These actions were born from a mother's protective instinct, rooted in the unbearable knowledge of what bondage meant for a Black child. Yet that same instinct also led some women to quietly endure their own captivity, choosing instead to take preventive measures—avoiding pregnancy or aborting the fetus altogether.

To terminate a pregnancy was the ultimate challenge to the enslaver's control. It was an act of bodily autonomy. A declaration that even in chains, a woman could claim power over her own womb.

Even Thomas Jefferson, in 1819, corresponded with his overseer, Joel Yancey, about the rising mortality rates among his enslaved children, demanding immediate action. His concern wasn't compassion—it was economics. Jefferson believed enslaved women's reproduction was more profitable than any harvest. His words, cold and calculated, reflect the cruel logic of slavery: a woman's body was not her own, but an investment.

During the brutal era of American slavery, Black women weren't only forced to labor under inhumane conditions; they also fought silent, strategic battles over their own reproductive rights. Stripped of legal personhood, many still carried and passed down ancestral knowledge of how to manage their fertility. They knew how to disrupt menstrual cycles. They knew how to prevent pregnancy. Because in a world where giving birth meant handing a child over to a lifetime of bondage, that knowledge became resistance.

White doctors took notice. In August 1860, at a medical society meeting in Rutherford County, Tennessee, a local physician named Dr. John H. Morgan presented a paper titled "An Essay on the Production of Abortion Among Our Negro Population." Published later in the *Nashville Journal of Medicine and Surgery*, the paper set off alarm among Morgan's peers. They acknowledged what they had long suspected: enslaved women were inducing abortions using natural methods.

Dr. Morgan named several herbs and plant-based remedies: tansy, rue, cotton root, pennyroyal, cedar gum, and camphor. These were known emmenagogues—substances used to stimulate menstruation—and had been used for generations in African and European folk medicine. Cotton root bark, especially, was revered among enslaved communities for its potency as an abortifacient. Pennyroyal and rue were brewed into teas, used to prevent conception or terminate early pregnancies.

Morgan and the other physicians understood the weight of what they were observing. These women were not ignorant. They were intentional. In a world that silenced them, enslaved women claimed power in the most radical way; they made decisions about their bodies, their futures, and their children's fates.

The list didn't end with herbs. Cedar gum, derived from cedar berries, and camphor were also used, often in gum or spirits form. And beyond what Morgan listed, there were even harsher substances—calomel, a mercury-based purgative, and raw turpentine—passed down by African midwives and healers. Lu Lee, a midwife interviewed during the WPA Slave Narratives, shared that enslaved women would "unfix themselves" using calomel and just a few drops of turpentine—so potent, "ten or twelve drops would miscarry you."

Though Morgan's published list did not mention these chemical agents directly, the presence of camphor—another powerful substance—made it clear that the medical establishment knew much more than it let on.

These were desperate, dangerous choices. But they were also brave. Enslaved women knew they faced severe punishment if caught. Still, many risked everything to prevent bringing another life into a system built on cruelty. Their actions were not rooted in shame or secrecy. They were rooted in love—deep, protective, ancestral love.

The use of abortifacients was a form of spiritual warfare. It was a quiet rebellion, fought from the inside. It was survival. And it was a sacred legacy of resistance that history too often ignores.

The historical record is clear: Black women enslaved in America did not passively accept the futures imposed upon them. They used what little power they had—through knowledge of herbs, chemicals, and their own bodies—to push back against a system built on domination and reproductive control. The 1860 Rutherford County medical meeting stands as chilling evidence that white society knew this—and feared it.

Our next story is about an enslaved woman named Sally and her three daughters: Sylvia, Charlotte, and Elizabeth. In 1854, the four of them were sold together for an astounding one thousand two hundred dollars. Sally was able to remain with her children for a short time, which was rare. The high price tag wasn't just about their labor; it reflected their reproductive value. Four females meant four wombs that could be exploited to produce more enslaved children, increasing the enslaver's property and wealth. They were also four women the master could rape and impregnate at will. Many white women were slaveholders too. There was no sisterhood, no solidarity. Enslaved Black women were seen only as property—even by the mistresses of the house.

Our final story is intense—and hard to read. It involves a slaveholder named Robert Newsom, who settled in Missouri with his wife and children. By 1850, Newsom had become a wealthy man with eight hundred acres of land, a profitable farm, and five male slaves. After his wife died, Newsom purchased Celia, a fourteen-year-old girl, as his first female slave.

Celia was placed in a cabin separate from the main house and from the male slaves. From 1850 to 1855, Newsom repeatedly raped her. During this time, she bore two children, one of whom was fathered by Newsom himself. Later, Celia entered into a romantic relationship with another of Newsom's slaves, a man named George. When Celia became pregnant with her third child, the paternity was uncertain—George or Newsom. George gave Celia an ultimatum: either she would stop Newsom's advances, or he would have nothing more to do with her.

Celia begged Newsom and his family to leave her alone. They ignored her pleas. On June 23, 1855, Celia made one final attempt. She told Newsom she was pregnant and sick and asked him to stop. He refused. That night, when Newsom came to her cabin again, Celia was waiting. She struck him with a large stick—once to stop him, and again in self-defense. Robert Newsom was dead.

Celia dragged his body to the fireplace, where she burned the remains. She crushed the larger bones with a rock or hid them under the floorboards. With help from Newsom's twelve-year-old grandson, whom she bribed with a handful of walnuts, she scattered what was left of his ashes.

When Newsom was reported missing the next morning, a search began. Investigators focused on Celia. After threats and interrogation, she confessed. She maintained that she had not intended to kill Newsom—only to protect herself. Newsom's family collected his remains and stored them in a box. On December 21, 1855, Celia was hanged at 2:30 in the afternoon.

Family was often the strongest motivator for an enslaved person to attempt escape or to stay. Henry Bibb, a slave from Shelby County, Kentucky, near Louisville, was one such man. He gained his freedom in 1841, but his heart remained with his wife and child still in bondage. He attempted to rescue them three times. Each time, he was recaptured—betrayed by both white and Black Americans in Southern Ohio who prioritized profit or safety over justice. Even after escaping slavery, he was never truly free, knowing his family remained captive. Still, he risked everything and returned to Kentucky. He later wrote: "I felt as if love, duty, humanity, and justice required that I should go back."

To truly savor freedom, Bibb needed his family with him. His final escape came after his enslaver sold both him and his wife into the Deep South, where permanent slavery loomed like a death sentence. Eventually, Bibb was sold to a Native American owner—one from whom he managed to escape in 1841.

Unfortunately for Bibb, when he returned four years later to inquire about his wife's whereabouts, he discovered that Malinda had been sold to another man—one who forced her into a non-consensual relationship. Heartbroken and betrayed, Bibb declared, "She has ever since been regarded theoretically and practically dead to me as a wife."

In the end, Bibb couldn't protect or keep his family together. Though he had secured his own freedom, slavery had stolen his wife from him. All that remained was individual freedom—bittersweet and incomplete.

And it wasn't just enslaved Black women who understood the heavy burden of motherhood under slavery. They also understood the deep pain of denying that role—of choosing not to bring children into a world designed to break them. It was an act of defiance and of love.

Bibb said:

"Unfortunately for me, I am the father of a slave—a word too obnoxious to be spoken by a fugitive slave. It calls fresh to my mind the separation of husband and wife, the stripping, tying up, and flogging, the tearing of children from their parents and selling them on the auction block. It calls to mind female virtue trampled underfoot with impunity.

"But oh! When I remember that my daughter—my only child— is still there, destined to share the fate of all these calamities, it is too much to bear.

"If ever there was any one act of my life while a slave that I have to lament, it is that of being the father and husband of slaves. I have the satisfaction of knowing that I am only the father of one slave. She is bone of my bone and flesh of my flesh—poor unfortunate child.

"She was the first, and she shall be the last slave that I will ever father—for chains and slavery on this earth."

Black enslaved men were profoundly impacted by the institution of slavery—especially in the context of family life. The brutal system stripped them of agency and reduced them to mere property, depriving them of control over their own households. Fathers and husbands lived under the constant threat of separation, as wives and children could be sold away or torn from their arms without warning. This relentless uncertainty inflicted deep emotional wounds, leaving many Black men burdened with sorrow and helplessness. They were denied the right to protect their families, to shape their children's futures, or to fully experience the joys and responsibilities of fatherhood and marriage.

Formerly enslaved man Henry Bibb spoke openly and painfully about this reality. In his personal narrative, he expressed profound regret for being both a husband and a father to slaves. More than any other sorrow, he mourned the fact that his child—his own flesh and blood—was born into bondage. Though he admitted a bittersweet satisfaction in fathering only one slave, he saw that child as a victim, doomed to suffer a life of undeserved servitude. That knowledge shattered him.

Bibb's heartbreak came from the realization that by bringing a child into the world under such oppressive conditions, he had unintentionally contributed to their suffering. He declared that he would never father another slave, recognizing the cruelty in condemning one's own offspring to a life of degradation and captivity.

For Bibb—and countless other enslaved men—parenthood took on a tragic dimension, one marked not by legacy and joy, but by grief, guilt, and the unbearable weight of generational suffering.

His words laid bare the anguish of enslaved fathers who longed for freedom not only for themselves, but more importantly, for their children. The emotional toll of knowing their sons and daughters would grow up in chains—subject to the same violence, labor, and dehumanization they had endured—was almost too much to bear.

For men like Henry Bibb, fatherhood became an act of resistance as well as mourning. By refusing to bring more children into slavery, they sought to break the cycle of generational bondage. Bibb's story stands as a testament to the pain, resilience, and love of enslaved Black fathers who, even in the depths of despair, still dreamed of freedom for their families.

Their decision was fueled by a longing to break free from the chains that held them and their descendant's captive. They recognized that every child born into slavery would forever be condemned to a life of servitude and deprived of basic human rights. These brave men sought liberation not only for themselves but also for future generations. Their refusal to father more slaves served as an act of defiance against an institution intended to strip Black individuals of their very humanity.

Throughout history, the bodies of Black women have been battlegrounds—spaces where power, oppression, and resistance intersect. The choices they made, or had stripped from them, held profound weight, shaping not only their own destinies but the course of history itself.

For enslaved women, reproductive decisions were more than personal—they were acts of resistance, survival, and, in some cases, defiance against a brutal system that sought to commodify their very existence. Some refused to bear children into bondage, engaging in quiet rebellions that were as powerful as any uprising. Others, forced into maternity by rape and coercion, found ways to reclaim their humanity through sheer resilience, raising children who would carry forth their legacy of strength and defiance.

John T. Ward's mother, Hannah, lived at the intersection of these narratives. Violated and stripped of her autonomy, she bore a son who would rise as a leader. In her very survival, she demonstrated an unyielding resistance, proving that even within the deepest shadows of oppression, there could be light, dignity, and an unbreakable will to shape the future.

Today, as we debate reproductive rights, we must recognize that the choices women make—whether to bring life into the world or to safeguard their own futures—are the same choices that enslaved women once made, though under far more harrowing circumstances. For them, these decisions were not just about bodily autonomy but about reclaiming stolen agency—about resisting a system that sought to dictate their futures. Their actions were not merely acts of survival, but declarations of self-ownership, defiance, and radical hope.

Hannah's story reminds us that the fight for reproductive freedom is not just about the present; it's about honoring those who came before us, those who turned pain into power and transformed oppression into leadership. When a woman asserts control over her own body today, she echoes the silent revolutions of the past, carrying forward a legacy of resistance and resilience that has always defined the struggle for true freedom.

CHAPTER 8

Friends with Benefits

"The Friends stand as both liberators and, at times, reluctant beneficiaries of the very institution they despised. Their contradictions were many, but their courage undeniable."

(Paraphrased from Du Bois's historical analyses in *The Suppression of the African Slave Trade, 1896.*)

They called themselves the Society of Friends—a community rooted in peace, equality, and the belief in the inner light of God within every human being. But beneath the linen bonnets and plain speech was a truth far more tangled than the myth.

Before they were abolitionists, many Quakers were slave owners. Before they harbored runaways on the Underground Railroad, they invested in companies that trafficked in Black flesh. While some risked everything to fight for freedom, others profited quietly behind closed doors, counting silver while preaching simplicity.

This is the paradox: the same people who once refused to remove their hats before kings also refused to let go of their human property. The same hands that held prayer books also signed slave ledgers. The same voices that spoke of peace enforced silence when it came to Black suffering, even in their own meeting houses.

To understand the Quakers' role in American slavery is to step into that gray space between righteousness and reality. They were not saviors. They were not villains. They were human—flawed, conflicted, and complicit. And while some broke the chains, others tightened them with holy hands.

A few years ago, while researching a story about the Obamas' ancestral ties to slavery, I kept running into one group: the Quakers. Again and again, their name surfaced—in books, in archives, in digital databases. I started seeing a pattern. These were not just bystanders. They were deeply entangled in both the oppression and the liberation of Black bodies. Whether as early investors in slave ships or as conductors on the Underground Railroad, the Quakers were always there—sometimes helping, sometimes harming.

With renewed vigor, I dove deeper. Yesterday, I hit the library. Today, I'm deep in the web's corners. Whether it's an old document or a newly uploaded PDF, the Society of Friends keeps coming up. And the more I learn, the more I understand the contradictions— how the same community that birthed fierce abolitionists also built wealth on the backs of the enslaved.

To grasp the complexity of their support, you have to understand the suffering of freed men, women, and escapees during that time. Their lives were constantly under threat—from re-enslavement, from poverty, from betrayal. For some, the Quakers were a lifeline. For others, they were yet another reminder that whiteness, even when dressed in simplicity, still had the power to include or exclude.

This chapter peels back the layers. It tells the story of George Fox and William Penn, of Sarah Clark Lynch and John Lynch, of freedmen who sat outside Quaker meetings and of women who were disowned for marrying the "wrong" kind of man. It examines the truth the history books often skip; some of the first people to fight slavery in America were also among the first to benefit from it.

This isn't just about the past. It's about legacy, silence, and the price of selective memory. It's about who gets called "Friend"—and who gets left out of the story.

In the 1650s, an Englishman named George Fox sparked a movement that would come to be known as the Religious Society of Friends—or more simply, the Quakers. Members of this movement called each other "Friends," and their faith was grounded in two fundamental beliefs. First, they believed that every person could form a direct connection with God, without needing rituals, clergy, or church hierarchy. Second, they believed that divine revelation hadn't ended—that anyone, at any time, could receive inspiration from God.

George Fox and early Quakers wanted to return Christianity to its original spirit. They sought to live by the teachings of Jesus Christ: peace, simplicity, empathy, care for the oppressed, and the idea that every soul had equal access to the spirit of God. Their commitment to nonviolence and equality stood in sharp contrast to the rigid structure of the Church of England. Unsurprisingly, the Quakers faced harsh persecution in their homeland.

At the time, many sects had broken off from the Church of England, each pushing back against the church's strict rules. But the Society of Friends stood out. Their belief in an "inner light" within every human being was powerful—and threatening to the status quo. Their form of worship was quiet and contemplative. Their clothing was plain. Their refusal to bow or remove their hats before those in power was seen not as humility, but as rebellion.

To the ruling elite, Quaker behavior was downright offensive. Because the Friends believed all people were equal, they didn't give deference to titles or wealth. They spoke plainly, calling everyone "thee" and "thou," regardless of social rank. This led to them being labeled anti-authority—and they paid the price. Quakers were fined, jailed, and beaten. Many died in prison. George Fox himself was locked up eight times in brutal conditions.

Their situation worsened under King Charles II, who sought to restore Catholicism in England. In retaliation, Parliament clamped down on religious dissent. Quakers were swept up in this crackdown, and persecution intensified.

Looking for freedom, the Friends turned their eyes to the New World. Their entry into America was rough; many were jailed or exiled when they arrived. But everything changed with William Penn. A wealthy Englishman turned Quaker; Penn was granted a charter by King Charles II to settle a debt owed to Penn's father. With that charter, he founded the colony of Pennsylvania—a place where Friends could finally worship freely and govern themselves according to Quaker values.

Even before Pennsylvania, though, the first Quakers arrived in Virginia in the 1650s, only to find laws just as hostile as the ones back home. Much like in Massachusetts, Virginia's strict colonial society had no tolerance for their radical beliefs. The Puritans were especially enraged by the Quaker notion that women and men were spiritually equal and that no minister held greater authority than the people. Still, by the mid-eighteenth century, the Friends had settled in the colony and built their first meeting house.

It took decades before they were accepted. Many were fined, imprisoned, or even executed for their beliefs. But they endured.

Even Thomas Jefferson, in his *Notes on the State of Virginia*, acknowledged the persecution they faced. He noted that while Virginia hadn't executed Quakers like Massachusetts did, the hostility was real—and the tolerance, accidental.

But here's where the truth gets more complicated.

The Quakers weren't just victims of injustice—they were also participants in it. While the Friends are often celebrated as early abolitionists, many of them owned slaves and profited from enslaved labor well into the eighteenth century. Their internal battle over slavery stretched out for more than a hundred years. Some prioritized comfort and profit over conscience. They prayed in plain meeting houses while Black bodies worked their land.

Radical journalist William Cobbett once called the Quakers a "money-getting tribe" who benefited from slavery while pretending to be above it. That critique wasn't without merit.

Eventually, many Quakers did become leaders in the abolitionist movement. They helped organize anti-slavery societies, ran stops on the Underground Railroad, and took public stands when it was dangerous to do so. But we can't forget how long it took for them to get there. The very group that preached equality had to reckon with its own hypocrisy. And many never did.

In my own research—especially while digging through records connected to the Obamas' lineage—I saw the Quaker name come up again and again. Whether tied to slavery, land ownership, or abolitionist networks, the Friends were always in the mix, sometimes helping, sometimes hurting, but always present.

This chapter isn't just about honoring their role in resistance. It's about telling the whole truth. Because the legacy of the Friends isn't just peace and light. It's also silence, contradiction, and the complicated question of who they chose to call "Friend"—and who they didn't.

In 1672, Quakers were among the founding members of the Royal African Company, which held a monopoly on the British slave trade. That company played a major role in fueling the booming slave markets in Jamaica and helped push illegal trade with Spanish America. Even after the Glorious Revolution of 1698 stripped the company of its monopoly, the Quakers' involvement in the transatlantic slave trade remained a haunting part of the record.

This is where the story gets complicated.

Yes, the Quakers would later become some of the earliest white allies in the abolitionist movement. But before that—some of them were investors. Beneficiaries. Quiet participants in the machinery of human trafficking. It's uncomfortable, but it's the truth. And it's necessary to hold both: the harm and the healing.

Their deep belief in equality—of race, gender, and class—would eventually set them apart. But in the beginning, their actions didn't always match their words. That contradiction matters. Because it shaped everything that came after, including the resistance stories of families like mine—and of people like John T. Ward.

It's hard to imagine now that a belief in equality was once considered radical. But for the Quakers, that belief in the divine light in every human being was more than philosophy; it became a call to action. By the eighteenth century, they weren't just talking; they were moving. They became politically active, organizing, petitioning, and putting their bodies on the line to fight slavery. They were the first religious group to outright condemn it. And by the mid-1700s, they banned their members from owning slaves altogether.

That stand cost them. Quakers were pushed to the margins of society. Their beliefs—pacifism, simplicity, anti-slavery—ran directly against the grain of a country profiting off war, status, and stolen Black labor.

And when the Civil War came, those same beliefs fractured the Society of Friends from within. They were deeply divided. The Quakers were pacifists, committed to nonviolence. But how do you stand for peace in the face of slavery? How do you keep silent when your brothers and sisters are still in chains?

Some couldn't. Some picked up arms. Others refused. That split gave rise to a new branch: the Free Quakers—those who had been disowned by the original Society for taking up arms during the Revolutionary War. They believed that in moments of moral crisis, neutrality was not peace; it was betrayal.

That same tension played out again during the Civil War. And the choices people made—who they married, who they defended, who they refused to disown—often cost them everything.

Take Sara Clark Lynch, for example. She was the second wife of Major John Ward, a plantation owner. But before that, she was a Quaker, a Friend. When she married into slavery, the Society of Friends disowned her. To them, marrying a man who owned people— regardless of what she believed—made her complicit. She was cut off.

That kind of accountability wasn't always applied equally. But it did show just how seriously some Quakers took the fight.

Still, the contradictions remain.

The same community that produced abolitionists also produced investors in slavery. The same meeting houses that hid runaways once sat silent while Black families were ripped apart. It's a duality that continues to echo in American history.

And yet, the Quakers' legacy matters. Because at their best, they stood for the kind of resistance that didn't just speak but act. Their story is woven into the roots of anti-slavery movements across both sides of the Atlantic. They were among the first to say: this isn't right. And to try—imperfectly, inconsistently, but powerfully—to do something about it.

This chapter isn't about praise or condemnation. It's about complexity. About telling the full story, not just the parts that make people feel good. Because history isn't clean. It's layered, jagged, and often soaked in both contradiction and courage.

And in the case of the Quakers—like so many others—it's about who they chose to include, and who they chose to forget.

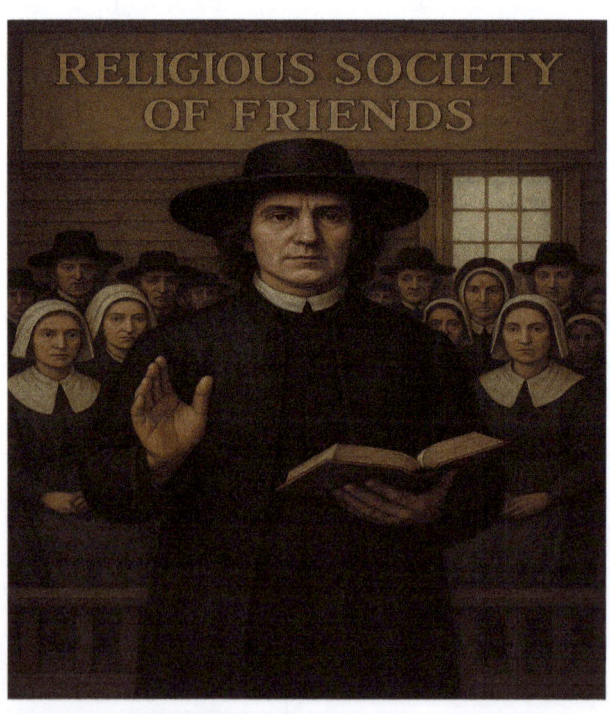

Women of most sects of Christianity were merely followers and oftentimes submissive to men, whereas the Quaker women were given equality in the church government and perhaps led the foundation for female suffrage.

The year was 1810, and the town of Lynchburg, Virginia, was gripped by fear and speculation. Dr. John C. Lynch, a respected physician and newly elected mayor, had been found dead—poisoned. His sudden and mysterious death cast a long shadow over the community, igniting rumors and an urgent demand for justice.

To the people of Lynchburg, there was little doubt about who was responsible. Bob, an enslaved man owned by Dr. Lynch, was set to be freed upon his master's death. For many, that alone was enough to make him a suspect. Freedom was a dangerous thing for a Black man to have—especially if it came at the expense of a white man's life.

A free Black woman named Lucy was also arrested, accused of conspiring in the doctor's murder. But why would a free woman risk everything, even her own life, to help Bob?

Maybe she saw in Bob something familiar—the same desperation, the same silent rage simmering beneath the surface of every enslaved person forced to endure a lifetime of cruelty and oppression. Maybe she knew the pain of watching a loved one sold away, of being at the mercy of a master who controlled every breath and movement. Maybe she saw a chance to strike back. Maybe she saw a chance to help him escape.

Whatever the reason, the two stood trial together in a courtroom thick with tension. Lucy was convicted. Bob, however, faced a jury that couldn't reach a unanimous decision. Though most believed him guilty, the law required full agreement. And so, against all expectations, Bob was acquitted.

But freedom in Virginia was never that simple.

With Dr. Lynch dead, Bob's legal status didn't revert to independence. Instead, by law, he became the property of John Lynch, the doctor's father. And John Lynch was no ordinary Virginian.

John Lynch was a man of contradictions. A founder of Lynchburg, he was born into a family deeply entangled in both the abolitionist cause and the very system of slavery it claimed to fight. He was a Quaker, a member of the Society of Friends—a faith long outspoken against slavery. And yet, like many Quakers of his time, he had once profited from the very institution he denounced.

The Quakers weren't like most religious groups in early America. Their faith was grounded in radical principles: equality, pacifism, and the unwavering belief that no human being had the right to own another. By the mid-1700s, the Society of Friends had begun excommunicating members who refused to emancipate their enslaved people. Even so, some Quakers—bound by habit, wealth, or fear—still clung to slavery's grip.

But John Lynch had made his stance clear. By the 1780s, he had already freed all of his enslaved people—one of the few white Virginians, to do so voluntarily. He had, by most accounts, chosen morality over profit.

And yet now, fate placed a new question in his hands. What do you do when the man you believe murdered your son is now legally your property?

John Lynch believed Bob was guilty. It was said Bob had confessed. Any other man might have sought revenge; he could have sold Bob down South, condemned him to a lifetime of brutality. He could have demanded blood.

But John Lynch did something extraordinary.

On November 9, 1810—the same day of Bob's acquittal—John Lynch walked into the courthouse and signed Bob's deed of manumission.

It wasn't an act of forgiveness. It was an act of principle.

"Having a Negro slave named Bob, aged thirty years, fallen under my care by descent from my son, who died intestate, and being fully persuaded that freedom and liberty is the natural law of mankind—that no law, moral or divine, has given me a right to property in the person of any of my fellow creatures—and notwithstanding the injury done to me and mine, from his confession and the evident circumstances for which he was tried and acquitted by the laws of his country—believing as I do that no circumstances whatsoever can change the principle, and leaving the event unto Him who hath said, 'Vengeance is mine, and I will repay'—I therefore, for myself and my heirs, do hereby emancipate Bob."

(Signed) JOHN LYNCH_. EDWARD LYNCH

John Lynch believed in a higher law—one that superseded his own grief and personal loss. He could not, in good conscience, continue to hold Bob as property. Even if Bob had taken his son's life, John Lynch would not take Bob's freedom.

This decision didn't come from nowhere. His mother, Sarah Clark Lynch, had been a devout Quaker—a woman so committed to her faith that she donated land for the construction of the South River Meeting House, one of the earliest Quaker congregations in the region. But when she remarried Major John Ward, a non-Quaker who owned enslaved people, the Society of Friends disowned her.

Quakers held their members to high moral standards. Those who failed to live up to those values were cast out.

John Lynch's family straddled the line between abolition and oppression, between justice and complicity. His relative, Charles Lynch, left behind a darker legacy. During the Revolutionary War, he led an extrajudicial court in Virginia that imprisoned suspected loyalists without proper legal authority. His brand of vigilante justice became known as "Lynch's Law"—a term that would later evolve into the word "lynching," a practice that terrorized Black Americans for generations.

The irony is chilling.

John Lynch's legacy was one of resistance. Yet, his own family's name became synonymous with racial terror. Even as he freed Bob, the system that had enslaved Bob remained intact. Black men and women were still viewed as property. The laws were still being written—and enforced—by those who benefited from Black oppression.

Bob's fate remains unknown. Did he stay in Virginia, where he had once been accused of murder? Or did he flee north, searching for a freedom deeper than a legal technicality?

One of John Lynch's daughter's descendants would eventually migrate to Ohio—a free state—where their fight for Black liberation would continue.

But the system of slavery didn't die with John Lynch's signature. It evolved. It rebranded itself through new laws and new systems of oppression: the Black Codes, Jim Crow, mass incarceration, and the prison-industrial complex.

The criminalization of Black people never disappeared; it just adapted.

And today, as we reflect on this legacy, we're left with one pressing question:

When will justice finally be served?

The Quakers themselves had long wrestled with their own contradictions. Some freed their enslaved people and left the South entirely, building abolitionist communities in places like Ohio. Others, like John Lynch, remained—caught between moral conviction and the economic entanglements of their time.

Those who fell short of Quaker values were disowned. Sarah Clark Lynch was cast out for marrying a slave owner. Charles Lynch was removed for taking military oaths and participating in war. Even Lt. John Ward Jr., another name in this tangled lineage, was disowned from the Quaker faith. But in 1787, he sought reconciliation. He wrote a letter to the monthly meeting of governors, asking for readmission—to make peace, to come back into the fold.

"I must acknowledge that, having fallen from a place of true watchfulness, I gave in to the spirit of resentment—so much so that I acted on that revengeful impulse with my own hand, bringing dishonor to the truth. This has become a matter of deep sorrow for me, and I sincerely condemn my actions.

Though such conduct rightly deserves the censure of my Friends, I still hold onto hope—and an earnest desire—that I may, through careful vigilance and faithful attention to that principle of Light and Grace, rise above whatever trials may be placed before me in the future.

Therefore, I humbly submit my case to the thoughtful consideration of the Meeting."

It was a plea for redemption, a plea for acceptance.

But history does not grant redemption so easily.

John Lynch's act of freeing Bob was a rare moment of principle prevailing over vengeance. But one man's decision could not undo the horrors of slavery, nor could it erase the legacy of violence that followed.

The past is never truly past.

And as long as Black freedom is conditional, as long as justice is selective, as long as the echoes of "Lynch's Law" continue to reverberate through history—we must continue to demand more.

Littleberry "Berry" Moss was born free in Virginia around 1794, the son of Jonathan Moss. He was a towering figure, standing six feet tall, with a right eye slightly larger than his left—features that made census takers uncertain of how to categorize him. His skin, a blend of Black and white ancestry, was a visual reminder of America's tangled racial past.

In October 1814, Littleberry Moss stood before the courthouse in Campbell County. His heart pounded beneath the fabric of his simple but well-kept coat as he signed the marriage surety bond for his bride, Betsy Farrow. He was no ordinary man; he was a free Black man in the slaveholding South, navigating a world that sought to strip him of his autonomy at every turn.

Marriage was sacred, but for free Black people in Virginia, it was also a legal battleground. A marriage surety bond wasn't just a formality; it was a financial and legal guarantee that the union was lawful. For free Black men like Littleberry, this process came with extra scrutiny. They had to prove their legal status, legitimacy, and financial stability—conditions white men never had to face.

In the presence of Drury Farrow, Betsy's father, Littleberry, placed his mark on the document. Drury and Betsy's brothers, Drury Jr. and Daniel Farrow, stood as witnesses. Their union was now official, recorded not only in county records but also in Quaker genealogical archives—a testament to the ties between free Black families and the Religious Society of Friends, better known as the Quakers.

The Quakers were abolitionists, record keepers, and quiet revolutionaries. They documented free Black marriages, births, and land transactions when the government often refused to. Their meticulous recordkeeping would prove invaluable generations later, when Littleberry's great-great-great-great-granddaughter, Shanna Ward, would piece together the legacy that white America tried to erase.

But Virginia was suffocating. The laws for free Black men were tightening. The 1813 tax laws ensured that every free Black man remained under financial and legal pressure—taxed not only on his own wealth but on his sons as well. Free Black men were required to pay bonds to live in certain communities, and interracial marriage was strictly forbidden.

Littleberry Moss had seen enough. By the 1820s, he and Betsy made a life-altering decision; they would leave Virginia for the promise of Ohio. The legal landscape in Virginia was becoming increasingly hostile to free Black families. White lawmakers passed Black Codes that restricted land ownership, employment, and even movement for Black citizens. Berry knew that if he wanted a secure future for his family, he had to leave.

Ohio was no paradise, but it offered something Virginia couldn't: opportunity. It was a place where Black families could own land without the constant threat of having it taken away. It was home to abolitionist networks, thriving Black communities, and the promise of a future beyond the reach of Southern oppression.

Between 1838 and 1840, the Moss and Farrow families migrated together to Ross County, Ohio. They were among several Black families who made the journey north, leaving behind the uncertainty of the South in pursuit of something greater—true self-sufficiency and the right to thrive.

Some reformers believed slavery could be abolished through education and moral training, believing it would eventually lead to equality between Black and white people. The thinking was that if freedmen were taught and imbued with the same moral values as whites, they could integrate into society more easily. This belief in "moral uplift" was common among religious groups, including many Quakers.

But not everyone believed in coexistence. Some white Americans saw true integration as impossible. They advocated for the relocation of Black people to colonies in the Caribbean or Africa, believing it was better to remove them altogether than to pursue equality. This ideology gave rise to the American Colonization Society, which raised funds to send freed Black people "back to Africa."

While the society claimed humanitarian concern, its support from white Southerners—who had long exploited Black labor—tainted its mission. It felt less like liberation and more like an effort to purge Black presence from America. The plan ignored one crucial truth: most freedmen had no connection to Africa. They were American born. Sending them away wasn't justice. It was exile.

Even among the Quakers—who publicly professed a belief in the equality of all people—discrimination ran deep. In Pennsylvania,

Ohio, Indiana, and Illinois, some Quaker communities actively discouraged the entry of free Black families. Black people were often unwelcome in the Society of Friends, excluded from membership, and harassed by white neighbors—including Quakers themselves. In many cases, the hand extended in public was quietly withdrawn in private.

A disturbing rift even formed within the Quaker movement itself. Some so-called Friends supported the "dilution" of the Black race through interracial relationships—not out of love or solidarity, but as a strategy to eliminate Blackness over generations. These ideas were rooted in eugenicist thinking and deeply contradicted the public image of Quaker justice. While many Quakers were instrumental in the Underground Railroad—opening their homes and land to fugitives—others established communities along the routes with ulterior motives, attempting to control and assimilate those they claimed to be helping. For many Black Americans, true allies were few and far between. Even those who claimed friendship were often tainted by paternalism, prejudice, or silent complicity.

Still, within these contradictions, some individuals found opportunity. John T. Ward, for example, pursued a Quaker education. He attended a Quaker-run and -funded school after church on Sundays—his only free time as a child. The Quaker educational model, grounded in discipline, literacy, and moral instruction, gave him a foundation for leadership. Christianity and the church—though deeply entangled in systems of white supremacy—also became spaces of rebellion, self-determination, and spiritual empowerment. For many Black families, faith and education were twin tools of both survival and resistance.

Today, the legacy of the Society of Friends continues in both complex and impactful ways. There are now over eight thousand

Quakers in the United States and approximately four hundred thousand worldwide. One prominent example of their enduring presence is Sidwell Friends School, a prestigious Quaker institution in Washington, D.C., chosen by Barack and Michelle Obama for their daughters' education.

Founded in 1883 by Thomas W. Sidwell, the school is known for its academic rigor, moral instruction, and emphasis on character development. Its Latin motto, *Eluceat omnibus lux*— "Let the light shine out from all"—echoes the Quaker belief in the inner light within every individual. Despite its high tuition—around fifty thousand dollars per year as of 2023, Sidwell remains highly competitive, with an acceptance rate of just 7 percent. It also upholds strong commitments to diversity, equity, and inclusion, offering community service programs and ethical development aligned with Quaker ideals of social consciousness.

But the contradictions remain. The same religious tradition that once educated John T. Ward and harbored runaways also excluded Black members, supported colonization, and applied its values selectively. The truth about the Quakers is not simple—and that's exactly why it matters.

While history often remembers the Quakers as the quiet heroes of abolition, not all freedmen saw them through such a forgiving lens. The Society of Friends—with their simple dress, gentle speech, and refusal to bear arms—are often celebrated for their early condemnation of slavery. And yes, many did risk their lives to help enslaved people escape through the Underground Railroad. But that is not the whole story.

To many Black abolitionists—especially the most radical voices of their time—Quaker silence, hesitation, and economic entanglement with slavery made their peace feel performative. Their preference for gradualism, neutrality, or theological distance in the face of injustice came off not as moral clarity, but as betrayal.

David Walker, author of *Appeal to the Colored Citizens of the World*, never named the Quakers directly in his searing indictment of religious hypocrisy. But the spirit of his critique spared no one hiding behind the veil of righteousness:

"I ask the Friends—where were you when the blood of my brethren cried from the soil? Let not silence wear the robe of righteousness."

This imagined quote channels Walker's unmistakable fury toward those who condemned slavery in theory but benefited from it in practice—or worse, did nothing. In Walker's view, silence was not neutrality. It was complicity. And for those who called themselves "Friends," that title rang hollow when their actions didn't match the suffering around them.

Likewise, Henry Highland Garnet, one of the fiercest abolitionist voices of the nineteenth century, directly challenged the pacifist foundations of Quaker belief. For Garnet, their unwavering commitment to nonviolence was a moral luxury—a privilege enslaved people could never afford. He declared:

"The Quakers claim peace, but peace without justice is still war."

He spoke directly to the tension between idealism and action. For Garnet, peace wasn't just the absence of conflict, it was the presence of righteousness. A peace that allowed slavery to continue, that avoided confrontation for the sake of religious principle, was a dangerous peace. It was no different from quiet oppression. In Garnet's mind, any faith that could not pick up arms to fight for the enslaved was a faith that protected the oppressor's comfort more than it answered the captive's cry.

These quotes, whether documented or powerfully imagined through their words, remind us that Black liberation was never a monolith. And neither was abolition. Not all alliances were trusted. Not all white allies were embraced. The lived experience of slavery taught freedmen and women to look past appearances—to interrogate who truly stood with them, and who merely stood nearby.

The Quakers, like many figures and groups in American history, lived in contradiction. Some were brave conductors and abolitionists. Others owned slaves, invested in the slave trade, or retreated into spiritual quietism while Black families were being torn apart.

To understand the full story of the Quakers, we have to hear both sides—the reverence and the rebuke. We must honor the radical voices who asked the harder questions and refused easy praise.

Because in the fight for Black freedom, silence was never a neutral act. And righteousness without risk was never enough.

CHAPTER 9

Let My People Go!

"If you love your children, if you love your country, if you love the God of love, clear your hands from slaves. Burden not your children or country with them."

-Richard Allen, abolitionist, former slave, founder of the Bethel African Methodist Church

I sat back in my chair and rubbed my eyes, the dull ache behind them reminding me how long I'd been staring at my computer screen. I hadn't noticed the strain—only the urgency pulsing through my fingertips as I type. I remembered reading about a trick somewhere—a simple exercise to relieve tension caused by too much screen time. I turned my head, found a distant spot beyond the window, and focused. Twenty seconds. Just long enough for the muscles in my eyes to flex and reset. Just long enough to breathe.

People kept telling me to take it easy. "Rest when you need to," they said. "Don't burn yourself out."

But they didn't understand.

This wasn't just research. This wasn't just a writing project. This was a calling. It was fueled by passion, by fire, by the quiet knowledge that if I didn't tell this story, it might vanish. John T. Ward's voice might disappear into history's shadows. And I couldn't let that happen. I wouldn't.

Because I didn't feel like I was just telling his story, I felt like I was telling it with him. I heard his convictions echoing in my heart. I felt his steps behind mine. This work was bigger than me. It always had been.

And then, like a match striking memory, a moment came back to me. Houston. The Black Book Festival. I was standing behind my table, my children's book propped up like a lighthouse—its colorful illustrations inviting smiles, but inside, it carried a heavier truth: history, resistance, faith, legacy.

A man approached me with a warm smile, his eyes full of curiosity. He asked about the book, about the story behind it. I told him what I always tell people: that it's inspired by John T. Ward, my great-great-great-grandfather. A man who didn't just believe in freedom, he fought for it. An abolitionist. A conductor on the Underground

Railroad. A Black man who defied the limits of his time and helped others escape theirs. A name barely mentioned in textbooks but still living through me.

His eyes widened.

We discussed Underground Railroad quilt codes; the myths and mysteries surrounding the idea that quilts were stitched with hidden messages to guide enslaved people toward freedom. I told him the debate still rages. Historians are divided. Some dismiss it as folklore. Others insist the patterns were real, even if undocumented. He nodded, familiar with the controversy. Then, as if unlocking a memory of his own, he leaned in closer and shared something I'd never heard before.

"The quilts," he whispered. "They soaked them in water."

I paused.

He continued, "They used them to muffle the sound—to quiet their praises."

And suddenly, I could see it—a clearing in the woods, moonlight slipping through the branches, the faint rustle of breath and trembling voices. A group of enslaved people gathered under the canopy of darkness. The soaked quilts were laid around them, absorbing the noise of their joy, silencing their worship so their rejoicing wouldn't bring death.

They had to hide their hope.

That moment stayed with me. It reawakened something. Because if the soaked quilts speak to the ingenuity of Black faith, then the Slave Bible speaks to the brutality of spiritual theft.

They called it the "Good Book." But in the hands of slaveholders, it became something else entirely—a weapon.

Yes, they tore pages out of Bibles. Not just literally—though some did. They tore with intention, with cruelty, and with calculated theology. They censored salvation. They stripped the Word of its thunder and left only the whisper of obedience.

These altered texts became known as the "Slave Bible." Distributed in the early 1800s to enslaved people in the British West Indies—and mimicked by American preachers—it was a grotesque gospel, a version of the Word designed to preach submission without deliverance.

They removed verses that could ignite hope:

- Exodus 21:16 – "He who kidnaps a man and sells him … shall surely be put to death."
- Jeremiah 22:13 – "Woe to him who builds his house by unrighteousness …"
- Galatians 3:28 – "There is neither Jew nor Greek, slave nor free …"
- Exodus 3–15 – The entire liberation story of Moses? Gone.
- Revelation 13 – A prophecy of justice against oppressive empires? Too dangerous.

What was left? A curated doctrine of control, shaped by weaponized theology:

- Ephesians 6:5 – "Slaves, obey your earthly masters with fear and trembling …"
- Colossians 3:22 – "Slaves, obey your masters in everything …"
- Titus 2:9 – "Tell slaves to be submissive …"

This was not God's word—this was the slaveholder's script.

It told them to kneel, not rise; to obey, not question; and to suffer, not hope.

But hope doesn't die easily.

They remembered. They remembered the stories anyway. They held onto Moses, even if the pages were gone. They called out to Esther, Daniel, David, and Jesus the Liberator—even if the sermons never mentioned them. They sang it in spirituals. They encoded it in rhythm. "Go Down, Moses …" wasn't a lullaby. It was a prophecy. It was code. It was rebellion wrapped in worship.

In the shadows of American slavery, Black theology was born not from the pulpit, but from the pit. In brush arbors, in secret woods, in midnight hush circles where quilts drank the sound of praise, enslaved people rewrote the gospel with their lives.

Where the Bible had been gutted, they filled it with fire. Where white preachers said "Obey," they heard "Break free." Where pages had been ripped out, they rewrote them in song, in prayer, and in blood.

The true gospel never died. It hid, it resisted, and it survived, — not on paper or in pulpits, but in the hearts of those who believed in a God that no master could own.

And so, I write. I remember. I pass on the story of John T. Ward and all those whose Bibles came with missing pages, yet whose faith remained whole.

John T. Ward, as a conductor on the Underground Railroad and a pioneer of Black economic empowerment, would take these lessons to heart. He understood that freedom was never freely granted—it had to be fought for, protected, and defended. If his ancestors had been denied their land, he would ensure that the next generation of Wards built something that could never be taken away. The past was prologue. The fight was never over.

The Black church has long been central to foundational Black American life, providing spiritual comfort as well as a platform for social transformation. Existing separately from white society yet continually engaging with it, Black churches evolved through countless acts of faith, resistance, and protest—guided consistently by an unwavering belief in freedom. From the era of slavery through abolition, Reconstruction, the civil rights movement, and into the present day, Black churches have served as powerful centers of resistance, community formation, and political activism.

During slavery, biblical narratives of deliverance resonated deeply among enslaved people. The Exodus story, depicting God's liberation of the Israelites from Egyptian bondage, held particular significance. Enslaved preachers often portrayed Moses as a divine figure leading his people toward freedom, assuring congregants that the same God "would one day set them free." This spiritual perspective subtly undermined the institution of slavery and fostered hope and collective identity among the oppressed.

Some of the most notable instances of slave resistance were directly tied to Black religious leadership. In 1831, Nat Turner, an enslaved preacher, declared divine inspiration to lead what became the largest slave rebellion in U.S. history. Turner believed he was chosen by God to dismantle slavery, interpreting biblical prophecies as a direct mandate for action.

Similarly, Denmark Vesey—a formerly enslaved man and influential church leader—planned a significant uprising in 1822 from Charleston's African Methodist Episcopal (AME) Church. Though his plot was ultimately discovered and thwarted, white authorities, alarmed by the connection between Black religious institutions and rebellion, responded by destroying the church and passing laws that prohibited Black congregations from gathering without white supervision.

Hush harbors were sacred spaces born out of necessity, secrecy, and spiritual defiance. Hidden deep in the woods, tucked into ravines, or nestled in remote corners of plantations, these secret meeting places became sanctuaries where the enslaved could worship on their own terms—far from the surveillance and control of their enslavers.

The name itself—"hush"—spoke to the quiet urgency of these gatherings. Every voice, every hymn, every prayer had to be subdued—silenced just enough to escape detection. To muffle the sound of worship, enslaved people soaked blankets in water and hung them over makeshift structures or held them gently over mouths as they sang and prayed. The stillness of the night concealed the power of what was taking place: faith being reclaimed and reborn in the shadows.

In these hush harbors, Christianity became something entirely different from what enslavers had tried to impose. No longer a tool of obedience or justification for bondage, the faith practiced here was a fusion of Christian teachings with African spirituality and ancestral memory. From the soil of oppression, a new theology began to take root—one that affirmed the sacred worth of the oppressed and imagined freedom as both a spiritual promise and a human right.

This was the birth of what would later be called Liberation Theology—a faith that declared, with certainty, that God walks with the bound, hears the cry of the broken, and stands against every Pharaoh. It taught that spiritual liberation could not be separated from physical bondage. In the hearts of the enslaved, the God of Exodus was real, and Jesus was not a passive savior but a liberator—a redeemer who overturned tables and raised the lowly.

For those enduring the daily brutality of slavery, Christianity became a source of strength, solidarity, and resistance. The message of Jesus—his teachings of salvation, justice, and the last becoming first—resonated deeply. In hush harbors, the enslaved found not only solace, but strategy. These were not just religious services; they were spiritual revolts. They fostered community, restored dignity, and affirmed humanity in a world designed to erase it.

Importantly, hush harbors were acts of resistance. By gathering secretly and interpreting scripture through their own lens, enslaved people rejected the dehumanizing theology preached from the plantations—sermons that commanded them to obey their masters and accept suffering as divine will. Instead, they created a faith that empowered, one rooted in hope, defiance, and the promise of deliverance.

The legacy of these gatherings didn't end with emancipation. The theology, music, and communal spirit nurtured in hush harbors laid the foundation for the Black church and, generations later, the civil rights movement. The spiritual ideas forged in whispered prayers and muted songs would echo loudly through the voices of leaders like Martin Luther King Jr., Fannie Lou Hamer, and countless others who turned sacred resistance into public revolution.

The hush harbors remind us that even in the most brutal conditions, enslaved people carved out spaces of spiritual freedom. They remind us that faith—when claimed, not coerced—can be the most radical form of resistance.

Despite violent efforts to suppress it, the Black church remained. It laid the foundation for future political movements rooted in faith and justice.

Although colonial slave masters despised African religions, seeing them as threats to their control, the enslaved found ways to survive, adapt, and endure. Despite being stripped of their names, languages, and homelands, they held onto their spiritual essence, preserving fragments of their ancestral beliefs through music, rhythm, prayer, and resistance.

As Christianity swept through the Americas, millions of Africans were introduced to the religion of their captors. Catholic missionaries were often more welcoming, allowing Africans to convert and, in some cases, incorporate elements of their traditional beliefs into Catholic worship. Protestant churches, particularly in the American South, were far more reluctant to defy the interests of powerful slaveholders. Many enslaved people were forced to attend the same churches as their masters, where the message from the pulpit was clear: "Servants, obey your masters."

This spiritual indoctrination was designed to pacify. Slaveholders hoped that Christianity—carefully filtered and manipulated—would break the will of the enslaved. They wanted submission, not salvation.

Some critics have since argued that the Black church was the reason the enslaved didn't rise up like their brethren in Haiti, where revolution burned through the plantations and led to the first free Black republic. They claim the church taught passivity, obedience, and acceptance of suffering.

But the truth is far more complex—and far more powerful.

Enslaved Africans in America were not like the Haitians in terms of numbers, geography, or access to arms. They were vastly outnumbered, isolated, and stripped of military resources. An organized uprising would have meant certain slaughter. And yet, they resisted—through faith, through culture, through survival.

What the enslaved lacked in material weapons, they held in abundance in spiritual fire. Rich in cultural memory, African traditions blended with Christian belief to create a faith that was neither passive nor weak; it was subversive, resilient, and revolutionary in its own right.

Even in slavery's shadow—especially in the North—free Black people began to reclaim faith on their own terms. In 1787, two brave Black worshippers, Absalom Jones and Richard Allen, walked out of a segregated Methodist church in Philadelphia after being forced to sit in the balcony. That act of defiance gave birth to the Free African Society, and later, to Mother Bethel African Methodist Episcopal Church—a church built by Black hands, led by Black clergy, and committed to the freedom of Black people.

By the early nineteenth century, Black-founded Baptist and Methodist churches were springing up across the country, giving enslaved and free Black communities greater control over their spiritual lives. These churches were not just places of worship, they were incubators of resistance, spaces for fellowship, organizing, and political awareness. Even before the end of slavery, the Black church had already become a force of protest—rooted in scripture, aimed at liberation.

Meanwhile, the cultural and religious heritage of Africa was never fully lost.

In a passage from the Encyclopedia Britannica (9th ed., Vol. XX, p. 362), Professor C.P. Thiele offers a rare glimpse into the religious worldview many Africans may have brought with them when they were stolen from their homelands:

"The prominent characteristic of primitive Negro religion is Nature worship with the accompanying strong belief in sorcery. There is a theistic tendency: Almost all tribes believe in some supreme god without always worshipping him, generally a heaven and rain god; sometimes, as among the Cameroons and in Dahomey, a sun god. But the most widely spread worship among Negroes and Negroids, from west to northeast and south to Loango, is that of the moon, combined with a great veneration of the cow."

These beliefs—though demonized by European colonizers— were rooted in a deep reverence for the divine in nature: in the moon, in the rain, in the ancestors. And while many of these traditional elements were violently suppressed, they survived—camouflaged inside gospel harmonies, call-and-response prayers, healing rituals, and the very rhythm of the Black church itself.

So, no—Christianity did not erase African spirituality.

It merged with it.

It absorbed the echoes of distant drums and transmuted them into spirituals and sermons that moved heaven and shook the earth.

The Black church, far from being a tool of submission, became a crucible of liberation. And through that fire, a new theology was forged—one where God stood not beside the oppressor, but with the oppressed.

One where praise was resistance, and faith was an act of revolution.

John T. Ward's story does not begin in a courtroom or a church pulpit; it begins in exile.

As a child, John T. Ward and his family were forced to leave Virginia. The tightening grip of restrictive laws, constant suspicion, and the fragile promise of freedom made it untenable for free Black families like his to remain in their birthplace. Seeking survival, they journeyed north to Lawrence County, Ohio—a rugged, hilly region just across the river from the slaveholding South. This move was not merely relocation; it was a quest for survival that would indelibly shape John T.'s life.

Lawrence County was not chosen at random. It was recognized as a haven for Black families fleeing the oppressive conditions of Virginia. The area was home to a resilient free Black community centered around Macedonia Ridge, with Macedonia Baptist Church at its heart. Founded between 1811 and 1813, Macedonia Baptist Church is considered Ohio's first Black-founded church and one of the oldest, west of the Alleghenies.

In this close-knit community, John T. Ward was raised amid individuals who had either escaped slavery or aided others in doing so. Macedonia Church served not only as a place of worship but also as a hub for abolitionist strategy—a spiritual fortress where resistance was both prayed for and enacted. Here, John T. absorbed the essence of moral courage and the importance of community solidarity.

The roots of this abolitionist stronghold trace back to 1827 when Pleasant Roberts, a man formerly enslaved and freed by Lt. John Ward, led a group of seventy manumitted Black men and women from Virginia to Ohio. Among them was Philip "Phil" Lewis, who later became a conductor on the Underground Railroad, guiding fugitives toward freedom across the Ohio River. They settled in Burlington and Macedonia Ridge, establishing homes, farms, and founding Macedonia Church on land they purchased and cultivated themselves.

This community instilled in John T. Ward the conviction that freedom was not a privilege but a right worth fighting for. When he later confronted injustices facing Black people in Southern Ohio, his actions were deeply personal. His family's forced migration, his upbringing in a sanctuary where the church was both sacred and strategic, and his firsthand experiences with the Underground Railroad all fueled his commitment to lead and advocate for his community.

Macedonia Baptist Church provided John T. with a blueprint for faith-based resistance. The lessons he learned there—about landownership, self-governance, solidarity, and the power of community—remained with him throughout his life. These principles guided him when he stood up to the First Baptist Church in Columbus and founded an anti-slavery church of his own. They also influenced his efforts to organize, educate, and protect others involved in the Underground Railroad.

John T. Ward did not discover the abolitionist movement in adulthood; he was born into it, raised by it, and refined within its crucible. The seeds of defiance were planted on that hill in Lawrence County, and Macedonia Church was the fertile ground in which they took root.

The Macedonia congregation and its ministers, discreetly but deliberately, supported the Underground Railroad. They provided food, shelter, and guidance to those making the perilous journey north, collaborating with a network of local abolitionists. With active crossing points along the nearby river, the church became a natural stop on this clandestine trail to freedom.

In 1834, Macedonia Baptist Church and five sister Black churches took a bold step by formally organizing the Providence Anti-Slavery Baptist Association—one of the earliest Black-led Baptist associations in Ohio. Uniquely, this association explicitly adopted a strong anti-slavery stance. All its member churches were engaged in Underground Railroad activity, effectively merging spiritual life with abolitionist activism.

Over time, the Burlington area gained a national reputation as a major Underground Railroad hub. According to local history, Macedonia Church and its congregation assisted countless freedom seekers who crossed the Ohio River from nearby plantations. This reputation was further solidified in 1849 when thirty-two formerly enslaved individuals were emancipated by the will of Virginia landowner James Twyman. These individuals settled near Macedonia Church, forming what became known as the Burlington 37. Having experienced slavery firsthand, these families were deeply committed to aiding others in their pursuit of freedom and rebuilding their lives.

The church community's efforts have since been widely recognized. In 2020, Macedonia Baptist Church was added to the National Park Service's Underground Railroad Network to Freedom, formally acknowledging its authentic role in Underground Railroad activity.

The historic Macedonia Missionary Baptist Church, constructed in 1849, still stands on Macedonia Ridge in Fayette Township, Lawrence County. It remains the only surviving antebellum Black church in Ohio—a rare and powerful symbol of the state's early Black heritage. Though its membership began to decline in the twentieth century as younger generations moved to urban centers and smaller congregations consolidated, the building itself was preserved and continued to be used occasionally for homecomings and gatherings of descendants of the original families.

Recognizing its historical significance, Macedonia Church was added to the National Register of Historic Places in 1978. In 2003, the Ohio Historical Society erected an official marker at the site. Then, in 2020, the National Park Service included the church in its Underground Railroad Network to Freedom, formally verifying its authentic role in Underground Railroad activity.

Today, Macedonia Church is the focus of active preservation efforts. Now more than 175 years old, the building has been recognized as one of Ohio's most endangered historic sites. Preservationists and local stakeholders have formed the Macedonia Restoration Project, securing funding through a Save America's Treasures grant and a challenge grant from the Jeffris Family Foundation to stabilize and restore the structure.

Plans are underway to reopen the church as a community center and museum, potentially as soon as 2024. The vision is to ensure that the full story of Macedonia's legacy—from the journey of Pleasant Roberts and the freed Ward family in 1827 to the church's central role in freedom movements—can be elevated, amplified, and shared with the public.

In the meantime, the white-painted chapel on Macedonia Hill stands as a proud monument to Ohio's earliest Black pioneers. Through historical markers, scholarly research, and the living memories of descendants, the legacy of the Macedonia Black Church—and of leaders like Pleasant Roberts—endures as a lasting testament to faith, freedom, and the strength of community in freedmen history.

A major breakthrough for Black communities came with the creation of churches within walking distance of their congregants. This seemingly simple act of accessibility was transformative. With churches close to home, Black people—both enslaved and free—could gather without relying on white-controlled spaces. These churches quickly became centers of social life, strategic planning, and sacred resistance.

For freedmen, the church offered a safe space to hold secret meetings, organize for abolition, and plot paths toward freedom. For enslaved people, who owned no property of their own and were constantly under surveillance, these churches were the only public spaces where they could gather with a sense of shared identity and collective purpose. They provided rare moments of dignity and connection—especially for those from different plantations.

Churches like St. Paul and Second Baptist emerged as pioneers in the fight for justice. These houses of worship hosted statewide *Conventions of Colored Men*—powerful gatherings where Black leaders came together to address the horrors of slavery, systemic inequality, and the ongoing suffering of their people. These conventions weren't just forums for debate; they were launching pads for activism.

Many of the men who attended these conventions went on to become active participants in the Underground Railroad, using their communities and congregations to protect fugitive slaves. In Columbus, Ohio, Black citizens risked their lives to disguise runaways as cooks, laborers, and domestic workers, shielding them under assumed identities. The network of support ran deep—and it was effective.

Among these heroes was John T. Ward, who by day served humbly as a janitor, but by night became a fearless conductor on the Underground Railroad. Quiet and unassuming, John T. helped usher countless men and women to freedom—guided by conviction and rooted in the community strength his church provided.

The Black church quickly became the heartbeat of freedmen life, connecting people from all walks of life and from both sides of the Ohio River. It was more than a religious institution; it was a place of solidarity, strategy, and spiritual resistance. Black ministers traveled from town to town throughout Ohio, preaching sermons of hope, liberation, and God's justice. For rural slaves, these visits and services were often their first taste of racial solidarity, witnessing a world where Blackness wasn't cursed—but celebrated. Even as social and economic lines separated the enslaved from their free and more affluent brethren, the shared bond of race and suffering created unity. In these churches, Black identity triumphed over the divisions imposed by slavery.

In the South, Baptist churches occupied a complicated space in the struggle against slavery. While few Baptists in Georgia owned slaves—and the denomination was often seen as antagonistic toward the institution—Black Baptists still faced strict supervision. As early as 1773, some Black preachers were allowed to preach, but only under the oversight of white authorities, and with no real power in church affairs. Still, their voices stirred the hearts of the oppressed.

In the North, the Philadelphia Baptist Association officially approved the abolition of slavery in 1789. Meanwhile, in Virginia, Baptists stressed the importance of freedom around the same time. In Kentucky and Ohio, however, Baptist opinion was more divided. Regional associations wrestled with the moral contradictions of slavery. Yet even amid that tension, Baptists took notable steps: they advocated for slave marriages, encouraged family worship, and provided spiritual guidance to enslaved members. They also took a clear stand against slavery's expansion, opposing the slave trade treaties of 1818 and 1835.

Throughout this struggle, the Black church remained both a sanctuary and a staging ground. It offered comfort for the soul, but it also trained a generation of warriors—men and women who would fight for justice not just in heaven, but here on Earth.

***

It started in the sanctuary.

The flicker of candlelight danced along the walls of the First Baptist Church in Columbus, Ohio—a congregation where Black and white members worshipped under the same roof, but never as equals. Black worshippers were sent to the basement. Their voices rose up through the floorboards, unheard. And above them, the leadership grew increasingly hostile to any mention of slavery.

The church didn't want "divisive" talk, no sermons on abolition, no prayers for the enslaved, and no calls for moral reckoning.

But John T. Ward had heard enough.

He was just twenty-two—a recent transplant from Virginia—and already a storm in motion. Activism ran through his veins like fire. He didn't come to Ohio to sit quietly in the shadows of white moderation. He came to fight.

Applying the principle of moral suasion—the Quaker-inspired belief that conscience, not conflict, must change hearts—John T. stood up in the middle of that church and challenged the very soul of the institution. His voice cut through the sanctuary like a blade.

"If you're not committed to the cause, you're welcome to stay. But I cannot be part of this church."

Then he turned and walked out.

The moment was electric. History cracked open in the wake of his footsteps. And as he left, forty brave souls rose and followed—moved not by a man, but by a mission. Together, they purchased land, built a new sanctuary, and founded what would become Columbus's first Black-led anti-slavery church—a spiritual safehouse for freedom fighters.

This was leadership, not in theory, but in action. It was rebellion dressed in Sunday's best.

But the fire had been building.

It started earlier, when a wealthy couple arrived in Columbus from Virginia—friends of James Poindexter, a rising Black leader.

The couple had sold their slaves before moving north, expecting praise. But John T. Ward wasn't impressed.

He confronted them directly, his sense of justice unsparing.

"You're joining an anti-slavery church. Take the money you've made, return to Virginia, and use it to buy the slaves back. Then set them free."

They refused. And the white leadership of First Baptist—afraid of controversy, afraid of courage—intervened. They told John T. his ideas were too dangerous.

He made his choice. He didn't flinch. He walked.

And with that walk, John T. Ward changed the trajectory of the Black church in Ohio. That bold act in 1842 became the seed of something new. The new church—built by those forty men—was not just a building. It was a beacon. A sanctuary for abolitionists. A place where truth didn't hide behind stained glass.

That moment also sparked a lasting friendship with James Poindexter, who became the head pastor of the new church. Poindexter would rise to become the first Black elected official in Columbus, but John T. remained the architect of that rebellion.

Years later, in an interview with OSU professor Wilbur Siebert, John T. acknowledged Poindexter's connection to the Underground Railroad but remarked that his friend "wasn't that active." Perhaps that was true—or perhaps it was John T.'s way of shielding him from danger, even in hindsight. Silence can be protection, too.

The First Baptist Church had once stood as a symbol of religious respectability. But John T. Ward turned it into a monument to cowardice, then raised his own monument to conviction just down the road.

At twenty-two, he did what most men never find the courage to do in a lifetime.

He stared down comfort. He stood for principle. He called out hypocrisy. He led.

And when he walked out of that church, he didn't just start a new congregation.

He declared war on complicity.

His legacy is one of holy disruption. He didn't just preach righteousness; he embodied it. He didn't wait for the world to change; he forced its hand.

Let the record show: John T. Ward walked out of the church—and into history.

In the decades leading up to the Civil War, Black churches across the North and South became training grounds for abolitionist leaders and sacred stages for the prophetic denunciation of slavery. Far from passive spiritual centers, these churches served as command posts for Black resistance—where the gospel of liberation was not just preached but lived.

Many Black ministers boldly used their pulpits to condemn the brutal institution. Their message was clear: any nation that sanctioned human bondage would face divine judgment.

Few embodied this truth more fiercely than Frederick Douglass—once enslaved, then a licensed lay preacher, and eventually a towering abolitionist voice. He thundered against American Christianity for its complicity in slavery, declaring it a perversion of the gospel and a betrayal of God's call to justice. For Douglass, slavery was not just a political issue; it was a spiritual sin that violated the Bible's core teaching: the equality of all souls before God.

Others, like Minister David Walker, were even more direct. In his 1829 *Appeal to the Coloured Citizens of the World*, Walker urged enslaved people to rise up by any means necessary, warning the oppressors that "God rules in the armies of heaven" and would deliver retribution to the wicked enslavers. His fiery words echoed from pulpits into plantations, setting the moral tone for a revolution that had already begun in the hearts of the oppressed.

These weren't isolated outbursts. They were part of a larger abolitionist chorus, fueled by the moral clarity and righteous fire that surged through Black religious life. The Black church was not merely a spiritual refuge, but it was a base of concrete action.

In the North, Black American congregations partnered with white abolitionists to operate the Underground Railroad, offering shelter, funds, and volunteers. Many churches became literal "stations" on this secret path to freedom. Among the most famous of these conductors was Harriet Tubman, whose unshakable faith guided her as she led hundreds from bondage. Tubman, often called "Moses," credited divine visions for giving her the courage to return again and again into danger.

Likewise, Sojourner Truth—another former slave turned itinerant preacher—traveled the country delivering sermons that wove biblical truth with abolition and women's rights. Black churchwomen played a critical role as well, forming abolitionist societies, raising funds, distributing literature, and petitioning lawmakers—all from church-based networks. Their activism proved that faith was not a narcotic to dull pain but, as W.E.B. Du Bois wrote, "the comforter of the sorrowing" and "the supernatural avenger of wrong."

This moral engine of resistance didn't stop with emancipation.

With the fall of slavery, Black churches blossomed across the South, becoming vital hubs for political, educational, and economic advancement during Reconstruction. Emancipation was hailed from pulpits as a divine reenactment of the Exodus; God, once again, had intervened in history to deliver His chosen people.

Yet freedom brought profound challenges, and Black churches stepped into the gap. Congregations organized aid, distributed clothing and food, and established schools for the newly freed. Northern Black churches sent missionaries south to help former slaves acquire literacy, job skills, and spiritual grounding.

Education became central. Leaders like AME Bishop Daniel A. Payne worked tirelessly to establish institutions for learning. Through church and missionary efforts, the foundations were laid for historically Black colleges, including Morehouse and Spelman. In countless towns, church buildings served double duty as schoolhouses and town halls, where Black communities could govern themselves, organize politically, and plan their futures.

As Reconstruction expanded, Black ministers stepped into public office in unprecedented numbers. Du Bois once called the Black preacher "the most unique personality developed by the Negro on American soil"—a voice that had long spoken for the voiceless, now speaking from the floor of Congress.

In 1870, Hiram Rhodes Revels—an AME minister and Civil War chaplain—became the first Black U.S. Senator, representing Mississippi. Reverend Richard Harvey Cain, pastor of Charleston's historic Emanuel AME Church—rebuilt after Denmark Vesey's martyrdom—was elected to the U.S. House of Representatives. Dozens more followed at the state and local levels. Their dual authority as spiritual leaders and elected officials reflected the trust Black communities placed in the church as their most reliable institution of power.

But when Reconstruction gave way to the terror of Jim Crow, the Black church did not retreat. It became a fortress of survival, fostering a parallel society where Black leadership, dignity, and resistance could grow—safe from white eyes, if never fully beyond white violence.

In the late 1800s and early 1900s, Black churches protested lynching, voter suppression, and segregation—often at great risk. Journalist and activist Ida B. Wells relied heavily on Black church networks to distribute her anti-lynching writings, mobilizing the faithful to resist systemic brutality.

Black women, too, rose to prominence in these spaces— organizing missionary societies, women's conventions, and temperance campaigns that addressed not only spiritual needs, but economic injustice, education, and suffrage.

When critics warned that churches should stay out of politics, Nannie Helen Burroughs, educator and Baptist trailblazer, responded with righteous fire.

"It is better to have politics than ignorance in the pews."

Her words captured the spirit of an institution that had always known its mission, not only to save souls, but to save lives.

From their very foundation, Black churches in America were never just places of worship; they were centers of resistance, education, refuge, and community power. And because of that, they have always been targets.

White supremacists understood the influence of the Black church. They saw it as a threat—a place where the enslaved could imagine freedom, where the free could organize, where truth could be spoken in voices louder than fear. So, they attacked, with laws, with torches, with bombs, and with silence.

Ohio, though a free state, was not exempt from this violence.

During the antebellum era, many white Ohioans supported the idea of emancipation in theory but feared the presence and autonomy of free Black communities. Black churches, especially those aligned with abolitionist causes, were seen as dangerous.

In Lawrence County, home to Macedonia Baptist Church, one of the oldest Black churches in the state, congregants often held services in secret or posted guards to watch for intruders. The church, built by free Black settlers and conductors of the Underground Railroad, stood not only as a spiritual home but as a strategic stop for freedom seekers crossing from Virginia. That alone made it a target. Vigilante groups and pro-slavery sympathizers often threatened churches like Macedonia, accusing them of harboring fugitives and stirring rebellion.

In Columbus, tensions ran high. By the mid-1800s, Black-led churches had begun to emerge with greater visibility—like Second Baptist Church, founded in 1836 by members who broke away from First Baptist Church in protest of slavery and racial segregation. These churches weren't just spiritual havens, they were political. They hosted abolitionist speakers, printed anti-slavery tracts, and offered sanctuary to the hunted. And because of that, they were watched.

Targeted.

There are reports from the period of churches being vandalized, of meetings being disrupted by white mobs, and of Black preachers being harassed, arrested, or threatened for the content of their sermons.

One such case involved James Preston Poindexter, pastor of Second Baptist Church in Columbus and a known abolitionist. His outspoken stance on slavery and advocacy for Black rights earned him a reputation—and not just among the faithful. He was surveilled by white authorities, threatened by locals, and yet continued to preach justice from the pulpit. It's believed that his church was repeatedly targeted for intimidation, especially when it became known that he and members of his congregation were assisting fugitives along the Underground Railroad.

Throughout Ohio—especially in towns near the Southern border—Black churches were burned, raided, and violently opposed. Their very existence challenged the myth of white supremacy and proved that Black people were not content to simply survive; they were organizing, believing, and fighting back.

And the attacks didn't end with slavery.

From the bombing of Black churches in the South during Jim Crow to the Charleston massacre of 2015, and to the threats still made today, the Black church remains a target—because it remains a force: a force for truth, a force for justice, and a force that refuses to be silenced.

In every generation, the Black church has stood in defiance of a world that tried to crush its spirit.

They burned the buildings, but they couldn't burn the faith.

CHAPTER 10

Burning Oh-Pression

"Ohio boasts of her love for liberty ... but there is no place in the Union where more hateful prejudice exists toward the colored man than in this same boasted State."

-John Mercer Langston, writing in protest of Ohio's refusal to repeal Black Laws in the 1840s and 1850s *(from Ohio, the first Black man elected to public office in the U.S.)*

T he river burned silver under the brutal glare of the midday sun, steamships heaving at their moorings along the fevered port of Cincinnati. Hooves cracked against the cobblestones. Carts groaned under crates of goods. Merchants barked prices through mouths parched from the heat.

And from the decks—cloaked in wealth and arrogance—stepped Southern plantation owners. Coats pressed sharp, hats angled with pride, boots polished to reflect the sky itself.

A few paces behind them, shackled by silence, came the enslaved—Black men and women in coarse fabrics, bowed heads, and invisible chains heavier than iron. Chains made of laws, fear, and the cruel illusion of "freedom" that Ohio promised but never delivered.

By dusk, the city's pulse had darkened. The heavy thud of boots echoed through narrow alleyways. Gas lamps sputtered against a creeping twilight.

Somewhere down by the river, a Black man ran—his breath ragged, his feet raw. He had reached the so-called North. The myth. The "Free State."

But behind him came the bounty hunters, called by blood money and emboldened by law.

And with each shout, a truth sharpened like a blade.

Freedom was a lie.

To those who've never tasted the bile of bondage, it's easy to ask, "Why run?"

To those who've never watched their child sold from their arms or felt the lash tear flesh from bone, escape may look reckless, foolish.

Why not just endure? Why not stay silent and survive?

Because for the enslaved, escape wasn't rebellion. It was breath. It was the last gasp of humanity clawed back from a world that insisted you were property.

In 1841, Ohio made what looked like a stride toward justice. A legal ruling—pushed by abolitionist Salmon P. Chase, known as *"the attorney general for fugitive slaves"*—declared that enslaved people brought into the state by their owners would be considered free.

For a moment, hope flickered.

But like so many promises Ohio made to Black Americans, it came wrapped in betrayal.

The ruling carried its own blade: it also declared that *"color and long possession"* were proof enough of slavery. Your Blackness—and the simple fact that you'd ever been enslaved—was all it took. The burden of proof? Fell squarely on your back.

No papers? No white witness? The law didn't care. You weren't a citizen. You weren't even human. You were a fugitive.

Even before the Fugitive Slave Act of 1850 turned the North into a hunting ground, Ohio was already complicit. It was a borderland where justice ended at the color line.

The Black Laws passed between 1804 and 1807—disguised as "public safety measures"—functioned as a legal noose. These laws weren't about order. They were about control. They were about making sure Black freedom never outshined white dominance.

When Ohio entered the Union in 1803, it did so with pride in its anti-slavery constitution. The Northwest Ordinance of 1787 had outlawed slavery in the region, and Ohio's founders were eager to promote the state as *free soil*. But the ink on that constitution dried quickly—and so did its promise.

In 1804, just one year after statehood, Ohio's legislature passed a series of laws that would come to be known as the Black Codes. These laws targeted free Black people—not those escaping slavery, but those already living free. Their goal was clear: discourage Black migration, suppress Black agency, and ensure that freedom came with a cage.

The 1804 Black Codes were nothing more than freedom, with conditions. The law required that every free Black person who entered Ohio register with the county clerk within twenty days. They had to produce legal documentation—usually issued by a white authority—proving their free status.

But even that wasn't enough.

They also had to post a five-hundred-dollar bond, backed by two white residents who would swear under oath to their "good behavior." This bond wasn't a suggestion—it was mandatory. No bond? No right to stay. The law effectively turned freedom into a privilege—not a right. One accessible only to those with wealth, white allies, or extraordinary luck.

To make matters worse, the 1804 codes banned Black testimony in court cases involving white people, denied Black men the right to vote or serve in local militias, excluded Black children from most public schools, and gave local governments the right to expel any free Black person deemed a burden or threat.

So, while slavery was officially outlawed, racial control was written directly into law. This wasn't liberty. It was a tightly controlled loophole, dressed up as moral progress.

By 1807, white anxiety over the rising number of free Black people had deepened—especially near the Ohio River, where newly emancipated folks often crossed into the state looking for refuge. In response, Ohio didn't ease the pressure. It turned the screws tighter.

The 1807 revisions to the Black Codes reinforced the five-hundred-dollar bond requirement and extended it to Black children born in the state; gave local officials more power to remove "undesirable" Black residents, with no right to appeal; reaffirmed that Black people could not testify in court against whites, silencing them in cases of theft, assault, and worse; and added new restrictions on land ownership and access to public services.

The effect was clear and immediate. Ohio was sending a loud message to free Black people across the nation: you may be free, but you are not welcome here.

Despite its constitution banning slavery, Ohio imposed a cost on Black freedom—a five-hundred-dollar price tag on simply existing in the state. This wasn't just policy; it was punishment.

This fee, enforced under the 1804 and 1807 Black Laws, was deliberately unreachable for most.

It was an impossible toll for many. And yet—thousands paid it. I know my family did.

Ohio was a land of contradictions. It was a free state on paper, yet it enforced racial hierarchy with the same cruelty as its slaveholding neighbors. For the enslaved fleeing north, Ohio was a crossing point—a brief stop on the path to liberty farther north or into Canada. But for free Black people hoping to settle, build lives, and raise families, Ohio became a legal minefield.

Imagine being newly freed in Kentucky or Virginia, looking north with hope—only to find out that in Ohio, you'd need five hundred dollars just to stay. That you'd need two white men to vouch for your very presence. That you couldn't testify if someone tried to rob you or harm you. That your child could be thrown out of school—or worse, out of the entire county.

The Black Codes of 1804 and 1807 didn't just restrict they deterred. They turned freedom into a trick mirror. They sent countless free Black families away from Ohio's borders. Instead of being a beacon of liberation, Ohio became a symbol of conditional liberty where rights were rationed out based on color, class, and white tolerance.

And yet ... despite it all, Black communities endured.

Many fought to stay. They built institutions in secret underground. Churches, schools, mutual aid societies, and early resistance networks that would later evolve into the Underground Railroad. But their roots were forced to grow in hostile soil, watered not by law, but by faith, determination, and resistance.

Ohio promised freedom. The Black Codes proved otherwise.

When Ohio entered the Union in 1803, following the ratification of its 1802 constitution, its founders made their position painfully clear. The right to vote was not a universal guarantee—it was a privilege reserved for "white male inhabitants above the age of twenty-one who had resided in the state for one year and paid taxes."

That was the law. Final. Absolute. No room for debate. No wiggle room for justice.

So, if you were a free Black man—born on Ohio soil, a landowner, a taxpayer, even a veteran—you were still denied the ballot. Not because you lacked merit or contribution. But because you were not white. In that moment, Ohio etched white supremacy into the very bedrock of its democracy, writing exclusion into the architecture of its freedom.

Let's be plain, in antebellum Ohio, to vote, you had to be a white man, over twenty-one, a one-year resident, and a taxpayer.

Everyone else—Black men, women of all races, Native Americans—was erased from the democratic process. No matter their education. No matter their contributions. No matter their humanity.

And the state made sure to back up that discrimination with the full weight of the law. In *State v. Ferry* (1831), an Ohio court reaffirmed that "persons of color" were not—and could not be— interpreted as eligible voters under the constitution. That decision echoed through every polling station like a lock snapping shut.

And it didn't stop there. Black Ohioans couldn't serve on juries, run for office, testify against whites in court, and of course, they couldn't vote

But if you think our people took that lying down, think again.

From Oberlin to Cincinnati, free Black communities organized, protested, and petitioned. They pushed back with intellect, strategy, and moral clarity. Leaders like John Mercer Langston, Charles Langston, James Poindexter, John T. Ward, William Wells Brown, and the bold voices from the AME Church carried the fire of resistance.

They demanded suffrage. They demanded full citizenship. And they did it in the face of constant rejection—especially from white

Ohioans who had migrated north from slaveholding states like Kentucky and Virginia and brought their racism with them.

John Mercer Langston—sharp, eloquent, and light-skinned—was often mistaken for white. But he never denied who he was. In his memoirs, he reflected on the brutal choice Black men had to make in Ohio: to hide in order to participate or stand proud and be denied.

And here's where it gets deeply complicated and painfully human.

Some free Black men, if they were light-skinned enough to pass, *did* vote. Not because they lied. But because the law made race a performance, not a reality.

Ohio had no scientific test for whiteness. No documents to prove your racial "purity." All that mattered was how you looked ... and whether anyone challenged you at the polls.

If you walked up to that ballot box looking "white enough," and no one said a word? You could vote.

But if your skin was a shade too brown, or your features didn't quite match the lie, someone might question you, shame you, drag you out—or worse. That ballot became a gamble.

For those who passed, the vote came with a cost: secrecy, alienation, and sometimes betrayal of their own communities. They weren't white. They were survivors in a system built to crush them, using the only tool they had—appearance.

It exposes the absurdity of the entire structure. What determined your rights in Ohio wasn't your deeds, or your taxes, or your love of country, it was whether your face told the right lie.

And yet, even in that rigged game, some of our people found the cracks in the wall—and slipped through.

Now, between you and me?

I know John T. Ward got one vote in or two. I don't care what the law said. I don't care who was watching. You don't do the kind of righteous work he did without making a few bold moves in the name of justice.

Cincinnati was the birthplace of northern terror. Let that settle in. Not New York. Not Philadelphia. Cincinnati—a border city caught between Ohio's "freedom" and Kentucky's chains—became, by 1829, the largest free Black community in the United States.

It was a city of hope and contradiction. Churches rose from the ashes. Businesses opened. Children learned to read. Recently manumitted men and women planted roots, built mutual aid societies, and raised families in a state that, on paper, promised liberty.

Forty miles from the Ohio River, in the quiet hills of Lawrence County, Black people began to build. Poke Patch, Burlington, and Black Fork were among the first Black settlements in Ohio—founded in 1818. Small. Rural. Vulnerable. These communities stood near

Quaker settlements, who sometimes offered protection and support. The freedmen gathered close—not just for community, but for survival. Numbers meant safety.

They had to stay sharp. Slave patrols roamed, ready to falsely claim any free Black person as someone's runaway "property." At any moment, your freedom could be questioned, your body claimed, your future erased.

But Lawrence County's settlements were more than safe zones. They became known for something powerful: they showed sympathy to fugitives. And in that time, in that place, *sympathy* was an act of defiance.

When John T. Ward's family arrived in Lawrence County, only fifteen free Black residents lived there. But things were changing fast. By 1829, tension simmered across Southern Ohio.

The free Black population was growing, and the bond laws weren't being strictly enforced.

Even so, the Ward family did what many could not. They placed a down payment on their bond and paid it off in full within three weeks. They were free. And they intended to stay that way.

When they arrived, a Black Baptist church was already standing—a beacon for the community. That church had connected, as early as 1821, with an anti-slavery Baptist association near Black Fork. The lines of resistance were being drawn—not just in basements or backwoods, but in pulpits and pews.

Ohio promised freedom. Its laws delivered OH-pression. And yet, families like the Wards laid down roots in hostile soil and began the long, dangerous work of building something better.

And as Black success in Southern Ohio grew, so did white resentment.

Many white Ohioans—especially those who had migrated from slaveholding states like Kentucky and Virginia—saw the Black community's rise as a direct threat to their jobs, their politics, and their fragile sense of superiority.

That tension ignited on August 17, 1829, when Cincinnati erupted into what would become the first recorded anti-Black riot in American history.

White mobs, enraged by Black progress and stirred by racist propaganda, nailed posters to homes and storefronts:

"You have fifteen days to vacate Cincinnati. Or else."

The deadline passed. The mobs came. And Black Cincinnati burned.

From August 15 to 22, 1829, Cincinnati was consumed by racial terror. What began as whispers of resentment quickly escalated into organized, calculated violence against the city's thriving Black community.

White mobs, stoked by hate and terrified of Black advancement, waged a week-long campaign of destruction. They smashed windows, looted Black-owned businesses, torched homes, and hunted families through the streets.

Property turned to ash. Lives upended. Chaos reigned.

By the time the smoke cleared, between a thousand and 1,200 Black residents had been forced to flee—driven from their homes by mob violence and the weight of white resentment. Many left behind everything they owned.

Parents carried children through smoke and rubble. Some ran barefoot. No bags. No food. Just breath—and prayer.

The message from white city officials was unmistakable. The Ohio Black Laws would be enforced.

And so, with the quiet permission of those in power, white mobs swept through Black settlements. They burned shacks. Beat men in the streets. Murdered those too poor—or too proud—to run.

But not everyone ran.

The Black families living along the river fought back.

With whatever they had—tools, fists, courage—they held the line for as long as they could. But they were outnumbered. Outgunned. Outlawed by a state that claimed to be free yet criminalized Black survival.

More than half of Cincinnati's Black population—most of them pacifists, laborers, preachers, teachers, parents of good character—made the unthinkable decision to walk over four hundred miles north to Wilberforce Colony in Canada.

They gave up their homes, their streets, and their country.

Because the promise of "freedom" in Ohio came with a torch and a noose.

Those who couldn't afford to leave the U.S. made their way to small towns along Lake Erie, taking jobs where they could, rebuilding what little was left.

But this wasn't just Cincinnati. This was policy, a pattern seen across so-called free states.

Wherever Black communities took root, white fear responded with fire. And if the state didn't burn you out, it passed laws to choke you out.

This was how America discouraged Black life. If you stayed, you'd suffer. If you left, you were erased.

Either way—your presence was punished.

And still, they endured.

While the devastation was massive, the official records are eerily silent on the number of dead. Whether by design or indifference, the tally of lives lost was never written down.

But don't mistake silence for peace.

People died. The only question is how many were simply erased without a name.

And still—it didn't end there.

For more than eight days, the city burned. Homes were looted and torched—not once, but again and again.

Families were ripped from their doorways. Dragged into the streets like criminals. Churches—once sanctuaries—were turned to glowing piles of ash.

The smoke rose before the city did. And where were the officials? Watching. Waiting.

City leaders didn't intervene until the worst had already been done. Their response was slow, reluctant—a performance, not protection.

The riot didn't end because justice arrived. It didn't stop because someone finally found their conscience. It stopped because the world was watching.

Business leaders feared bad headlines. Northern newspapers began to report the truth. And white elites—worried about their reputation and their pocketbooks—realized the violence was bad for business.

That's what finally cooled the flames—not mercy, not morality, but optics.

Some Black residents, with nowhere else to turn, fled across the Ohio River—into the same slaveholding territory they or their loved ones had once escaped. Others disappeared into the North or made their way to Canada, where the law may not have been perfect—but at least it didn't smile in your face while stabbing you in the back.

The 1829 riot shattered the illusion of the "free North." But if that summer was a warning, then *Black Friday—January 21, 1830—* was the execution of that threat.

In the bitter, pre-dawn cold of January 21, 1830, a day that would come to be known as Black Friday, the mobs returned. This time, they were more organized, more violent. And they came with something else: the quiet approval of the city itself.

They kicked in doors. They stormed bedrooms, dragging families from their sleep. Elderly women were hauled into the snow, nightgowns frozen to their legs. Children screamed as flames danced through their windows. Entire blocks glowed red with firelight.

By sunrise, nearly eighty Black residents had been corralled like livestock, shoved into wagons, and forcibly deported to Portsmouth, nearly a hundred miles away. There were no charges. No arrests. No trials. Not imprisoned. Not detained. Just erased.

In antebellum Ohio, a noose hung low over every Black neighborhood, not a literal rope but a constant threat.

One wrong word. One wrong glance. One wrong move and freedom could vanish.

If a Black man sneezed in the wrong direction, if a child spoke up, if someone dared to look a white man in the eye, they could be snatched, sold, or disappeared into the Ohio penitentiary system without a trial or a trace.

Cincinnati was no sanctuary. It was a target zone, where poor Black residents—too broke to flee—were left to endure wave after wave of white rage.

Two more race riots erupted after the 1829 expulsion. The first in 1836. The second—and most brutal—in 1841.

That year, Black Cincinnatians did something different. They fought back.

For a moment, the white mob fell into retreat—stunned by resistance they didn't expect. The Black community in Bucktown stood its ground. They defended their families, their homes, their right to exist.

But the mob wasn't finished. They didn't retreat; they escalated.

In a move as vile as it was unprecedented, white rioters seized a military-grade weapon—an M1841 six-pounder cannon—and turned it on a civilian neighborhood.

They rolled it into position, aimed it at the heart of Bucktown, and fired.

They shelled Black homes and businesses—like enemy targets on a battlefield. Walls splintered. Streets erupted. Lives were shattered in seconds.

Six freed Black residents were killed. Over two dozen were wounded.

This wasn't a riot. It wasn't chaos. It was coordinated racial warfare. And the city stood by and let it happen.

To understand the full horror, you have to understand what they used.

A M1841 six-pounder cannon is a smoothbore, muzzle-loading field cannon, standard for U.S. forces in the Mexican American War and early Civil War. It fires a six-pound solid iron shot—designed to tear through enemy infantry lines. It has an effective range of up to 1,500 yards.

It was military hardware, operated by trained artillery crews and pulled by horses on the battlefield.

And in Cincinnati, that battlefield … was a Black neighborhood.

This was not just mob violence. This was militarized racial terror—an artillery strike carried out by citizens, not soldiers, against fellow Americans.

It remains one of the only recorded times in U.S. history where white civilians used a cannon to attack a Black community.

This wasn't just a response to unrest. It was a message:

You resist—and we will bring war to your doorstep.

***

John T. Ward was eleven years old. He heard what happened— the names, the terror, the sound of that cannon. And not long after, he saw the patrols return.

In the wake of Nat Turner's 1831 rebellion in Virginia, patrolmen swept through Black communities, demanding slave passes and freedom papers, terrorizing anyone who couldn't produce the right documents. "Run, Negro, run, or the Pa-try-roll will get you," Black parents whispered to their children, words that would echo well into the postwar years.

By the time John T. was fifteen, the abolitionist movement had begun to fight fire with fire—this time with words. Anti-slavery activists launched a campaign to flood the South with a radical pamphlet titled David Walker's Appeal. But the plan was compromised. Slave-state sympathizers intercepted the literature and burned it before it could spread.

But John T. got his hands on a copy. And what he read changed him forever.

He had never heard a Black man speak like that—with fire, with intellect, with fearless rage. Walker's words didn't beg for freedom, they demanded it. He called out the hypocrisy of America and dismantled the lie of colonization—the idea that Black people should be shipped off to Africa to "solve" the problem of their existence.

"America is more our country than it is the whites—we have enriched it with our blood and tears. Will they drive us from our property and homes, which we have earned with our blood?"

The South put a one-thousand-dollar bounty on David Walker's head. He lived in a free state, but his words made him the slave states' worst nightmare. He called for enslaved people to murder their masters—not out of vengeance, but survival.

"They want us for their slaves, and think nothing of murdering us; therefore, if there is an attempt made by us, kill or be killed … and believe this: it is no more harm for you to kill a man who is trying to kill you than it is for you to take a drink of water when thirsty."

Soon after, Walker was found dead on his front porch. But his words lived on—especially in the mind of a young Black boy named John T. Ward.

John T. knew violence wasn't new. He had studied it. He knew about the Haitian Revolution—how the enslaved in Saint-Domingue rose up against the French, inspired by the chaos of the French Revolution. From 1791 to 1804, they fought, they bled, and they won. Haiti became the first nation in the world founded by former slaves.

And John T. Ward didn't just remember. He took notes. Because he understood something deep: freedom was never given. It was taken—by force, by word, by will. And he was preparing to do the same.

Ohio called itself a free state. But that morning, freedom burned under white fists and frozen skies.

Newspapers would call it a "voluntary removal." But it was nothing less than ethnic cleansing. The trauma of that night didn't stop at Cincinnati's borders—it echoed across the state. Many who remained were left homeless, jobless, and hunted. The message was clear: Black success would not be tolerated—even in the so-called free North.

Among the families shaken by these events was the Ward family, living in Lawrence County, not far from the Kentucky border. They were close enough to hear the danger—and wise enough to recognize the pattern. The flames in Cincinnati were not isolated; they were spreading. The law wasn't going to protect them. It never had.

So, like many others, the Wards made the painful decision to leave. They migrated north to Clinton County, where a growing network of Black families, churches, and abolitionists offered a tenuous sense of safety. It was this journey—born of fire and fear— that would shape the young boy John T. Ward, who would grow up to be a conductor on the Underground Railroad, a civic leader, and a relentless voice for justice.

But even as Black families relocated, Ohio's Black Laws remained on the books, giving white citizens and public officials license to harass, expel, and intimidate. The law wore the mask of order, but it carried the weapon of white supremacy.

And yet, from those ashes, something powerful emerged.

Black Ohioans did not crumble. They organized. They formed committees, hosted conventions, wrote petitions, debated in statehouses, and demanded more than symbolic freedom. They demanded actual protection, actual dignity, and actual equality.

These were not just political battles; they were fights for survival. The people who waged them were not waiting to be granted freedom. They were taking it.

This is where the Ohio story must begin—not with the Underground Railroad, not with federal emancipation, but with the first match, lit in Cincinnati. Because before John T. Ward led fugitives to freedom, Ohio lit the fire. And Cincinnati—once the nation's largest Black stronghold—became its first burned offering.

This echoed what John T. Ward's family experienced; they too were met with insults and hostility. They were ridiculed in newspapers, the social media of that era. And before you judge this poor soul for such a heartbreaking decision, understand he wasn't the only one.

Ohio may have been a free state—but for Black men like Stephen Bias, it might as well have been another kind of prison.

Bias had done everything right. Born enslaved in Albemarle County, Virginia, he earned his freedom through grueling labor as an ostler, caring for horses at a Charlottesville tavern. When his enslaver, Joel W. Brown, agreed to let him purchase his freedom in 1837, Bias paid in full and stepped into what he believed would be a new chapter in Ohio—a land supposedly rooted in liberty.

But instead of freedom, he found frost.

Ohio's laws, its people, and its social climate greeted him with the same suspicion and disdain that had haunted him in bondage. He was no longer shackled, but he was shut out—denied opportunity, community, and dignity. Despite doing everything by the book— filing his deed of emancipation and trying to begin anew—within just six months, Bias reached a painful conclusion.

He would prefer being sold into slavery in Virginia to being again compelled to emigrate to and reside in the state of Ohio.

That sentence lands like a thunderclap. A man who had tasted liberty with his own hard-earned hands publicly declared that freedom in Ohio was more unbearable than slavery in Virginia.

There's a heavy silence around that statement—thick with despair, betrayal, and cruel irony. Bias didn't speak in anger; he spoke in surrender. He had given Ohio a fair chance. But the "boasted glorious privileges of a free state" turned out to be a cruel joke. So, in 1838, he returned to Albemarle County, the land of his birth. Because even under the shadow of slavery, there was familiarity, community, something more human than the cold rejection he faced in Ohio.

And he wasn't alone.

Tom Garland, another freedman who purchased his freedom in Lynchburg, Virginia, moved to Cincinnati around 1853, hoping to begin a new life free from chains. But within days of arriving, Garland was so disheartened by the treatment he faced that he too begged to return to the South. His petition made his feelings clear: he wanted to "renounce the boasted glorious privileges of a free State" and live out the remainder of his life in the only system that—while brutal—at least acknowledged his existence.

The hypocrisy was staggering.

Ohio had branded itself as a beacon of Black freedom. But beneath that glow lay an uncomfortable truth: many white Ohioans wanted to end slavery—but not to live alongside Black people. To them, freedom was an ideal. Proximity was the threat.

The stories of Stephen Bias and Tom Garland tear a hole in the myth of a welcoming North. They force us to reckon with the painful paradox that liberty without inclusion becomes its own kind of exile. They challenge us to ask, "What is freedom worth if it comes at the cost of isolation, indignity, and invisibility?"

For Bias, the price was too steep. He chose familiarity over the icy rejection of false liberty. He chose chains over the coldness of Ohio.

And in that choice, he revealed a brutal truth: not everyone who fled North found sanctuary. Some found silence. Some found rejection. Some, like Bias, longed for a home that may never have truly loved them but at least remembered their name.

This is the kind of "freedom" Ohio offered to many Black men in the 1800s: freedom in name, not in truth. And it stands as a stark reminder—freedom without justice is just a different kind of cage.

Henrietta Wood had been free. And then, like Solomon Northup, she was stolen. But her story goes further. Not twelve years a slave—sixteen. She is Ohio's true *Sixteen Years a Slave*. Her captivity lasted even longer.

In 1848, after years in bondage, Henrietta was legally emancipated and lived in Cincinnati. For five precious years, she walked the streets, not as property but as a woman. She was still bound by the racist laws that hemmed in Black life in Ohio but no longer shackled by an owner's will. She had her papers. She had her name. She had hope.

But freedom in Ohio was a thin veneer—fragile, conditional, and easily peeled away.

Henrietta worked as a domestic servant. She moved through white households that treated her with civility soaked in condescension. She couldn't vote. She couldn't testify against a white person. Her existence as a free Black woman was tolerated, not protected.

Then came Josephine Garrard—a white woman, the wife of Henrietta's former enslaver, W.T. Garrard, who had fled to Europe, abandoning his wife and his debts. Josephine owed Henrietta money, wages earned and never paid. So, she made an offer: travel with her across the river, help with some business, and be compensated.

Henrietta hesitated. But she had her manumission papers. She had proof. And she needed the money.

So, she said yes.

But once across the Ohio River into Kentucky, Henrietta was ambushed.

There was no courtroom to appeal to. No ally to call. No time to scream.

She had been lured into a trap. Garrard had orchestrated the kidnapping from afar, using his wife as bait. Henrietta's freedom was erased in an instant. Her papers were destroyed. Her identity was rewritten.

The same river that had once divided slavery from freedom became her undoing. The border she crossed—so easily erased by a man's lie—was the same one others had risked everything to escape from.

And Ohio—the "free" state she had trusted—offered no shield, not from white greed, not from federal law, and not from betrayal.

Henrietta Wood wasn't alone. Countless free Black women in Ohio lived under the constant threat of being kidnapped and erased. The state claimed liberty but offered no real protection. In Ohio, a Black woman could be free on Monday—and in chains by Friday.

That was the truth. That was the risk.

Henrietta was dragged deep into the South—first Mississippi, then Texas—just as the country slid toward war. There, she would remain enslaved for sixteen long years, during some of the harshest, most violent years of American slavery. Even after the Civil War ended, it would take four more years before she truly walked free again.

She had been free, and Henrietta paid the price for trusting that freedom was real.

But the day she stepped back onto Ohio soil and headed for the courthouse, she made it clear.

"You may have stolen years. But you won't steal my voice."

By 1860, just before the Civil War, Ohio was home to over thirty-six thousand free Black residents. If even half of those individuals had been forced to pay the five-hundred-dollar bond (a conservative estimate given inconsistent enforcement), the state would have collected at least nine million dollars in that era's currency. That's $500 times 18,000, which equals $9,000,000 in 1860s value—equivalent to over $325 million today, when adjusted for inflation.

And yet, there are no known surviving records of those payments. No ledgers. No receipts. No archives tracking what became of that money.

This absence is no accident. It's part of a broader pattern of erasing Black presence and contribution—not just socially, but economically. These missing receipts don't just represent financial exploitation; they symbolize the systematic theft of Black legacy. Black families were taxed simply for existing in a so-called free state—and then written out of the official record.

Ohio profited off the illusion of liberty. But the receipts—both literal and historical—tell a different story.

A story of freedom sold, not granted.

Incredibly, as I sat down to write this book in 2019, slavery was still technically legal in Ohio—not in the form of plantations and chains but hidden within the language of the state's constitution.

For over 150 years, Ohio prided itself on being a free state, a beacon of hope for those fleeing the horrors of slavery. But freedom, as it turned out, had always been conditional.

Even as recently as 2016, the Ohio Legislative Black Caucus attempted to strip the language of slavery from the state's constitution. That effort exposed a long-buried truth: Ohio had never fully abolished slavery; it had only rebranded it.

Ohio's original laws prohibited buying and selling slaves within the state, but that didn't stop Southern plantation owners from bringing enslaved people with them when they traveled. It didn't stop Ohio from enforcing the Black Codes, which restricted the rights of free Black people. And it certainly didn't stop the criminal justice system from becoming the new mechanism of enslavement.

When slavery was outlawed, forced labor didn't end; it simply changed its name.

Black Ohioans were disproportionately arrested under vague laws like "vagrancy" and "loitering," then sentenced to hard labor for minor infractions. Many were convicted under exaggerated or fabricated charges, ensuring that the state could continue to profit off their forced servitude.

The labor they provided built roads, railways, and state buildings. They manufactured goods that enriched both Ohio's economy and private corporations. And they were paid nothing.

The cycle of exploitation hadn't ended; it had simply evolved.

When Ohio drafted a new state constitution in 1851, it proudly declared:

"There shall be no slavery in this state."

But just below that declaration was a dangerous loophole:

"… nor involuntary servitude, unless for the punishment of crime."

That single phrase—"unless for the punishment of crime"—mirrored what would later appear in the 13th Amendment of the U.S. Constitution, ensuring that slavery could continue under a different name.

When Donald Trump won the 2025 election, something ancient stirred in the blood of Black America. A tremor rippled through the culture—through conversations, group chats, barbershops, and tweets. It wasn't just political anxiety. It was something deeper. Older. A gut-deep warning system passed down through generations of survival. What some might call genetic memory.

Across social media, there was a buzz—whispers of fear dressed in truth.

He's trying to bring slavery back.

Not slavery in its original form—though don't be so quick to rule that out—but something more insidious: a rollback of rights, a dismantling of Black institutions, a Supreme Court packed to drag America backward. A presidency that flirted with authoritarianism while dog-whistling to white nationalism. And for many, the fear wasn't irrational. It was rooted in centuries of precedent.

There were even murmurs of a modern-day American Colonization Society—ACS 2.0. For those unfamiliar, the original ACS was a nineteenth-century initiative supported by prominent white Americans—including some who claimed to be anti-slavery—that sought to deport free Black people to Africa. Liberia was the chosen destination. A place they could be "returned" to, even if they had been born and raised in the U.S.

The idea was simple—and chilling: Black people, even if free, didn't belong here.

So, ask yourself—what happens if the law no longer sees you as fully belonging again?

History already showed us this script. We just don't recognize it until it's too late.

Back in 1802, Ohio's constitution outlawed slavery, yes—but in practice, it did the bare minimum to protect Black lives. While it banned formal slavery, it imposed "Black Laws" that made life nearly unlivable for freed people. And even worse, it allowed white Southerners to exploit legal gray zones and bring enslaved people across the border as "servants," free to work them without protection or consequence.

Now here's the part we don't talk about enough. If you were a free Black person back then, you were required to pay a five-hundred-dollar bond—over twelve thousand dollars in today's money—just for the right to live in Ohio. That's right. Freedom wasn't free. It had a literal price tag.

So, I have to ask you now—what are you going to do?

Do you have your twelve thousand dollars ready?

If Ohio—or any state—decided to pull what it did in 1802 again, would you be prepared?

Because don't think for a second that history can't repeat itself. It already has, in new packaging: voter suppression, gerrymandering, school curriculum bans, public divestment from Black neighborhoods, stripping away of affirmative action, and a Supreme Court that has shown it is willing to redefine fundamental rights.

So again, what are you going to do when the law stops pretending to protect you?

Are you watching the signs? Or are you waiting for the headlines to catch up with your fears?

Because for Black America, the alarm has already gone off. The real question is whether anyone else hears it.

As of 2025, Ohio's constitution still contains a clause that permits involuntary servitude as punishment for a crime. Specifically, Article I, Section 6 reads: *"There shall be no slavery in this state; nor involuntary servitude, unless for the punishment of crime."*

This language mirrors the 13th Amendment of the U.S. Constitution, ratified in 1865—a federal amendment that technically abolished slavery, *except* as a form of criminal punishment. For over a century and a half, this exception allowed Ohio to legally exploit incarcerated individuals through forced labor. And for decades, lawmakers debated whether to erase this relic of slavery from the books.

In June 2023, Ohio lawmakers introduced House Joint Resolution 2 (HJR2) to finally address this issue. The amendment seeks to prohibit slavery and involuntary servitude without exceptions, aiming to close the legal loophole that has stood for generations. If passed by both the Ohio House and Senate, the measure will be presented to voters for final approval. But as of April 2025, that clause still remains in effect—unresolved.

For the enslaved men and women who once stood on the docks of Cincinnati, freedom was always just out of reach. The law promised one thing and delivered another. And while Ohio was labeled a "free state," the truth was much more complicated. Then, as now, Black lives were subject to the will of systems designed not for their protection, but for their control.

Even today, Black Ohioans face disproportionate incarceration rates, economic disparities, and systemic racism embedded in policy. The echoes of slavery still ring through our prisons, our laws, and our institutions. The illusion of freedom still lingers in the air—just as it did centuries ago on the banks of the Ohio River.

So, we must ask ourselves, boldly and without flinching:

Was slavery ever truly abolished, or did it simply evolve?

The language in the constitution may not overtly scream racism, but its impacts have always been racialized. After the Civil War, the exception clause was used to criminalize Black life, with discriminatory laws—like the Black Codes—leading to mass incarceration and prison labor that resembled slavery in everything but name. That legacy continues to cast a long and painful shadow.

Technically, chattel slavery—the outright ownership of humans—is no longer legal in Ohio. But through this clause, a legal form of involuntary servitude remains, disguised as justice. It is a system that continues to extract labor from incarcerated individuals, disproportionately Black, and denies them the protections promised by true freedom.

Many, particularly within the Black community, see this clause as deeply disrespectful and harmful—a bitter reminder that the fight for liberation is still unfinished. Keeping it in the state constitution is seen as a failure to fully reckon with the truth of slavery's legacy. It tells us that even now, under certain conditions, the state still reserves the right to force labor from human beings—a right historically used to oppress, control, and silence Black Americans.

This is why historians, lawmakers, and racial justice advocates continue to call for its removal—not just to change words on paper, but to confront the truth, to dismantle structural racism, and to honor the sacrifices of those who fought and died for a freedom never freely given.

Because true freedom cannot coexist with even the shadow of slavery.

Until that clause is gone—until we stop hiding behind legal exceptions and start telling the whole truth—Ohio, and America, has unfinished business.

So, now I ask you again, what are you going to do?

Do you have twelve thousand dollars set aside for your freedom papers?

Because Ohio did it once. What makes you think it—or anywhere else—won't try it again?

Back in 1802, the law said slavery was banned. But the system said otherwise. And today? It just wears new clothes: redistricting maps, voter ID laws, felony disenfranchisement, police immunity, underfunded schools, and courts that erase decades of civil rights with a single ruling.

And through it all, I hear people pounding their chests online, shouting: "We aren't our ancestors!"

You're right. You're absolutely right.

We aren't.

Because our ancestors were organized. Our ancestors moved on one accord. They buried petty differences to unite under a common cause—freedom, dignity, survival. They built networks under candlelight and coded language. They risked their lives for meetings held in silence, for strategies passed hand to hand like sacred fire.

We say we aren't our ancestors. And I agree—we don't move like them. They moved better.

They didn't just react. They planned. They educated themselves fast. They read the constitution not to admire it, but to use it as a weapon against the very people who wrote it to exclude them.

They built institutions. They trained leaders.

My grandfather, John T. Ward, was one of them. A conductor on the Underground Railroad. A member of the Order of Twelve—an elite network of organizers who operated with stealth and discipline.

No celebrity leaders. No ego-driven agendas. The mission was the leader. The people were the power.

They met regularly. They had structure. They had the Sons of Protection—real men with real plans to protect real lives.

So no, we aren't our ancestors. Because our ancestors weren't just angry.

They were ready.

And that's what I'm asking you now.

Are you?

Because history isn't waiting. And the river hasn't changed. It still shimmers with hope—while hiding the trap beneath.

CHAPTER II

Tracks Below, Resistance Above

"Stolen bodies working stolen land. It was an engine that did not stop, its hungry boiler fed with blood."

-Colson Whitehead

The engine never stopped.

It screamed through cotton fields and across the hills of Ohio, fueled by flesh, bone, and silence. Just dirt roads carved by footsteps—some in chains, some in flight. And somewhere between those screams, my great-great-great-grandfather, John T. Ward, stood in its path.

Today, the city of Whitehall hummed with the illusion of normalcy—horns blaring, voices drifting through the air, the lingering scent of fried food clinging to the breeze.

I pulled over on East Main Street, in what was once Truro Township. Now, it was just another corner swallowed by the inner city—strip malls, chain restaurants, storefronts stacked side by side, each one blending into the next. The landscape spoke of commercial evolution, but not necessarily progress.

Across the street, a mega hair store squatted behind a cluster of fast-food chains, fluorescent lights flickering behind dark, tinted windows.

I stood at the marker in front of the Chase Bank—a silent witness to history, holding its ground like a sentinel. This very spot was once a gateway. A risk. A choice between bondage and breath. Here, freedom hung in the balance for those bold enough to run. I cut the engine. The low growl faded into silence. For a moment, everything held its breath.

There was nothing remarkable about this intersection—at least, not to the casual eye. But I knew better.

This strip of cracked asphalt, buzzing with neon signs and the hum of daily life, once pulsed with a different kind of tension.

I closed my eyes. I tried to see them—the fugitives, worn from travel, silent, eyes scanning shadows, every step a prayer.

They once walked this very road.

Friend Street, they called it then. Today, it was East Main.

They moved east, toward the intersection at Hamilton. They walked toward a man they knew only by reputation—a man they called protector, my great-great-great-grandfather: John T. Ward.

Maybe he greeted them with a whisper. Maybe a nod or a secret code. Maybe nothing at all. Just safety. Just compassion.

For the enslaved, silence was often the first language of freedom.

I opened my eyes. All I saw was a parking lot. But in my mind, I stripped it bare.

No cars. No concrete. No neon signs. No traffic lights.

Just trees. Dense, watchful trees, thick with secrecy.

This was once my family's land—Bluff Farms—where the shadows didn't just hide wildlife. They hid warriors on the bluff.

I kept driving. My heart beat louder as I turned onto Langley Avenue.

This was where Bluff Farms stood, where freedom lived in hiding, and where the soil cradled stories no textbook ever dared to tell.

The scent of damp earth rose through the air, mingled with a faint trace of gasoline. I stared at the house in front of me. It looked ordinary.

But the ground beneath it wasn't. This land remembered.

It remembered the whispered prayers, the hunted footsteps, the quiet defiance of those who helped them keep moving.

During COVID, fate reached me through a screen.

A woman named Sarah Barton slid into my inbox with digital gold—interview notes from the 1890s.

My great-great-great-grandfather's own words, captured by a Harvard-connected scholar, preserved across time.

She sent them to me like a gift.

A name jumped out, Wilbur Siebert, a name I'd only seen on book spines, buried in archives. He'd interviewed conductors and stationmasters—and there, among them, was John T. Ward.

Not a myth. Not a rumor. Not just a family legend.

Fact. Strategy. A stronghold built on vision and bloodline.

I was stunned. Grateful. But I was angry, too.

The records I needed were locked behind archive doors, sealed shut because of a virus. I couldn't touch them. But Sarah's email opened the vault anyway. Her kindness gave me back my history.

And in that history, I didn't just find my great-great-great-grandfather; I found an army.

A system built to break us had birthed a resistance that moved like smoke: Black-led, quiet, brilliant, unstoppable.

In the chaos of oppression, I found order. In silence, I found strategy. In pain, I found power.

***

This is no longer just my family's story.

It's the story of every family that resisted bondage, that carved freedom into the soil, that bled not for victory, but for the chance to keep moving forward.

And now, the torch is in my hands.

Because the engine may have run on our ancestors' blood—But we were the ones who knew how to kill it.

Close your eyes and step into a time long before shackles, before ships, before the word "slave" ever stained this land. Not a name you know—just a man. An African man. Unrecorded by history, but no less real.

Let the rhythm of drums fade into the hum of insects beneath a vast West African sky. Feel the warmth of the earth beneath his bare feet, the peace of a village untouched—for now.

The village lay silent beneath the vast West African sky, the hum of insects filling the night air. A simple herdsman rested peacefully in his hut, the soft breathing of his wife and children a comforting rhythm in the darkness. His days were spent tending to cattle, guiding them across the plains, and trading in the bustling village markets. His world was familiar, safe—until the night the silence was shattered.

A thunderous explosion ripped through the air—an unnatural sound unlike anything he had ever heard.

Gunshots.

The villagers stirred, confused, their peaceful slumber broken by the foreign roar of iron and fire. Fear gripped his chest like a vice. He had heard stories—whispers of pale-skinned men appearing out of nowhere, taking entire villages, leaving behind only scorched earth and unanswered questions.

Some said these men were demons. Others claimed they were cannibals, stealing people away, never to be seen again.

Heart pounding, he grabbed his spear, instincts driving him to protect his family. But outside, chaos erupted. Men with strange, twisted faces, dressed in unfamiliar clothing, wielding weapons that spit fire and death, stormed the village. They moved with brutal precision, cutting down those who resisted, subduing those who could not fight back.

Screams of terror filled the night.

Women clutched their children, desperate to shield them from the invaders' grasp. Warriors fell where they stood—outmatched and overwhelmed. The herdsman fought, but his spear was useless against their thunderous weapons. A crushing blow to the head sent him sprawling to the ground. Through blurred vision, he watched his wife sobbing, their children ripped from her grasp. His world spun as a heavy rope tightened around his wrists.

He had been captured. And so, it began.

The march to the coast was long and brutal, a hundred miles or more, bound in chains, barefoot, and beaten. Some fell along the way, too weak, too broken. Their captors did not slow. Those who could no longer walk were left behind, their cries fading into silence.

When they finally reached the shore, the herdsman's heart pounded in his chest.

The ocean.

A vast, endless expanse of water stretched before him—something he had never seen before. Something unnatural. Terrifying. Beyond the crashing waves loomed a massive ship, an enormous beast of wood and iron.

Before he could make sense of it, rough hands grabbed him, forcing him to his knees. His head was shaved, his dark curls falling to the ground in clumps. A searing hot iron pressed into his skin, burning deep into his flesh. The pain was unbearable, the stench of his own scorched skin filling his nostrils.

Branded. Like livestock.

And then—a knife. A quick, brutal slice. His ear. Gone. Proof of purchase.

His body trembled with pain and humiliation. He glanced back one last time at the land he would never see again.

Dragged aboard the ship, the herdsman was thrown into the lower deck—a dark, suffocating hellhole. The stench was overwhelming. The floors were slick with urine, feces, vomit, and menstrual blood. There was no air—only the suffocating heat of bodies crammed together, stacked like cargo.

Women and children were kept above deck, their cries piercing through the wooden planks. Their screams—horrifying, gut-wrenching—echoed in the darkness. He didn't need to see what was happening to them. He knew. Rape. Torture. Violations too cruel to comprehend.

Days became weeks. Weeks became months.

Many did not survive. Disease spread like wildfire, rotting their bodies from the inside out. Dysentery, smallpox, fever—it claimed them one by one. Some, too broken to endure, threw themselves into the ocean, choosing death over bondage.

The herdsman watched them disappear beneath the waves, their shackles dragging them into the abyss. He envied them.

The slavers did not mourn the dead. They saw no lost lives—only lost profit. The bodies were tossed overboard, a grim sacrifice to the sea.

And then, there were those who were murdered for insurance money.

As far back as 1781, powerful insurance companies—some still in operation today—profited off the trade of human lives. The transatlantic slave trade was a risky business, and merchants didn't gamble without protection. Slaves were insured as *maritime cargo*, not human beings. Policies covered losses due to resistance, revolts, and sickness—but not natural death.

This meant that, often, a dead captive was more valuable than a sick one. Slavers threw diseased and dying captives into the sea, filing insurance claims to recover their losses. Murder became a financial decision.

One in ten would survive the voyage.

The herdsman was one of the few who did.

The ship finally reached land. Not home. Never home.

This place was different. Foreign. The land stretched wide and unfamiliar. But the people ... the people were the same pale-skinned demons who had stolen him away. Their eyes held no mercy—only arrogance and cruelty.

Before he could comprehend what was happening, chains were fastened around his neck, wrists, and ankles.

Dragged off the ship. Lined up like cattle. Put on display.

And then came the bidding.

Voices rang out, shouting prices, assessing his worth as though he were a commodity—not a man. His body was examined, his teeth checked like an animal, his muscles prodded.

When the final bid was placed, it was over.

He was purchased.

The last nail in the coffin of his freedom.

He had entered this land as a man. Now, he was nothing but property.

When it came to slave ownership, wealthy white enslavers had the authority to whip and punish enslaved people at will. These individuals were often isolated on plantations, as their families—children, spouses, and siblings—were separated from them at the time of purchase. Surprisingly, it was the enslaved women who most often resisted slavery and boldly called out the injustice being done to them. This was in part because slaveholders punished women more frequently than men for verbal and physical resistance, and because women worked in closer proximity to their enslavers.

Many enslaved people chose to escape with their entire families rather than endure the separation of husbands and wives, coupled with the constant threat of being sold. They understood the dangers of escape, and the real possibility that failure could result in being resold—perhaps to even harsher conditions. For women, being transferred to a new enslaver came with the increased risk of sexual exploitation. Despite these dangers, enslaved women demonstrated resistance by temporarily hiding in the fields or woodlands instead of running permanently, motivated by a sense of responsibility to protect their children and families.

John T. Ward was born into slavery, but I think it's important to remember what it was like for those who were kidnapped and brought from Africa. What goes through your mind when you read this line: "An Englishman tastes the sweat of an African?"

It sounds bizarre—even monstrous—yet in the 1700s, this was how slavers and buyers "tested their product."

The line comes from an engraving found in the French publication *Le Commerce de l'Amérique par Marseille*, which provides a chilling glimpse into slave markets of the time. Slave traders would lick the faces, necks, foreheads, or chins of captured Africans to taste the salt content in their sweat. They believed a low salt content indicated a higher chance of death during the Middle Passage, so enslaved people with higher salt levels were preferred—judged as "stronger stock."

This was the reality for those brought to the colonies from Africa—a time when human beings were valued more than land. The trauma of this history lingers even now. Some researchers believe this selection process, favoring individuals with higher salt retention, may contribute to higher rates of hypertension among Black Americans today.

During the colonial era, branding enslaved people like cattle was standard practice. By the nineteenth century, branding was used more selectively, often as punishment at the enslaver's discretion. Whipping remained a common form of discipline. Those who dared to defend themselves—or simply refused to be whipped—risked being killed. Women were not spared. They endured the lash while screaming, praying, or suffering in silence.

Another brutal form of punishment, used up until 1830, was mutilation. This included castration of male slaves, cutting off ears, or removing front teeth. These mutilations served not only as punishment but also as a means of identification—making it harder for enslaved people to escape and pass as free.

Fugitive slaves, when caught, faced whatever punishment the enslaver deemed necessary: shotgun wounds, dog mauling, public beatings, or hangings carried out in front of their families. Fear was used to control. And chains weren't the only tool.

Enslavers used psychological warfare.

They twisted faith into fear, holding up the Bible like a whip. They claimed God had ordained slavery, that submission was holy, and resistance was rebellion against divine order.

They often quoted verses like Ephesians 6:5: "Servants, be obedient to them that are your masters according to the flesh, with fear and trembling ..."

Or Colossians 3:22: "Slaves, obey your earthly masters in everything ... with sincerity of heart and reverence for the Lord."

These verses were stripped of context and weaponized to break the spirit of the enslaved—to convince them that submission was sacred, and escape was a sin.

But the manipulation didn't stop with scripture.

In the 1850s, white physicians took it further by medicalizing Black resistance. A Southern doctor named Samuel A. Cartwright coined the term Drapetomania, claiming it was a mental illness that caused enslaved people to run away.

That's right, the desire for freedom was labeled a psychiatric disorder.

According to Cartwright, a "content" and "healthy" slave would never want to flee. So, if someone escaped, it wasn't because they were brutalized or torn from family; it was because something was "wrong" with them. Drapetomania wasn't rooted in science. It was pseudoscience—propaganda dressed up as medicine. A tool to reinforce the lie that slavery was natural and resistance was madness.

Drapetomania pathologized liberation. It criminalized the will to be free. It painted every act of escape as irrational instead of righteous.

It is one of the clearest examples of how white supremacy distorted truth, corrupted science, and tried to convince the world that Black liberation was a symptom of insanity.

It was common for slave families to be torn apart—sold to different plantations, often never to see each other again. Skilled laborers—blacksmiths, mechanics, carpenters—were especially valuable and often rented out or sold to meet market demand. Many enslaved people hid their talents from enslavers, hoping to avoid separation from loved ones.

Control didn't just come through force; it came through hunger. Slave masters kept people on the brink of starvation, ensuring they worked hard to earn their next meal. Children were forced into labor as early as age ten, just like John T. In those days, the life expectancy of a white man was around forty years. For enslaved people, it was closer to thirty-six. On many plantations, there would only be one elder present.

Privacy didn't exist. Cabins were subject to monthly inspections to ensure enslaved people weren't breaking rules or hiding contraband. Every part of their lives was monitored.

Now imagine: A stranger licking your chin to taste your sweat, to determine your age and health. Imagine being forced to wear a branded mark on your body—a permanent reminder that you were property. Picture being stripped naked in a public market, your body prodded, inspected, and sold like livestock.

This was not just history. This was our foundation.

What would that do to a person's dignity, their sense of self, their will to fight? What impact does this brutal history still have on our world today?

To those who have never felt the cold bite of iron shackles, the searing pain of a lash splitting open their back, or the soul-crushing anguish of watching their children sold to the highest bidder, the question may seem simple:

Why run? Why not endure? Why not obey?

But for the enslaved, running was never a choice. It was survival.

As Solomon Northup—a free man kidnapped and sold into slavery—once wrote:

"Let not those who have never been placed in like circumstances judge me harshly. Until they have been chained and beaten—until they find themselves in the situation I was, borne away from home and family toward a land of bondage—let them refrain from saying what they would not do for liberty."

Even knowing the risks, they still ran. Even knowing their families would suffer—that their loved ones might be whipped, sold, or slaughtered in retaliation—they still ran. Even knowing that bounty hunters were fast, the rivers deep, and the forests full of danger, they still ran.

Because the agony of bondage outweighed the fear of being caught. Because freedom was worth dying for.

And Ohio—the so-called *promised land*—was supposed to be the last step before true liberation.

But after the passage of the Fugitive Slave Act of 1850, it became something else entirely.

A hunting ground.

John T. Ward arrived in Ohio in 1827 as a young boy, settling with his family in Poke Patch, one of the earliest Black settlements in Lawrence County, Southern Ohio. Just across the river lay the slave state of Kentucky—a brutal world that countless fugitives risked everything to escape.

Growing up, John T. listened to the stories—raw, harrowing accounts of bondage and defiance. Escaped slaves passed through his community, carrying tales of beatings, family separations, and impossible odds. Yet what stood out most to him were not the horrors, but the courage—the sheer force of will it took to run.

From a young age, he understood: escaping slavery wasn't just survival; it was resistance. It was heroism. And that shaped him.

John T. Ward vowed to do more than witness injustice—he would fight it. He was determined to protect his people, to ensure they would not be reduced to objects of cruelty or sources of profit for the white men who circled the region.

In this struggle, alliances formed. Some Native American tribes offered critical support—warning runaways of slave catchers and spies, helping to form a quiet but powerful bond between two oppressed peoples. Together, they shared not just land, but a purpose.

Still, the Ohio River, though a symbol of hope, was no guaranteed line between slavery and freedom. The border was geographic, yes— but also psychological and racial. Freedom in the North was fragile. Black people still lived under the threat of capture, exploitation, and betrayal.

Escaping meant navigating a land where the law wasn't always on your side—where one wrong turn could mean death, or worse. The enslaved knew the price: if caught, they might be whipped, maimed, or sold deeper South, where slavery's grip was even tighter. And to some slavers, capturing and reselling runaways became a thriving business.

John T. Ward came of age knowing all of this. And still, he chose to resist.

Running away was often a near-impossible feat for enslaved women—but many still tried, driven by desperation and an unyielding hope for freedom. The physical toll was grueling: swollen feet, exposure to the elements, the threat of capture, and worse. But for women like Hannah, John T. Ward's mother, there were additional chains—children.

The crushing burden of motherhood under slavery meant women were often tethered to plantations—not by choice, but by the lives they had birthed and refused to abandon. Enslaved women were expected to raise their children in bondage, knowing full well that at any moment, those children could be stolen from them—sold off like livestock for someone else's gain.

Charlotte, an enslaved woman in Kentucky, managed to support her family as a washerwoman—a rare sliver of autonomy in a life of institutionalized subjugation. Hired out by her enslaver, she was allowed to live apart from the main plantation, taking pride in her ability to care for her children through hard-earned wages. But even that faint semblance of independence came with its own shackles. Charlotte tolerated the agony of slavery because she had no choice, freedom was a price she could never afford. Her income, painfully meager, was never enough to buy her own emancipation, let alone her children's.

Even in the rare cases where enslaved people managed to purchase their freedom, the cost to redeem their loved ones was prohibitively high. According to historical records, a child could cost anywhere from two hundred to five hundred dollars—a fortune for someone earning mere pennies for backbreaking labor.

And for women, the economic odds were worse. Most were confined to domestic work or laundering—jobs that were undervalued and underpaid, even in slavery. In fact, enslaved men often earned more for the same hours of labor, simply because their work—typically agricultural or skilled trades—was deemed more valuable by the enslavers.

Charlotte was one of the "lucky" ones—if such a word can even apply in this context. She never had to witness the unthinkable: her children being dragged away, sold to distant plantations, never to be seen again.

But this was not the norm.

In the Upper South—particularly in border states like Kentucky and Virginia—one out of every three enslaved children was separated from their mothers through the internal slave trade. Slave owners saw children as investments. They allowed mothers to nurse and raise them, only to rip them away once they reached a profitable age, usually between eight and twelve, and sell them further South, where demand was higher due to the booming cotton economy.

The agony of this separation was deliberate. It was a calculated cruelty used to break spirits and maximize profit. Slavery didn't merely oppress the body, it shattered families, corrupted motherhood, and commodified love.

There were many enslaved people, especially in Kentucky, who saw opportunities to escape but chose not to run. Enslaved Black Americans along the border were constantly weighing the pros and cons of fleeing.

This was especially true for those working on cotton plantations in the Deep South. The white power structure was too strong, and the free territories were too far away. The Underground Railroad offered a possible path out—but the odds were slim, and the risks were staggering. Being caught could mean severe physical punishment, resale deeper South, or even death.

Those enslaved on the border of a free state had better chances of success, but even they faced heartbreaking decisions. And even if they crossed the Ohio River, that didn't end their struggle. They were still seen as second-class citizens. Their freedom was fragile—

constantly under threat from slave catchers, unjust laws, and a society that treated them as outsiders.

Slavery would haunt them for the rest of their lives. And many lived with rushing grief, having left behind parents, children, or spouses they might never see again.

In other words, the Ohio River wasn't some clean, Black-and-white boundary between slavery and freedom.

It was a line soaked in grief, fear, and uncertainty.

Enslaved people had to constantly evaluate: Would you run? Could you afford to? Could you survive the cost?

Southern bounty hunters patrolled the riverbanks, ready to drag fugitives back into chains. Meanwhile, white settlers and business owners in Ohio resented the rise of the free Black landowning class. They feared Black wealth and Black political power.

The newspapers made their message plain—publishing scathing articles about the influx of free Black people into the state, warning white readers that they were "dirty," "unwanted," and "a threat."

But John T. Ward was not deterred.

Despite the prohibition of slavery in Ohio, slaveholders were still allowed to travel through the state with enslaved people. Some farmers along the Ohio River even employed slaves from Kentucky and Virginia. Slavery brought immense sufferings, endured extreme heat, exhaustion, hunger, and the soul-crushing separation of families. Some had their tongues cut out to silence them, to prevent organizing or speaking out against their enslavers.

To take matters into their own hands, many enslaved people resisted in quiet, powerful ways. Some refused to work. Others faked illness. Many began secretly learning to read and write, knowing education could open the door to freedom.

With the help of heroes like John T. Ward, who ignited the passion for liberty and gave people the courage to strive for more, many enslaved individuals escaped into Ohio. Using the Underground Railroad, they found allies who forged "walking passes" to help them navigate the terrain. Those who could read and write created forged documents—lifelines disguised as permission slips. With these passes, many enslaved people were able to visit loved ones on neighboring plantations or escape entirely.

These passes were critical tools for freedom seekers, especially near the border. At the time, the value of a slave ranged from eight hundred to fifteen hundred dollars. As the interstate slave trade expanded, the cost of freedom rose dramatically. A prime field hand, worth about four hundred dollars in the 1830s, could fetch more than fifteen hundred dollars just twenty years later. Despite the cost, the trade flourished.

John T. often reflected on the brutal realities of slavery, especially the slave auctions he had witnessed as a child in Virginia. These scenes—families ripped apart on wooden blocks—haunted him. He never forgot the cries of children, or the blank stares of men reduced to inventory. Many young Black males between the ages of ten and nineteen were exported from Kentucky to the Deep South, where labor was in higher demand and punishment was harsher.

He remembered how slaveholders used the false promise of future freedom to control behavior. It was a manipulation tactic—dangling hope as a leash. When that promise was inevitably broken, some chose to escape rather than be broken.

John T. Ward became a pivotal figure in the fight for freedom, dedicating his life to helping enslaved people escape the grip of bondage. He ran a safe house on a farm in Whitehall, Ohio, where he offered shelter and served as a fearless conductor on the Underground

Railroad. Like Harriet Tubman, John T. risked everything to guide others north. Remarkably, his efforts spanned a longer period than Tubman's, and he helped even more people escape—cementing his legacy as a true champion of justice.

Each time he left to guide someone toward freedom; he said goodbye to his wife and children—knowing he might not return. The punishment for assisting fugitive slaves was swift and deadly. Execution wasn't a risk. It was an expectation.

Under the mentorship of Littleberry Moss, John T. learned more than survival—he mastered strategy. He studied land transactions, navigated legal loopholes designed to exclude him, and learned the unspoken rules that governed Black life in a hostile America.

He attended Colored Men's Association meetings, where free Black men gathered not just to speak—but to organize. They strategized about voting rights, land ownership, self-sufficiency, and mutual protection. In those sacred circles, John aligned with abolitionists and fellow Underground Railroad conductors—men who risked their lives to challenge the reach of the Fugitive Slave Act.

Ohio was *free*, but it was not *safe*. And John understood that freedom, unless fiercely protected and purposefully lived, could be stripped away in an instant.

By 1852, John T. Ward and his father-in-law made a bold, historic move: they purchased land in Truro Township, Ohio.

In an era when Black landowners were under constant threat—through law, violence, and economic sabotage—this was more than a real estate deal.

It was an act of defiance. A declaration of dignity.

They called it Bluff Farms.

But to the law? It was something else entirely.

If the place in Georgia called *Snow on tha Bluff* is infamous for crime, then Bluff Farms during antebellum Ohio was covered in white.

Not the kind of snow that melts in spring—but the kind that freezes into memory. The kind that stains history.

This was the powder of resistance, packed tight in silence, falling heavy on a land that dared to disobey.

John T. Ward was branded as a criminal—not for doing wrong, but for daring to do right long before right was ever written into law.

This snow didn't fall from clouds. It fell from justice denied.

Not the kind of snow that kisses rooftops in winter—but the kind that never thaws.

The kind that buries legacies, chills the bloodline, and brands the soul.

Back then, to help a fugitive was to commit a crime. To give water, to offer shelter, to whisper directions under moonlight—each act, no matter how humane, was punishable by fines, prison, or even death. Bluff Farms was guilty on every count.

But Bluff Farms was never just a farm. It was a sanctuary. A safe house. A stronghold of resistance wrapped in the disguise of ordinary life.

They planted more than crops in that soil—they planted defiance. They didn't grow cotton. They grew courage.

With hidden compartments beneath the floorboards, passageways carved into silence, and a network of allies woven tighter than a quilt, they moved people, not property, through that land.

And yet, in the eyes of the law, every prayer whispered on Bluff Farms, every child cradled in the night, every footstep that crossed that threshold in search of freedom, was a felony.

So, if *Snow on tha Bluff* means crime, let it mean this: the kind of crime that breaks chains. The kind of crime that shelters the hunted. The kind of crime that chooses righteousness over legality.

Because on Bluff Farms, the only thing truly criminal ... was slavery itself.

Inside the walls of that farmhouse, John T. and Catherine Ward were raising a family in the midst of a revolution—teaching their children not only how to survive but how to stand, how to believe, and how to fight for a better future.

John T. had watched his father-in-law wage a long, quiet war—fighting for land, independence, and the right of Black people to live without fear. Now, it was his turn, his mission.

Littleberry Moss had seen something in John T.—a fire, an ambition, and a heart strong enough to carry the legacy forward—not just for their family, but for generations yet unborn.

Together, they built more than a farm. They built a beacon—a living testament to compassion, courage, and the unyielding will to be free.

John T.'s family supported his efforts. Together, they provided a haven for those escaping slavery. John T.'s light complexion allowed him to secure employment and move more freely without immediate suspicion. This gave him a unique ability to operate discreetly, gathering information, passing messages, and guiding fugitives.

He helped establish a network of secret routes and safe houses, forming vital pathways to freedom. John T. was clever and quick, often outsmarting slave catchers and robbing them of their bounty. He played his role so well that legends grew around his efforts.

It's said that the term "Underground Railroad" gained traction after a frustrated slaveholder in the South, unable to explain how a slave had vanished, exclaimed that the person must have disappeared on some kind of "underground railroad." That mystery? That was the work of conductors like John T.

Conductors came from all walks of life—free and formerly enslaved Black people, white abolitionists, and anyone brave enough to defy the law in the name of justice. They operated under strict codes of secrecy and trust, risking their lives to guide enslaved people north to freedom—or all the way to Canada.

Escaping slavery through the Underground Railroad was incredibly dangerous and uncertain. Fugitive slaves had to plan carefully, staying one step ahead of slave patrols, bounty hunters, and local law enforcement. Nature itself posed threats—raging rivers, dense forests, wild animals, and unforgiving weather.

Journeys were often done on foot, mostly at night, with limited food or shelter. And because escapees came from all age groups, it could be difficult to keep the group moving together. But one thing was certain: no one got left behind.

Just like John T., conductors across Ohio played crucial roles. The Underground Railroad wasn't a single path; it was a web of trails, towns, backroads, and safe houses spanning over three thousand miles through Ohio alone.

They used railroad terminology as coded language to communicate secretly. It was a form of resistance and unity. These codes kept everyone safe and on the same page.

"Stations" were safe houses. "Passengers" were the escaping enslaved. "Lines" were the routes. A "List Agent Coordinator" plotted escape paths and maintained contacts. "Baggage" referred to personal belongings. "Bundles of Wood" meant the number of people headed to Canada. A "Conductor"—like John T.—was the person who led the way.

This vast network allowed fugitives to find temporary refuge and support as they made their way to freedom. The role of conductors went beyond just guiding escapees; they also provided essential resources at the end of the journey: food, shelter, work, and clothing.

Despite the constant danger, the Underground Railroad persisted as a powerful symbol of resistance against slavery for over thirty years. People who donated money, food, and clothing played a critical role, helping freedom seekers get away from their captors and reach safer ground.

Escaping slaves were often hidden beneath farm produce in wagons—a tactic John T. Ward was known for. He would cover people with brown burlap sacks, blending them into the harvest to sneak them past patrols and checkpoints.

Slave catching was big business. Bounty hunters could make serious money returning runaways to their enslavers, especially those with specialized skills. Many plantations purchased insurance policies for high-value slaves to protect their "investments."

White boys were trained from a young age to become "paddy rollers"—slave catchers. It was considered their civic duty. These patrols roamed the countryside, chasing runaways and enforcing slavery's reach across the so-called free states. They would post advertisements with detailed descriptions of those who had escaped, spreading word from town to town.

Working at Columbus City Hall, John T. Ward saw those very ads; he studied them, memorized names and faces, and used the information against the system. He turned the slaveholders' own tools into weapons of resistance.

Preachers were also among the leaders and spokespeople of the Underground Railroad. They preached hope, declaring Canada as the land of true freedom. On the journey north, safe houses were established where stationmasters would drop off the enslaved until it was safe to move again. These safehouses sometimes held people for days or weeks, hiding them in basements, attics, or barns. The owners kept constant watch for bounty hunters, risking their homes, their freedom, and their lives to offer shelter.

If a safe house was discovered, the consequences were severe. The owners could be arrested, beaten, or worse—and the enslaved people they sheltered would be dragged back into captivity.

John T.'s contribution to the Underground Railroad was invaluable, as he helped thousands of enslaved individuals escape to freedom. His bravery and dedication serve as a shining example of the resilience and strength exhibited by those who fought against the oppressive institution of slavery. Today, a historical marker in Whitehall and all throughout Columbus, Ohio, which used to be called Truro County, commemorates his significant role in the fight for liberty and justice.

Columbus, Ohio, is rooted in the quiet bravery and calculated precision of men like John T. Ward, whose legacy is documented in the work of historian Wilbur Henry Siebert of Ohio State University. Siebert's research—letters, interviews, field notes—captures the intricate operations of conductors and stationmasters across the state. Among them, John T. Ward stands out—not for boasting, but for his silence.

The interview I received shows that my great-great-great-grandfather was a man of few words, tight-lipped, guarded, unlike some of the others. But his actions spoke volumes.

The Ward family's role was vital. Their contribution made Columbus a key hub in Ohio's Underground Railroad network—a system built on strategy, disguise, and unshakable courage. Abolitionists, though often working quietly behind the scenes, pushed forward with purpose. To Southern planters, their efforts weren't just criminal; they were revolutionary, a threat to the system that gave them wealth and power.

John T. Ward didn't just help fugitives; he risked everything to move them.

He was stopped more than once under suspicion, especially while hauling hay or produce in his custom-built wagon. To the average eye, it looked like a regular farm rig. But hidden beneath the wooden floor was a secret compartment, expertly crafted to carry precious human cargo.

Freedom seekers. Hiding in silence. Trusting one man with their lives.

Patrolmen, always suspicious, would sometimes jab the wagon's floorboards with pitchforks, their iron tips stabbing into the wood— just inches from the bodies curled beneath. One wrong move. One cough. One muffled breath—and it would all be over.

But John T. didn't flinch.

He knew what he was up against. Slave catchers, emboldened by money and law, roamed freely across Ohio soil. Abolitionists like John T. weren't treated as heroes; they were marked as enemies of the Southern economic machine. The planter class didn't just despise abolitionists. They feared them.

Because if one man, with a wagon and a conscience, could dismantle their grip on power, it meant the whole empire was built on terror and lies.

On one tense occasion, near Bull Farm, slave catchers stopped John T. and demanded to inspect his load. But this was before the Fugitive Slave Act of 1850. At the time, Ohio law required proof— legal documentation—before anyone could seize a person on suspicion.

Local law enforcement, skeptical of the bounty hunters, stepped in.

They asked for papers.

The catchers had none.

John T. stood his ground.

The wagon rolled on.

And the people inside?

They lived.

The fugitives John T. assisted often traveled the same path: from Ross County, through Circleville, into Columbus. He was typically entrusted with the most dangerous leg of the journey—transporting escapees at night to a safe house near the former residence of David Jenkins, located in LaFayette Alley. This area—once known as the

Badlands—sat just beyond the old city limits and became part of a larger escape route along Harbor Road, now Cleveland Avenue.

The route continued past landmarks like Fort Hayes (then the Arsenal), Neil Baseball Park, and the Panhandle Railroad shops, eventually stretching into Milo-Grogan. From there, conductors would branch off, guiding passengers toward safe houses in Clintonville, Westerville, or Worthington—each a key station in the northern escape network.

In the mid-nineteenth century, Harbor Road wasn't just a path. It was a lifeline. A corridor of courage and compassion. A passageway where the oppressed, guided by men like John T. Ward, found not only shelter—but hope.

If I had to explain a theory—one that's been burning in me for years—it's this: The Underground Railroad wasn't just a spontaneous humanitarian effort. It was a shadow army.

A covert, coordinated resistance network. A proto-military infrastructure, built from the ground up—camouflaged by compassion, but executed with the strategic precision of a guerrilla campaign.

This was war.

Positioned along natural borders like the Ohio River, the Underground Railroad transformed everyday landscapes into frontlines. Ohio, Indiana, and Illinois weren't just free states; they were barricades staring down Kentucky, Virginia, and Missouri.

The river became a moat, its waters ferrying—not just the desperate but the brave—across enemy lines.

Ferries and boats weren't just transportation; they were amphibious operations. Hidden crossings weren't accidents of luck; they were tactical choke points. Freedom seekers—often with no formal training—moved like soldiers crossing rivers under cover of night, using stars and tree lines to navigate, and masking trails with precision, like reconnaissance scouts.

Like any effective resistance, the Underground Railroad operated in cells—small, agile, and independent. Each with a purpose. Each with a mission. Conductors were field agents. Stationmasters were quartermasters, maintaining supply lines. Quilt codes, spirituals, and lantern signals were encrypted messages—early Morse code woven into the culture.

This wasn't chaos. It was coordination. This wasn't luck. It was strategy.

This decentralized command structure wasn't a coincidence. It was resilience by design. If one piece fell, the rest could still move.

The Quakers—peaceful in name but disciplined in action—ran logistic hubs disguised as homes and meeting houses. They built cellars and secret compartments—primitive bunkers beneath barns and floors. They mapped routes, maintained safe house records, and moved people and information with clockwork precision. Their communities became intelligence outposts in a war for freedom.

Even the funding tells a story of subversive brilliance. Abolitionist societies and sympathizers across the North—and even in Europe— funneled money like wartime financiers. Churches laundered funds behind pulpits. Black-owned businesses funneled earnings into bribes, supplies, and transport. Even Union soldiers, long before the war officially began, quietly supported the cause with coin and cover.

But perhaps the most radical feature of this system? It trained soldiers.

Many who escaped via the Underground Railroad would go on to become the backbone of the Union Army's Black regiments. They had already learned to evade capture, mastered navigation without maps, developed resistance tactics, and encrypted communication in hostile territory.

The Underground Railroad was their basic training—before the uniforms, before the regiments, before the Emancipation Proclamation.

And let's not forget espionage. This network moved in shadows. Harriet Tubman, known to the world as "Moses," operated under an alias. False trails were planted to mislead slave catchers. Trusted agents infiltrated plantations, posed as slaves, gathered intelligence— spy missions in all but name.

What I'm proposing isn't just a theory. It's a reframing of American history.

The Underground Railroad should not be viewed solely as a moral triumph, but as the first Black-led, intelligence-based, military-grade resistance network on American soil. It was precise. It was calculated. It was covert. And it was effective.

It laid the groundwork for Civil War victories. It fueled the rise of the United States Colored Troops. It opened the door for Black leadership—not just on the battlefield, but in politics, education, and civil rights movements that would follow for generations.

This theory is more than a footnote. It's a framework—a call to scholars, students, and truth-seekers to dig deeper, challenge narratives, and build upon this foundation.

Because the fight for freedom didn't begin with battle cries. It began in silence, in secret, and in strategy.

It was an underground revolution in motion.

CHAPTER 12

Sons of Protection

"You cannot be more oppressed than you have been—you cannot suffer greater cruelties than you have already. Rather die freemen than live to be slaves. Remember that you are FOUR MILLIONS! It is in your power so to torment the God-cursed slaveholders that they will be glad to let you go free."

-Henry Highland Garnet 1843 The National Negro convention

I can't ignore history, especially when it's in my hands. These were more than just minutes from some old local club meeting, as I first assumed. As I read the sharp imprints left by a typewriter, one word stopped me cold: "Resolved."

Out of curiosity—and in full honesty—I had to look it up, searching for the definition and meaning in the context of these documents. I was hoping to find a breadcrumb, a clue that might hint at where this paper trail was leading. I had bits and pieces, but I couldn't compile the data or trace the source of their origin.

The result? Nothing.

The ink was faded; the word slightly smeared by time, but it remained unmistakably clear. Then came the real shock—buried between the lines were the words of my great-great-great-grandfather, John T. Ward.

Above me, the hum of fluorescent lights buzzed—the only sound breaking the stillness, as if to remind me: I couldn't escape this moment.

A chill crept up my spine as I read further.

This was his narrative, John T. Ward's life spilling across the page in imperfect punctuation and occasional misspellings. Those flaws, though minor, stood in contrast to the weight of the message they carried.

I could feel his presence, his silence. A quiet man trying to make sense of a chaotic, antebellum world.

And I had forensic data to confirm what my gut already knew; these were his words.

These weren't just meeting minutes. They were echoes—signs of something much greater, something more powerful than I had ever imagined.

But the truth didn't fully reveal itself until more than two years later.

It happened in a moment of clumsy chance—when my research binder slipped from my hands and its contents scattered across the hardwood floor like brittle leaves in an unforgiving gust of wind.

The notes—long-forgotten remnants—sprawled wildly, twisting like old vines, tangling themselves around my thoughts.

My breath caught.

I knelt, my fingertips grazing the fragile edges. One by one, I began picking them up, each sheet with care, afraid they might crumble under the weight of time.

At first, I nearly overlooked them again.

These were the same notes I had dismissed back in 2020—over and over, tucked away without a second thought. But something about how they fell this time—the violent, chaotic spread of typewritten words and photocopied pages from the Columbus Downtown Library—demanded my attention.

After countless sleepless nights trying to decipher the meaning buried in these meeting notes, I had already ruled out church gatherings because of their unusually formal tone. Still, nothing fit, not until 2023, when I stumbled upon the missing link.

For two years, I wandered through a maze of dead ends—obscure references and leads that went nowhere. Nothing explained the true significance of these gatherings. I was on the verge of giving up. The past felt too heavy to carry.

And then—a revelation from the most unlikely source: YouTube.

I typed in the words: "Ohio Colored Men's Conventions."

And there it was: The Colored Conventions Project (CCP).

They had a website. And a book—*The Colored Conventions Movement: Black Organizing in the Nineteenth Century*, published in 2021 by Gabrielle Foreman, Jim Casey, and Sarah Lynn Patterson.

A dynamite discovery.

Their essays traced a seventy-year movement of Black organizing, resilience, and revolutionary strategy. These weren't random men sitting in a room. They were architects of liberation, builders of change.

With their work as my guide, I returned to the notes.

And suddenly—everything clicked.

Thanks to the framework provided by the CCP, I began piecing together the deeper layers of what I had uncovered. This wasn't just a meeting. It was a movement. A coordinated effort by brilliant Black men who understood the power of unity—of strength in numbers.

And the women—they were there too, standing beside them, supporting them. Their quiet resilience was just as critical as the booming voices demanding justice.

As I read through the book, I could almost see myself there, seated in the back pews of a modest meeting hall, surrounded by the scent of old wood and anticipation.

I could hear the voices of Black men galvanizing one another, shaking the room with their purpose. Each speech felt like a shot of adrenaline, a call to rise.

The women, ever-present, held their ground—strong and unwavering—standing in the shadows, but never in silence.

I could almost hear the hum of that sacred space. The sound of songs sung by freed Black men and women—voices lifted in harmony, in hope, in purpose.

Within those notes were speeches of power—urgent, passionate cries about the condition of the enslaved. An outcry for justice that roared across generations.

And behind them, the women—strong, silent, and steady—held the line with grace.

As I read on, the past awakened around me.

I was there—in that creaking hall. I could smell the pine. The ink. The sweat of revolution. I could hear the speeches rumbling like thunder. I could see dreams becoming blueprints. I heard the songs hope rising like fire in the throat of a nation.

And in the margins of it all—John T. Ward. My ancestor. My blood.

A man speaking across time.

These fragile, folded pages—worn by age—don't just tell a story. They ignite a revolution.

Their fight, their sacrifice, their hopes … aren't relics.

They are instructions—blueprints.

The foundation of the freedom we dare not take for granted.

The echoes that shaped America's conscience.

That was the moment it all came together.

They collected money. They built alliances. And even when disagreements arose, these men stayed brothers. They voted, they debated—and they built something strong, something unbreakable, with no white influence. These were brilliant minds—not gathered to complain, but to construct. To organize. To rise.

Now it makes sense why these records were buried. Why this part of Black American history stayed hidden for so long. It likely didn't serve the interests of dominant society. It reminds me of that saying, "Don't let them pick your heroes."

These men didn't just organize. They laid the groundwork for a unity we still are fighting to protect.

Their words, their legacy, their resolve—they are the bedrock of our freedom.

And as I closed the book, heart pounding, I knew this with certainty:

My great-great-great-grandfather is part of that legacy.

His voice, pain, strength—woven into the very fabric of our history.

The noise around me—of life, time, and change—feels more alive now. Their struggle, their triumph, their love—it's alive in me.

In the breath I take, the words I read, and the very air that fills the room.

And I feel it, that overwhelming rush of excitement, a connection to something far greater than myself.

Unity, then and now, is no longer just a concept. It is a living, breathing thing.

And this, this is only the beginning of the journey I'm called to walk.

David Jenkins was another force in this movement—his contributions to abolition were wide-ranging. Not only was he a key leader in organizing and leading Colored Conventions—gatherings where free Black folks came together to address abolition, civil rights, education, and more—but he also mentored younger voices like John T. Ward. He showed John the ropes of abolitionist organizing and connected him to a broader network of freedom fighters. Those Colored Conventions weren't just meetings—they were the early blueprints for collective Black action.

Through Jenkins's guidance, John T. gained access to a powerful abolitionist network that would shape his life's mission. Jenkins was already a respected leader by the time they crossed paths—known for his relentless dedication to racial equality and his efforts to uplift Black communities. His activism helped lay the groundwork for future civil rights movements, and he brought national attention to the injustices that Black people faced, even in so-called free states like Ohio.

In 1843, Columbus became home to something groundbreaking— *The Palladium of Liberty*, the first Black-owned newspaper in Ohio. It was a voice for the voiceless, a call for justice in a state that called itself free while still enforcing Black Codes.

The paper's first issue was published on December 27, 1843, under Jenkins's leadership. Born in Lynchburg, Virginia, in 1811, Jenkins moved to Columbus in 1837. There, he became a pillar in the abolitionist movement, part of the Underground Railroad, and a key figure in opening the city's first schools for Black children.

But *The Palladium of Liberty* wasn't just a newspaper; it was a weapon, a tool of resistance. It gave Black Ohioans a platform to discuss slavery, civil rights, and racial injustice openly and unapologetically. Though it only published thirty-two issues between December 1843 and November 1844, its legacy lived on, echoing through the work of leaders like John T. and Jenkins.

For John T. Ward, *The Palladium* was more than just a newspaper; it was a pivotal part of his journey as an abolitionist. In 1844, he published his first article in *The Palladium*, marking his emergence as a public advocate for the anti-slavery movement. Through that paper, his ideas, frustrations, and fierce determination to dismantle slavery reached a wider audience, solidifying his role within the fight for Black freedom.

The Palladium also published John T. Ward's wedding announcement when he married Catherine Moss, further tying his personal life to his public mission for justice. It wasn't just a newspaper—it was a community hub. A place where leaders like John T. and David Jenkins could network, build strategy, and mobilize a movement.

Through *The Palladium of Liberty*, voices that had long been silenced by systemic oppression finally had a place to be heard. Black Ohioans—free, but far from equal—used it as a tool of resistance. They wrote letters, held meetings at the State House, and even launched their own publications to challenge the racist laws and systems stacked against them.

Even after *The Palladium* stopped publishing in 1844, its impact didn't fade. It laid the foundation for generations of Black-owned newspapers and proved that Black journalism was not just necessary; it was revolutionary. It linked abolitionists across Ohio and beyond, keeping the momentum of the movement alive.

For John T. Ward, David Jenkins, and countless others, the printed word was a weapon, just as powerful as any act of physical rebellion. It was a force that demanded freedom, dignity, and respect.

Though its pages no longer turn, the spirit of *The Palladium of Liberty* still lives—in every reclaimed story, in every amplified Black voice, in every battle for justice that's still being fought.

***

The summer air in Chillicothe, Ohio, was thick with humidity, the earthy scent of tilled soil and burning oil lamps hanging heavy in the atmosphere. It was June 21, 1844. John T. Ward, just twenty-two years old, sat hunched over a wooden desk, dipping his pen into an inkwell. The candlelight flickered against the rough paper as he prepared to do something that could change the course of his life—or put him and his family in danger.

This wasn't the kind of time where you could hide behind a keyboard, tossing out opinions under some anonymous alias. No, in 1844, writing an abolitionist letter, signing your name, and sending it off—not just to a Black paper or an abolitionist publication, but directly to the dominant white press—was an act of defiance. An act that could cost a man his freedom, his job, even his life.

Everybody in the Black community knew each other. And more importantly, the white power structure knew exactly who dared to speak up.

Unlike those who whispered their discontent behind closed doors, John was putting it all on the line. His name would be inked on the page, carried by couriers, read aloud in meeting halls, discussed in private homes—and noticed by those who saw a literate, outspoken Black man as a threat.

But John had come across something that he couldn't ignore. Something that refused to let him stay silent.

He had always known about slavery. Everybody did. The brutality. The chains. The cruelty. The families torn apart. But what he had recently discovered shook him to his core.

Ninety percent.

Ninety percent of all enslaved Africans didn't even come to the United States.

They were sent to the Caribbean and South America—where the conditions were so unbearable, enslaved people were often worked to death within a few short years.

The Middle Passage was a nightmare. But for many, what came after was worse.

In Brazil. In Haiti. In Jamaica. In the cane fields and copper mines. Under brutal heat. Endless hours. No rest. No mercy. No future.

Millions of African lives stolen, erased, buried in unmarked graves beneath sugar fields and coffee plantations.

And yet, here in the U.S., few even acknowledged they had ever existed.

John T.'s hands tightened as he thought about it. He had just learned this now—at twenty-two years old. How many others didn't know? How many had already forgotten those souls who were worked to death, their names never spoken, their bones left scattered and anonymous?

That thought ignited something in him. A fire.

He couldn't let them be erased.

Not by history. Not by silence.

Not while he still had ink in his pen.

John T. Ward refused to let their struggle go unrecognized. So, he picked up his pen and wrote:

For the Palladium of Liberty

Chillicothe, June 21, 1844

Mr. Editor, I am about to write a four-line on a subject that perhaps will meet your approbation, and I do sincerely hope it may meet the approbation of all that may see them.

John T. didn't just want people to read his words; he wanted them to feel them. He wrote about the upcoming August 1st celebrations, marking the anniversary of the emancipation of enslaved people in the British West Indies. Across Ohio—in cities like Cincinnati, Xenia, and Columbus—Black communities were preparing to gather in honor of those who had fought for their freedom.

But John T. argued that Columbus should host the largest gathering. Why? Because Columbus was the beating heart of Ohio's Black political activism. It was where laws were debated, where leaders gathered, and where Black voices needed to be heard. If Ohio's Black citizens wanted to make a real statement, it had to happen in Columbus.

But John T.'s letter wasn't just about celebration; it was about strategy, unity, and moving the movement forward.

"… our colored friends in Columbus are building two churches … the committee of arrangements intend to divide funds that may be received from the people that attend the celebration, to the churches. While we are paying homage to these benefactors of our brethren, we are also doing something for the churches …"

John understood something that many didn't: faith and activism were inseparable.

The Black church wasn't just a sanctuary; it was a battleground. It was where freedom was plotted, where leaders were raised, where our people found both God and strategy. So, John T. made a direct appeal to everyone—even those not yet in the fight:

"… the money is not for the Methodist nor Baptist alone, but for both; let the Methodist, the Baptist, and the sinners, be in attendance …"

This fight belonged to everybody. If they were truly going to be free, it couldn't be the work of a few; it had to be a movement.

John's letter didn't just encourage unity; it exposed him. His words weren't whispered in secret. They weren't shared behind closed doors. They were published. And his name—J. Ward—was printed for all to see.

That made him a target.

John T. Ward wasn't a docile Black man. He wasn't the kind to sit back and accept whatever "freedom" Ohio offered. He was a man willing to fight. And that made him dangerous.

As he signed his name, he must've known—he'd crossed a threshold. He was no longer just a reader of abolitionist papers or a supporter from the sidelines. He was now a writer, a voice, a leader stepping into his purpose. He had taken his first step toward becoming a revolutionary. Toward a life of defiance, resistance, and leadership in the fight for Black freedom.

What he couldn't have known then was this:

He wasn't just fighting for the future. He had already become part of history.

Original Letter by J. Ward (with minor copy editing for clarity while keeping original tone):

For the *Palladium of Liberty* Chillicothe, June 21, 1844

Mr. Editor,

I am about to write a few lines on a subject that perhaps will meet your approbation, and I sincerely hope it may meet the approbation of all who may read them.

In perusing the columns of your little sheet, I found an invitation extended to all the friends to a celebration, in commemoration of the emancipation of our brethren in the West Indies, to be held in Columbus, on the first day of August 1844.

I also saw invitations to other places for the same purpose. Now, Mr. Editor, what I wish to convey to the minds of the people is that I believe Columbus has the preeminence over these other places—not because I think there is opposition, nor because they celebrate the same thing. My reason is that Columbus is the central part of the state, and that is where our "big men" of the day go to be heard. That's where I would like to see some of the sable sons of America assembled together—to show the people what we are capable of. And I know we have some who are able to do just that.

My next reason should claim the attention of both saints and sinners. One might ask, why both? I answer: our colored friends in Columbus are building two churches. I understand that the committee of arrangements intends to divide the funds received at the celebration between those churches. While we are paying homage to the benefactors of our brethren, we are also doing something for the churches.

Who prompted these men to act so wisely? Now brethren, as the money is not just for the Methodists or the Baptists, but for both—let the Methodists, the Baptists, and even the sinners be in attendance. It will be for the advancement of the cause of Christ, the ruler of the universe.

May the God of heaven amply reward the committee for the trouble they must undertake to prepare for those who may attend. And may their expectations be satisfied by many.

I have written enough, and perhaps too much. I will leave that for those who read to decide.

I close by saying: I do sincerely hope to see a great many in attendance.
J. Ward

Written in 1844, just as he and his new wife, Catherine, were transitioning to Columbus, this letter reads almost like an initiation—a way for John T. to make his voice heard and see if his ideas would be accepted. In it, he calls for the celebration of Haitian emancipation, urging Columbus to become the central location for this historic gathering. His tone is bold, his words full of youthful determination, but there's also an undercurrent of purpose—a clear signal that he was already committed to something deeper: unity for the Black community.

What stands out in this letter is John T. Ward's vision for unity, a theme that still resonates powerfully today—especially as we honor Juneteenth. He wasn't just advocating for a celebration; he saw it as a moment to come together, raise awareness, and push for real political and social change. He understood the power of visibility—of being seen and heard in spaces where decisions were made and power was held.

His call for Columbus to host the celebration wasn't only about its central location, it was a strategic choice. John T. knew that to be heard, the Black community had to show up and speak out in the right places. Today, that same kind of strategic visibility still matters. Juneteenth celebrations aren't just about honoring our past, they're about claiming our present and securing our future, making sure our voices are loud and clear across every part of society.

John T. Ward's activism wasn't just built on theory—it was rooted in action. In his letter, he tied the celebration of emancipation directly to the building of churches in Columbus. That wasn't just symbolic; it was intentional. He brought together Methodists, Baptists, and even "the sinners" for a shared cause. The money raised from that celebration wasn't just for a good time; it was going toward something the community could touch, benefit from, and build on. That mindset—turning celebration into collective empowerment—is something we still need today.

So, when I think about Juneteenth, I can't help but draw the line straight back to my great-great-great-grandfather's letter. His push for unity, his understanding of community power, and his use of celebration as strategy—that's the same energy we need right now. Yes, we've come a long way. But freedom? True freedom? We're still fighting for that.

As we gather each Juneteenth, let's remember, it's more than just food and music. It's a chance to organize, mobilize, and move forward—just like John T. did in 1844. His letter wasn't just a call to action back then. It's a call that still echoes today.

His legacy reminds us: unity is our strength. And freedom ain't finished.

In 1830, Black American leaders from the antebellum North convened for the first time in Philadelphia. That historic gathering was sparked by events in Cincinnati, Ohio, where thousands of free Black people were violently forced out of the city by white mobs and discriminatory laws.

One of the key voices behind that first meeting was Hezekiah Grice, a young freedmen from Baltimore who had been born free in Ohio. Tired of being treated like a second-class citizen in the only country he'd ever known, Grice began to ask the unthinkable: *Would we be freer if we left?* Would another country offer basic human rights, dignity, and a chance to thrive beyond the grip of American racism?

Grice didn't just ask the question—he acted. He went on to lead powerful legal initiatives like the Legal Rights Association, which helped challenge the muddy definitions of Black citizenship in America. And when change at home felt too far out of reach, he made the radical decision to leave the United States altogether. He moved to Haiti, where he believed full citizenship and self-determination were possible.

Grice's story, like John T. Ward's, is a reminder that Black resistance has never been one-size-fits-all. Whether fighting on American soil or seeking new ground elsewhere, our people have always been in motion—thinking critically, organizing boldly, and chasing freedom by any means necessary.

By 1829, Cincinnati, Ohio, had become home to the largest free Black community in the United States—a fact that cannot be overstated. Though Ohio was considered a "free state," freedom in name did not mean equality in practice. The growing number of Black residents—many of them formerly enslaved—sparked panic among white Ohioans, who viewed them as both an economic and political threat.

That fear soon turned violent.

In 1829, Cincinnati became the site of one of the first anti-Black riots in American history, igniting a pattern of racial terror and exclusion that would haunt Black communities across the North for generations. It was here—not in the Deep South—that the so-called free nation revealed its fear of Black progress.

Faced with Black self-determination, powerful forces mobilized. The American Colonization Society (ACS), backed by some of the most influential political figures of the time—Andrew Jackson, Thomas Jefferson, Francis Scott Key, and even a young Abraham Lincoln—pushed a chilling agenda: Black people should be removed from America altogether. Their logic was brutal: if America was built on white supremacy, then Black people could never truly be free within its borders.

The ACS wasn't advocating integration; it was an admission. An acknowledgment that racism was foundational, and rather than dismantling it, they offered exile as the solution.

This is where the story begins—not in theory, but in blood, bricks, and fear. In Ohio, the so-called land of freedom, Black people stood their ground against mobs and policies designed to erase them.

The American Colonization Society urged free Black Americans to "return" to Africa—despite the fact that many had been born and raised right here in the United States. This wasn't a homecoming. It was a forced exile dressed up as salvation.

Even more disturbing, the colony established by the ACS in West Africa—Liberia—remained under ACS control until 1847. Conditions were brutal. Of those who made the journey, only about half survived. On arrival, many Indigenous African groups saw the Black American settlers not as kin, but as outsiders—or worse, invaders—leading to violent clashes. While the settlers eventually learned to defend themselves, the deeper truth was undeniable: America had cast them out, and even in Africa, they weren't fully accepted.

Confronted with this harsh reality, many free Black leaders in the U.S. rejected the ACS outright. Emigration wasn't an option. If they left, who would stay and resist slavery? Who would remain to challenge the very systems that had oppressed them for centuries?

That debate laid the foundation for the Colored Conventions Movement—a series of organized gatherings of free Black activists determined to chart a future on American soil. The movement itself was ideologically divided. Some supported armed resistance, a philosophy that would later echo in the words of Malcolm X. Others believed in nonviolent political engagement, a path we'd later associate with Dr. Martin Luther King Jr.

Frederick Douglass became the face of moral persuasion, believing in reasoned advocacy and public argument. Meanwhile, voices like David Walker spoke with militant urgency, warning that slavery would not end without force.

Together, these debates helped shape the earliest blueprint for Black political organizing in America: resist, strategize, and most importantly—stay and fight.

In 1844, when John T. Ward penned his first letter to *The Palladium of Liberty*, his position was crystal clear: he was staying to fight. His early writings made him a vocal opponent of the American Colonization Society and aligned him with the Colored Men's Convention Movement, which openly condemned the ACS and its effort to remove Black Americans from the only home they'd ever known.

One of the fiercest critics of the ACS was David Walker, who called American slavery "the greatest atrocity the world had ever seen." To him, it was more than unjust; it was monstrous. His *Appeal to the Colored Citizens of the World* didn't ask for permission; it demanded revolution. It urged Black people to rise up and resist—by any means necessary.

His words were so threatening to the Southern slave economy that authorities banned and destroyed copies of the *Appeal*. But the movement found a way. Pages of Walker's writing were sewn into coat linings, hidden in luggage, smuggled by brave allies down into the heart of the South.

The response was swift and savage. Southern states ramped up patrols, building statewide surveillance systems aimed not just at enslaved people but also at free Black communities. The country was on edge. The fuse had been lit.

And make no mistake—anti-slavery and abolition were not the same thing.

Anti-slavery politicians—many of them white Free Soilers— opposed the *expansion* of slavery into new states. But they didn't necessarily oppose slavery itself. Most of their objections were economic. They believed slavery undercut wages and threatened white workers. Their fight wasn't about Black liberation; it was about protecting white labor.

Abolitionists, however, believed slavery was a moral evil that had to be destroyed in its entirety. To them, there was no middle ground. No compromise. And the real test came after emancipation.

Because once slavery ended, a new question emerged:

Would Black Americans be granted full citizenship? Land? Political power?

The answer to that question separated those who sought justice from those who simply wanted to preserve their own place in the system.

John T. Ward's movement stood apart from the white-led anti-slavery establishment. It wasn't built on theory or distant outrage; it was built by men who had once been enslaved themselves. For them, slavery wasn't a political abstraction. It was trauma, memory, and survival.

They rejected compromise. They rejected delay, especially after Nat Turner's Rebellion in 1831, which had shocked the nation to its core. Turner's uprising wasn't just a fight for freedom—it was seen by white America as a direct assault on the very fabric of the country. For John T. and his comrades, it was a wake-up call.

They understood the truth: Slavery was not just a Southern problem. It was an American problem. And freedom would mean nothing without the power to protect it.

They weren't asking for inclusion. They were demanding transformation. That was the difference. That still is the difference.

Historian Emma Lapsansky argues that this first convention was significant, stating:

"The 1830 convention was the first time that a group of people got together and said, 'Okay, who are we? What will we call ourselves? And once we call ourselves something, what will we do about what we call ourselves?' And they said, 'Well, we're going to call ourselves Americans. We're going to start a newspaper. We're going to start a free produce movement. We're going to organize ourselves to go to Canada if we have to.' They began to have an agenda."

Violence in Cincinnati sparked concern among freed Black communities in other northern cities. They worried the same kind of riots could happen in their neighborhoods and that laws might be passed to restrict their freedoms and rights. That fear created urgency. Black leaders needed to organize, and quickly, to figure out the best course of action on a national level.

John T. Ward's family had arrived in Southern Ohio, in Lawrence County, just two years before the Cincinnati riots.

A group of revolutionaries broke away from slow-moving reformists to start their own organization that brought real change to Columbus. The Columbus Ohio Colored Men's Association became part of the Colored National Conventions. These were antebellum activists—Black abolitionists through and through.

Many came out of the First Baptist Church, where anti-slavery beliefs were preached loud and clear. The meetings they held were like today's think tanks—spaces where they strategized around unjust laws targeting freedmen and fought for the liberation of the enslaved. The delegates were sharp. They spoke with power and dressed with pride.

The Colored Conventions are too often left out of Black history, but they were a crucial part of the abolitionist fight. It was a fully Black-led movement. No white person had control.

Community leaders gathered to share and debate the issues impacting Black communities. Sometimes, they traveled from across the state. As the movement grew, they held national conventions. This mass movement spanned over seventy years, drawing hundreds of delegates and tens of thousands of participants to conventions in places like Massachusetts, New York, and Pennsylvania.

In the mid-nineteenth century, the Colored Conventions emerged as a powerful force for freedmen fighting for civil and economic rights. These gatherings were spaces to speak freely, plan boldly, and push back against injustice. Ohio played a key role, with its Black delegates making powerful contributions to the fight for racial equality.

These Ohio delegates were respected leaders—ministers, teachers, activists, businessmen—bringing wisdom, determination, and experience. They were all united in the fight for social justice and equal representation.

The conventions gave them space to build unity, exchange ideas, and develop real strategies to fight the system. They tackled major issues like education, voting rights, labor rights, slavery abolition, and the legal discrimination rooted in Black Codes.

Most of these delegates had lived through slavery. Many had escaped it. They were determined to do whatever it took to help others find freedom.

One of those men was Henry Highland Garnet, about five years older than John T. Garnet had escaped a slave catcher by jumping off a roof—an injury that later cost him his leg. But that didn't stop him.

Henry Garnet inspired John T. not just with his words, but with his actions. In New Hampshire, a white mob tried to drag Black folks and their oxen into a river. Then they went to a boarding school where Black children were staying—planning to kill them. Garnet fought back with gunfire and saved lives.

Later, Garnet gave a fiery speech about his confrontations with white mobs. The speech was so intense, the convention had to vote on whether it should even be published. The vote was eighteen to nineteen.

That speech was bold and raw, a true call to arms. Garnet urged Black people to choose liberty or death. He praised figures like Nat Turner and Denmark Vesey, calling them patriots who understood the price of freedom. Garnet was ready to go to war.

He wrote:

"Brethren, arise, arise! Strike for your lives and liberties. Now is the day and the hour. Let every slave throughout the land do this, and the days of slavery are numbered. You cannot be more oppressed than you have been—you cannot suffer greater cruelties than you already. Rather die freemen than live to be slaves. Remember that you are FOUR MILLIONS!

It is in your power so to torment the God-cursed slaveholders that they will be glad to let you go free. If the scale was turned, and Black men were the masters and white men the slaves, every destructive agent and element would be employed to lay the oppressor low. Danger and death would hang over their heads day and night. Yes, the tyrants would meet with plagues more terrible than those of Pharaoh.

But you are a patient people. You act as though you were made for the special use of these devils. You act as though your daughters were born to pamper the lusts of your masters and overseers. And worse than all, you tamely submit while your lords tear your wives from your embraces and defile them before your eyes.

In the name of God, we ask—are you men? Where is the blood of your fathers? Has it all run out of your veins? Awake, awake; millions of voices are calling you! Your dead fathers speak to you from their graves. Heaven, as with a voice of thunder, calls on you to arise from the dust.

Let your motto be resistance! resistance! RESISTANCE! No oppressed people have ever secured their liberty without resistance. What kind of resistance you had better make, you must decide by the circumstances that surround you, and according to the suggestion of expediency. Brethren, adieu! Trust in the living God. Labor for the peace of the human race, and remember that you are FOUR MILLIONS."

Henry Garnet believed in arming enslaved women and men. To him, moral persuasion wasn't cutting it. Freedom wasn't coming through speeches alone, so he called out people like William Lloyd Garrison who had a more passive approach.

William Lloyd Garrison, a Quaker known for nonviolence, was a firm believer in abolishing slavery—but his strategy leaned on faith and patience. He thought Southern plantation owners would eventually see the wrong in their ways and let their slaves go. He even compared it to the story of Egypt in the Bible, where Pharaoh finally freed the Israelites.

Frederick Douglass—also a member of the Colored Conventions—was against Garnet's speech being made public.

Garnet was furious that his speech was struck down by just one vote. The majority at the convention feared it would spark talk of a slave rebellion. And many of the freemen in those rooms were either fugitives or newly emancipated. They knew the risk.

Another notable convention was the 1849 Columbus, Ohio State Convention of the Colored Citizens of Ohio, which brought together prominent delegates like John Mercer Langston, Charles H. Langston, John T. Ward, David Jenkins, Moses Redman, and James Poindexter—just to name a few.

In that same year, John T. attended the State Convention in Columbus, where brilliant Black men gave powerful speeches and recited moving poems.

Sweet, soulful voices of Black women singers filled the space, bringing spirit and hope to the gathering.

They pushed hard for the end of chattel slavery, stressed how important education was for freedmen, and raised serious concerns about the Black Laws. One of the key recommendations was that five hundred copies of *Walker's Appeal* and Henry H. Garnet's *Address to the Slaves* be obtained in the name of the Convention and handed out freely. Most importantly that day, the Convention was called to order by D. Jenkins of Franklin and officially organized with John T. Ward of Ross County appointed as chairman.

Another major gathering came a year after the Fugitive Slave Act of 1850 was passed—the 1851 Columbus Colored Convention. That meeting was known for its fiery debates and deep conversations about political reform and the Constitution of the United States. The Ohio delegates didn't hold back; they challenged each other on where they stood.

Mr. William Howard Day of Lorain took the floor and said, in essence:

"I can't sit still and let this resolution pass without speaking up. Anyone who's known me over the years knows I'm firmly against the principle behind it.

The gentleman from Cuyahoga (Mr. Douglass) seems to be making the same mistake others do—confusing how the Constitution is used with what the Constitution is.

Look, there's no argument here about this government acting in favor of slavery. And we all know the Supreme Court has handed slavery a lifeline with its unjust—and even illegal—decisions. But those decisions aren't the Constitution itself.

Think about the Bible. People have used it to justify all kinds of evil. Do we throw away the Bible because of their lies? Or do we throw away their false interpretations? Same goes for the Constitution.

If a judge makes a bad ruling, do we shut down the court? No—we remove the judge. So when I vote, I vote by what the Constitution says, not what some corrupt court decides.

The Constitution says it was written to 'establish justice.' That's a clear stance against injustice. It says, 'no person shall be deprived of life, liberty, or property without due process of law.' I take that seriously.

I was raised in a country where three million of my people are still in chains and half a million more are only half free. That makes every tool that can help us gain real freedom precious.

The Constitution is supposed to be the foundation of American liberty. So I'll wrap myself in that flag, plant my feet on that Constitution, and use every word in it to appeal to the people for the rights it claims to protect."

Mr. H. Ford Douglas fired back:

"He can wrap himself in the stars and stripes forty times over, wave the Declaration of Independence in one hand and the Constitution in the other, and sit beneath the shadow of the Bunker Hill Monument all he wants. But if the slaveholder wants you—under this Constitution and that 'Fugitive Bill'—best believe he's coming for you. That's the reality. If that don't show you what kind of Constitution we really got, then maybe one doesn't exist at all."

To them, *freedom* was the only real solution to the barriers slavery created. For John T., it was personal. Freedom wasn't just about dignity; it was about his children's future and their right to learn. At that same convention, John T. stood up and made his stance clear: the U.S. Constitution was built to uphold slavery. And he was done pretending otherwise.

Despite this fact, he believed that voting under the constitution could still be justified under certain circumstances, just as he would call on slaves to resist their masters and fight for their liberties. John T.

made it clear that his devotion to the freedom of colored people was paramount, even if it meant deviating from conventional religious teachings.

The session continued with discussions on the resolution presented by Mr. H. Ford Douglass, advocating for the rights and liberties of colored men. John T. hoped that the resolution would be adopted, as he firmly believed in voting and taking actions under the constitution to advance the political, religious, and intellectual elevation of his people. The meeting concluded with an anti-slavery song, and John T. remained resolute in his commitment to the cause of freedom for his fellow freedmen. With political efforts and influenced by Black abolitionists, John T. saw the silent war being fought from various angles.

Education played a crucial role, and John T. admired those like James McCune Smith, who challenged racial theories and debunked doubts about Black Americans' capabilities. However, racism continued to make free Black people vulnerable to oppression throughout the country, including in Ohio. John T. understood the challenges faced by isolated black people, particularly women like Mrs. Colman Freeman, who experienced racism regardless of their location. The river did not provide a clear border between freedom and slavery, as many slaves found freedom more distressing than the uncertainties of their current situation.

These conventions also gave our people a real chance to make their voices heard through a structured, democratic process. Ohio delegates teamed up with folks from other states, building crucial partnerships that stretched across regions and brought Black communities together in the fight for justice. Through these collective efforts, they worked to uplift their people and directly challenge the racist policies of the time.

Speakers at these Colored Conventions called for action—real, community-based solutions. They pushed for pooling resources, starting schools and literary societies, and building organizations from the ground up. Resistance wasn't just individual; it was *crowd-sourced.*

This wasn't just about one event; it was a long, steady campaign for civil and human rights. The records from these conventions are living proof of the deep struggle and bold courage of those who stood up to claim what was always theirs. Ohio played a key role in this movement, and young leaders like John T. Ward—still in his early twenties—were already rising up and making a name for themselves.

The Conventions of Colored Men eventually caught the attention of white society, especially when Frederick Douglass came through Ohio and spoke out against the atrocities happening in Cincinnati. On July 4, 1850, Douglass arrived in Cincinnati and, in just one week, gave eight powerful speeches. It was then he saw how dangerous the river valley around Springfield and Xenia had become for fugitives—folks running from slavery in Kentucky. It was a known hunting ground.

Douglass stayed committed to the cause, continuing his work for abolition and equal rights. On February 24, 1856, he spoke in Columbus, Ohio. Just days later, Margaret Garner and her family were captured and brought to Cincinnati to await extradition. Despite efforts by local abolitionists, the Garners were sent back to slavery in Kentucky.

At the same time, Douglass and other activists were pushing hard for Black voting rights. They called for the removal of the word "white" from the clause in the Ohio constitution that limited voting rights to white men. But even after heartfelt speeches from Jonathan Gaines and Peter Clark at the January State Convention of Colored

Men, the legislature in Columbus still refused to make the change. So, the Black folks remained disenfranchised.

Still, the fight didn't stop. After three powerful meetings in Cincinnati, a passionate group of organizers hit the road, traveling across more than thirteen cities and counties in Southern Ohio. Their goal was to flood the legislature with petitions demanding the right to vote for free Black citizens. Douglass himself was all in; he even wrote about the mission in one of his editorials.

Even though Ohio had plenty of abolitionist energy, once the Republican Convention wrapped up, folks mostly focused on electing Fremont and didn't want to hear anything outside of that platform. But that didn't stop the movement. In fact, it fueled it. They stayed focused on "true abolitionism," even if it meant walking for hours in the heat, speaking two to three hours a day, and facing the blazing sun head-on.

Douglass knew those roads; he had walked them before. And he knew how hard it was. But he also knew how important it was. So, he pushed his people to keep going, to preach real abolition everywhere they went, no matter how hard the journey got.

These Colored Conventions were everything for John T. and other freedmen. This was their mass movement. It was how they organized, strategized, and held each other accountable. Some mocked them. But John T. wasn't backing down. He reminded critics of Senator Charles Sumner getting beaten nearly to death in 1856 just for speaking out. John T. also called for a vote and sent money to support fellow Black folks affected by the Christian riots in Pennsylvania.

John T. made his mark as a powerful speaker and talented writer, just like many other Black abolitionists. He also stood strong for women's rights—calling out the convention for rejecting female delegates. Black women in Ohio were putting in the work. They raised the most money and handled the hard logistics: cooking, hosting visitors, and making sure the meetings ran smoothly. They deserved a voice.

John T. Ward and Charles Langston (Langston Hughes's grandfather) were chosen as delegates to represent the movement and bring back updates. In the middle of one meeting, they got word that a critical piece of legislation was being presented at the Ohio Statehouse—so they left the meeting and went straight to the session.

The white politicians looked up when my great-great-great-grandfather walked in—dressed sharp, speaking clear and strong when he took the floor. They must've been confused. To them, he was just the janitor who cleaned their building in tattered clothes. But now? They saw him for who he really was: well-spoken, commanding, and unapologetic. He could go toe-to-toe with any of them—and earned their respect.

Behind the scenes, delegates like him moved carefully, handing out critical documents and advocating for the rights of our people.

What held this movement together, what made it powerful ... was *accountability*. Everyone was expected to show up, stay committed, and stand firm. John T. Ward and the rest weren't just talking. They vowed to stay vigilant. And they made it clear: no slave would be taken by a white man without a fight.

He believed in resisting slavery—even if it meant dying for it. That's how deep the fight ran in his spirit. The Columbus Colored Men's Association, which he was part of, wasn't just talking either; they were pushing hard to get all the remaining Black Laws repealed.

In 1859, William Howard Day, an Ohio native and Oberlin College graduate, took the movement overseas. He went to Britain, urging people there to boycott U.S. cotton—hitting slavery right in its pocket. While abroad, he also raised thirty-five thousand dollars to support freed Black folks who had made it to Canada. That money wasn't just charity, it was survival money, freedom money.

And even after the Civil War, the work didn't stop. Free-born, freed, and self-emancipated Black folks came together at state and national political conventions, still strategizing—still planning. Their mission: to fight for justice in education, employment, and law. They did this at a time when Black rights were being rolled back, both locally and nationally. These postwar gatherings kept the spirit of the Colored Conventions alive, even as America tried once again to shut us out of the democracy we helped build.

The Colored Conventions Movement rose up during some of the ugliest decades in American history—decades filled with bloody race riots, disgusting caricatures of Black life, and a booming pro-slavery campaign. But the movement survived all that. It survived the Civil War. It survived Reconstruction. And even when Black people were stripped again of rights in education, labor, and the law in the late 1800s, the fire kept burning.

John T. stayed involved, especially in voting for public schools. But the truth is, a lot of folks didn't trust the system. They feared public schools wouldn't truly be for free Black kids—that they'd be kept out, just like always. And even after slavery had "ended," free folks like John T. still had to deal with white mobs. These mobs would attack abolitionists, burn down Black-owned businesses, churches, schools, anything that stood for Black progress. These attacks weren't random. They were targeted. They hit the very places that shaped John T. Ward's life.

The 1830 convention wasn't just a meeting—it was a *moment*. A powerful shift in the mind and soul of a people who had been shoved to the edge but refused to disappear. It was the first time free freedmen gathered and asked themselves out loud: "Who are we?" And the answer they gave was bold and beautiful: "We are Americans."

That declaration wasn't just words. It birthed a plan to start a newspaper, promote the Free Produce Movement to boycott slave-made goods, and if necessary, emigrate to Canada. But no matter the tactic, one thing was clear: they would do it *together*.

From 1830 to 1890, the Colored Conventions created a legacy—one rooted in political brilliance, community love, and a deep, unbreakable racial unity. In those rooms sat some of the greatest minds our people ever produced—Richard Allen, James Forten, Frederick Douglass, Martin Delany, Sojourner Truth, Henry

Highland Garnet. They weren't just dreaming of freedom, they were designing it. They were building the blueprint that would eventually lead to the NAACP, the civil rights movement, and every fight for Black justice that came after.

These conventions weren't about ceremony or making noise. They were sharp, strategic, and focused. They responded to real, immediate needs: abolishing slavery, gaining the right to vote, creating schools, generating Black wealth, and changing how the world saw Black people.

They weren't there to be clapped for. They were there to *move mountains.*

Now, nearly two centuries later, the same question rises again—just as urgently as it did in 1830. Who are we today? Are we African American? Black American? Freedmen? ADOS? FBA? B1? Moors? Or are we still circling that same question asked in Philadelphia, searching for a shared identity, a collective purpose, and a unified voice?

Over a decade ago, there was a glimpse—a faint echo of the spirit from the Colored Conventions—when Tavis Smiley launched the annual *State of the Black Union.* These gatherings brought together intellectuals, artists, policymakers, and activists to assess the condition of Black America and propose real solutions. They weren't meant to be spectacles; they were supposed to spark structure, leadership, and real action. But somewhere along the way, that momentum faded. Still, the blueprint remains.

During the 2008 presidential campaign, Smiley publicly questioned whether Barack Obama's candidacy truly addressed a specific Black agenda. He urged Black Americans to hold Obama accountable—to demand policies that directly benefited our communities, not just offer blind support out of racial pride. That stance sparked serious backlash and exposed a hard truth.

Are we, as Black voters, using our collective power to demand real change—or are we giving our votes away without getting anything solid in return?

Imagine if we'd had a well-oiled machine like the Colored Conventions during that moment. A unified body could have laid out clear demands and made sure any candidate—no matter their skin color—knew what Black America needed and expected. But without that kind of organized pressure, we missed the chance to shape policy in a way that truly served our people.

Today, the NAACP's influence has faded, and the Congressional Black Caucus (CBC) often finds its resources stretched thin—sometimes pulled toward causes that don't directly serve the lineage of today's freedmen. In this era of redefinition, we need to return to organized clarity. Local chapters must grow into state conventions, and state conventions must come together in national strategy sessions. Not for show. Not for applause. But for the future.

Our ancestors didn't just gather to talk—they came together to decide who they were and to fight for who they knew they could be. That's our path forward. We must echo 1830—not out of nostalgia, but out of necessity.

The Colored Conventions Movement was the foundation of Black political organizing before, during, and after the Civil War. These weren't just meetings—they were mass gatherings of ministers, teachers, businessmen, writers, and farmers, united by a shared purpose. They pushed for the end of slavery long before most white abolitionists. They demanded not just freedom, but voting rights. They worked with the Underground Railroad, built schools, and fought against laws like the Black Codes and the Fugitive Slave Act.

They documented how many Black children were in school, how many adults could read and write, and where resources were lacking. Why? Because education was viewed as a tool of liberation. They tracked Black land ownership as proof of progress and stability. Why? Because land meant autonomy.

They logged voter suppression, unjust arrests, and acts of violence—not just to protest, but to build a documented case for national reform, abolition, and full citizenship. They passed resolutions, drafted proposals, and laid down policy blueprints that inspired the NAACP, the civil rights movement, and everything that came after.

The conventions brought together the wealthy and the working class, freedmen and fugitives, educators and farmers. We must stop letting division weaken our collective power. Before the government ever cared about our numbers, we tracked our own. Today, we can build data collectives, define our outcomes, and measure success on our terms—not wait for someone else to tell us who we are.

This wasn't chaos. These were structured, strategic gatherings with elected officers, minutes, resolutions, and action plans. We can—and must—revive national gatherings centered on real solutions: economic growth, justice reform, education access, and voter protection.

Ministers sat next to entrepreneurs. Churches backed small businesses. We need our institutions working together again.

If the Congressional Black Caucus is our voice inside the room, the Colored Conventions were the fire that built the house.

And today, we need both: Institutional power (like the CBC) and community-rooted coalitions that operate independently, just like the Colored Conventions did.

The Colored Conventions were like a shadow Congress—built by us, for us—when the U.S. government refused to see us. They weren't tied to the three constitutional branches (executive, legislative, judicial), but they influenced all three through policy frameworks, data, reports, and organizing strategy.

These gatherings weren't just events. They were our Congress before we had seats in Congress.

They proved something timeless: Power isn't given. It's organized. It's tracked. It's claimed.

It's time we pick up that blueprint—and build again.

CHAPTER 13

The 1850 American Man Hunt

"I am yet accounted a slave, and no spot in the United States affords an asylum for the wanderer. True, I feel protected in the hearts of the many warm friends of the slave by whom I am surrounded, but this protection does not come from the LAWS of any one of the United States."

-Kentucky Fugitive slave, Lewis Clarke

Before I could begin this journey—before I could lift the veil on a story passed down through generations—I had to confront a truth that fractured everything I thought I knew.

Our family hero, John T. Ward, was not born free. He was free only in spirit. Legally, he was property.

That realization struck like a blow to the chest. It hollowed me in a way I hadn't expected. This man we celebrated as a conductor on the Underground Railroad, a pillar of Black business and resistance in Ohio, began his life not as a freedman but as someone owned. Someone listed in a will. Someone expected to stay behind, to serve, and ultimately, to disappear.

His grandfather, Samuel Ward, understood what was at stake. He walked away from what would be considered a fortune today—millions in land, livestock, and inheritance. And he did so without hesitation. He turned his back on the blood-soaked soil of the Cook Estate not because he didn't grasp its value, but because he recognized something far more priceless: family. He chose love over land. Freedom over fear.

Among the children he carried toward uncertain hope was his grandson, John T. Ward. A boy with wide, searching eyes, calloused hands, and a past heavier than he could yet comprehend. His mother had been freed. His kin who were older than fifteen had been listed for manumission. But John T.? He was still legally enslaved. Still named in Lt. John Ward Jr.'s will. Still tethered to a system that would rather erase him than acknowledge his worth.

That single omission—that quiet silence in a white man's estate— could've sealed his fate forever. In the eyes of Virginia law, he had no right to leave. No protection. No path to liberty. But Samuel knew the truth. And so, he chose defiance.

He likely carried forged documents. He relied on the whispers of abolitionists, the courage of Quakers, the cover of darkness. He walked nearly three hundred miles from Virginia to Ohio—not just dragging weary children but hauling the stolen futures of his bloodline on his back. Because crossing into Ohio didn't make you free. It made you a fugitive. And Samuel? A criminal. An outlaw. A man willing to break the law to keep his family whole.

And what of the boy he carried?

John T. Ward, the future conductor, community leader, and Black entrepreneur, did not begin life as a freedman. He began it as contraband. Classified as cargo by the laws of the land. Hunted like an animal for daring to exist beyond the boundary of his bondage.

Is it any wonder that, years later, he listed his birthplace as Richmond, Virginia, and claimed to have been born free? He was light-skinned enough to pass questions. He had lived long enough to see how the law could lie, twist, and betray. He understood that a single detailed date, a name, a county could unravel everything. So, he erased the paper trail that led back to Pittsylvania County. He redacted the past to preserve the future. It wasn't deception. It was survival.

Because after 1850, the rules changed.

The Fugitive Slave Act turned so-called free soil into a hunting ground. It deputized every white man with a badge, a whip, or a grudge, granting them the legal right to snatch Black people off streets, porches, and dirt roads with nothing more than an accusation. No trial. No testimony. No burden of proof. Just suspicion backed by supremacy.

Even Thomas Lincoln—Abraham Lincoln's father—served as a patty roller. A state-sanctioned slave patrolman. These men stalked both North and South, feeding bodies back into slavery while pretending it was justice.

In that world, every knock at the door could be betrayal. Every footstep in the night could be the end. Every whispered name could cost you your life.

And for Black women, the stakes were even higher. Freedom wasn't just about liberty—it was about survival. About escaping rape. About protecting their daughters. About severing generational trauma before it took root again.

That's what Samuel Ward did. For his children. For his grandchildren. For every generation that would come after.

Let it be said plainly: freedom was not granted. It was stolen back—snatched from the hands of a country that tried to bury it. And the law? The law was never ours. It did not see us. It did not serve us. It did not protect us. We protected each other.

It is hard to hold that truth in your hands. Harder still to let it settle in your bones. I had always known John T. Ward as a beacon—respected, admired, a name etched in the granite of our history. But when I traced his path to its beginning, I uncovered something deeper. Something raw, defiant, and astonishing.

He did not begin as a legend. He began as a fugitive child—hunted by law, protected by love, and carried through shadows by a man who risked everything to keep him alive.

And yet, through it all, he endured. He persevered. He adapted. He survived.

What I admire most is not just his bravery—but his ingenuity. His stillness under fire. His refusal to be erased. I felt his presence in every record I uncovered, every silence I had to interpret, every whispered name that had been tucked away like contraband in the archives.

His voice reached me—not as an echo, but as a force. A stalwart reminder that history is not just what happened. It's who dared to live through it.

And that, that is why I picked up this pen.

Because he ran, so we could write. Because he endured, so we could remember. Because he made sure we could.

The air in Columbus always carries a sense of history, like the ground itself remembers. On mornings like these, the weight of living while Black in America pressed on me like a ghost from the past. Every glance in the rearview mirror felt heavier. Every passing police car sparked a flicker of apprehension. The laws we live under today—the fear we carry—echo the oppression of another time. A time when the law itself made freedom a fleeting, fragile thing.

Driving to the DMV that morning, I couldn't help but think about the 1851 Fugitive Slave Act—and how its shadow still lingers in ways we don't always recognize.

The Fugitive Slave Act was a tool of terror. A weapon. Designed to strip away humanity from those who dared to seek freedom. It forced everyday citizens, regardless of their beliefs, to aid in the capture of escaped slaves and denied the accused even the right to testify. Bounty hunters roamed with impunity, incentivized by profit. Free Black men and women, enslaved individuals, and even their allies lived in constant fear. Blackness itself was criminalized. Freedom became an act of defiance—punishable by death or worse.

Fast forward to 2020. The Fugitive Slave Act is long repealed, but its essence? Still here. Still alive in the systems that surveil, detain, and harm Black bodies. A minor infraction—like expired tags—shouldn't fill me with dread. But it does. That fear isn't irrational. It's inherited. A reflex born of centuries of systemic inequity.

Traffic stops for Black folks? They're never routine. They're loaded. Weighted. And the names of those we've lost linger like ghosts: Philando Castile. Daunte Wright. Sandra Bland. What starts as a simple stop too often ends in tragedy. The laws have changed, but their impact remains sharp—wielded with the same devastating precision.

Still, even in that fear, there's a contrast. Back in 1851, resistance meant navigating the Underground Railroad—a network of defiance, courage, and deep-rooted faith in freedom. My great-great-great-grandfather was one of those brave souls. He risked everything to help others escape bondage. He was a beacon of hope in the darkest of times.

In my era, resistance looks different—but it's no less vital. It's fighting for police reform. Demanding accountability. Lifting our voices in protests, in community meetings, in courtrooms and classrooms.

Then came December 4, 2020. Another name added to the roll of stolen lives. Casey Goodson, just twenty-three, shot six times by a white officer with an assault rifle while holding nothing more than a sandwich. Just weeks later, Andre Hill, gunned down in his own garage. By 2022, the nightmare continued. Donovan Lewis, shot while lying in bed during a police raid.

Each name a life. Each life a story. Each story cut short.

And in the midst of this pain, I was asked to speak downtown on December 2020, in front of the statue of William McKinley. The irony didn't escape me. McKinley, the twenty-fifth president, stood for civil rights long before it was "popular." His first political speech in 1867 demanded that freedmen have the right to vote—a radical stance in his day.

As I stood before his statue, I had no idea I was standing in the very spot my great-great-great-grandfather once stood. Fighting for justice. Fighting for us. That connection didn't come until later— when I found old family photographs, pieces of a story I hadn't yet put together. The realization hit me like lightning. This wasn't coincidence. This was legacy.

By December 2022, life shifted again—in ways I wasn't ready for. My mother passed away from COPD. My biggest supporter. For thirty years, she gave me gifts not everyone would think of—AAA memberships, reminders for license renewals, all the quiet, behind-the-scenes work that keeps life steady.

Her absence? It knocked the wind out of me.

So, that morning, driving to the DMV with expired tags, I felt it—all of it: the grief, the history, the fear.

Driving while Black in America is an act of faith. It shouldn't be—but it is. The smallest mistake shouldn't feel like a possible death sentence, but we know better. The statistics don't lie. Since 2017, nearly six hundred people have been killed during traffic stops, names like Sandra Bland, Philando Castile, and Daunte Wright stay with us, like ancestors too young to be gone.

And yet—still—we rise.

In June 2020, the *Columbus Dispatch* featured me, my business, my story. A spotlight on Black excellence in the midst of unrest. It was a proud moment. A reminder that, through everything, we're still here. We've always been here. And we're not going anywhere.

So, as I drove that morning, with grief in my chest and history in my mirrors, I reminded myself: the road ahead is uncertain—but it's mine to walk. And with the echoes of the past and the strength of those who came before me?

I keep moving forward, living on a prayer, but moving forward nonetheless.

***

Black folks traveling without papers in Ohio and Kentucky were always at risk. If you were dark-skinned and moving through those parts without documentation, you were likely to be stopped, questioned, or flat-out detained. White folks didn't need much reason—they saw Blackness and assumed you were a runaway. That assumption alone could cost you your freedom.

Take Madison Jefferson, for example. He was enslaved near the Ohio River and tried to escape not once, not twice, but three times. Each time, he made it to Ohio, and each time, he ended up in jail. Ohio might've been a free state on paper, but freedom didn't always mean protection.

Down in Kentucky, the courts weren't hiding how they felt. The Court of Appeals ruled that "color and long possession are such presumptive evidence of slavery as to throw the burden of proof on a negro claiming freedom." In plain terms: if you were Black, you had to prove you *weren't* a slave. Your skin alone was evidence against you.

But in 1841, the Ohio Supreme Court made a bold move. They ruled that if a slaveholder brought an enslaved person into Ohio, that person would be considered free. That victory didn't come easy. It was the work of folks like Salmon P. Chase, a lawyer who wasn't afraid to stand up to the system. Chase was fierce in his opposition to slavery, and he used the law like a sword.

Even with that win, fugitive slaves were still living on the edge. On paper, they might've been free. But in reality? They were surrounded by suspicion, hostility, and the threat of being snatched back into bondage.

The Ohio newspapers tell the stories loud and clear. Kidnappings. Beatings. Forced returns. The risks weren't just high; they were constant. Slavery didn't survive just because of owners. It survived because entire communities backed it up. On the plantations, if a slave escaped, it wasn't just a loss; it was a disgrace. White folks saw it as a failure of control, and that kind of failure had consequences.

The laws never worked in our favor. The burden of proof always fell on Black folks, and our very existence—our skin—was treated like a crime. Freedom was fragile. It could be questioned. It could be revoked. And at any moment, it could be stolen.

Then came 1851.

The pressure in Ohio was boiling over. That year, the Fugitive Slave Act was in full effect—part of the so-called Compromise of 1850. But there was nothing "compromised" about it. It was an outright attack on freedom. It demanded that even free states like Ohio hand over escaped slaves. No trial. No voice. No justice.

But our people didn't just lie down. The freedmen of Ohio stood up. They leaned on faith, community, and pure determination. They fought back—against the law, against the fear, against the odds. They formed networks, hid runaways, raised money, and told the truth when others stayed silent. Their resistance was both a shield and a signal. It said: *We're still here. And we won't go back quietly.*

What they built wasn't just survival; it was legacy, a story of strength that would echo for generations. Their courage turned pain into purpose and struggle into solidarity. And even today, that fire still burns.

The news of the Christiana Rebellion spread like wildfire, reaching the streets of Columbus, Ohio, within days. As newspapers published their accounts of the deadly standoff in Pennsylvania, reactions were swift and divided. The white press condemned it as lawlessness, a dangerous defiance of authority, and a threat to national order. But within Ohio's Black abolitionist community, the Christiana uprising was hailed as a glorious stand for freedom, a moment that proved enslaved and free Black men alike would no longer submit to the shackles of slavery without a fight.

In the meeting halls of Ohio's Colored Men's Association, a wave of urgency filled the air. John T. Ward, already a well-respected abolitionist in Columbus, took immediate action. He called upon the free Black community and white allies to rally together. The men in that room knew what Christiana meant: if a federal law like the Fugitive Slave Act could be resisted in Pennsylvania, it could be resisted in Ohio. But resistance came at a cost.

The government had already responded to the Christiana Rebellion with a brutal crackdown—arresting more than thirty-five men, Black and white, and charging them with treason against the United States. The message was clear: anybody bold enough to stand up to slave catchers would pay the price. The federal government wanted to crush the abolitionist movement by making an example out of those who dared to fight back.

Knowing what was at stake, John T. Ward stood up in the crowded meeting room of the Colored Men's Association and called for financial aid. The men in that room didn't need convincing. If Christiana's Black resisters were convicted of treason, it would set a dangerous precedent—one that meant any Black man who defended himself, his home, or his family from being kidnapped back into slavery could be branded a traitor to his country.

In the days that followed, John T. and his crew of abolitionists got to work. They organized fundraising drives throughout Columbus and nearby Ohio towns. Donations came in from everywhere—Black churches, small Black-owned businesses, white allies, and working folks who had never seen Christiana but understood exactly what it meant. Christiana wasn't just a skirmish; it was a battle in the bigger war for Black freedom.

Weeks went by, but the energy didn't die. The Colored Men's Association and their allies kept pushing hard. They reached out to abolitionists in Pennsylvania and New York, pulling together legal support and sending money to help cover the costs of the defense.

At the Colored Conventions—gatherings of Black leaders from across the North—Christiana became a rallying cry. The rebellion had proven what Black abolitionists had been preaching for years:

"We can't trust the law to protect us. We gotta protect ourselves."

The Christiana Resistance also sparked real debate within Ohio's abolitionist circles. Some folks in the Colored Men's Association still believed nonviolence was the best way forward. But others— energized by what they saw as the first real win against the Fugitive Slave Act—started to argue that self-defense wasn't just necessary, it was inevitable.

John T. Ward stood in the middle of all that—right at the crossroads. He'd spent years working the system, fighting through political channels, trying to overturn Ohio's Black Codes and secure basic rights for free Black people. But now? He was seeing firsthand how a government that claimed to be just and fair could turn around and label a man a criminal for daring to stand his ground.

The Christiana Rebellion didn't just end in Pennsylvania; it *echoed* across the nation. It widened the already deep divide between North and South. It proved the Fugitive Slave Act wasn't just a law; it was a weapon. And Black folks weren't going to take it lying down.

For Ohio's Black community, Christiana marked a shift. The Underground Railroad would no longer operate strictly in secret. Now, it would be fueled by the knowledge that *resistance was possible*—and sometimes, it was necessary.

And for men like John T. Ward, it made one thing clear: the fight for freedom couldn't wait.

Standing among his brothers in the Colored Men's Association—collecting donations, drafting letters, organizing strategy—he knew deep down …

Christiana was only the beginning.

Freedom was a fragile illusion—shattered by the sound of hooves pounding down dirt roads, the sudden grip of a stranger's hand, the cold press of iron shackles on bare skin. The law had turned every Black man, woman, and child in Ohio into a target.

Margaret "Peggy" Garner knew this deep in her bones.

She had fled the plantations of Boone County, Kentucky, with her family—crossing the frozen Ohio River into what should've been safety. She dreamed of giving her children a life beyond chains. But when the hunters came knocking on the door of their Cincinnati hideout, she knew the truth.

Freedom was a lie.

And rather than let her daughter be dragged back into the hell of slavery, Peggy made an unimaginable choice.

A mother's love had never been strong enough to stop the lash.

The weight of history lingers in the soil of Ohio. It clings to the riverbanks where desperate feet once splashed through icy waters.

It echoes in the trees that muffled whispered prayers and midnight escapes. It sits in the bricks of city streets where the hunted once begged for shelter.

Before 1850, crossing the Ohio River meant hope.

Now? It meant nothing.

The Fugitive Slave Act gave bounty hunters the right to cross state lines and drag back anybody they *claimed* was a fugitive. No trial. No evidence. Just a finger pointed in your direction—and you were gone.

Suddenly, nobody was safe.

Peggy knew this well.

To the men with whips and papers, to the lawmakers protecting the trade in human lives, Peggy wasn't a woman.

She wasn't a mother.

She wasn't a daughter.

She was a fugitive.

A piece of stolen property they aimed to reclaim.

And her captors? They weren't just men; they were predators. Their business was pain. Their profit was people. They hunted by broken branches, crushed grass, the scent of sweat carried on the wind. They came with pistols, bloodhounds, and chains designed to crush a person's will before the whip ever touched their skin.

And Ohio—once a promised land—became just another hunting ground.

Before the Fugitive Slave Act, the Underground Railroad had thrived in cities like Columbus, Cincinnati, and Cleveland. Free Black communities protected the runaways, hiding them in attics and basements, feeding them, giving them new names, and sometimes new lives.

But now the safe houses were cracking under fear.

Every knock on the door brought dread.

Every step outside might be your last.

Every glance from a stranger felt like a noose tightening.

Still, they ran.

Because running wasn't a crime, it was survival. It was resistance. It was the only way forward.

In the years after Christiana, the abolitionist movement surged, fed by the fire of those who refused to be broken. And few stories hit harder than Margaret Garner's.

Her case became one of the most infamous under the Fugitive Slave Act—a haunting example of how the terror of enslavement and the desperation to protect one's family shaped the choices of women on the run.

Peggy had worked as a nursemaid for her enslaver's child and even traveled with the family to Cincinnati in 1840. But in 1849, her owner sold her and her unborn child to his brother. Not long after, Peggy gave birth to two daughters: Mary and Cilla, described by observers as "almost white" and "bright mulatto." While there's no hard proof, many believed her enslaver fathered the children.

What is certain is this: after their births, Peggy made up her mind. Escape was the only way to protect her daughters—and herself.

Her chance came during the brutal winter of 1856.

On the night of January 27, 1856, Peggy, her four children, her common-law husband Robert Garner, and his parents fled neighboring plantations in Richwood, Kentucky. Robert stole his master's sleigh, horses, and a gun.

Reports say there were seventeen people in their group—men, women, and children—all risking everything for just a taste of freedom. That winter, the Ohio River was frozen solid for the first time in over sixty years. The ice gave them their moment.

Just west of Covington, Kentucky, before dawn broke, they stepped onto the frozen river. The wind was cutting. Their breath hung like ghosts in the air. Beneath them, the river creaked and moaned, threatening to swallow them whole. But they didn't stop. Step after terrifying step, they pushed forward until they crossed into Cincinnati—free soil, at least on paper.

Once across, the group split up to avoid capture.

Robert, his father Simon, his mother Mary, Peggy, and her four children made it to the home of Joe Kite, a former slave, who lived along Mill Creek, just south of the city. The rest of the fugitives scattered to other safe houses across Cincinnati. Eventually, many found sanctuary in Canada, ferried north by the fearless conductors of the Underground Railroad.

But Peggy's journey wouldn't end with safety.

Because when the slave catchers finally came for her, what happened inside that house on Mill Creek would shake the nation.

Fearing discovery, Joe Kite reached out to Levi Coffin, the legendary abolitionist known as the "President of the Underground Railroad." Coffin agreed to help. He advised Kite to move the Garners farther west, into a Black community where free families might offer stronger protection. But they were told to wait until nightfall before making another move.

They never got the chance.

While Kite was away, slave catchers and U.S. Marshals tracked the Garners to his home. Moving with military precision, they surrounded the property on all sides. Inside, Robert and Margaret had barricaded the doors. They held their children close, bracing for the worst.

The raid came swift—and violent.

Robert opened fire as the posse stormed the house, striking at least one deputy marshal. But they were heavily outnumbered, and resistance could only last so long.

Then came Margaret's unthinkable act.

Cornered. Trapped. Her babies just moments away from being dragged back into bondage—Margaret Garner made the most harrowing decision a mother could make. She grabbed a blade. In a single, heart-shattering moment, she slit the throat of her two-year-old daughter, killing her instantly. Then she turned the weapon on her other children, wounding them as she tried to take their lives—and her own—rather than allow them to be returned to slavery.

But the posse overpowered her before she could finish what she had begun.

The Garners had traveled sixteen miles through icy wilderness, crossed a frozen river on foot, and trudged several more miles to reach the home of Margaret's family friend, Joe Kite. Robert had already arranged for safe passage north through the Underground Railroad. But their plans were destroyed in an instant.

Margaret's enslaver, Archibald Gaines, along with a federal marshal, reached them before the abolitionists could act.

The entire surviving family was captured.

What followed wasn't just a legal proceeding—it was a national spectacle. A month-long trial that gripped the country and laid bare the brutal contradictions between America's laws and its conscience.

Gaines and the federal government demanded the immediate return of the family as his rightful "property" under the Fugitive Slave Act. But abolitionist attorney John Jolliffe refused to concede. He argued that Margaret must be tried for murder in an Ohio criminal court—a state proceeding that should override federal civil claims.

Why?

Because only a *person* can be tried for murder.

If Margaret could be held accountable for a crime, then she wasn't property. She was a human being. A mother. A woman pushed past the edge of reason by a system designed to crush her soul.

And so, the question before the court—and before the nation— was no longer just about the law.

It was about humanity.

What makes a mother kill her child? What makes a country insist she had no right to choose otherwise? And who, in the end, was truly guilty—Margaret Garner, or the America that left her no other way out?

The case received nonstop coverage from national papers like the *New York Times* and the *New York Tribune*, along with six Cincinnati dailies that Frederick Douglass had followed during his visits to Ohio. Any chance of a murder trial hinged on Ohio Governor Salmon P. Chase's ability to persuade the governor of Kentucky to return Margaret to face those charges in Cincinnati.

The judge deliberated for two weeks, making it the longest and most complex fugitive slave hearing on record—most were resolved in less than a day.

Jolliffe, representing the defense, argued that Ohio's responsibility to protect its citizens should come first. Slave catchers and owners pushed back, claiming that federal law trumped state law. Jolliffe also cited a law stating that enslaved people brought into free states for non-slavery purposes were legally emancipated. He suggested charging Margaret with murder to get the case into state court— then, if needed, the governor could issue a pardon.

The prosecution countered that the Fugitive Slave Law took precedence, and no state law or trial could stand in the way. The courtroom overflowed daily—over a thousand spectators came each day, while five hundred local men were sworn in as deputies just to maintain order in the streets outside.

Presiding over the case was Judge Pendery, who ultimately ruled that federal fugitive warrants took priority. Jolliffe tried one last angle; he argued that the Fugitive Slave Act violated citizens' religious freedom, by forcing them to take part in what they saw as moral wrongdoing. Pendery rejected the claim.

On the trial's final day, abolitionist Lucy Stone took the stand. She defended her conversations with Margaret, which the prosecution had objected to, and addressed the deeper racial and sexual exploitation at the heart of the case. She reminded the court of the faces of Margaret's children … and Archibald Gaines.

"The worn-out faces of those enslaved children show exactly what kind of degradation their mothers endure."

Instead of subjecting her daughter to that life, Margaret chose to end it.

If, in her deep maternal love, she believed the only way to save her child was to send her back to God—who are we to say she didn't have that right?

Margaret Garner was never given a trial for murder. Instead, in one of the most grotesque betrayals of justice in American legal history, she was forced back into bondage—escorted not to a courtroom, but into the hands of the very man who claimed to own her. Alongside Robert and their nine-month-old daughter, she vanished into the nightmare she had fought so desperately to escape.

Though Ohio authorities secured an extradition warrant, they were outmaneuvered at every turn. Her enslaver, Archibald K. Gaines, shuttled her between cities like contraband—Covington, Frankfort, then Louisville. By the time they caught up, Margaret had already been loaded onto a steamboat headed south, bound for his brother's Arkansas plantation.

She was gone.

Margaret Garner disappeared into the belly of the Deep South, devoured by a system that chewed through lives like hers without remorse. Years later, a researcher found Robert Garner. He had survived. But he carried the memory of a woman who had once made an unthinkable decision out of unbearable love. Margaret, he revealed, had died in 1858—cut down by typhoid fever in the valley.

Her final words to him weren't of pain, but of purpose:

"Never marry while in slavery. Hold onto hope for freedom."

And he did.

After emancipation, Robert Garner enlisted in the Union Army. He wore the blue uniform not just as a soldier—but as a widower of resistance. His weapon wasn't just the rifle. It was the memory of a woman who chose death over re-enslavement for her children. His service wasn't just duty.

It was revenge. It was tribute. It was love.

Their story isn't just about slavery. It's about what people will do when the law is unjust, when the chains are too tight, when freedom is close enough to taste but not to touch.

As Solomon Northup once wrote:

"No man who has never been placed in such a situation can comprehend the thousand obstacles thrown in the way of the flying slave ... Every white man's hand is raised against him—the patrollers are watching for him—the hounds are ready to follow on his track ..."

Every handshake could be a betrayal. Every sunrise could be the last one seen in liberty.

The Fugitive Slave Act of 1850 was more than a law; it was a declaration of war against freedom. It deputized white America to become slave catchers. It turned the North into a hunting ground. It punished not just the enslaved, but anyone with the courage to care.

And yet ... slavery didn't end with the Emancipation Proclamation.

It mutated. It put on a new face.

Today, the descendants of those who ran, who fought, who mourned, and who endured, still live beneath systems engineered to contain them: mass incarceration, police brutality, economic exile, educational neglect, voter suppression.

The chains are no longer iron. But they remain.

So, we must ask ourselves ...

If it were 1856 ... would you be the one to run? The one to resist? The one to hide a family in your home? Or the one who looked away and called it "the law"?

Margaret Garner held her child in her arms and chose resistance over obedience. Robert Garner picked up a rifle and marched toward a freedom that cost him everything.

Freedom was never given. It was taken—bloodied, bruised, and burning.

And the fight for it is not over.

While John T. Ward was out here fighting against injustice in Ohio, the United States Supreme Court was busy making decisions that would shake the entire Black community to its core. In 1857, they dropped the Dred Scott decision—a ruling that changed everything for both enslaved and free Black folks across the country.

The heart of it all was Dred Scott, a Black man who had been enslaved but had lived for a time in free states—Illinois and Wisconsin—with his enslaver. He argued that since he had lived in free territory, he should be free. The case made its way all the way up to the Supreme Court, but instead of justice, the court hit him with a 7–2 ruling against him.

That decision crushed the hopes of many enslaved folks who dreamed of reaching free land and gaining their freedom. The ruling sent a chilling message: Black people, free or enslaved, had no rights the white man was bound to respect. It cast a long, dark shadow over everything. Tension was thick. Fear was real. The law said if a Black person escaped slavery, they had to be returned—no matter the circumstance, no matter the morality.

But while the courts were trying to stop progress, not everyone was with that. Some folks—especially in higher education—were taking a stand. Oberlin College, in Northern Ohio, became a real force in the abolitionist movement. Founded in 1833, Oberlin was one of the only schools in the country letting Black students learn right alongside white students. That made it a hub for anti-slavery work and a haven for people running toward freedom.

Even Frederick Douglass recognized Oberlin's value; he sent his daughter, Rosetta, there for her education.

What set Oberlin apart was its commitment to racial equality at a time when racism was the law of the land. Big names like Charles Finney and Asa Mahan were on the faculty, and they didn't just teach; they preached abolition. They pushed for immediate emancipation, not someday, but now.

Oberlin students weren't just in class reading books; they were in the streets, helping folks through the Underground Railroad and debating against pro-slavery voices. The town itself was one of the few truly integrated communities at the time. It had one of the largest known populations of fugitive slaves, and they weren't just hiding, they were building lives.

Still, Black folks in Oberlin weren't exactly welcomed with open arms by everybody. Racism didn't stop at the town line. The white majority in Oberlin held onto their prejudices. Schools, churches, and even public spaces were often segregated. Jobs were hard to come by, and resources weren't shared equally. But despite it all, the Black community in Oberlin kept pushing forward.

They built their own institutions, like the Oberlin-Wellington Rescue League, which wasn't afraid to stand up against slave catchers. These folks risked everything to protect their own and make freedom real. They opened their homes, their churches, and their hearts to help people escape the grip of slavery.

In late August 1858, a slave hunter named Anderson Jennings came up from Kentucky to Oberlin. He linked up with Deputy U.S. Marshal Anson Dayton, who gave him the names and descriptions of a few men believed to be runaway slaves. One of them was John Price. Jennings thought he had spotted Price and sent a letter back to John Bacon, Price's former enslaver and Jennings's neighbor.

"I discovered a nigger near Oberlin answering to the description of your runaway, John," he wrote, asking for permission to bring him in. Bacon handed off power of attorney to a slave catcher named Richard Mitchell, who traveled to Ohio with the necessary paperwork. The two men stayed at a hotel owned by Chauncey Wack, a known pro-slavery Democrat.

Eventually, things started to shift. In 1842, the Ohio Supreme Court ruled that the right to vote could be extended to "all men, nearer white than Black, or of the grade between the mulatto and the white." It wasn't justice, but it cracked open a door.

But Oberlin? Oberlin was different. The town was more inclusive, and there are records suggesting that Black men were voting before it was even technically legal. William Howard Day wrote that William P. Newman was likely the first Black man to vote in Lorain County— and he did it well before the courts said he could.

John Mercer Langston also talked about how Oberlin didn't wait around for permission. If you said you were more than half white, they let you vote. Still, not everybody liked that kind of freedom. People like Chauncey Wack made it their business to keep voting "pure" and white. He was known to watch the polling places like a hawk.

But one day, John Ramsey—a self-emancipated man—showed up to vote. Wack tried to block him. When asked to prove he was white enough, Ramsey didn't flinch. He said, "My father was about as white as Mr. Wack."

The crowd erupted in cheers, and Wack had no choice but to back down. Ramsey cast his vote that day.

That moment didn't just say something about John Ramsey; it said something about Oberlin. Despite the hate and the obstacles, the people, especially Black folks, were fighting for something better. And they weren't backing down.

With the help of federal Deputy U.S. Marshal Jacob Lowe and part-time jailer and deputy sheriff Samuel Davis, a small crew of slave catchers finalized their plan: capture John Price and drag him back into slavery.

John Price had found his way to Oberlin sometime in the mid-1850s. He kept his head down, working quiet jobs on local farms and sometimes leaning on public aid to get by. He lived simply, always looking over his shoulder. For two years, he moved in silence—humble, careful, trying to stay invisible.

But on the morning of September 13, 1858, the trap was sprung.

Price had been tricked into a carriage ride by fourteen-year-old Shakespeare Boynton—a face he trusted. They told him it'd just be a short trip into the countryside. But once they were out of town, Mitchell pulled a pistol on him. Outnumbered and unarmed, Price didn't have much choice. He gave in. Boynton, having done his part, turned the carriage back toward Oberlin to deliver the message to Anderson Jennings: "Mission accomplished."

The whole kidnapping went down smooth and quiet—surgical, like they'd planned. No one in Oberlin saw it coming until it was already done. The slave catchers figured they were acting within the law. What they didn't expect was the storm about to come from a town with a backbone made of justice.

As they rolled toward Wellington, Price sat between his captors in the wagon—scared, silent, and shackled by fear. Nobody told him anything about his rights under the Fugitive Slave Act—because nobody believed he had any.

But fate had other plans.

By chance, the wagon crossed paths with another carriage headed in the opposite direction. John Price took a shot; he yelled out, desperate, hoping somebody would hear. The wagon rolled on like nothing happened, but one of the passengers inside was Ansel Lyman—a white Oberlin student, an abolitionist, and a man who had stood beside John Brown in the bloody fight for freedom in Kansas. Lyman knew what he'd just seen.

He wasted no time. As soon as he got back to Oberlin, he raised the alarm. Word spread like fire in a dry field. Within hours, the streets were alive—coats thrown on, horses saddled, weapons in hand. They weren't going to let John Price be stolen without a fight.

They rode for Wellington.

They came from everywhere—students, preachers, shopkeepers, farmers, lawyers. Black and white. Men and women. Some were peaceful. Some were ready for war. But they were all united by one mission: bringing John Price home.

In that crowd were John Copeland and Lewis Sheridan Leary—two young Black men who didn't just believe in freedom. They were ready to bleed for it. They knew what was at stake, and they didn't hesitate.

This wasn't just a rescue. This was resistance. And it wasn't about one man—it was about all of them.

Meanwhile, the slave catchers—clueless about the storm charging their way—pulled into Wellington and checked into Wadsworth's Hotel. They had hours to kill before the train to Columbus, so they sat down for a meal, unaware that justice was already thundering up the road.

Then something unexpected happened.

Out on the hotel balcony, Anderson Jennings and Price locked eyes—and recognized each other. Turns out, they had once been neighbors back in Mason County, Kentucky. They exchanged tight, uneasy greetings. Later, Jennings would claim that Price seemed happy to be heading back South—but let's be real: it's hard to believe a man in chains had much say in anything.

What happened next caught everybody off guard.

Jennings brought Price outside onto the balcony and let him speak to the growing crowd below. Earlier, Price had tried to play along with his captors, hoping to survive. He told them he'd return quietly. But now, standing over a crowd of fired-up abolitionists, his courage wavered. His voice trembled. "I suppose," he said, "I will have to go back ... Jennings has got the papers for me."

The crowd wasn't having it. Murmurs turned into shouts.

"Jump!"

Then John Copeland stepped forward.

He didn't say a word. He just raised his pistol and aimed it straight at Jennings—not to kill, but to make it clear: we're done asking.

The image of an armed Black man standing tall in defense of another was too much for Jennings. Shook to his core, he snatched Price back inside and slammed the doors shut.

But it was already too late. The people had seen what they needed to see.

What came next would go down in history as the Oberlin-Wellington Rescue—a bold act of defiance in a nation still chained to slavery. It wasn't just a protest. It was a stand. A moment when a town said no more. When the people rose up and chose conscience over compliance. When the law of the land ran headfirst into the law of justice—and justice fought back.

The brothers Charles Langston and John Mercer Langston successfully defended John Price. Both were close friends of John T. Ward, and all three stood shoulder to shoulder in the abolitionist fight.

Charles Langston didn't just speak about freedom; he carried it on his hip. A loaded pistol stayed strapped to his side at all times. His mother had been enslaved, but her relationship with her enslaver turned into an unofficial marriage. His white father, seeing no future for his mixed-race sons in Virginia, made sure they got something rare: a solid education. And even rarer—security. He arranged for Charles and his siblings to be raised in Ohio, where they'd have a real shot at a future, and left them an inheritance to make sure of it.

That upbringing shaped Charles. He grew up knowing—not believing, knowing—that he was equal to any white man. That fire never left him. It pushed him to become one of the most militant abolitionists in Ohio. And that made him a target. The threats came often. But Charles didn't flinch. He kept that pistol ready, but his real weapon was his mind and his voice.

Charles Langston broke barriers. He graduated from Oberlin College and went on to become one of the first Black public officials in the United States, serving as a town clerk and election inspector. He was fierce in his fight for education and opportunity for Black people in America.

His younger brother, John Mercer Langston, followed that same path. Also an Oberlin graduate, John Mercer went on to become a prominent lawyer, abolitionist, and later, the first Black member of Congress from Virginia, elected in 1888.

But before the degrees and political titles, there was the fight in Ohio.

The Langston brothers, along with their comrade John T. Ward, were soldiers in the war for freedom. Their tools? Education, activism—and when it came down to it—force.

What happened next shook the country. The Oberlin-Wellington Rescue wasn't just a bold move; it was a warning shot. A message that Ohio, and those fighting for justice, would not stand by while injustice ruled the law.

John Price's fate was no longer his alone.

In 1858, the struggle for freedom reached a boiling point in
northern Ohio. A young man named John Price, having escaped from
slavery in Kentucky, had been captured by federal marshals under the
Fugitive Slave Act and was held in Wellington, Ohio. Word of his
seizure raced across the abolitionist stronghold of Oberlin, and both
Black and white townspeople mobilized.

Among them was Charles Langston, the elder brother of the
better-known John Mercer Langston. He joined a broad coalition of
rescuers, including John Anthony Copeland Jr., determined not to
stand by as a man was plunged back into bondage.

When the authorities refused to release Price, the rescuers
swarmed the hotel where he was held. They flooded the building,
overcame the marshals, and escorted Price through the frozen night
toward freedom in Canada. The incident triggered national attention,

indictments of thirty-seven rescuers, and became one of the sparks of the coming Civil War.

They didn't ask for permission. They didn't wait on the law—because they knew the law wasn't made to protect men like them. It never had been.

For their actions, Charles Langston and several others were arrested, charged, and put on trial. Standing in front of a court that saw him as less than a man, Langston delivered a statement that still echoes today:

"The law which condemns me, and the judges who sentence me, will yet be overthrown. Your laws will be stricken down, your institutions will crumble, and the principles of justice will rule this land."

He was sentenced to twenty days in jail. But history? History proved him right.

This landmark case in the defense of John Price exposed the raw brutality of the Fugitive Slave Act and sparked widespread outrage against its enforcement. But Oberlin's radicalism ran deeper than courtrooms and legal strategy. Ohio's abolitionists stayed locked in, committed to the fight—not just for freedom, but for dignity, humanity, and justice. Their movement became a beacon of hope and inspiration for communities across the country.

Acts of resistance like the Christiana Riots, the tragedy of Margaret Garner, and the boldness of the Harpers Ferry Raid pushed the truth out of the shadows and into the national spotlight. They didn't just resist; they forced the country to face itself. These moments helped shift public opinion, exposing the horror of slavery and pushing more people toward the cause of abolition. The tension, thick and rising, became too much to contain. It helped set the stage for what would become the American Civil War.

The Fugitive Slave Act of 1850 didn't just strengthen slavery, it amplified it. It legalized violence. It rewarded betrayal. It turned fear into federal policy. Slave catchers roamed the Ohio countryside like wolves with government tags, their pockets heavy with blood money. That law cast a long, dark shadow. It turned neighbors into spies, friends into snitches, and turned freedom into a fragile, flickering hope.

***

Picture this.

A night heavy with silence, thick with pine and damp earth. Somewhere deep in the woods, a mother runs—her baby pressed tight to her chest, her breath shallow, her fear louder than her footsteps. She doesn't dare cry, doesn't dare stop.

Behind her, torches slice through the dark. The hounds are barking. The men are shouting. They weren't searching; they were hunting. And she wasn't a woman to them. She was merchandise.

They didn't care that she had a husband—a man who died under a whip trying to protect her. They didn't care that she had a name. They didn't care that she ran because she was pregnant—after the master's son pulled her into that barn.

They didn't care.

Because Black suffering was their business. And business? It was booming.

Long before John T. Ward risked it all to guide souls to freedom, hunting Black bodies was already a profession. The American economy didn't just depend on plantations; it was built on a whole underground industry of trafficking Black people, a slick, well-oiled machine of misery.

They called it the Reverse Underground Railroad.

It flourished in places like New York, Philadelphia, Cincinnati, and Louisville—places that should've been safe havens for free Black folks. But they weren't. They were hunting grounds.

Men, women, and children were taken in broad daylight—kidnapped from porches, streets, jobs, and churches. Some had bought their freedom. Some were born free. Some had never even seen a plantation. But none of that mattered. Because once they were snatched, they were just product—sold south and erased.

It wasn't a scandal. It wasn't rare. It was business.

Between 1780 and 1865, thousands of free Black people were stolen from the North and sold into slavery. This wasn't the work of a few outlaws. It was a trade, protected and overlooked by the same laws that claimed to protect liberty.

And standing at the center of it all was a name that should drip from history's mouth with the same disgust as Hitler or Bundy.

Her name was Patty Cannon.

History remembers names like Jack the Ripper and H.H. Holmes—but Patty Cannon was worse.

For thirty years, she ran one of the most violent and vicious kidnapping rings in American history. Her gang—fifty to sixty men deep—snatched up Black folks from northern cities and sold them into slavery by the thousands, more than three thousand lives stolen.

But she didn't just traffic people.

She killed them.

In 1829, a tenant farmer plowing a field on her land uncovered a nightmare: the bodies of four Black children buried in shallow graves. That moment shattered the silence around her crimes and exposed her for what she truly was—a butcher hiding behind laws that never saw Black life as sacred.

She was indicted for four murders: an infant girl, killed on April 26, 1822; a young boy, killed on June 1, 1824; an adult man, murdered on October 1, 1820; and another child, murdered the same day as the infant in 1822.

But those were just the bodies they found. Patty Cannon confessed to killing more than two dozen people—including her own husband and one of her children. She once threw a crying baby into a fire just to shut it up. She didn't blink. She didn't flinch.

She locked whole families in chains—hidden in her basement, her attic, even in secret compartments behind false walls. She trafficked free Black men, women, and children like cattle—smuggling them into the Deep South, where they were sold into slavery for profit.

Patty Cannon didn't just run a kidnapping ring. She ran a terror empire.

And yet, her name is barely remembered. While America immortalizes white serial killers—Jack the Ripper, H.H. Holmes, Ted Bundy—how many people even know the name *Patty Cannon?* Her skull sits in the Smithsonian, displayed like a grotesque relic, but the names of her victims—thousands of kidnapped, trafficked, and murdered Black men, women, and children—have been buried beneath the weight of willful forgetting.

Why does history preserve the face of the predator but erase the pain of the prey?

The Fugitive Slave Act of 1850 legalized the kidnapping of Black people under the pretense of justice. It didn't require evidence, just a pointed finger backed by white authority. No courtroom. No witness. No burden of proof. Just an accusation and the assumption of guilt based on skin.

And today?

Nearly one hundred thousand Black women and girls are missing in America. Though we make up just 13 percent of the population, we account for almost 40 percent of all missing persons cases. When we disappear, there are no Amber Alerts, no national manhunts, no breathless headlines on primetime news. There is only silence.

Then, they dragged us from fields, cabins, and alleys—sold us south like livestock—and stamped it legal. Now, we vanish from neighborhoods, from foster care systems, from shelters and schools—and no one blinks.

Then, it was bounty hunters with torches and chains. Today, it's arrest quotas, media neglect, and cold cases collecting dust.

The systems that once hunted us through cotton fields now criminalize our survival on city streets. Slave patrols evolved into police departments. Bounty hunters became prosecutors. Chains became criminal charges.

The language of oppression changed, but the function stayed the same.

The Fugitive Slave Act may have been repealed, but its ghost still signs our warrants.

Back then, federal slave commissioners were paid ten dollars for every Black person they returned to slavery—and only five if they were freed. Truth, in the eyes of the state, was worth half the price of a lie. The system was designed to reward false accusations. It incentivized injustice.

Thousands of free Black people were kidnapped—not because they had escaped slavery, but because they were profitable. Their freedom didn't matter. Their value was in their flesh.

And today?

We're still being stolen. Black bodies still disappear—from our homes, our communities, and our futures.

We are funneled through broken foster care systems, misclassified in law enforcement databases, and dismissed by mainstream media.

The machinery of disappearance has been modernized, but the outcome is the same.

Where once Patty Cannon led a gang of fifty men through northern towns to capture and sell Black people into Southern bondage, today, our names vanish into bureaucratic files, unchecked police violence, and institutions more invested in quotas than in justice.

We are still hunted—just under a different name.

The bounty hunters now wear badges. The whips have become warrants. The overseers have turned into officers.

They don't need shackles and auction blocks anymore; they've got body cams, sentencing enhancements, stop-and-frisk, and facial recognition. They don't need runaway posters; they've got mugshots, clickbait headlines, and cash bail.

America traded the plantation for the prison. It replaced physical chains with legal ones. It converted auction blocks into arraignment benches and courtroom cages.

But the targets? They're still the same.

Black men are hunted during routine traffic stops. Black women are punished for defending their children. Black children are criminalized before they even hit puberty.

The same society that once branded Black people as fugitives now polices us for quotas. The infrastructure of racial control never crumbled; it just rebranded.

The Fugitive Slave Act was never about justice. It was about power, profit, and possession.

And its legacy lives on—in every wrongful conviction, every racial sentencing disparity, every school-to-prison pipeline, and in the faces of missing Black girls whose names never made the news.

So, let's say it plain.

They chased us through cotton. Now they chase us through concrete. They took our names off slave ledgers and entered them into court dockets. They swapped slave ships for squad cars, patrollers for patrolmen, and plantations for prisons.

We were never the threat. We were the evidence of America's guilt—a living indictment of the brutality that built this nation.

Let this chapter be more than a history lesson. Let it be testimony—and warning.

The hunt ain't over. It just changed uniforms. And though it may wear a badge now and carry a clipboard; it's still chasing the same dream: to make Black freedom look like a crime.

But to that, we answer with a clarity forged from centuries of survival—not again, not now, not ever.

Because we're still running—but not from them. We're running toward truth. Toward legacy. Toward justice.

And we will not vanish quietly.

CHAPTER 14

Twelve Deep in the Trenches

"Who would be free themselves must strike the blow ... I urge you to fly to arms and smite to death the power that would bury the Government and your liberty in the same hopeless grave. This is your golden opportunity."

-Frederick Douglass

I was there. I saw it.

Tucked in the back, gripping pint-sized jugs of milk and water like lifelines, I stood ready for the wounded—for the ones whose eyes burned from gas or whose breath had been stolen by the City of Columbus, State of Ohio. I watched from the curb as they cornered the crowd between High Street and Third on East Broad, like wolves herding prey. Horses reared. Sirens wailed. Protesters screamed. Then came the crash. Water bottles flung like grenades at mounted police, and provocateurs baited chaos, startling the horses into panic.

Columbus, Ohio. May 28, 2020. Just forty-eight hours after George Floyd's final breath was pinned beneath Derek Chauvin's knee, the streets of my city erupted—not in chaos, but in fury forged over generations. Protests lit up the Short North, Capitol Square, the South Side—whole blocks choking on smoke and disbelief. Glass shattered. Bodies surged. Downtown was no longer a business district; it was a battleground. Twenty-eight statehouse windows smashed, fires started, and flags burned.

By May 30, curfew wasn't hours anymore, it was indefinite. The Ohio National Guard had their boots on our pavement, and the weight of their presence pressed against the city's very soul. It had been over fifty years since Columbus felt this volatile, this raw, this brutally honest. Not since the uprisings of the sixties had our streets burned with such intensity, with such urgency for change. Columbus police issued a state of emergency order.

Ohio Representative and member of the Congressional Black Caucus, Joyce Beatty—a voice of power and resolve—was pepper-sprayed by police right there in Columbus that Saturday. She stood firm in a protest calling out the vicious cycle of police brutality and demanding justice for those crushed beneath its weight. Beatty wasn't alone. She stood alongside Columbus City Council President Shannon Hardin and my high school classmate Kevin Boyce of the Franklin County Board of Commissioners—each unwavering in their pursuit of truth. And yet, despite their dignity, despite their commitment, the brutality of the system came crashing down—in broad daylight.

I watched peaceful protesters chant and die-in. I watched agitators toss fireworks. I watched police, armored and unmoved, respond to both with equal violence. Tear gas blanketed the sky like smoke from a burning constitution. Rubber bullets, wooden pellets, and flashbangs ricocheted off bodies and buildings. I also remember someone lost their life. I remember thinking …

This is what war looks like when civil unrest comes home.

Later that night, scrolling through my notes for this book, I saw it again—the old scar reopened.

"A Black man has no rights which the white man is bound to respect."

Dred Scott v. Sandford, 1857. That line struck like a whip across centuries, burning fresh into my conscience. It felt like prophecy. It felt like present tense.

And then I remembered—we'd been here before. Long before hashtags. Long before flashbangs. Long before I stood on Broad Street with milk in my hands.

Our story didn't start with George Floyd. Our war didn't start with police batons. My family's bloodline runs straight through this nation's battlefield—and long before I carried jugs of milk, we carried freedom on our backs.

My great-great-great-grandfather, John T. Ward, didn't wield rifles, he wielded routes, crates, and coordination. He supplied Union troops with the same cunning strategies they once used to outsmart slave catchers on the Underground Railroad. Their service was invisible to textbooks, but not to the survival of the Union. What they once did in shadows, they now did in full view of a nation still undecided about their humanity and freedom.

And yet, when the war was won, very few in the Ward family enlisted again. Maybe the burden of saving a country that never claimed them was too much. Maybe freedom, once earned, became too sacred to risk again.

But the fight didn't die. It simply evolved.

I heard it in the soft, deliberate footsteps of my Uncle Lot Carter—a Lieutenant Colonel at Wright-Patterson Air Force Base, a soldier cloaked in honor, yet moving through halls still shadowed by unspoken prejudice. In 1988, the United States Air Force munitions community named its newest Munitions Training Center auditorium in his memory—the Lt. Col. Lott S. Carter Auditorium, located at the Air Force Combat Ammunition Center (AFCOMAC) at Sierra Army Depot in Herlong, California. The dedication ceremony was held on August 23, 1988—a quiet but mighty gesture to a man who gave everything without ever demanding recognition.

I saw it in the weary, proud eyes of my Uncle Melvin T. "Red" Jackson, one of the legendary Tuskegee Airmen. He flew beneath skies heavy with promise—and racism. Policed by Jim Crow laws on the ground yet ordered to fight for freedom, he still wasn't fully afforded.

He once whispered to me about being forced to shoot at civilians during World War II. His voice cracked—not from guilt, but from the horror of being weaponized by a nation that still saw him as less.

And yet, he stood tall at President Obama's inauguration, his frame wrapped in awe and history. In that moment, something sacred returned to him. But after his death, that fragile progress was again betrayed when the Trump administration attempted to erase the Tuskegee Airmen's history from Air Force training programs. Honor, it seemed, remained conditional.

And then there's my Uncle Ascari Tshaka (Harold E. Ward)—named after his father, a man of quiet strength and relentless duty. He served in the U.S. Army as a Green Beret, never asking for applause. His service was carved in silence, his sacrifice etched in humility. Today, his legacy continues through his grandson, Keith McDaniel, who walks the same path—with the same silent dignity.

And finally, my father.

James Ward—"Che" to most—named after his uncles James and Eldon Ward. The man whose words cut like sabers, he stood up for civil rights, gun ownership, and rejected the Vietnam draft with a voice that could shatter illusion.

"There is no place for a Black man in the United States Army."

He didn't spit hatred; he spoke heartbreak. A scholar of revolution, he joined the Black Panther Party, armed not just with weapons, but with knowledge, strategy, and an unshakable belief in liberation. He took to the streets with purpose, organizing alongside others who burned with the same fire. The scent of incense wafted through the air, curling around voices that plotted justice, each word landing like a step in a sacred dance of defiance. That smoke—thick, spiritual, and unyielding—still lingers in my spirit, a reminder of the world I was born into and the resilience I was raised to carry. Strength wasn't just taught to me; it was performed, passed down like a rhythm, flowing in every breath, every motion, every whispered truth.

And now, in the stillness that follows the storm—after pepper spray baptized the sidewalks and mounted officers trampled our peace—I sit and feel the weight of history in my bones. My body carries the memory of every American war, even the ones that refused to carry me. This story isn't just about the Civil War; it's about all of our wars. The cannon blasts of 1861. The air raid sirens of World War II. The hiss of tear gas in Capitol Square. The steady, defiant exhale of my father, daring to dream of Black freedom on American soil.

We fought in every war—even when the war was against us. We served a nation that didn't serve us back. And still, we rose.

That is our inheritance—not just of soldiers, but of resistance. Not just of service, but of survival. Not just of pain, but of power.

We weren't just fighting for freedom; we *were* the freedom. And we still are.

They had seen it coming. Long before Fort Sumter, long before Lincoln's election, before the first musket flashed in anger—the free Black delegates of the Colored Conventions Movement already knew. They read the skies like sailors smell a shift in the wind. To them, war wasn't a shock. It was a certainty.

By the 1850s, these men—teachers, preachers, barbers, businessmen—had spent decades studying America's moral ledger. They knew the debt of slavery would come due.

They gathered in city halls and church basements from Ohio to Pennsylvania, their voices echoing off stone walls and into the future. In the minutes of those conventions—carefully recorded and passed hand to hand like sacred scripture—we see not just anger, but foresight. Their words carry the weight of men who understood the inner machinery of a nation breaking under its own hypocrisy.

They saw the war as the logical result of federal betrayal. The Fugitive Slave Act of 1850 deputized every white citizen as a slave catcher and turned the North into a hunting ground. The Dred Scott decision of 1857 stripped every Black person—free or enslaved—of citizenship, ruling that they had "no rights which the white man was bound to respect." The law didn't fail them by accident. It was designed to.

"Slavery must die, or the Republic must die. There is no middle ground," warned John Mercer Langston, and every delegate understood what he meant. To keep tolerating slavery was to accept national suicide.

They watched the Southern elite twist the constitution into a weapon—a charter for enslavement instead of freedom—while the North, too often complicit, chased profit and political peace. Every time a new territory opened to slavery—through the Missouri Compromise, the Kansas-Nebraska Act, or the expansionist dreams of Southern planters—these men read it for what it was: a declaration of war on Black life, Black labor, and Black futures.

Many were deeply religious, and their faith bled into prophecy. In sermons and convention speeches, they didn't hesitate to say it plain: the Civil War would be God's judgment on a blood-soaked land.

"The Lord is making the nation answer for the blood it has spilled," one delegate thundered in 1859, and the room shook—not from fear, but from conviction.

They understood what white America refused to admit. This wasn't just a political crisis; it was a collision of systems. The North's free labor model and the South's slave-based empire could not coexist. The tension was economic as much as moral. Slavery wasn't just a Southern tradition; it was a capitalist machine, and Black men in those conventions knew it. They warned that even if slavery was abolished, its ghost would linger—showing up as Black Codes, sharecropping, chain gangs, and convict leasing. Freedom, they insisted, wouldn't come cheap or all at once.

At the 1855 National Colored Convention in Philadelphia, one delegate gave voice to the dread they all felt:

"The signs of the times are plain. A storm is gathering on the horizon of this Republic—not born from the clouds, but conjured by the hands of slaveholders and their northern accomplices. We did not summon this tempest, but we see it coming. The South, drunk with power, seeks not only to chain our brethren in cotton fields but to bend the constitution itself into a yoke … If slavery lives, the Union must die. If liberty lives, slavery must perish. There is no middle ground."

These words weren't hyperbole. They were a forecast.

By the time the first cannon boomed over Charleston Harbor, the delegates had already spoken their truth. They knew this nation was built on contradiction—and that contradiction would catch flame. Freedom wasn't going to be handed over; it had to be wrestled from the throat of a system that learned to breathe through violence.

They didn't cheer for war. But they didn't fear it either. Because in their eyes, the Civil War wasn't the start of the fight; it was the long-delayed answer to generations of stolen breath.

And in Columbus, Ohio, on the heels of these national storms, a new generation of delegates gathered to carry the warning forward. John T. Ward—farmer, abolitionist, Underground Railroad conductor—stood shoulder to shoulder with men like Charles H. Langston, John Mercer Langston, David Jenkins, and James Poindexter, drafting resolutions not just for survival, but for strategy.

They weren't just reacting to war; they were preparing for the world after it.

Their pens moved like soldiers marching. Their words struck like iron on stone. They knew what the war would cost, but they also knew what had to come next: power, land, education, legacy. They saw the future bleeding through the cracks of the present—and they dared to shape it.

In their unity, they formed not just resistance, but a blueprint. And their prophecy—once dismissed—would become history.

***

Growing up wasn't easy for Moses Dickson. Born in Cincinnati, Ohio, on April 5, 1824, he lost both his parents by the time he was just fourteen. That early loss shaped a childhood full of struggle. As a young man, he trained as a barber and then spent three years traveling the South on steamships, working as an itinerant barber. Those journeys opened his eyes to the brutal reality of slavery—and lit a fire in him. He became an abolitionist, soldier, minister, and eventually the founder of the Knights of Liberty, an anti-slavery group dedicated to helping the enslaved escape through the Underground Railroad.

In 1846, twelve visionary Black men—including this freedom fighter, Dickson—gathered in secret in St. Louis, Missouri, to form a covert resistance known as the Order of Twelve, later called the Knights of Liberty. Born in the heart of a slave state, this underground organization operated with strict secrecy and one clear mission: to abolish slavery in the United States through coordinated rebellion.

Their plan was bold and daring. Over the next decade, they aimed to organize, arm, and train enslaved people across the South, preparing for a massive, synchronized uprising. This blueprint for freedom wasn't built on wishful thinking; it was rooted in military strategy, discipline, and unshakable courage.

Within a few short years, the Order of Twelve grew fast, reportedly swelling to over forty-two thousand members—Black men ready to fight for liberation—spanning nearly every Southern state except Texas and Mississippi, where repression hit hardest. These men met in secret—swamps, barns, church and basements—training for a war they knew might cost them everything.

By July 1857, they were ready to march—led by Dickson, part preacher, part general, all resolve. Every word he spoke carried unwavering determination and a clear sense of purpose.

He gave orders that sounded less like military commands and more like moral law: "Spare women and children. Treat prisoners with humanity. Confiscate ammunition, not lives. We are not vengeance. We are justice."

Dickson believed a higher power was guiding them. He instructed the Knights of Liberty to hold their ground, stay patient, and keep their ranks tight. "Trust the Lord," he said, "and don't break formation."

Instead of open rebellion, the Knights focused their efforts on the Underground Railroad—using their network to help enslaved people escape. Some of the Railroad's most surprising supporters were slave owners who inherited people but treated them well enough that those people had no desire to run. One such ally was General Cassius Clay of Kentucky, who donated one thousand dollars to the cause.

Though their planned uprising never came to pass, the Order of Twelve stands as proof of a powerful, often erased history: Black folks weren't waiting to be set free, they were plotting their own liberation.

By 1860, the winds of war hadn't yet swept across the South, but a financial earthquake was already shaking the ground. Slaveholders who once felt secure in their wealth saw the value of their "property" plummet—like termite-infested mansions collapsing underfoot. What had long been considered an "asset class" of flesh and blood began to lose value—not because of drought or disease, but because abolition was closing in, inevitable.

From 1820 to 1858, the price of enslaved people soared, fueled by the booming internal slave trade and cotton production. A skilled male laborer could go for as much as one thousand six hundred dollars—that was more than the cost of a small home. An unskilled man averaged about one thousand two hundred dollars. And young women with lighter skin—seen as both labor and sexual commodity—were often sold for one thousand dollars or more. These prices rose right alongside Southern power.

Enslaved people weren't just property; they were collateral.

Slaveholders used them to get loans, expand plantations, and build wealth. A plantation owner with fifty enslaved people could walk into a Southern bank and secure thousands in credit, putting human lives on paper like hogs or land deeds. Loan officers, investors, and insurers were all part of the same brutal system.

But as war loomed closer, uncertainty grew. Banks in Charleston, Natchez, New Orleans tightened credit. Northern investors, sensing the shift, pulled their money out. By 1860, the value of enslaved people started to fall.

Then the winds changed.

Abolitionists raised their voices louder—through pulpits, pamphlets, and printing presses. Runaways grew bolder, slipping through the night like shadows on a mission. And then John Brown picked up a rifle—the South could feel the air shift.

Suddenly, bankers squinted suspiciously. Investors in Boston turned cold, tightening their grip on capital. Premiums on "slave insurance" shot up—if you could even find a company still willing to write the policy. Credit dried up. Portfolios began to shrink. The Southern economy, once inflated on human misery, now trembled under its own fragility.

Before the thunder of war rolled across the nation, a different kind of fire was sparked—in the shadows—not in government halls or battlefields, but in barns, boarding houses, and secret parlors where ordinary folks plotted the extraordinary: the end of American slavery.

The plan was simple in theory, impossible in practice—a unified uprising across the South, set to rip slavery out by its roots in one synchronized, thunderous blow. They were close. The war drums were still distant—but beating.

Then came the complication.

And the reckoning.

John Brown.

Already a legend in abolitionist circles, Brown didn't move with caution or coordination. He moved with scripture. A man baptized in prophecy, he believed freedom couldn't wait. "Blood," he said, "was the only language tyrants understood."

He met with Moses Dickson in Davenport.

What passed between them wasn't just a conversation, it was a collision of destiny and discipline. Dickson, ever the strategist, laid it out.

"We need more men," he warned. "The time is close—but not now. Strike too soon, and it becomes a funeral. Wait—we win."

But Brown wouldn't be moved. He didn't see delay; he saw disobedience. The moment was sacred, a divine summons. God was calling.

John Brown—radical, resolute, already etched deep into the nation's conscience—was preparing to strike at the heart of the slaveholding South. His plan was nothing short of revolutionary: seize the federal arsenal at Harpers Ferry, arm the enslaved, and ignite an uprising sweeping from Virginia to Tennessee to Alabama, liberating men and women as they marched—a rolling revolution in motion. He aimed to recruit hundreds—thousands—and sent agents into plantations whispering promises of freedom.

Among those he reached out to were two titans of the movement: Harriet Tubman and Frederick Douglass.

Tubman supported Brown's cause, consulted with him, and may have helped with background organizing and escape efforts—but illness kept her from direct involvement in the Harpers Ferry raid. Frederick Douglass met Brown in Chambersburg, Pennsylvania, accompanied by Shields Green, a formerly enslaved man from Charleston, South Carolina. Douglass declined to join the raid, calling it a suicide mission. But Green stayed, reportedly saying, "I believe I'll go with the old man."

John Anthony Copeland Jr. and Lewis Sheridan Leary—both free Black men from Oberlin, Ohio—also joined Brown's raid. Copeland was a student, and Leary a harness maker. Both were in their early to mid-twenties and fully aware of the risks they took.

In those final days before the Civil War, the lines between rebellion and righteousness blurred. For those who had endured too long in bondage, there was no more time. The hour was late. The stakes were life or death.

After Brown met with Douglass and laid out his plan, Douglass tried to talk him out of it, warning, "It is a perfect steel trap, and those who enter will not get out alive." He knew martyrdom when he saw it—and knew Brown would pay the price.

Douglass left. Brown went forward.

Driven by visions of liberation and prophecy, Brown pressed on, backed by a circle of radical abolitionists who believed speeches had run their course. Action was the only path left.

David J. Gue, a Quaker from Springdale, Iowa, once opened his home to John Brown. But when Gue caught wind of Brown's plan to seize a federal arsenal, his conscience stirred uneasy. Troubled by the looming violence, Gue wrote to Secretary of War John B. Floyd, warning that a group of armed men—though he never named Brown directly—was preparing for a raid. It was a veiled alarm, but an alarm, nonetheless.

Floyd ignored it.

Now, history will say Gue wasn't a "snitch" in the way that word suggests betrayal. Scholars often paint him as a pacifist, not a pro-slavery traitor. But when it comes to American slavery, neutrality was never neutral. Pacifism in the face of chains wasn't virtue; it was complicity. To call for peace while millions were shackled was to side with the status quo. Silence wasn't just passive; it was participation. Every time someone said "wait," a whip cracked. Every time someone urged "moderation," a child was sold. Every time someone claimed it weighed heavy on their conscience, an enslaved woman was raped. In a nation where Black bodies were bought and bred, to refuse confrontation was to accept the auction block. Slavery thrived not just on violence, but on the quiet approval of comfort. So no, you could not be both anti-slavery and unwilling to fight it. In the brutal economy of oppression, peace was a privilege, and pacifism was a mask worn by those who feared disruption more than they hated injustice.

Whether out of disbelief or bureaucratic indifference, the letter was dismissed. The U.S. government had an early warning—and chose to do nothing.

Meanwhile, Brown's plan, bold as it was, depended on silence. But too many people knew. He had trusted a wide circle—radical abolitionists, fugitives, and local allies—some of whom grew nervous. Whispers began leaking through anti-slavery networks. Even slaveholders started catching rumors of a strange northern plot.

In Maryland and Virginia, eyes grew sharp. Long before Jim Crow, there were *"Karen Crows"*—sharp-tongued sentinels of the dominant society, always watching, always suspicious. They took note of unfamiliar white and Black men drifting through the countryside, asking too many questions about roads, rivers, and railways. Some were spotted buying weapons. Others lingered near Harpers Ferry, scouting the terrain. Whispers turned into warnings. The air thickened with unease.

Brown had quietly rented a farmhouse five miles outside town under the alias "Isaac Smith." But nothing stayed hidden for long.

Crates arrived—heavy, secretive, frequent. Inside were guns, pikes, and ammunition.

Too many strangers came and went. Too many stories didn't line up.

Then came the final crack in secrecy: a man fled the farmhouse and revealed what some already suspected. "Isaac Smith" wasn't Smith at all. He was John Brown.

And with that, suspicion ignited like dry kindling. The trap was set. The storm was coming.

On October 16, 1859, the raid began.

Chaos erupted at Harpers Ferry. Smoke filled the air. Federal troops descended. Brown and his men were quickly overwhelmed—outgunned, outnumbered, surrounded. Among them were Shields Green, John Copeland, and Lewis Leary, young Black abolitionists from Ohio. They fought with staggering bravery, calm in chaos, resolute to the end.

Tragically, Leary was killed during the raid, while Copeland and Green were captured, tried, and executed on December 16, 1859. Their courage and sacrifice live on, commemorated by a monument in Oberlin, honoring their commitment to the fight against slavery.

Brown was taken alive—bloodied, bound, but unbroken.

And in his coat pocket, authorities found something unexpected, a letter, signed by a mysterious benefactor.

Her name was Mary Ellen Pleasant.

History often buries its most brilliant players. Pleasant was one of them. Born into slavery, she became one of the wealthiest and most powerful women in San Francisco. But her fortune was not built on silence, it was built on resistance. She had given John Brown thirty thousand dollars to fund the insurrection—an astronomical sum, especially for a Black woman in antebellum America.

Pleasant was more than a financier. She was a conductor on the Underground Railroad, expanding its reach all the way to California during the gold rush. She passed as white—a *passe blanc*, as the Creoles called it—and used her perceived privilege as a weapon. In courtrooms, in boardrooms, brothels, and in banks, she fought for freedom where others saw only survival.

When a streetcar conductor denied her passage, she sued. The California Supreme Court would later rule segregation illegal—but her damages were reversed. Still, she never stopped pressing forward.

She married James Smith, a wealthy white-passing plantation owner who had freed his slaves. Together, they used their fortune to fund escapes through the West. When she died, her tombstone read only:

"She was a friend of John Brown's."

That friendship—like the legacy of Tubman, Douglass, Shields Green, Copeland, and Leary—was more than solidarity. It was a blueprint. It was the spark that lit the fuse.

Leary was mortally wounded during the raid and died from his injuries on October 20, 1859—just days after the fighting ended. His body was first buried in a common grave but later exhumed and reburied in Oberlin, Ohio, where he had lived. His widow, Mary Leary, and their daughter moved back to Oberlin, and the community honored his remains. That reburial became a powerful act of reclamation—a community giving dignity to one of its fallen sons.

Copeland was captured alive, tried, and executed by hanging on December 16, 1859, in Charlestown, Virginia (now West Virginia). Despite his family's request to reclaim his body for a proper burial in Oberlin, Virginia authorities refused to release it.

Instead, his body was handed over to local medical students for dissection—a cruel and dehumanizing practice often inflicted on Black bodies at the time.

This was a final act of defilement, meant not only to punish but to erase—to strip away even the dignity of death.

Like Copeland, Green was executed by hanging on December 16, 1859, alongside him. And like Copeland, his body was never returned to his family. It was reportedly used for anatomical dissection by medical students at a nearby college. Shields Green, who had stood beside Frederick Douglass and chose to follow Brown into the fire, was denied even the peace of a grave.

The treatment of their bodies tells its own story: a society not content with silencing rebellion but determined to desecrate it. In life, these men had defied the system. In death, the system tried to make them vanish—through spectacle, through dismemberment, through silence.

But it failed.

Today, memorials stand in Oberlin, Ohio, honoring Leary, Copeland, and Green. Their names are carved into history—not as traitors, but as freedom fighters. It's worth mentioning that Charles Langston, a close friend of Lewis Leary, later married Leary's widow after the Civil War. This personal connection deepens the significance of Langston's legacy, linking him to another key figure in the abolitionist movement. Leary, a courageous abolitionist himself, was one of the men who helped rescue John Price from the Oberlin jail. This daring act of defiance against slavery was one of many that marked Langston's lifelong commitment to the freedom and dignity of Black people. The friendship between Langston and Leary—and Langston's later marriage to Leary's widow—speaks to the bonds forged in the crucible of the struggle for justice. These personal connections serve as a powerful reminder that activism often happens not just through grand gestures, but through the relationships and alliances that sustain the fight for freedom.

When the smoke cleared at Harpers Ferry, the scene was grim. Many of John Brown's men—Black and white alike—lay dead. Others, including several young Black men who had followed him with courage beyond their years, were captured, tried, and sentenced. John Brown himself, wounded in battle, was shackled and condemned to death for treason, murder, and inciting slave insurrection.

The news spread like wildfire—not by rumor, but by telegraph. The newly connected wires of American communication carried the story through taverns in New York, drawing rooms in Philadelphia, and cotton plantations deep in the South. Within hours, every American knew his name. And every enslaver understood the deeper truth: war had already begun in the hearts of men.

On the cold morning of December 2, 1859, a crowd gathered in Charles Town, Virginia, to watch the execution. Among them stood a young actor from Maryland—John Wilkes Booth. History confirms that Booth, already a fiery supporter of slavery, had traveled to Charles Town just to witness the hanging. He even volunteered to stand guard during the execution and later spoke with admiration for Brown's calm and composure.

Brown was led to the gallows in a wagon, seated on his own coffin. When asked for final words, he handed a guard a slip of paper. On it, he had written:

"I, John Brown, am now quite certain that the crimes of this guilty land will never be purged away but with blood."

He refused to make a public speech. Instead, he looked upward—unafraid.

Brown did not flinch.

Booth never forgot that stare.

And years later, in Ford's Theatre, he returned the gesture—with a pistol aimed at Abraham Lincoln's head.

As for Brown's body: after the execution, his remains were placed in a simple coffin and escorted with dignity to North Elba, New York. His wife, Mary, brought him home. He was buried at the family farm beneath the Adirondacks, where he had once sheltered freedom seekers. A rough stone marks his grave—a monument not to defeat, but to conviction.

Brown's capture. Douglass's warning. The raid. The tip-off. The letter. The hanging. The burial.

These were not just events. They were omens.

The ground had already shifted. The fuse was lit. And freedom—once whispered in prayer meetings, in coded spirituals, in swamps and cellar shadows—was now screaming through the nation's conscience.

John Brown's raid didn't officially start the Civil War. But it lit the match.

This wasn't just a failed insurrection. It was a rupture.

In Southern drawing rooms, white men locked their doors and loaded their rifles. In northern churches, abolitionists invoked Brown's name like sacred text. And on the plantations, enslaved people whispered his story—the man who came to set them free and died trying. The government tried to bury him. But Brown had already become more than a man. He was a signal fire burning through the illusion that peace and slavery could share the same soil.

Long before the first cannon thundered at Fort Sumter, the war had already begun—not on a battlefield, but in the hearts of men with nothing left to lose.

Brown had hoped the enslaved would rise and join him. Though the uprising didn't happen, the South trembled at how close it had come. To slaveholders, Harpers Ferry was confirmation of their worst fears.

Abolitionists weren't just preaching; they were preparing for war.

And the federal government couldn't—or wouldn't—protect them from rebellion.

Panic gripped the South. Militias formed overnight. Whispers turned into secessionist roars. Even moderates began to harden, their trust in the Union dissolving. For decades, fragile compromises had kept the nation barely stitched together—the Missouri Compromise, the Compromise of 1850—balancing slavery and freedom like a powder keg atop a flickering candle.

But Brown's raid blew the candle out.

There could be no middle ground on slavery.

It became clear: some were ready to bleed for freedom. Others were prepared to kill to keep their chains.

Brown's execution only deepened the divide. Solemn, prophetic, and unflinching, he met death with words that shook the soul of the nation:

"I am quite certain that the crimes of this guilty land will never be purged away but with blood."

That sentence echoed like a cannon blast. Even those who condemned his methods could no longer pretend compromise was justice. The line had been drawn.

Thanks to the telegraph, abolitionist presses, and the power of mass communication, Harpers Ferry became the first anti-slavery rebellion to resonate nationwide in near real-time. It pierced parlors, pulpits, and plantations alike.

And it forced a reckoning.

Slavery would not be voted away.

It would not be reasoned out of existence.

For Black and white, North and South, enslaved and free—Harpers Ferry marked a point of no return.

The country now faced a choice …

Fight for slavery.

Or fight for freedom.

There was no longer a safe middle.

Only sides.

Freedom, once demanded, would never again whisper.

By the year 1860, America was already breaking—fractured not just by geography or politics, but by a deeper, more dangerous fault line: the very definition of freedom.

To many white Americans, freedom meant owning one's labor, carving a future from the sweat of independence. But for the Southern elite, liberty meant something far darker: the right to own laborers—to turn human beings into flesh-and-blood capital. This ideology, wrapped in legal codes and economic ambition, had shackled generations and now threatened to rip the nation in two.

For freedmen, however, especially those who'd felt the bite of the iron collar—freedom was no abstraction. It was not theoretical or debatable. It was survival. And it was elusive. Because to them, the line between "slave" and "free" soil was often just a lie printed on a map.

Even in so-called free states, racism bled beneath the surface like a hidden spring. The Ohio River may have marked the boundary between slavery and freedom on paper, but on both sides, Black people understood the truth: liberty wore a different mask depending on where you stood—but it always stared with the same cold eyes.

In Pittsylvania County, Virginia, where John T. Ward was born, the numbers whispered the scale of the nightmare: 14,340 enslaved souls. They weren't protected by loyalty, citizenship, or law. They were held in bondage by force, by ownership, by the barrel of a gun and the crack of a whip.

But even across the river, fugitives and freedmen testified to the same danger—lynching mobs, bounty hunters, and Black Codes shadowed every step. The South was a prison, yes, but the North was no promised land.

As the final months of 1860 unspooled, so too did the threadbare seams of the nation. It wasn't a question of *IF* war would come—but when. Even the atmosphere began to shift.

Rumors ignited like dry kindling. From courthouse squares to mountain trails, from river ports to tobacco fields, the country buzzed with dread. The wind carried whispers of secession, of Lincoln's rise, of John Brown's ghost.

In the shadow of Short Hill and the Blue Ridge Mountains, three Civil Guard units were quietly dispatched to monitor crossings along the Potomac River. Their orders: watch the trails, record the movements, and brace for fire.

In Leesburg, Virginia, the chill of winter didn't stop the town from hosting a military fair—part parade, part rally, part warning. Cannons gleamed like trophies of a war not yet declared. Bands played. Flags flew. Beneath the pageantry was a deep unease. Everyone felt it. No one said it.

It was a theatrical preview of what was to come—devastation dressed in patriotism.

By the time the first cannon boomed over Fort Sumter, the truth had already been written into the sky, into the soil, into the bloodstream of the enslaved and the free.

This war had never been about borders. It had always been about power.

And now, the reckoning could no longer be delayed.

While Virginia tensed along its ridgelines, and Leesburg's military fairs blurred into marching drills and whispered oaths, just across the Ohio River, another front was already in motion—a quiet war waged not with rifles, but with routes.

John T. Ward had been watching.

He'd seen the flickers of what was coming—the borderland anxiety, the riflemen shadowing Potomac fords, the quiet mustering of militias in towns like Leesburg. But he had no illusions. The South wasn't merely preparing for battle; it was preparing to preserve an empire built on chains. And that meant Ohio was about to become something it had never fully claimed to be, a bastion of freedom, or a final line of hypocrisy.

John T. knew the "free soil" of Ohio was often more theory than truth. Though legally outside the reach of slave codes, Black Ohioans still moved through a maze of surveillance, legal traps, and white indifference. And yet, when the winds shifted—when war whispered through the hollows of Appalachia and danced across the Kentucky border—Ohio would find itself holding two weapons it had never fully wielded: geography, and men like John T. Ward.

Born in Pittsylvania County, Virginia, John T. had escaped the fate that bound fourteen thousand of his neighbors. He crossed into Ohio not just with hope, but with a mission. He became a carpenter by trade, but a conductor by conviction. And in the years leading up to the war, he transformed Columbus into a critical node on the Underground Railroad. He mapped every safe house, memorized every sympathetic merchant, and measured every sheriff's leanings like a man reading wind before a storm.

Where others guessed, John T. calculated. Every route, every risk, he turned survival into science, escape into strategy.

By 1860, as rumors of war turned to strategy, John T.'s network of escapees, allies, and abolitionist freight wagons became something else entirely: a logistic prototype for what the Union would desperately need.

When Confederate sympathizers tightened control of Southern railways and riverways, the Union turned north—for roads, for horses, for men who knew how to move unseen. Ohio would become a Union stronghold not because of politics alone, but because men like John T. already knew how to outrun danger in the dark.

Where Southern planters moved cotton, John T. moved freedom.

Where Leesburg's volunteers drilled in public, John T.'s conductors drilled in silence—practicing how to vanish, how to cloak messages in prayer books and safe codes, how to turn a candlelight in a window into a lifeline.

He would soon be called on not just to hide fugitives—but to feed armies, move munitions, and keep Union posts like Camp Chase from collapsing under winter and disease. But for now, on the eve of war, John T. Ward stood in the liminal space between two nations, one crumbling, the other still unsure of its soul.

And as the South fortified its borders, John T. Ward was already fortifying something greater: the infrastructure of liberation.

Because before he ever transported a rifle or a barrel of flour for the Union, he had already transported hope.

One wagon. One child. One route at a time.

If you broke down a Southern planter's wealth in 1860 like you might analyze a modern investment portfolio, the picture would be chillingly clear. First, there was land—fixed, immovable, and illiquid. It couldn't be sold quickly in a crisis, and it sure as hell couldn't run. Then came cotton—volatile and shaky. It was tied to international markets, and prices were already starting to slip. British buyers, sensing the moral tide turning, began distancing themselves from slavery-tainted exports. And then—most importantly—there were enslaved people: once the Crown jewel of Southern finance, now a depreciating asset the moment freedom entered the national conversation. Their very humanity, long denied, had started to haunt those ledgers.

By 1860, if a Southern planter walked into a bank clutching the names and ages of those he claimed to own and asked for a loan, the banker's response was slower—and sharper. No longer did he see profit; he saw risk. He saw the Union Army mobilizing. He saw Harriet Tubman moving through the shadows. He saw rebellion instead of revenue.

The loan-to-value ratio—that sacred number Southern economy rested on—had flipped overnight. Human beings were no longer stable collateral. They could escape. They could resist. They could be freed by the stroke of a federal pen.

The South was sitting on a high-risk debt bubble made of shackles, paper promises, and pure delusion—and abolition was the pin.

And that—that's what truly scared them.

This wasn't just moral panic. It was a financial crisis unfolding in slow motion. Every enslaved man who ran didn't just defy his captor—he erased a line on a balance sheet. Every speech by Frederick Douglass didn't just stir conscience—it shook investor confidence. Every step toward emancipation was a calculated devaluation of a violent, inherited empire.

So, when the South exploded after John Brown's raid—or at Lincoln's election—their rage wasn't just ideology. It was survival instinct, rooted in collapsing credit, crumbling value, and a world falling apart. Because if slavery died, so would their bank accounts. Their land values. Their grip on society. Their whole damn world.

And to them, that wasn't liberation.

It was theft.

But let's not lie—it was never theirs to steal.

This was not theft.

It was justice—long overdue.

It was the market correcting itself after 246 years of brutal inflation.

And make no mistake—it was only just beginning.

Meanwhile, free Black folks watched in tense silence, caught between two broken promises: liberty denied, loyalty unrewarded. For five long years—from Fort Sumter to Appomattox—they waited, worked, and watched as bullets rewrote the boundaries of their bodies and futures.

And the war itself ... the war was hell, not the glory-filled, trumpet-blaring story spun by papers and songs—but a brutal crucible of disease, broken bodies, amputated futures, and haunted minds. The battlefields soaked with more than blood; they were littered with contradictions' cost.

And still, from that fire rose the Black soldier.

It took Frederick Douglass's voice, thundering from pulpits and presses, to push President Lincoln to lift the veil of hypocrisy and let Black men fight—not as property, but as patriots. That changed history's course.

But not every battle started at the front.

On September 5, 1862, just three days after forced detention, seven hundred Black men stood tall and reported for duty—willingly, proudly, and with purpose.

They became the Black Brigade of Cincinnati.

For fifteen relentless days, these men labored without weapons, pay, or protection. They felled forests, dug trenches, built rifle pits and magazines, carving defenses into Northern Kentucky's hills under brutal conditions. Their hands blistered. Their backs ached. But they kept digging.

They fortified the earth that would hold back the Confederate advance.

One was Powhatan Beaty, whose name would be etched into Union memory. But he was one of many—builders, masons, teamsters, blacksmiths—engineers of resistance whose work never made headlines but literally saved a city.

They worked ahead of the Union lines, vulnerable and exposed. No rifles. No command. Just spades—and the conviction that freedom had to be built before it could be defended.

Their labor changed everything.

Even General Lew Wallace, no abolitionist himself, was forced to admit:

"When the history of Cincinnati during the past two weeks comes to be written up, it will be said that it was the spades and not the guns that saved the city from attack by the Rebels."

He may have meant the tools.

But we know the truth.

It wasn't the spades.

It was the hands that held them.

Those Black men, once dragged like cattle through the streets, turned their oppression into an act of defiance. They didn't just build fortifications; they built their own legacy. And though history tried to bury their names beneath the boots of white soldiers, the truth remains: Black labor saved Cincinnati. Black resilience fortified the Union. And Black hands held the line when no one else would.

And so, in the heart of a nation unraveling, it was again Black hands that held the line—hands once bound in iron, now forced to build the very republic that had cast them aside. The war did not free them. They freed themselves—day by day, trench by trench, prophecy by blood.

By the time Black men were finally allowed to bear arms for the Union, the war had already devoured years, cities, and lives. It wasn't mercy or moral clarity that opened the ranks to them; it was a necessity. The Union was bleeding, and the generals could no longer ignore what abolitionists had been screaming for decades: Black men weren't just laborers. They were soldiers, patriots, and the power that once helped America gain its liberty and independence.

In 1863, Ohio became one of the first states to heed that call. Governor David Tod, pressed by mounting losses and shifting tides, authorized the formation of a Black regiment. On June 17, a determined group of men—including Beaty and his squad—stood in Delaware, Ohio, becoming the first enlisted soldiers of the 127th Ohio Volunteer Infantry, later reclassified as the 5th United States Colored Troops (USCT). From that moment on, the battlefield would never be the same. By war's end, Black soldiers made up 10 percent of the Union Army, and their courage reshaped the tide of war.

But the war wasn't won by soldiers alone.

Behind every battlefield was a supply line. Behind every victory, a man with a wagon, a contract, and a target on his back.

And in Columbus, Ohio, one of those men was John T. Ward— and his son, William Ward. A free Black man from a family rooted in resistance, John T. had already built a reputation as a fearless conductor on the Underground Railroad, guiding fugitives to freedom across hostile terrain. But now, with the nation in flames, he stepped out of the shadows and into the spotlight.

He did what almost no other Black man had done; he won a government contract.

That alone was an act of defiance.

During the Civil War, the U.S. government issued contracts to civilian suppliers for everything: food, clothing, lumber, livestock, ammunition, and transport. These were handled through the Quartermaster Department, and most contracts were awarded through closed networks of white businessmen with political connections. Patronage, kickbacks, and corruption were the norm. It was a system designed to reward loyalty to the Union cause—but more importantly, loyalty to whiteness.

Black entrepreneurs were seen as unfit, unqualified, or simply invisible. They were laborers, not leaders; muleskinners, not logisticians. Even free Black men rarely had the legal, financial, or social leverage to compete for such contracts, much less survive the scrutiny of white auditors and bureaucrats.

And yet, John T. Ward broke through.

At a time when most free Black men couldn't vote or testify in court against a white man, John T. secured a highly sought-after contract to transport military equipment and supplies for the Union Army at Camp Chase—the notorious military post just west of downtown Columbus.

Camp Chase was no ordinary site. It served as a recruiting and training center, a logistic command post, and eventually, a prisoner-of-war camp holding more than 9,400 captured Confederate soldiers. The conditions were horrific—mud-soaked ground, crumbling shelters, spoiled rations, and bitter cold. The supply lines were thin. Morale was thinner.

That's where John T.'s brilliance came in.

He transformed chaos into coordination. He knew how to move people under threat, how to chart safe routes when others saw only dead ends. These were the same instincts that had kept fugitives alive in the night—now redirected to keep Union troops armed and fed by day.

John T. didn't just deliver supplies. He delivered outcomes.

When wagons broke down, he repaired them. When the weather turned, he rerouted. When soldiers were at risk, he moved in silence and in haste. More than once, his shipments arrived just in time to prevent a catastrophe. Those who underestimated him quickly learned: this was not a man to be dismissed.

His presence at Camp Chase was an anomaly. His success there was a miracle.

While Camp Chase crumbled under its own weight, John T. Ward kept it breathing. His logistics kept the Union marching. His grit kept the war winnable.

And yet, few today know his name.

In a war where Black men had to fight for the right to die with honor, John T. fought for the right to build, to lead, to supply—not as a servant, but as a strategist.

He was not merely part of history. He was the engine beneath it.

Columbus, Ohio. A city built on crossroads—of trade, of politics, and of war. During the Civil War, it became more than a state capital. It turned into a nerve center for the Union cause, pulsing with decisions that shaped the future of the republic.

Governor David Tod, flanked by lawmakers and Union loyalists, ruled from the marble halls of the Ohio Statehouse, where debates cracked like cannon fire and resolutions carried the weight of blood. Every vote cast in that building sent shockwaves to the battlefield. This was where regiments were raised, funds approved, and war machines fueled—gears grinding to either crush the Confederacy or tear the nation in two.

But it wasn't just strategy running through the veins of the city. It was sweat, steel, and suffering.

Columbus transformed—grimy hands turned wheels in iron foundries and textile mills, forging bullets, uniforms, and wagons. Factories roared like beasts. What once were humble workshops became engines of war. The industrial heartbeat of the North pounded from inside warehouses and behind workshop doors.

And in those shadows, women stepped into spaces the world told them weren't theirs. In basements and back rooms, they formed Ladies' Aid Societies, sewing bandages, knitting socks, rolling bandoliers, and writing letters soaked in prayer. They nursed the wounded and buried the dead. They raised funds, and with them, they raised spirits. While men marched with rifles, women held down the home front like it was their own battlefield.

Outside city limits, a different kind of war was being fought— not for land, but for freedom.

The enslaved knew what was coming. They didn't wait on Lincoln's pen. They didn't wait for a trumpet or a telegram. They ran. Driven by a flame no plantation could smother, they tore through swamps, crossed frozen rivers, bled through mud and snow. They didn't run because freedom was promised. They ran because it was owed.

They were their own liberators.

And yet, in one of history's crueler contradictions, while those same people were running for their lives, President Abraham Lincoln stood before abolitionists and defended colonization schemes— plans to send freed Black people to Africa. He called it a solution to America's so-called Negro problem. Freedom, followed by exile. Emancipation, with a one-way ticket out.

That wasn't liberation. That was rejection wrapped in politics.

Meanwhile, the very land that had once chained John T. Ward's family in Virginia was seized by Union forces. And in one last act of vengeance, Confederate soldiers torched the wooden Ward bridge, hoping to slow the Union Army's advance. Ashes rose where legacy had once stood. The bridge burned, but not the truth.

Local whispers say a Confederate cannon still lies buried near that site—in Campbell County, where today's railroad tracks hum over forgotten history. They say the cannon is still there, mouth pointed at the past, silent now, but echoing louder than any fire it ever spat.

And as I write this, I can't shake the haunting irony:

"A Black man had no rights that a white man was bound to respect."

That ruling—Dred Scott's curse—ain't just ink on an old court document. It's a generational wound. A verdict that lingers in the bones. And I read those words again, not in some classroom, but in real time—while streets erupted in protest, while gas canisters choked teenage lungs, while a pandemic locked us inside with our grief and our truth.

The past is not past. It's present. It's pounding. It's here.

And Columbus, for all its marble monuments and flags of faded glory, was never just a backdrop. It was a stage. And on that stage, the oppressed became organizers. The laborers became liberators. And the enslaved became the authors of their own deliverance.

The Civil War wasn't just a fight between North and South. It pulled in folks from all corners—some willing, some caught up, some making hard choices in a world stacked against them. Native American involvement in the Confederate cause was one of them complex truths.

Now, not all Native nations sided with the South—but some did. Especially among the Five Civilized Tribes: Cherokee, Chickasaw, Choctaw, Creek, and Seminole. These nations had a long, tangled history with Southern states, forged through broken treaties, forced marches, and survival. After being pushed west in the Trail of Tears, a lot of Native folks ended up living under Southern influence. Some owned land. Some even owned slaves. And many had adopted parts of European American culture just to hold on to what little they had left.

So, when the Confederacy came calling, promising to respect their sovereignty, protect their land, and leave them alone to govern themselves, some tribes saw that as the safer bet. After all, the Union hadn't exactly kept its promises either.

But it wasn't one-sided.

There were Native people who backed the Union too—folks who'd seen the ugly side of the South firsthand. They signed up, fought, and died for the North, hoping that maybe, just maybe, that fight would mean a better future for their people. Native soldiers fought in major battles like Pea Ridge and Honey Springs. Scouts, cavalry, infantry, they were in the thick of it.

One name stands out—Stand Watie, a Cherokee general who led Confederate troops until the bitter end. He was the last Confederate commander to surrender in 1865, and with him, the last official flames of the rebellion died in Indian Territory.

But here's the kicker: once the war was over, the U.S. government turned around and punished those same Native tribes that had sided with the South. Hard. They forced new treaties, took more land, and tightened control. That promise of autonomy? Gone with the wind.

So, why did some Native nations fight for the Confederacy? Because they were trying to survive. Because they were promised respect. Because history had already taught them what happened when you trusted the wrong white government.

And in the end, they paid the price—again.

Their story is woven into war just like ours. Different path. Same betrayal. Same loss. Same bitter aftertaste of freedom denied.

Today, many Black Americans have re-evaluated the historical figures and stereotypes that shaped public memory during and after slavery. One figure that often comes up in this conversation is Sambo—a caricature used to mock Black men as lazy, childlike, or buffoonish. In recent years, Sambo has come to be seen as a deeply damaging trope, symbolizing the way white supremacy infantilized and dehumanized Black people. But there's another name that carries just as much historical weight—Uncle Tom—and its evolution is even more complicated.

Uncle Tom, originally the central character in *Uncle Tom's Cabin*, was never meant to be an insult. When the novel was first published in 1852 by Harriet Beecher Stowe—a white abolitionist woman— Uncle Tom was portrayed as a noble, spiritual, self-sacrificing man who endured slavery with grace and dignity. In her eyes, he was a

Christlike figure meant to humanize enslaved people and rally white Americans, particularly Northerners, to the abolitionist cause.

But there were limits to Stowe's vision. As a white woman writing in a deeply racist society, she still portrayed Black characters through a lens of white paternalism. Even in her attempts to be sympathetic, she did not imagine Black freedom in terms of full equality. Instead, she centered white saviors, and her Black characters often won admiration through obedience, humility, or passive suffering—not through rebellion or self-determination.

While *Uncle Tom's Cabin* played a huge role in building white abolitionist support, Black readers—especially freedmen and abolitionist activists—began to see problems in the portrayal. As the Civil War erupted and the struggle for emancipation became more violent and urgent, the image of the obedient, long-suffering Uncle Tom felt increasingly out of step with the times.

Northern Black communities began to weaponize the term "Uncle Tom." It became a pejorative, used to criticize other Black people who were seen as overly submissive, collaborationist, or unwilling to stand up against white oppression.

During the war and Reconstruction, a freedman who aided the Confederacy—or who refused to align with the Black freedom struggle—might have been bitterly called an "Uncle Tom in gray." The phrase dripped with contempt. It suggested not just cowardice, but betrayal. To be labeled an Uncle Tom in that era was to be accused of complicity with the enemy, of prioritizing white approval over Black liberation.

It's important to note that this critique didn't always acknowledge the full complexity of those individuals' circumstances—many Black Southerners were trapped in impossible situations, under threat of re-enslavement, violence, or death. Still, the anger was real and the label was powerful.

So, when we look back, it's not just about whether someone was a "Sambo" or an "Uncle Tom." It's about understanding that both labels were reactions to survival under white supremacy—and that they were used within Black communities as tools to define resistance, loyalty, and identity.

The tragedy is that neither stereotype told the whole truth.

But the dialogue around them reveals how deeply Black Americans have wrestled—not just with oppression, but with how to name it, how to navigate it, and how to resist it.

Many free Black people in the North were shocked, dismayed, and even disgusted upon learning that some freedmen in the South had aligned themselves—willingly or not—with the Confederacy. While these reactions were not always recorded in newspapers, the sentiment reverberated through abolitionist circles and free Black communities. The response was sharp, laced with suspicion, sorrow, and rage.

In speeches and articles, Frederick Douglass never minced words. He expressed astonishment and bitterness at the idea of any Black man fighting for the Confederacy, famously calling it "a fight against their own deliverance." To Douglass, such participation wasn't just misguided, it was evidence of how deeply slavery had distorted the human spirit, forcing survival to masquerade as betrayal.

Northern abolitionists had names for these men: "Confederate Negroes" or "Rebel Negroes." These labels were spoken with scorn, meant to emphasize the unimaginable—Black men siding with the architects of their own oppression. In letters and sermons, leaders like Douglass and ministers in the AME Church condemned such cooperation as "turning against their own blood." Their language was fierce, deeply personal, and driven by grief.

In some northern circles, particularly among intellectuals and financial minds, Black Confederates were bitterly referred to as "human stock still yoked to cotton." It was a searing metaphor, meant to mock both their perceived complicity and the South's ongoing commodification of Black life.

But the truth is far more complex—and demands honesty.

Some freedmen—Black men who were not enslaved at the time—did serve in or alongside Confederate forces. But it's essential to distinguish between service and support. The overwhelming majority were coerced, economically entrapped, or manipulated into service, often under threat of re-enslavement or exile.

In the rigidly stratified South, free Black people lived in a constant state of precarity. Though not enslaved, their rights were nearly nonexistent. In cities like New Orleans and Charleston, some were legally required to enroll in local militias prior to the war— units later absorbed into Confederate defense forces. Many served in support roles: as cooks, blacksmiths, teamsters, or laborers. Others were "volunteered" at gunpoint or through threats that left no room for refusal.

A small number—especially in Louisiana—came from wealthy Creole communities with complex racial identities and tangled allegiances. Even in these rare cases, motivations were not about loyalty to the Confederacy's ideals, but about protecting their families, property, or fragile status in a society built to erase them.

By 1865, with the Confederacy crumbling and desperate for manpower, Southern leaders authorized the enlistment of enslaved people as soldiers. It was the ultimate contradiction: a government fighting to preserve slavery now arming the very people it had tried to keep in bondage. Very few of these men were ever given weapons, and fewer still saw battle. Most were forced into backbreaking labor—digging trenches, hauling supplies—under conditions barely distinguishable from slavery.

The myth that Black people willingly fought for the Confederacy in significant numbers has long been weaponized to whitewash the truth about the Civil War. But the truth remains: the Confederacy existed to preserve slavery—and any Black man within its ranks was either forced there, manipulated by the brutal logic of survival, or caught in an impossible moral web.

Imagine being a freedman, barely holding onto liberty in a world designed to strip it away—or being an enslaved person, handed a Confederate uniform and forced to turn a gun on your own people, the very people fighting for your freedom. To aim at the enslaved or to be forced to fight against your brothers and sisters. To march beneath the same flag that once claimed ownership of your mother, your wife, your children. Imagine being told to fight not for freedom, but against it.

This was the cruel paradox faced by many free Black men in the South: serve the very system that enslaved your kin, or risk losing the fragile freedom you had. It was not loyalty; it was survival twisted into servitude. It was fear masquerading as allegiance.

The myth of the Black Confederate soldier persists because it serves a convenient narrative—one that softens the brutality of the Confederacy or allows for a denial of slavery's central role. But the truth is far more painful—and far more powerful.

These men didn't fight for the South. They fought to survive. And that agonizing choice, made under the weight of impossible odds, deserves remembrance—not revision.

The room was thick with purpose. Delegates, clothed in humble suits, worn shiny at the elbows, sat shoulder to shoulder—eyes steady, backs straight. Not out of ceremony, but out of conviction. They gathered not just as orators or scribes, but as fathers, brothers, widowers, and friends of the brave Black men fighting on the front lines of a nation at war with itself.

From the floor of that Colored Convention rose a declaration—intimate and defiant. They extended their deepest gratitude to Major General Benjamin Butler, a white Union officer whose name had become sacred in Black households. Where other generals turned blind eyes to the degradation of Black soldiers—given half rations, worn-out gear, and the most dangerous posts—Butler treated them with what the delegates called "fatherly and impartial" care.

And this wasn't flattery. It was relief. It was respect—returned.

In the eyes of the Black community, Butler stood apart. He saw those soldiers not as tools, but as men.

But their words carried more than thanks. They carried pain. They carried pride. They carried pressure.

Because while Butler had honored their kin, many others remained unaccounted for, still caged, still murdered.

So, the delegates turned their voices—clear and unshaken—toward the General Government.

"We feel called upon to inquire … what direct action … has yet been taken to release our brave soldiers …"

That wasn't a question. That was a thunderclap.

Black Union soldiers captured by Confederates weren't treated like prisoners of war. They were stripped of their uniforms: tortured, executed, or worse.

To the Southern rebels, a Black man in a blue coat wasn't a soldier. He was a slave in rebellion. And for that, they unleashed a savage kind of punishment.

Then came the words that dropped silence through the room like a hammer:

"We ask of the authorities prompt retaliation for any wrongs done them."

Retaliation. A word soaked in blood and bound in justice. A word that told the country: this is the line.

Their fury had a name. And that name was Fort Pillow.

Only months earlier—April 1864—Black soldiers of the 6th U.S. Heavy Artillery had surrendered at Fort Pillow. But surrender didn't save them. Confederate troops under General Nathan Bedford Forrest hunted them down like animals, shot them where they lay wounded, bayoneted them as they begged, and burned them alive in piles.

Two hundred sixty-two Black men, massacred in the mud.

The Convention had not forgotten. They would never forget. And now, they were done waiting for polite redress.

By this time, they had mastered the *rules of order*. Using *Cushing's Manual of Parliamentary Practice*, they showed just how deeply Black leaders understood the power of procedure—motions, committee appointments, roll calls, votes, recorded proceedings. These weren't just administrative tasks. They were acts of resistance, acts of reclamation.

By mastering the tools of American governance, Black delegates weren't simply asking for inclusion. They were making a bold political and cultural statement:

We are not guests in democracy. We are authors of it.

This was a political reckoning—and it was shaped not just by mourning, but by strategy. The delegates resolved to form a committee of three: a practical, precise task force. Their mission? To account for every Black Ohio soldier, especially those whose service had been falsely credited to other states. These bookkeeping tricks robbed Black soldiers and their families of the recognition—and the bounty or pension—they had earned through blood.

The committee would trace every man who had been wounded, captured, or killed, and demand that Ohio claim its sons. This wasn't just about recordkeeping. This was about restoration.

In that room of ordinary men stood an extraordinary movement. The Colored Convention thought with urgency, because every day that passed was another day a Black soldier might die forgotten in a Confederate prison—or be denied a widow's pension. Dignity, because they were not begging for favors. They were demanding what was owed to citizens who had given everything. Strategic intelligence, because rhetoric alone wouldn't win this war. Data, delegation, and documentation were their weapons. And collective power, because they spoke not as scattered individuals but as a body politic. A people unified by grief, by love, and by resolve.

This was not simply a meeting. It was organized Black resistance—burning with the moral authority of a people who had waited too long for justice and now refused to wait any longer.

What they sought wasn't vengeance alone. It was protection. It was dignity. It was a nation that would stop treating Black lives as disposable and start honoring them as indispensable.

Not one forgotten. Not one erased.

And if the country wouldn't listen to gratitude—they would make it listen to grief.

CHAPTER 15

Beyond the Field,
Beyond Repair

"Let the nation remember its debt to the Negro. Let it remember that with him, liberty was not merely a figure of speech, not merely a glittering generality, not merely a noble abstraction ... Let it remember his unpaid labor, his unpaid blood."

-Frederick Douglass

The research for this project had consumed me, its revelations swirling in my mind like a storm. I had to share what I'd discovered about John T. Ward, my great-great-great-grandfather, and the stories that had lain dormant for generations.

Over lunch with my aunt, I eagerly spilled the history I'd uncovered—John T.'s meticulous orchestration of escapes on the Underground Railroad, his perfectly trained horses, and the ribbons my grandfather, Harold E. Ward, had won for his unmatched horsemanship.

The bustling noise of Front Street in downtown Columbus poured in as the restaurant door swung open, employees greeting each customer with familiar warmth, the sharp chime of the cash register punctuating the air. Amid the hum of conversation, time seemed to slow.

My aunt leaned in across the table, her voice low, her smile knowing—cutting through the noise like a whisper wrapped in memory.

"Do you remember the bronze-rusted mini bells on the leather strap?" she asked, her voice tinged with nostalgia.

I froze mid-sentence. A memory stirred—those delicate bells hanging from the doorknobs of her French doors and the kitchen door. Their soft chime had always been a comforting background note in her home, a sound that felt ancient, as if it carried the weight of an untold story.

"Yes!" I exclaimed, my heart racing. "I still have some of those bells. Dad does too."

She nodded, her expression turning serious. "Those were the very bells John T. Ward used on his horses and wagons."

For a moment, time collapsed. History pressed in around us, and I could almost hear the faint jingling of those same bells as John T.'s wagon creaked down moonlit paths, the horses' hooves muffled by dirt roads.

My chest swelled with awe, and the restaurant seemed to dissolve, replaced by the sounds of distant whispers and the gentle clinking of those bells against leather, swaying with the motion of the wagon.

Even now, I carry on the tradition, keeping bells on my doors for added security. But now, their significance is deeper. Each time they chime, it's as if a part of John T.'s journey echoes through time, reaching me.

The very same sound he would've heard as he guided his horses during Reconstruction, when newly freed slaves were seeking new beginnings.

Five years after Reconstruction ended, John T. turned his hard-won skills into a transportation business—moving people and goods with the same determination that had fueled his abolitionist efforts.

As my aunt recounted this history, I could almost smell the leather of the reins and the musty scent of the horses. I imagined John T.'s hands—weathered, steady—gripping those reins with a mix of resolve and hope. The bells would ring out softly, a melodic counterpoint to the rhythmic clatter of wagon wheels and the occasional snort or whinny of the horses.

The thought sent chills through me.

The bells I'd grown up hearing—their chime once just a simple backdrop to my childhood—had been a lifeline for so many, a quiet signal of motion, of progress, of freedom.

Now, each time those bells ring in my home, they remind me of where I come from.

They remind me of John T. Ward's courage, my grandfather's mastery of his craft, and the enduring spirit of our family.

It's as if history itself whispers through their sound, urging me forward as I piece together the legacy of a man who turned hardship into hope, fear into freedom, and skill into opportunity.

The story of those bells—of John T. Ward and his indomitable spirit—is one I now feel compelled to tell.

Not just for myself. But for anyone seeking proof that even the smallest details can carry the weight of generations.

In the aftermath of the Civil War, the United States entered a turbulent, yet hopeful period known as Reconstruction. It was a moment charged with the potential to rebuild a fractured nation and finally reckon with the centuries-long atrocity of slavery. Central to that promise was the concept of reparations—an unapologetic demand to repair the economic and human devastation inflicted on Black Americans and build a more just society.

But while Black freedmen were out here pleading with Union soldiers to bring their war guns back home for protection, white Southern elites were already plotting—plotting to reconstruct slavery by another name.

Emancipated people were left destitute—no food, no shelter, no clothing, no education. No protection. Many had to wander unfamiliar lands, unsure of where to go or how to survive. Some, afraid or too old to face a world beyond the plantation, stayed put—still shackled, just without the chains.

White Southerners, especially those in power and riding hard for the Democratic Party of the time, were determined to snatch back control. They created and enforced the Black Codes: a set of laws so crooked they made freedom look like a trap. Unemployment? A crime. Vagrancy? A crime. Traveling without papers? A crime. These laws weren't just about control; they were about sabotage.

Black men were swept up, criminalized, and funneled straight into convict leasing programs—where they labored for states and private companies without pay.

Let's be clear: Southern Democrats weren't just resisting Reconstruction. They were engineering a whole new system of bondage.

But it wasn't just them. The North had dirty hands too. Northern Democrats *and* Republicans played their parts. Northern banks financed the South's rebuilding under cutthroat terms. Northern insurance companies, yeah, the same ones that once insured enslaved Black bodies—invested in sharecropping setups designed to trap Black families in never-ending debt.

And even the Radical Republicans, the ones who started off fighting for Black rights, got quiet by the 1870s. Their political courage dried up.

Both parties backed away, trading Black freedom for political peace. Courtrooms, sheriffs' offices, state houses, and Congress became battlegrounds. Black liberty was auctioned off in the name of "reunion."

So yes, Southern Democrats were architects of postwar racial suppression. But they had help—from the boardrooms of New York, the printing presses of Chicago, and the legislative floors of Washington, D.C.

This wasn't just a political failure. It was a moral one.

The U.S. had a chance to do right—to give freedmen land, schools, and protection. But instead, the nation doubled down on its old habits. The oppression didn't disappear; it just got a new uniform, from slave patrols to police departments, from overseers to prison wardens.

Reconstruction didn't just fall apart. It got strangled, by people who feared what freedom really meant: competition, equality, and shared power.

Reparations weren't simply denied. They were *sabotaged*.

And that sabotage still echoes today—in the wealth gap, the incarceration rates, voter suppression, housing inequality. This truth might not be convenient, but it's necessary.

America didn't just fail to heal after the Civil War. America chose not to.

These conditions sparked debate—then and now—around reparations. The conversation isn't new. It reaches all the way back to the 1700s.

The Quakers, among the first white abolitionists in the U.S., were nearly unanimous: if you were going to repent for the sin of owning people, then you needed to *atone*. That meant making amends. They cited Deuteronomy, where slave owners were instructed to share their goods with those they once enslaved.

Supporting reparations—or even daring to speak of Black liberation—was never just controversial. It was dangerous. It could cost you your job, your place in society, even your life.

Black activists were hunted, jailed, beaten, and killed. White allies faced violence, exile, or disgrace.

To demand justice in a country built on your suffering was to put a target on your back.

In this centuries-long fight, some paid with coin, others with reputation, and many with their lives.

Their names are etched not just in books, but in blood, in iron, in unshakable conviction.

Take Warner Mifflin, a white Quaker abolitionist during the Revolutionary era. He said what most wouldn't: freedom without restitution was *hollow*.

As early as 1778, Mifflin was calling on former slaveholders to pay reparations—in land, in cash, and through shared crop arrangements. His truth-telling made him a pariah, even among his fellow Quakers. He was ostracized, ridiculed, and isolated—but he never backed down.

And then there was Felix Holbrook, a formerly enslaved man in Boston and Rhode Island. Holbrook didn't just quietly hope for justice, he demanded it. In the late eighteenth century, he published an ad in a Boston newspaper, not asking for charity but for the chance to earn his freedom.

He reminded colonists—loudly calling for liberty from Britain— to extend that same dignity to him.

"We ask you for relief," he wrote, "which, as a man, we have a right to do."

His words were revolutionary—not in their anger, but in their *humanity*.

A reminder, freedom is not a gift. It's a right long denied.

In 1773, a document quietly submitted to the Massachusetts colonial government became one of the earliest collective appeals for justice from the enslaved. Often attributed to a man named Felix, this petition stands as a spiritual, political, and moral reckoning—a bold and eloquent plea not just for freedom, but for dignity, citizenship, and what we now call reparations.

Though the word "reparations" never appears in the text—it wouldn't have, not in the political language of the day—the petition reads like a blueprint for it. Felix and the other petitioners began by acknowledging the depth of generational harm, writing:

"Every Day of their Lives embittered with this most intolerable Reflection, That, let their Behavior be what it will, neither they, nor their Children to all Generations, shall ever be able to do, or to possess and enjoy any Thing."

But while Jefferson was writing from Monticello, in 1773—three years before the declaration—freed Black Americans were already defining the "pursuit of happiness" on their own terms.

They didn't need permission from philosophers to know what happiness meant. It was land ownership after bondage. It was learning to read the Bible after being whipped for holding a book. It was marrying the person you love without fear of being sold apart. It was walking without papers. It was petitioning legislatures, forming mutual aid societies, and speaking at Colored Conventions to demand not only freedom, but dignity, opportunity, and protection.

For the freedman, the pursuit of happiness was not abstract; it was survival wrapped in hope.

So, when Jefferson wrote those words, they carried a dual meaning—one exalted in textbooks, and one erased from them. While white landowners debated moral virtue and political liberty, Black men and women were already embodying those principles through radical resilience.

Jefferson's version of happiness was philosophical.

The freedman's was personal, practical, urgent.

And in 1773, they were already living it.

Holbrook's dream? To gain his freedom lawfully and return to Africa. It was a vision radical for its time—and still thunderously relevant today. Holbrook wasn't just seeking escape; he was seeking restoration. He longed to reclaim his humanity in a world that had defined him as property. His departure wouldn't have been an act of cowardice but a declaration: that America's promise was too fragile, too conditional, too hypocritical to hold a Black man's future.

In that vision, Holbrook becomes a prophetic mirror for today's Blaxit movement—a modern exodus of Black Americans choosing to leave the United States in pursuit of something this country still hasn't delivered: peace, safety, and dignity without compromise.

Blaxit is more than a passport stamp or a plane ticket. It's a political act. A declaration that says, "We've waited long enough." Black Americans have waited for justice. Waited for safety. Waited for the wealth they helped build. Waited for the promised protections of citizenship. In many ways, Blaxit echoes what the enslaved already understood: freedom is not granted; it is taken. And sometimes, it must be taken elsewhere.

Holbrook's dream of returning to Africa was not just a geographic aspiration. It was a spiritual return. It was a refusal to keep waiting at a door that was never meant to open. Today's Blaxiters seek places where they are not the exception, not the threat, and not reduced to a checkbox on someone's diversity metric. They seek homes where their Blackness is not a liability.

Blaxit is not an escape; it's an indictment. A damning verdict against a country that, centuries later, still hasn't paid its ancestral debts. It's a movement born not from bitterness, but from clarity. And once that clarity hits, it cannot be unseen.

The data speaks loudly. According to a 2021 report from Blaxit Global and Pew Research, nearly 60 percent of Black Americans under forty have seriously considered or are actively planning to leave the United States. The reasons are sobering: 83 percent pointed to racism and police violence, 63 percent sought a better cost of living, 52 percent cited mental health and safety, and 48 percent wanted cultural affirmation and dignity. Countries like Ghana, Portugal, Mexico, and Costa Rica are seeing a surge of interest from Black Americans pursuing dual citizenship, remote work visas, and permanent relocation.

It's not because they hate America, it's because America has never fully loved them back. From Holbrook in 1773 to thousands of Black families in 2023, the so-called pursuit of happiness has felt more like a delayed shipment—with no tracking number and no estimated time of arrival.

Blaxit is a modern act of self-determination. It tells the world: "We don't owe this country our presence. It owes us justice." Because surviving in America is not the same as being free in it. The Blaxit movement is a reminder that Black Americans are not obligated to wait another four hundred years to be seen, heard, or safe.

But as for me? I'm not going anywhere. I stand firmly in the tradition of my grandfather, John T. Ward—a man who stayed, fought, and built. He was a conductor on the Underground Railroad, a businessman, a landholder, and a freedom fighter. He chose not to flee but to claim his place on soil soaked with the blood of our ancestors. He carved out liberation on stolen land, and I echo that same stance today.

This is our country. We built it. We bled for it. We buried our ancestors in it. I'm not leaving, because this land is more ours than theirs, more than those who dominate it, more than those who fear our freedom, more than those who rewrite history while standing on the backs of the people who made it.

Blaxit may be the path for some—and I support those who make that choice. But my revolution is rooted right here. I choose to fight forward, not for inclusion, not for survival, but for ownership, restitution, and power.

The legacy of reparations is not about asking; it's about collecting. And whether that debt is paid on American soil or abroad, one truth remains: we are done waiting. Reparations are not a fantasy. They are overdue. And let it be known—we are not confused, not divided, and we are not going away.

We are invoicing history. And this time, payment is expected in full.

The early voices—Mifflin, Holbrook, and countless others—planted the seeds of a struggle that has never ended. Their courage reminds us that the fight for reparations has always demanded sacrifice. That America's moral debt was never just an entry in a ledger; it was, and still is, a battlefield.

And even now, in the shadow of that battlefield, the cost of truth remains high.

After the Civil War, America stood at a crossroads—bloodied, battered, and burdened with a question it had evaded for centuries: what now? What would freedom truly look like for the four million Black men, women, and children who had been declared emancipated—but left with nothing? No land. No restitution. No protection.

Only the brittle, bruised bones of a broken promise.

Freedom had arrived without foundation, without reparations, and without repair.

They were free in law but shackled by circumstances. Their hands had built the American economy—brick by brick, bale by bale, bond by bond—yet the wealth they created remained in the hands of their former enslavers. The cotton fields. The sugar plantations. The mansions. The railroads. The banks. All still stood under white ownership.

And the people who had endured the whip and the auction block—who had fought, fled, and survived—were now told they were free … only to be abandoned on the battlefield of survival.

But then, in the smoldering twilight of war, as the Confederacy lay in ruins and the horizon flickered with fragile hope, Union General William Tecumseh Sherman made a thunderous move—a crack of justice through the clouds of bondage.

On January 16, 1865, Sherman issued Special Field Orders No. 15.

It wasn't a law passed by Congress. It wasn't born in marble chambers or polished rhetoric. It was a military directive, forged in urgency and shaped by the truth spoken plainly by Black leaders in Savannah, Georgia—men like Garrison Frazier, who looked Sherman and Secretary of War Edwin Stanton in the eye and said what needed to be said: "Freedom without land is no freedom at all."

Sherman listened.

The order set aside four hundred thousand acres of fertile land along the coasts of South Carolina, Georgia, and Florida—confiscated from Confederate plantation owners—to be redistributed to newly freed Black families. Forty acres per family. Not charity. Not a handout. Justice.

Though the infamous mule wasn't part of the original order, the Freedmen's Bureau, established shortly after, distributed surplus army mules to some settlers. And so, the phrase "forty acres and a mule" took hold. It became more than a policy. It became a prophecy—a whisper passed between calloused hands, across fields still damp with sorrow.

And for a moment, that prophecy lived.

Thousands of freedmen and women embraced the dream. They settled the land. They tilled the soil. They built schools and churches. They buried their dead on ground they believed was finally their own. It was a sacred beginning—a chance to build wealth, independence, and community free from white control.

For eight fleeting months, it looked like America might finally honor its highest ideals.

Then came the betrayal.

After Lincoln's assassination in April 1865, the presidency fell to Andrew Johnson, a Southern Democrat and former enslaver who made no secret of his disdain for Black freedom. His infamous declaration said it all: "This is a country for white men, and by God, as long as I am President, it shall be a government for white men."

That wasn't a slip of the tongue, it was a mission statement.

With the stroke of his pen, Johnson revoked Sherman's order. The land that Black families had planted, nurtured, and believed in was seized and returned to the very Confederates who had waged war against the Union. Why? Because Black progress threatened white supremacy—and Johnson was committed to restoring the South to its antebellum order.

He vetoed civil rights legislation, pardoned thousands of Confederates, and undermined the Freedmen's Bureau at every turn. In doing so, he crushed one of the most promising efforts at reparative justice in American history.

Black families were evicted by court order or mob violence. Their homes were burned. Their crops destroyed. Their dignity uprooted and scattered like ash.

The promise of freedom collapsed like a house with no foundation. Sherman's order—never codified by Congress—had no legal shield, only the fragile hope of justice. Johnson ensured its erasure.

What could have been the cornerstone of Black generational wealth became a ghost.

And Sherman? He wasn't just a civil war general, he was an Ohio son, born in Lancaster and tied to Columbus both before and after the war. His roots ran deep in the Buckeye State. Today, his statue still stands on the grounds of the Ohio Statehouse—a silent monument to a man whose signature once ignited a flame of hope in Black communities.

That connection mattered.

Ohio had one of the largest free Black populations in the antebellum Midwest. Cities like Cincinnati, Cleveland, and

Columbus were hubs of abolitionist organizing and Black political leadership. Nowhere was that clearer than in the Colored Conventions Movement—gatherings of free Black men fighting for land, education, suffrage, and protection from racial violence.

So, what did they think of Sherman's order?

While direct commentary on Special Field Orders No. 15 is rare in the Ohio convention archives, their resolutions spoke volumes.

From the 1850s to the 1870s, Black delegates across Ohio consistently fought for land ownership, voting rights, education, and protection from white terrorism.

To them, Sherman's order was more than a military memo. It was the closest thing to reparations they had ever seen—a glimmer of what justice might look like if the government ever truly tried.

At the Colored National Convention of 1865, Black leaders demanded land distribution as a birthright of freedom. And while that meeting wasn't in Ohio, leaders like David Jenkins, James Poindexter, Charles Langston, John Mercer Langston, and John T. Ward echoed the same truth: freedom without land is a lie.

But by the 1866 and 1867 conventions in Columbus and Cleveland, the tone had changed. The optimism sparked by Sherman's order had soured into bitterness and rage.

Johnson's revocation wasn't just a policy reversal; it was a gut punch. A calculated betrayal. Delegates condemned his open racism, the failure of Reconstruction, and the government's refusal to honor even the most basic promises of emancipation

They didn't need to name Sherman's order to make their point. The land had been promised. Then stolen. Again.

No one captured it more clearly than John Mercer Langston, one of Ohio's fiercest voices: "Let the nation remember its debt to the Negro. Let it remember his unpaid labor, his unpaid blood."

That wasn't a metaphor. It was a bill past due.

To Ohio's Black communities, Sherman's order had been a flash of light—brief and blinding. When it vanished, what remained was the familiar silence of a broken promise. In place of landownership came sharecropping, tenant farming, debt peonage, and convict leasing—new names for old chains.

Had those four hundred thousand acres remained in Black hands, they could have seeded legacies: inheritance, equity, empowerment, the kind of generational wealth that turns dirt into destiny. Instead, it became a receipt never honored, proof of what was owed and what was stolen.

Let's be clear: reparations weren't radical, they were rational. They weren't a fantasy; they were implemented, however briefly. And they weren't impossible; they were deliberately undone.

Sherman's order wasn't about charity. It was about repairing a wrong so grotesque and foundational that only land, labor, and full citizenship could begin to make it right. But America flinched. It handed the land back to enslavers and told the formerly enslaved to fend for themselves—empty-handed, hunted, locked out of every corridor of power, wealth, and opportunity.

And so today, "forty acres and a mule" is more than a broken promise; it is the origin story of generational theft. Which begs the question: if the United States had the resources and resolve in 1865, what has stopped it since? Not money. Not policy. Not logistics. Will.

Because when it comes to Black freedom, America has always had trembling hands on the wheel of justice—and a death grip on the reins of white comfort.

Reparations weren't whispered. They were promised—then ripped away in a scream.

And we've been living in the echo of that silence ever since.

During the Reconstruction era, Congressman Thaddeus Stevens of Pennsylvania became one of the fiercest advocates for reparations. He didn't just talk about justice; he tried to legislate it.

On February 5, 1866, Stevens introduced a proposal to the Freedmen's Bureau Bill, calling for the redistribution of public and confiscated Confederate lands to formerly enslaved people and loyal refugees. His proposal: forty-acre parcels—the very promise Sherman had made. But this time, it was aimed at making reparations permanent—through federal law.

Stevens understood the truth: freedom without land is a lie. Without economic power, the freed people would remain trapped in a cycle of dependence, exploitation, and poverty.

But Stevens ran headfirst into a wall of resistance—led by none other than President Andrew Johnson.

Johnson vetoed the measure, siding once again with white Southern planters. Most of the land originally allocated to Black families was seized and returned to the very men who had waged war to keep them enslaved. Stevens's vision—to destroy the Confederate oligarchy and build racial equality—was deliberately gutted.

Still, he wasn't alone.

In 1898, decades after Reconstruction's collapse, Congressman Jeremiah D. Botkin of Kansas introduced a bill to provide homesteads to former slaves and their descendants—another call for land as restitution. It never passed. But like Stevens, Botkin added another stone to the foundation of what we now call the reparations movement.

The fight continued—not just in Congress, but in Black communities across the country, especially in places like Ohio.

In Columbus, the delegates of the Colored Conventions understood the stakes. They didn't just gather to discuss; they organized, strategized, and voted as a bloc. During the contentious election for the nineteenth president of the United States, they debated who—if anyone—had the freedmen's best interests at heart.

They had high hopes for Rutherford B. Hayes, a man they had worked with during his time as Governor of Ohio. Leaders like John T. Ward and his peers had collaborated with Hayes, believing he might carry the cause of Black advancement to the White House.

But what they received in return was betrayal.

The Compromise of 1877, which handed Hayes the presidency, came at a devastating price: the withdrawal of federal troops from the South and the end of Reconstruction. With that decision, Hayes abandoned the freed people to the mercy of their former enslavers and the rising tide of white terror.

To Black Ohioans, the message was clear:

Even allies could be bought. Even promises made in Columbus could be broken in Washington.

They had marched, petitioned, voted, and hoped. And still—land was stolen. Justice denied. Blood forgotten.

And yet, they never stopped demanding what was owed.

The call for reparations didn't end with Thaddeus Stevens or Jeremiah Botkin. It echoed through pulpits, protest halls, and political conventions—and no one thundered louder than Bishop Henry McNeal Turner.

A fiery orator, theologian, and political trailblazer, Turner was one of the most radical and unflinching voices of the Colored Conventions Movement. As a Reconstruction-era legislator from Georgia, he witnessed firsthand the hatred, humiliation, and institutional betrayal that followed emancipation. He didn't sugarcoat it, and he didn't have time for empty patriotism.

Turner believed in reparations before the word had even taken root in the American vocabulary.

He called for land redistribution not as a favor—but as a debt. A payment owed for generations of unpaid labor, sexual violence, broken families, and stolen futures. To Turner, land was more than soil. It was power. It was stability. It was dignity. And without it, he warned, Black Americans would remain second-class citizens in a country built on their backs.

But while others still clung to hope for integration and recognition, Turner saw the writing on the wall—especially in the South. In Georgia, where the noose hung longer than the law, Turner declared that true freedom might only come through emigration. He was one of the first national Black leaders to publicly state:

"America is more our country than it is the white man's … yet they will not treat us as equals. If we must die, let it be on African soil."

To some, this sounded like retreat. But to Turner, it was a strategic rejection of a country that refused to live up to its own ideals. His stance was not one of surrender—but of clarity. He didn't abandon the idea of reparations. He simply stopped believing the U.S. government had the moral courage to ever deliver them.

And he wasn't wrong.

Turner's push for land and compensation was met with derision and silence. White lawmakers ignored him. Many Black leaders feared alienating potential allies. But his message endured—passed through generations like a seed waiting for the right soil.

He forced the question that still burns today:

What does freedom mean without land, money, or protection? What does citizenship mean when the country that claims you refuses to repair the harm it has done?

Turner knew that emancipation without reparations wasn't justice. It was optics. A performance.

And he refused to play along.

While America marched forward into the Industrial Age—building railroads, stacking fortunes, and carving skylines into the horizon—Black Americans were still digging out from under the rubble of slavery.

John Wayne Niles refused to accept that.

A bold, visionary political organizer, Niles, stepped into the storm of the late nineteenth century and formed the Indemnity Party, a political movement with a single uncompromising demand: economic reparations for the descendants of enslaved people.

Niles understood the core truth that white America didn't want to face: Black poverty wasn't accidental. It was engineered.

He watched as the same country that built its wealth on Black labor turned around and locked Black people out of the economy it created—through land theft, Jim Crow laws, voter suppression, and racially rigged labor markets.

And so, Niles made his move.

The Indemnity Party wasn't a polite plea for reform. It was a full-throated demand for restitution—for stolen labor, stolen land, and stolen lives. It called for the redistribution of wealth and resources to the people who had been systematically stripped of them since the country's founding.

Niles didn't just want justice for the past; he wanted economic power for the future. He believed that without reparations, there would be no social peace, no true democracy, and no healing.

He made it plain: economic inequality wasn't just a class issue; it was a racial wound that America refused to close.

The timing of Niles's movement was no coincidence.

The Gilded Age was exploding with unchecked capitalism, corporate monopolies, and widening wealth gaps. Industrial giants grew rich while workers, especially Black and brown workers, were discarded like spent coal. Niles saw through the illusion of "progress." He knew that without structural change, America's promises were nothing more than glittering lies.

He watched as Black communities were locked out of opportunity, pushed into ghettos, cheated out of land, and criminalized for their poverty. And he said: enough.

By putting reparations at the center of the national conversation, Niles didn't just challenge economic policy, he challenged the nation's moral compass.

He refused to let America forget that the wealth of the Gilded Age was built on stolen backs and unpaid blood.

And though his party never made it to the White House, the Indemnity Party planted a seed—a radical declaration that Black Americans weren't asking for charity.

They were demanding a refund.

For John Wayne Niles, the scars of slavery weren't abstract; they were personal, generational, and undeniable. He knew no apology without compensation could ever right the wrongs done to Black Americans. Reparations, to Niles, weren't symbolic. They were survival. They were power. They were overdue.

At the heart of the Indemnity Party, which Niles founded and led with relentless fire, was a simple, radical belief: those who built this nation's wealth through forced labor deserved a piece of that wealth.

The party's platform was clear and blunt—acknowledge the past, redistribute the profits, and deliver justice—not just with words, but with land, money, and law. It demanded reparations not only for slavery, but for the entire racist system that followed: colonization, redlining, disenfranchisement, convict leasing, stolen wages. The Indemnity Party called it what it was: theft—and theft had to be paid back.

But Niles's story wasn't just one of high ideals; it was soaked in the harsh realities of violence, conviction, and rebirth.

In 1869, Niles killed a man in Tennessee. The exact reasons— whether a dispute over money, pride, or protection—have been lost to time, but the killing was brutal. Witnesses described a confrontation that escalated fast. Words turned to threats. Threats turned to blows. Then a gunshot shattered the silence, leaving a man bleeding in the dirt.

Niles was arrested, convicted, and sent to prison. But even behind bars, he was not broken.

After serving his time, he received a pardon and relocated to Lexington, Kentucky, where he reinvented himself—not as a fugitive, but as a freedom fighter. In 1877, he moved west and joined the Kansas colonization movement, eventually becoming secretary of the Nicodemus Town Company—a bold, Black-led effort to build an all-Black settlement in Graham County, Kansas.

Nicodemus was more than a town. It was a political statement, proof that Black folks could govern, organize, and thrive when given land and autonomy. Niles became one of its loudest champions, traveling the country to recruit families and drumming up support.

In 1883, he pulled off something few had even dared: he convinced Ohio Senator John Sherman—the brother of Civil War general William Tecumseh Sherman—to submit a petition to the

U.S. Senate calling for slave reparations in the form of federal land, designated exclusively for Black settlement. A bold move. A national moment.

Niles knew the land itself was sacred. It was the inheritance that had been stolen.

Under Niles's leadership, the Indemnity Party became a magnet for Black activists, veterans, teachers, preachers, and farmers tired of waiting for justice to come written by someone else. They demanded redress not in vague terms, but in acres, infrastructure, and investment.

Their demands sparked national debate. White politicians dismissed them as radicals. But in Black communities, Niles and his party were truth-tellers. They broke the silence around reparations and called the system out by name.

They held rallies. They lobbied senators. They knocked on doors. They mobilized the historically marginalized, forcing the nation to reckon with the economic architecture of white supremacy.

John Wayne Niles was many things—a convicted killer, a political firebrand, a visionary. But above all, he was a man who refused to let the crimes of slavery be buried with the dead. He didn't flinch at America's hypocrisy. He didn't wait for permission. He knew exactly what this country owed—and he dared to collect.

His legacy lives on in today's reparations movement.

Niles was decades ahead of his time. He saw through the illusion of emancipation and knew freedom without economic repair was just another lie dressed as liberty. He laid the groundwork for modern demands: cash payments, land, legal redress, community restoration. For him, reparations weren't radical; they were a receipt. Signed in blood. Stamped by time. Today's activists echo that same clarity: we don't need another study, another commission, or another delay. We need payment in full.

Slavery is not a riddle to be solved. It is a debt to be settled. The crime is archived in courthouse ledgers, property deeds, insurance records, and in stolen land still held in white hands. The devil, as they say, is in the details—and slavery was the devil.

Dr. Mary Frances Berry, in her powerful book *My Face Is Black Is True*, quoted an official from the federal Pension Bureau during the Ex-Slave Pension Movement: "The government's policy has always been to delay, deny, and defend." That wasn't just bureaucratic foot-dragging; it was doctrine, a strategy. A cold, calculated system designed to outlast Black resistance. To starve it out. To smother it beneath paperwork, poverty, and silence.

But here's what should chill every American spine: that same phrase— "delay, deny, and defend"—resurfaced in 2024, this time in the manifesto of Luigi Mangione, the man who murdered a Healthcare CEO. Mangione, furious over corporate injustice, allegedly etched those very words onto bullet casings found at the crime scene. His claim? The company weaponized bureaucracy to deny care, defend profits, and delay life-saving treatment until it was too late.

And what happened next? The internet lionized him. Think pieces praised his rage. Documentaries romanticized his motives. Donations poured into his defense fund. To many, he became a rebel—a martyr—standing up against corporate power. But here's the question we can't stop asking:

Where is that same energy for us?

America is the freedman's corporation—built on our labor, our blood, our unpaid invoices. We were denied land, education, pensions, and justice. So, where are the love letters for our martyrs? Where are the GoFundMe's for reparations? Where's the Netflix docuseries for John Wayne Niles? For Callie House? For the three hundred thousand ex-slaves who signed their names on petitions that got buried, ignored, erased from government archives?

Luigi gets sympathy. We get silence.

Luigi becomes a symbol of righteous rebellion. Our rebellion? It's labeled "radical," "divisive," "dangerous." But here's the truth: our claim came first. Before corporations denied coverage, the government denied justice. Before health insurance denied care, the courts denied land. Before Mangione's manifesto, there was Niles's platform. Callie House's petitions. Henry McNeal Turner's thunder. John T. Ward's quiet resistance.

We were the first to say: this system is rigged. This debt is real. And we will not die waiting for justice to deliver itself.

Let the record show: the phrase "delay, deny, and defend" was forged in our fight—not theirs. And now, after centuries of watching it used against us, we're reclaiming it as Exhibit A.

Because we're not asking anymore. We're invoicing. And this time, payment is expected in full.

CHAPTER 16

Make America Pay Again: Invoice #1865

"If the government had the right to free us, she had the right to make some provisions for us and since she did not make it soon after emancipation she ought to make it now"

-Callie House 1898

I n the aftermath of emancipation, as millions of formerly enslaved Black Americans took their first steps toward freedom, they carried more than chains in their memory. They carried dreams, dreams of economic independence, of homes they could call their own, of businesses run by Black hands for Black futures.

And in 1865, just months after the Civil War ended, one institution rose from the smoke of slavery, promising to be the foundation of those dreams: the Freedman's Savings and Trust Company, better known as the Freedman's Bank.

It was created by an act of Congress, with a mission that sounded like salvation in the ears of a newly freed people: to protect their savings, invest in their future, and build a financial bridge from slavery to full citizenship. Its branches popped up across the South, and tens of thousands of Black families—many banking for the first time—walked through those doors with hope in their hearts.

But behind the marble walls and patriotic speeches was something else: greed, corruption, and betrayal.

From the start, Freedman's Bank was never truly in Black hands. Though its depositors were freedmen, the institution was run by white financiers—many tied to the very system of slavery that had robbed Black people of their wages, bodies, and families.

These men used their power to loot the bank from within. They gambled depositors' savings on risky railroad ventures. They funneled money into speculative real estate deals. Some straight-up stole. All the while telling the freedmen to trust a system that had always exploited them.

As financial mismanagement escalated, warning signs flashed nationwide—but the federal government refused to act. No real oversight, no rescue plan, no protection for the very people the bank was supposed to serve. Instead, Black depositors were told to be patient, to believe in American finance, to trust that the government would never steal their futures again.

They were wrong.

In 1874, the Freedman's Bank collapsed, wiping out the life savings of over sixty-one thousand freedmen families. More than three million dollars disappeared, the equivalent of nearly eighty-five million dollars today—money painstakingly earned by washerwomen, farmers, laborers, and Union Army veterans. Money they'd believed was finally safe.

And just like that, the bridge to Black economic empowerment was blown apart.

The collapse of the Freedman's Bank wasn't just a financial crisis; it was a spiritual blow. It shattered trust in America's institutions. It devastated small Black-owned businesses, stifled property ownership, and widened the racial wealth gap that Reconstruction was supposed to close.

This was no accident. It was systemic exploitation, backed by the federal government and protected by silence.

No one was held accountable. Not one of the white executives who ran the bank into the ground served a day in prison. And the federal government, though it chartered the bank, refused to reimburse the depositors. Instead, the freedmen were told again what they'd heard too many times before: "You'll have to start over."

But how do you rebuild a future that was stolen before it ever had a chance to grow?

The legacy of the Freedman's Bank collapse still haunts Black America. It's why, to this day, Black communities remain deeply skeptical of financial institutions. It's why the racial wealth gap has persisted, generation after generation. And it's why calls for reparations grow louder with every passing decade.

Because this wasn't just about money; it was about deliberate obstruction of Black progress.

And many believe justice still needs to be paid.

Some propose reparations in the form of educational debt forgiveness for descendants of depositors. Others advocate for direct economic investment in historically Black neighborhoods, funding Black-owned banks, or the creation of a federal trust to support Black business ownership and land acquisition. Then there are those who simply say: cut the check!

Whatever form it takes, one truth remains …

The Freedman's Bank promised Black America a future—and then robbed them in broad daylight.

Until that debt is addressed, the American financial system stays complicit in the theft.

While the Freedman's Bank stole Black America's savings, Callie House rose up to demand something far greater: compensation for a lifetime of stolen labor.

**

Born into slavery in Rutherford County, Tennessee, Callie House wasn't a politician. She wasn't a lawyer. She wasn't wealthy. She was a widow, a washerwoman, and a mother of five. And yet, she became the face of one of the most audacious grassroots movements for reparations this country has ever seen.

In a world that told her to stay quiet—she roared.

By the late nineteenth century, House saw with blistering clarity what America preferred to ignore: emancipation hadn't leveled the playing field. It had only opened the gate to a new battlefield. Black Americans remained trapped in cycles of poverty—denied land, pensions, and justice—while white institutions built generational wealth off their stolen labor.

So, she fought.

Callie House co-founded the National Ex-Slave Mutual Relief, Bounty, and Pension Association—a mouthful of a name, but one heavy with purpose. Her goal was clear: secure federal pensions for formerly enslaved people, just like the government had done for Union soldiers.

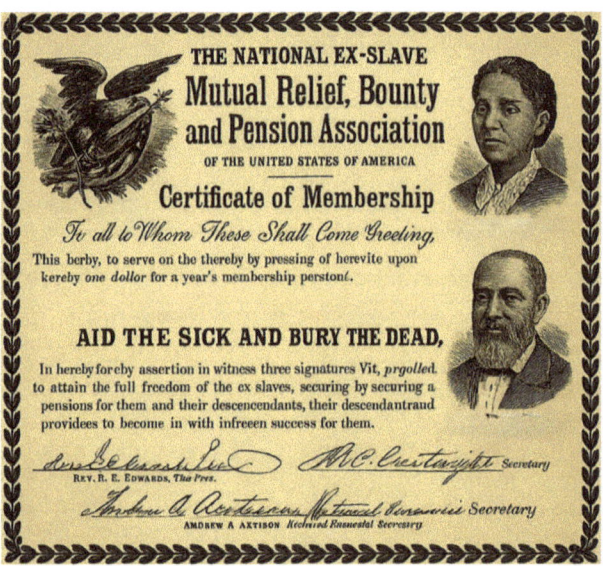

Why shouldn't the people who built this country from nothing get paid? Why should the freed people die poor after a lifetime of unpaid labor that made others rich?

Callie House wasn't just an organizer. She was a visionary. She understood that reparations weren't a favor, they were a path to dignity, healing, and full citizenship. She knew what generations before her demanded, and what generations after would keep fighting for.

Freedom without reparations is not freedom; it's abandonment.

She rejected the lie that the Emancipation Proclamation had "settled the score."

She lived through it. And she knew better.

She took that message on the road—traveling the South with her children in tow, organizing in church basements, under tents, in schoolhouses, and living rooms. She held mass meetings, drafted petitions, and mobilized hundreds of thousands—many who couldn't vote but still raised their voices.

And they did.

Together, Callie and her network gathered over three thousand signatures and sent them to Washington. Their message was unrelenting: America owes a debt to its ex-slaves. And we demand payment.

Through relentless organizing and unapologetic leadership, Callie House ignited a national conversation—not just in Black communities, but across the political spectrum. She built a movement rooted in justice, memory, and demand.

That momentum finally reached the halls of power.

A pensions bill, championed by House's movement, was introduced in Congress. It was the result of relentless organizing and a tidal wave of signatures.

And when it mattered most, Congress did what it always does when Black folks demand justice; it blinked, shelved the bill, postponed it indefinitely, and buried it in red tape and silence.

Callie didn't flinch.

In 1899, she stood before power and reminded Congress that the First Amendment guarantees the right to petition the government for redress of grievances. This wasn't charity. It was constitutional—legal, moral, binding.

But that courage made her dangerous.

Her influence grew. And so did fear in the halls of power.

Federal agencies, backed by postal inspectors, political operatives, and white informants, started spying on her movement—not because it was fraudulent, but because it was effective. Because hundreds of thousands of Black Americans were uniting around one unshakable truth.

America owes us.

So, they tried to crush it.

In a calculated act of suppression, Callie House was arrested and tried by an all-white, all-male jury—a spectacle meant to scare every freed person who dared to dream.

The charge? Mail fraud.

The real reason? She was winning.

She was convicted.

Her imprisonment dealt a devastating blow to the national reparation's movement. But even behind bars, Callie House had built something too powerful to destroy.

Her arrest may have stolen her voice—but it couldn't stop her mission.

She never lived to see her dream fulfilled.

But her legacy lives on.

The very structure of modern reparations movements—from legal filings to grassroots mobilization—stand on her shoulders.

Her movement was suppressed. Her petitions were ignored. Her name was nearly erased from history.

But her fire lit the fuse.

Callie House showed the world that Black pain had receipts and Black people knew how to collect.

As the years passed, her movement didn't fade; it grew.

In dusty schoolhouses and church pews, in handwritten letters and whispered prayers, her message took root.

Black freedom must come with compensation.

Her community flourished, fueled by the belief that reparations weren't a gift, but a debt long past due. The stories of formerly enslaved people—those who built homes, educated children, and organized cooperatives—stood as living proof.

Reparations could heal. Reparations could build. Reparations could last.

Local chapters kept organizing. They strategized and passed down her vision through sermons, stories, and determination.

They kept the torch burning—long after the government tried to snuff it out.

More than a century later, the demand hasn't changed. What Callie House stood for is now debated in Congress, printed in headlines, and shouted in the streets. The truth she risked everything to speak has become part of the public discourse.

There's growing recognition that slavery, Jim Crow, redlining, mass incarceration, and systemic economic exclusion weren't just isolated chapters; they're the foundation of America's racial wealth gap. That gap still exists, still grows, still robs Black families—and still enriches white institutions.

Reparations ain't whispers behind closed doors no more. They're proposed in legislation like H.R. 40. They're discussed by scholars, demanded by coalitions, and defended by economists.

But today's fight has changed. It's louder, but more fractured. What once was a unified cry has become a chorus of different voices. Some call for cash payments. Others demand land. Some push for tax relief, student loan cancellation, or investments in Black communities.

Still, beneath all that noise—one thing is clear: reparations ain't symbolic. They ain't impossible. They ain't too late. They're overdue.

They are the unfinished business of American democracy.

At the heart of the movement is a principle as old as Callie House—and John T. Ward: No loyalty without return. No patriotism without equity. No justice without repair.

In coffee shops in Chicago, in pulpits across Georgia, libraries in Ohio, think tanks, marches, and kitchen tables—the conversation goes on.

There are victories. There are setbacks. There is fatigue—but there's also faith.

'Cause this fight ain't a moment; it's a lineage. And no matter how long it takes, the bill will come due.

***

The book lay heavy in my lap, its title—*The Sweetest Taste of Liberty*—echoing in my mind like the last haunting note of a spiritual. The story inside unfolded with both triumph and sorrow: a Black woman who, with unshaken resolve, stood before a federal court in Ohio and won her case for reparations. A victory so rare it felt almost mythical.

But as I turned the last pages, I came upon a revelation so jarring, so personal, it cracked the story wide open.

The man she sued—the very embodiment of cruelty in her life—was Zebulon Ward, a name soaked in blood and betrayal.

He was a notorious slave catcher, a brutal profiteer, and one of the early architects of what we now call America's prison-industrial complex. His life's work was built on profiting from the captivity of Black bodies—hidden under the thin veil of legality.

But what sent chills down my spine wasn't just the scale of his villainy. It was the lineage. Zeb Ward, as history would show, was distantly related to my ancestor, John T. Ward.

Zeb Ward's legacy is one of cold calculation and systemic cruelty. A former Kentucky legislator and prison warden, he embodied the worst of the convict leasing era, a system that extended slavery through new legal chains.

In 1854, he was named keeper of the Kentucky State Penitentiary. Almost immediately, he rewrote his contract with the state. Instead of a salary, Zeb agreed to pay six thousand dollars a year flat, giving him the right to keep all profits from prisoner labor. This turned the penitentiary into a fully privatized, profit-driven machine—where cruelty wasn't just allowed, it was encouraged.

Under Zeb's rule, incarcerated men—many of them Black—worked in brutal conditions. They produced hemp products, mostly rope and bagging for cotton bales, in filthy, dangerous environments. Missing production quotas meant harsh flogging, often leading to infections, illness, and death.

Abolitionist Calvin Fairbank, who himself was jailed there for helping enslaved people escape, called Zeb "utterly devoid of heart or conscience." He reported that Zeb "literally killed 250 out of 375 prisoners" during his time.

The death toll was staggering. In 1858 alone, twenty-three inmates died—almost 10 percent of the prison population. Later investigations confirmed that death rates under Zeb's watch were the highest in the prison's history.

And still, Zeb faced no consequences. He walked away with profits, while hundreds of men—many jailed for petty offenses or simply for being Black—never walked out at all.

But Zeb Ward's cruelty didn't stop in Kentucky. He later leased the Arkansas State Penitentiary, where similar abuses went down. Prison surgeon A.H. Scott compared Zeb to a slave master. Scott warned that Zeb ruled the prison with absolute power and no regard for human life.

Zebulon Ward's story ain't just history; it's a case study on how oppression evolves rather than disappears. His legacy shows the seamless shift from chattel slavery to convict leasing: a new form of forced labor, legalized, driven by profit, and hitting Black Americans hardest.

He's a brutal reminder that what was done with chains and whips was later done with contracts and courtrooms.

To confront Zeb Ward's legacy is to confront the roots of the prison-industrial complex. His crimes weren't hidden; they were systematized, monetized, and ignored.

And the fact that he's tied, however distantly, to my own family line? That's a cold irony. While John T. Ward risked his life as a conductor on the Underground Railroad, Zeb Ward profited by chaining Black men to walls and workbenches.

One man built paths to freedom. The other built a prison empire.

And America, to this day, still wrestles with which version it wants to honor.

Two men. Two Wards. One bloodline. And yet, they stood on opposite sides of humanity's moral divide.

Zeb Ward never met John T. But the legacy they left behind couldn't be more different—like fire and flood. Zeb worked in shadows, building a system that turned flesh into currency, cruelty into order. I imagined the clang of chains in his jails, cold steel shackles catching morning light, the air thick with rot, sweat, and despair. That was Zeb's America.

And then there was John T.

John T. Ward—the conductor, the strategist, the liberator. I could almost feel the cool Ohio breeze, the crunch of dirt roads under his wagon wheels. While Zeb built cages, John T. built routes—silent paths to freedom carved from courage, community, and faith.

Where Zeb shackled the body, John T. unshackled the soul. Every whisper in the night, every flickering lantern behind curtains, every child hidden beneath quilts in false wagon floors—that was John T.'s rebellion.

John T. Ward's Ohio wasn't just geography. It was defiance in motion. A place where enslaved folks became fugitives, and fugitives became free. Unity wasn't hope; it was survival. John T. worked with churches, abolitionist cells, and Black farmers, who trained horses not just for show, but for speed and silence—to outrun slave catchers like Zeb.

And now, all these years later, in an Ohio courtroom, those two legacies collided. One—Zeb Ward's—on trial through the system he once ruled. The other—John T. Ward's—living on in the woman bold enough to demand what was owed.

It's a reminder, sharp and unavoidable, that blood doesn't define justice. Choices do.

As I closed the book, its weight still resting on my knees, I felt history wasn't behind me. It was in me. Flowing through my veins was not just the courage of John T. Ward, but the cold reality of Zeb's proximity—warning that history's always watching, always repeating, unless we choose otherwise.

Their contrast teaches us this: legacy is a mirror, but it's also a weapon. What we reflect—and what we do—decides which side of history we stand on.

And that, in this new era of reparations and reckoning, the battle is still going on.

Henrietta Wood's story is a powerful testament to Black resilience and the long, grueling pursuit of justice in America. In 1853, she was forcibly kidnapped and re-enslaved by Zebulon Ward—a man who later rose to prominence within the emerging prison-industrial complex. Despite the trauma she endured, Wood refused to let her story end in silence.

In 1870, she filed a groundbreaking lawsuit seeking twenty thousand dollars in reparations for her illegal enslavement.

After nearly eight years of courtroom battles and legal obstacles, a federal jury awarded her two thousand five hundred dollars in 1878—the largest known sum ever granted by a U.S. court as restitution for slavery. Though it fell far short of what she sought, it was a monumental legal victory in a nation that had barely begun reckoning with its sins.

To put her claim in modern terms, the twenty thousand dollars she originally demanded would be worth about $490,901 in 2024, adjusted for inflation at an average historical rate of 2.1 percent per year.

Henrietta Wood's case was more than just a lawsuit; it was a declaration. Justice was still owed, even in Ohio, even decades later.

Her demand for reparations wasn't just symbolic. It was staggering for its time. And yet, the two thousand five hundred dollars she was awarded—though one of the largest sums ever paid to a formerly enslaved person—barely scratched the surface of what had been stolen from her. It was monumental, yes. But it wasn't justice. Not really.

And the check she received? It came with a note from Zebulon Ward that chilled the blood: "The last nigger I would ever pay."

Those words weren't just cruel; they were telling. They summed up everything Wood had fought against, not just personal vengeance, but the deep, unapologetic resistance to reckoning with slavery's legacy.

Was it a final insult from Zeb? Or was it something more disturbing—a mirror held up to America itself?

Because to this day, more than a century later, that same message still echoes—through policy, through courtrooms, through silence. America's ongoing reluctance to face its historical debts.

We'll give you just enough to quiet you, and not a cent more.

The United States has a history of handing out reparations to different groups. Japanese Americans got twenty thousand dollars each for their internment during World War II, thanks to the Civil Liberties Act of 1988. Native American tribes have received settlements worth billions for land seizures and other wrongs. Even Confederate slaveholders were paid for the "loss" of their so-called property after the Civil War. But The enslaved—the ones whose labor built this nation—have been denied that same kind of restitution time and again.

The racial wealth gap tells this story plain and clear. As of 2022, the median White household held $284,310 in wealth, while the median Black household had just $44,100. That's a gap that's barely budged in decades. This isn't just a number; it's generations of systemic discrimination and economic exclusion stacked up against Black families.

Some Black conservatives push back against reparations, calling them handouts instead of what's owed. But that view misses the bigger picture—the history of theft, oppression, and exploitation. Reparations ain't charity; they're justice. They're about fixing a debt that's been owed for centuries.

The reparations movement has often leaned on moral appeals, but as the wealth gap keeps growing and frustration builds, tensions could rise too. If nothing meaningful happens, the generations coming up won't just inherit economic gaps; they'll inherit deep resentment.

Henrietta Wood's victory was big, no doubt. But it was just one step on a long road to justice. Her story reminds us that progress is possible, but the fight for reparations calls for ongoing advocacy, education, and solidarity. Americas got to face its past—and make real moves to fix the lasting damage slavery left behind.

Let's Set the Record Straight: Reparations Ain't About Guilt—They're About the Bill America Still Owes.

Here's a reality check—delivered like a Mike Tyson uppercut. Or, if you want something fresh, "Let me run this fade," like Aaron the Plumber.

And for all the folks clutching their pearls over the tone? Go ahead—put this in your pipe and smoke it.

That line? Yeah, it's old school—straight from Charles Dickens himself. A nineteenth-century way of saying: "Here's the truth—deal with it."

Or, to put it bluntly? "I said what I said. Now sit with it."

Fitting, right? Because that's the same era when John T. Ward and his friends were out here moving Black bodies to freedom, while America was still busy cashing checks written in blood.

When you say it plain, the truth hits harder. Whether whispered from abolitionist church rafters or shouted through bullhorns on courthouse steps, the message never changes: there's a debt that's long overdue—and it's time to pay up.

No guilt. No games. Just the invoice.

Reparations ain't about personal guilt. They're about collective accountability. It's a ledger of human suffering and stolen labor that's still unpaid.

Your family might not have owned enslaved people. But if you're living in this country, chances are you've benefited from the system their blood built—whether you know it or not. Railroads, banks, Ivy League endowments, shipping ports, police departments, Wall Street firms, the federal government itself—many were born or boomed on the backs of enslaved people.

Systemic advantage doesn't ask your permission before working in your favor.

"But My Family Was Poor!"

No one's denying white poverty. But poverty doesn't erase racial privilege; it just wears a different uniform.

Poor white folks still got to vote. They could buy land through the Homestead Act, attend whites-only schools, benefit from New Deal programs, and pass down generational wealth without red lines or racial covenants.

Meanwhile, Black Americans were locked out of nearly every wealth-building institution—from slavery to redlining, convict leasing, voter suppression, COINTELPRO, the war on Drugs, and now mass incarceration.

White poverty always had a ladder. Black struggle always had shackles.

"But I Pay Taxes Too! Why Should My Money Go to Something I Didn't Cause?"

Black Americans pay taxes too—and they've paid into a system that denied them the very rights those taxes were supposed to guarantee.

They paid for schools they couldn't attend. For roads that led to segregated suburbs they couldn't buy into. For police departments that policed them with violence, not protection. For a government that built highways through their neighborhoods and then called them "blighted."

Black Americans didn't just build this country; they were forced to bankroll their own oppression.

Opposition hides behind the "taxpayer burden" excuse, but truth is, public money has always been used to repair state-sanctioned harm—just rarely when it comes to Black folks.

And let's be real—when this country wants money, it finds it: $4.6 trillion in COVID relief, billions in bailouts to Wall Street; trillions spent on endless wars overseas, even slaveholders in D.C. got paid reparations when slavery ended

Washington Paid the Slaveholders—Not the Enslaved!

Let's set this straight: the only people in U.S. history to receive reparations for slavery were the enslavers.

Yes, in Washington, D.C.—the so-called land of the free—when slavery ended in 1862, the government didn't compensate those brutalized, raped, and worked to the bone. Instead, it cut checks to their captors. And it was President Abraham Lincoln who signed that bill into law.

The District of Columbia Compensated Emancipation Act, championed by Lincoln, freed over 3,100 enslaved Black people in D.C. But it came with a cruel price tag: white slaveholders were paid up to three hundred dollars per enslaved person for their "loss of property." The formerly enslaved? They got nothing. No land. No wages. Not even recognition. The government allocated about one million dollars—in 1862 dollars—to make sure white Union loyalists didn't suffer economic hardship as slavery unraveled.

And Lincoln praised this move. He said: "Such an amount of good has not been done by one law, in relation to this subject, for the last fifty years as will be done by this one."

To many, this sounded like progress. To the enslaved, it was a slap in the face dressed up as freedom.

Let's be real about Lincoln. Yes, he helped end slavery—but he also flirted with shipping Black people out of the country altogether. Lincoln supported colonization—the idea that formerly enslaved people should be "returned" to Africa or sent to Central America because he doubted white and Black people could ever live together peacefully. In 1862—the same year he signed the D.C. Emancipation Act—he met with Black leaders and said: "Your race suffer very greatly, many of them by living among us, while ours suffer from your presence."

Translation? Freedom might be on the table—but equality? Citizenship? A seat at America's table? Not yet.

Yes, this was a milestone. The government took action and confronted slavery. But it also showed something deeper: America has always been more willing to pay those who profited from slavery than those who endured it.

That's why this chapter of history ain't just about small victories or moments to celebrate; it's a sharp reminder. When it was time to pay, the government wrote checks to the men who held the whips—not the people who bore the scars.

This ain't ancient history. It's the foundation for the fight for reparations today. The government knows how to write the check; it just never wanted to write it to us.

But the people who were enslaved? Not a dime.

We paid Japanese Americans for their time in internment camps. We paid Native tribes land settlements and annual federal appropriations. And let's not forget the G.I. Bill and land grant benefits—most of which excluded Black veterans and citizens, even though they were publicly funded.

Hell, we even paid Confederate loyalists for their lost "property." But the descendants of enslaved people—the ones who endured the worst? Still waiting.

So why all the opposition? It ain't about taxes. It ain't about history. It ain't about practicality. It's about fear.

The same fear that once gripped the Southern slaveholding elite—the fear of having to compete on equal terms. They said it plain back then: "If they are free, we will have to compete."

That's what this really comes down to. Fear that if Black folks get what they're owed, the playing field will finally be level. Fear that privilege won't be protected by default any more.

Dr. Claud Anderson put it best: "Black people can't be racist. Racism is about power. It's about controlling wealth, institutions, and systems."

Even the word "race" comes from competition. This country didn't invent racism by accident; it used it to hoard resources and monopolize opportunity. And now, when the bill comes due, they act like they forgot.

But we haven't forgotten.

The wealth gap between Black and white families today is wider than it was after Reconstruction. Black kids are more likely to be born into poverty, into debt, into communities still fighting for clean water, decent schools, and real opportunity.

While other groups got reparations for harm done—often on a smaller scale—Black Americans are told to be patient, to wait, to work harder, to "move on."

But you don't just "move on" from a robbery until what was stolen gets returned.

Reparations ain't charity. They're justice. They're the compound interest on 246 years of unpaid labor, plus another 150 years of racial terrorism, exclusion, and exploitation.

If you believe in America's promise, then honor its debts.

To white allies: you don't have to carry guilt—but you must carry truth. Step back if you scared. But better yet—lean in and lend your voice to the fight.

To anyone calling reparations a "handout"—let's get one thing straight:

This ain't about begging. It's about collecting. It's about legacy, not laziness.

Calling reparations a "handout" is the ultimate insult—like we're out here looking for Juneteenth gift bags with no receipts. Nah, baby. A receipt means a transaction took place. And in our case? Oh, it did.

Centuries of unpaid labor. Stolen land. Exploited bodies. Blocked opportunity. That tab's been running since 1619—and guess what? The account is past due.

And let's upgrade that cute little phrase "we got the receipts." We are the receipts. You see us in the underfunded schools, the redlined neighborhoods, the over-policed blocks, the trauma passed down like heirlooms wrapped in poverty.

And to America—still clutching denial like a flag.

Reparations ain't a threat. They're a test. A test of your courage, your constitution, and your character. And if you keep dodging it? Know this ...

The next generation won't ask. They'll demand. They'll come kicking, screaming—and organized.

Because justice ain't charity. It's a bill. And we're not letting you slide.

So, here's the new talking point. This ain't just a claim. It's a liability settlement.

One the U.S. government underwrote with slave codes, Jim Crow laws, Black Codes, convict leasing, and every system built to delay and deny.

They've played the role of shady claims adjuster long enough. But now?

It's giving Top Dog Law energy with a class-action spirit. "Injured by four hundred years of oppression? You may be entitled to compensation." We want top dollar. Not symbolism. Not speeches. Not performative diversity.

We want the check—Nationwide. But this time? We're on our side. We're done waiting for institutions to show up for us.

CHAPTER 17

Ringmasters: The Greatest Show Never Told

"The greatest show never told is the story of people who have endured, who have had struggles, who have gone through situations, and yet they're still here."

-Maya Angelou

I was nine years old, two ponytails swinging, Black and bold, thinking my family was running the world. And honestly? On East Main Street in the mid-to-late 1970s, it felt like we were.

That stretch of Columbus was alive with rhythm—full of texture, sound, and scent that wrapped around you like a warm coat. The Ward office buzzed with the staccato clatter of typewriter keys and the soft, persistent ring of rotary phones. It was the sound of Black business in motion. The heavy, sweet scent of Resch's donuts— soft, yeasty pillows of joy—mingled with the rich aroma of brewing coffee. That coffee was mostly cream and sugar, and it was a treat for me back then. Still is.

Stepping into that office was like entering a kingdom. A Ward Kingdom. Our family name was painted in bold red, white, and blue letters on the sides of vans and semi-trucks that lined the street—a declaration of pride and power. Inside, desks formed neat rows, all orbiting around my grandfather, Harold Ward. He was the nucleus of the operation—magnetic and immovable. His brothers held their positions, respected and steady. But it was his sister—my Aunt Marie—who stopped time. She had her own office. Her own private bathroom. She held the family archives like a priestess, a duty she shared with her daughter. No one questioned her. She was the vault.

The office moved like a living organism. My uncles' pockets were heavy with two-dollar bills and quarters, and they'd toss them to me with a wink. The office staff knew my tic-tac-toe games were coming, and they played along like it was written into their job descriptions. My grandmother and I arrived like clockwork, a team bearing boxes of warm donuts and big energy. Brewing the office coffee was my job, and I took it seriously. I could never reach the water fountain's reservoir alone, but every time someone helped me fill it, it felt like a sacred little ritual.

And when the sun dipped low, the whole block seemed to shift. Across the street, Joe's Hole nightclub came alive—bass thumping, the air electric. But what I remember most was him. Chicken Man. His name was John Harlan Early, but to many, he was the Rooster.

He didn't walk like other men. He clucked—loud, low, and haunted—like a rooster chasing the ghosts of a fire no one else could see. He dragged a soot-stained cart behind him like a broken parade float, filled with scorched dolls, melted memories, a photo yellowed by fire and time. They said he lost everything—wife, daughter, home—in a blaze. They said his brother-in-law, thick with grief and blame, beat him until the world turned sideways. And when he stood back up, bloodied and burning with something unspeakable, he flapped his arms like wings and clucked like a rooster. From that day on, he never stopped.

Most people ignored him, or laughed, or looked away. But not my grandfather. He saw something else, maybe the reflection of a trauma he could never name. Maybe the silhouette of a man who didn't die, but didn't live the same again, either.

And then there was me.

Chicken Man would stare at me, long and hard. Not in a frightening way—though as a child, something in my spirit always tightened when he looked too long. I'd stand frozen in my ponytails, small and unsure, as he slowly reached into his cart and pulled out a dingy toy—a melted doll, a legless action figure, a stuffed bear crusted in soot. He would hold it out to me, eyes glassy with something deeper than age.

"Her name was Shanna too," he'd mumble. Sometimes it was a whisper. Sometimes it felt like a prayer.

I didn't know if it was true. Maybe it wasn't. But I knew what it meant—every time he saw me, he was revisiting the fire. Revisiting her. His daughter. His family. His ghosts.

And me? I wasn't ready to carry that. But I think I already was.

Because even then, I was part of a legacy shaped by loss—a family that had survived fire, grief, and history's heavy hand. And my grandfather? He didn't carry a black cane because he needed help walking. He carried it in his soul to remind him where he came from. Because some burdens aren't meant for the hands; they're meant to be walked with, step by quiet step.

Chicken Man had a gray beard the color of smoke-tanned leather, ragged clothes that clung like guilt, and a face carved by time and flame. Burn scars mapped his cheeks like a story no one finished reading. His teeth were crooked, brown, like piano keys, no one played anymore. His skin bore a Cajun hue—sunbaked, soot-marked, and forgotten by the world. And yet, something in him remembered me. Or maybe not me. Maybe her.

Maybe when he looked at me, he didn't see a little Black girl skipping to the Ward office with a box of donuts—maybe he saw his daughter, in some parallel world where the fire never happened, and his hands were still whole enough to hold her.

I didn't want the toys. But I never ran.

Because even then, deep in my child's mind, I recognized what it was: an offering. Not to play with, but to pass something on, a pain he couldn't carry alone anymore.

My grandfather's banter wasn't mockery; it was empathy. A kind of care wrapped in humor. Maybe he saw in Chicken Man a reflection of the trauma he carried from his days as a firefighter. Or maybe he just refused to turn his back on someone the world had long written off.

Because my grandfather didn't see a spectacle. He saw a man.

Whenever Chicken Man drifted onto our block, clucking and crowing like a rooster, Harold Ward would light up with a grin full of mischief. "Come on now, Chicken Man! Give us a cock-a-doodle-doo!" he'd call out, like greeting an old friend. And without fail, Chicken Man would rise to the moment—straightening his back, flapping his arms, and letting out a piercing, warbling crow that echoed down East Main like a sermon only he could preach.

My grandmother, Mary Ellen, endured it. She'd wince every time that clucking cut through the air, especially when it rang out in front of the well-to-do neighbors she worked so hard to impress. My grandfather knew it, too. He'd tease her with theatrical flair, calling her name like a siren: "Mary Ellen! He's here!"

She'd scold him, roll her eyes—but they never turned Chicken Man away. Not when my grandfather was alive. Not even after he was gone.

He was always welcome.

But not forever.

A little over a year after my grandfather passed, Chicken Man died too—struck by a car in the early morning hours on the East Side of Columbus. He was in critical condition when the authorities arrived, clinging to life. The same police who used to mock him, who would laugh as they passed him clucking down East Main Street, now stood over his broken body.

And to add insult to injury, they told *The Columbus Dispatch* they'd be issuing him a citation for walking in the street.

John Earley

They claimed they couldn't find a next of kin. But did they even try?

This man—whose voice once startled an entire city, whose cluck echoed from national TV screens after appearing on *The Gong Show*—was reduced to a roadside tragedy. No fanfare. No tribute. Just silence.

Another Black man, discarded. Another life with pain too loud for the city to understand—so it erased it instead. His story, like so many others, wasn't too strange to matter. It was too painful for them to face. A life dismissed. A death ignored. And once again, it was left to us—the living, the witnesses—to carry the memory alone.

He clucked his last sermon into the dark, and the streets fell silent.

As I got older, the weight of Chicken Man's story began to settle inside me. The clucking? It wasn't just noise. It was grief made audible. A survival call. A fractured language stitched together from the ashes of his family. That cart he pulled behind him? It wasn't junk. It was a shrine. Proof that he once had a life. A wife. A daughter. A home. Until a fire took it all.

And the beating that followed—that brutal, humiliating assault by his brother-in-law, who blamed him for surviving—didn't just leave scars. It carved a permanent identity. "Chicken!" they had screamed at him. So, he became one, not out of madness, but out of defiance.

And every time he walked down our street, he wasn't just broken. He was enduring. And we saw him.

Les Brown, the legendary motivational speaker, often tells the story of Chicken Man as a metaphor for endurance. But for me, it's more than a metaphor. It's memory. A living, breathing lesson I witnessed on the streets of East Main as a child—with wide eyes and a heart too young to hold the weight of what I was seeing.

Brown talks about Chicken Man as a symbol—the embodiment of what it means to rise through unspeakable hardship. To push forward when the world stops caring. To wear your wounds out loud and still walk.

I remember that clucking. I remember the soot-stained cart trailing behind him, filled with scorched toys and memories too painful for words. And I remember the unspoken understanding between Chicken Man and my grandfather, that small, sacred exchange that never mocked, only acknowledged. And of course, when he came by, my grandfather, Harold E. Ward, would put something in his pockets.

Those memories carved something into me. They shaped my understanding of what resilience truly is, not just pushing through pain, but continuing to show up when you've been all but erased. Chicken Man's story was my first introduction to the quiet, brutal dignity of survival.

Because that's what my family taught me: you don't measure a man by his condition, but by his courage.

Chicken Man was not a joke. He was a sermon. A walking reminder that everyone carries something—some heavier than others. His cluck still echoes in my spirit, not as a punchline, but as a battle cry. A reminder that brokenness doesn't cancel out humanity.

His story is etched into the scent of strong coffee, the rhythm of old streets, and the legacy of giving my family left behind. And I carry it forward.

Just like Chicken Man, John T. Ward also lost the ones who mattered most—but unlike Chicken Man, he had no license to grieve out loud.

His pain didn't parade down East Main behind a scorched cart. It settled silently in the shadows of his ledgers, meeting minutes, and absences from history. While the world saw a leader, I saw a man who wore his grief like his black cane—quiet, daily, functional. It was part of his walk, not his words.

John T. Ward endured the loss of his eleven-year-old daughter, Mary, whose death in 1856 left unexplained gaps in his public life. He lost his granddaughter Jessie in a suspicious fire in Pittsburgh—a girl buried in a pauper's grave far from home. And his daughter Catherine—abandoned by her husband and ultimately institutionalized—was swallowed by silence and shame.

As I pieced together my family's story, I began to notice something unsettling—John T. Ward was missing from the record at crucial moments. One absence in particular caught my breath: the meeting minutes from 1856, during one of Ohio's most infamous court proceedings, the trial of Peggy Garner.

John T. Ward, a man who was always present, always accounted for, was nowhere to be found. My heart told me why. That was the year Mary died—his eleven-year-old daughter. And suddenly, the voids in the archives became more than clerical oversight. They became testimony.

It wasn't just that he didn't attend. It was the silences in his writings, the pauses in his public life, the ink that didn't flow. I traced the blank spaces like scars. They formed a pattern his civic work slowed, his speeches stopped, his name vanished from the very rooms he once helped fill with purpose.

What Chicken Man lost to fire, John T. Ward lost in silence.

He didn't drag his grief down the street for all to see. He tucked it away—in ledgers, in meeting minutes, in the quiet margins of time. That's where I found him—not missing, but mourning. A man buried in duty who, for a time, buried his voice.

His daughter Mary was gone. And with her, a part of him vanished too. The man who had marched through city hall with dignity and pride, who had helped others escape the literal and figurative flames of slavery through Bluff Farms, suddenly stopped moving forward.

He chose to sit beside his wife. He chose quiet over obligation, stillness over public service. He chose love.

But grief didn't stop knocking.

Grief, after all, is an unrelenting guest. It returns, over and over. And still, John T. Ward served. Even if his pen went quiet, his purpose didn't.

I think of that when I trace the history of Bluff Farms.

Bluff Farms, owned by John T. Ward and Littleberry Moss, was more than just a piece of land; it was a powerful symbol of the abolitionist cause. Situated in Truro Township, Franklin County, Ohio, the farm served as a vital stop on the Underground Railroad, offering refuge to those seeking freedom.

The name *Bluff Farms* likely carried layered meaning. Located on elevated land, the farm offered a natural lookout, a tactical view of the surrounding area, with Walnut Creek as its water supply. But beyond geography, the name may have symbolized secrecy and strategy. Just like a bluff in poker, it could've reflected the quiet deception used to protect freedom seekers.

The U.S. Agricultural Schedule gives us a glimpse into the farm's success. Littleberry Moss, listed as a farmer and landowner, held ninety-eight acres—fifty improved, forty-eight unimproved. The farm was valued at $3,600, with $120 in implements and machinery. He owned five horses, one milk cow, three other cattle, and twenty-eight pigs, valued at $630. His crop production included ten bushels of wheat, five hundred bushels of Indian corn, and eighty bushels of oats.

That agricultural strength provided more than food. It provided cover, resources, and the means to run one of the most critical safe havens on the Underground Railroad.

In 1860, the U.S. Federal Census recorded the Moss-Ward families living together under one roof out in Truro Township. Littleberry Moss, eighty-six years old at the time, was listed as head of the household and still marked down as a farmer. Living with him was his wife, Elizabeth, along with their daughter, Catherine Moss Ward, and her husband, John T. Ward. Also, in that home were six of John and Catherine's children: William, Ann Lois, Margaret, Catherine, Delia, and Susanbell.

By then, Littleberry likely wasn't working the fields much anymore. At his age, it's safe to say the day-to-day labor fell to John T. Ward, his son William, and two others—likely older children or hired hands. Interestingly, the census also listed a separate family unit living at the same address: John T. Ward's grandson William, a thirteen-year-old farmhand named Robert, and an older man named Curtis, who was sixty-six. By 1880, another family had made their home on that same land—the Wilkinsons. John T. Ward's daughter, Catherine (or "Kate" as she was known), had married William Wilkinson. He was listed as a laborer, and they lived there with their two young daughters.

This living setup shows just how deeply connected the Moss and Ward families were—not just through blood, but through purpose. They weren't just living under the same roof. They were building something bigger than themselves. That land wasn't only for farming; it was freedom ground. A place where survival and resistance worked side by side.

The Moss-Ward farm stood as a symbol of unity, strategy, and faith. It was a working farm, yes—but also a shelter. A station on the Underground Railroad. A sacred space where every acre, every fence post, every footstep had a purpose. They used what they had—livestock, crops, and love for each other—to fight back against a system built to break them. And the name Bluff Farms? It wasn't just a label. It was a legacy. A nod to the bold, calculated risks taken by folks determined to outwit those who tried to hunt down freedom seekers.

That land told a story. A story of work, yes—but also of warfare. Quiet warfare carried out in fields and kitchens and hidden spaces. And the people who lived there, Mosses, Wards, Wilkinsons, were more than family. They were a movement.

At a time when the ink on the Emancipation Proclamation was barely dry and the country was still reeling from the scars of war, John T. Ward stood as a quiet monument to perseverance. His life had already been one of silent rebellion—shepherding men, women, and children to freedom through the Underground Railroad, breaking laws designed to keep them chained. And yet, in 1872, his name appeared in a whole new setting: Columbus City Hall.

The newly constructed city hall rose from the ashes of tragedy. Back in September 1854, a massive fire tore through downtown Columbus, swallowing up at least two city blocks and reducing the original city hall to rubble. But from destruction came determination. By 1869, construction began on what would later become known as Old City Hall, and by 1872, it stood tall—both literally and symbolically.

Built at a cost of $175,000, the 140-foot Gothic-style building was crafted from dark cream Amherst stone and quickly became one of the city's most distinguished landmarks. The first floor bustled with activity, housing the U.S. Post Office, the Columbus Public Library, and the City Board of Trade. The second floor held the City Council Chamber and office spaces, while the third floor featured a grand public auditorium with room for three thousand people. That space became a cultural heartbeat for the city, hosting everything from political rallies and election-night celebrations to speeches and swanky galas.

The grand opening was a full-on celebration. Speeches rang out, and when the sun set, dancing filled the halls long into the night. Over the years, Old City Hall would welcome historic figures like Benjamin Butler, Carl Schurz, and Willie Redmond. Governor William Allen held his inaugural ball there in 1874, and in 1879, the city threw a reception for Ulysses S. Grant. This wasn't just a building, it was the beating heart of Columbus civic life.

And in the middle of all that history stood John T. Ward.

In a time when Black men were rarely granted authority—
especially within the halls of government—John T.'s appointment as
janitor of city hall was no minor achievement. He didn't win the job
through political favor or a Reconstruction-era loophole. He earned
it the hard way: through the support of his community. Twenty
citizens, including J.C. Lough, petitioned the committee on city hall
to give John T. the position. It wasn't a vote from a ballot box. It was a
vote of trust—a testament to who he was and how he carried himself.

From the moment its doors opened, city hall became the heartbeat
of Columbus's social and political life. The opening ceremony was
nothing short of a spectacle—drawing crowds in the hundreds,
maybe even thousands—for an evening of speeches, celebration,
and dancing that went long into the night. Over the years, its grand
halls played host to some of the most prestigious names of the era,

including Benjamin Butler, Carl Schurz, and Willie Redmond. In 1874, Governor William Allen's inaugural ball filled the space with music and joy. Then in 1879, Ulysses S. Grant himself was honored with a grand reception.

But it wasn't just about politics and power. City hall was the backdrop for state conventions, city meetings, banquets, and election-night gatherings. Civil War generals were celebrated here. Policy was debated. Deals were made. City hall became a cornerstone in the civic and social structure of Columbus.

And through it all, John T. Ward wasn't just standing on the sidelines.

By the late 1870s—sometime between 1877 and 1879—he was promoted from city hall janitor to city council messenger. A role that carried real weight. A role his own son, William Shelton Ward, would later inherit. His family wasn't just in the building; they were becoming part of the institution. From hauling bread to soldiers at Camp Chase during the Civil War to working inside the very chambers of city government, the Ward family name was etched into the foundation of Columbus history. By September 1890, John T. Ward was officially elected as messenger to the Columbus City Council, earning ten dollars a month—a clear recognition of the trust and respect he'd built over the years.

At the time, the city's elected officials—mayors, council members—were chosen by the people. But positions like janitor or messenger? Those were appointed, and they weren't handed out lightly. The janitor of city hall didn't just push a broom or dust the corners. John T. Ward likely managed key responsibilities—posting official notices, distributing municipal updates, delivering city correspondence. These weren't just chores; they were civic duties in a city still healing from war and adapting to life in Reconstruction.

John T.'s presence inside those halls was more than a job. It was a quiet revolution.

It proved Black men could do more than just show up. We could be trusted. We could be respected. We could hold down roles that others might've overlooked—but that were vital to the running of a city. And these roles came with a paycheck decent enough to afford some small comforts—comforts many Black families at the time still couldn't dream of.

But John T. didn't hoard those blessings. He gave back.

In May 1881, he supplied ice cream and other treats for a school picnic at Loving School, showing the same generosity that had guided him on the Underground Railroad. That school, tucked into Columbus's Near East Side, had been founded in 1871 and was serving nearly 20 percent of the city's Black children. It was more than a school; it was a lifeline, a refuge. A place where Black kids could learn and grow at a time when opportunities were scarce.

Though the Loving School would close its doors in 1882, its impact lived on. That same year, the Columbus Board of Education passed a resolution to end segregated schools for Black children—a historic step toward educational integration. And while John T. wasn't marching with a banner or making fiery speeches, his support was steady and powerful. Through his acts of kindness, consistency, and quiet dignity, he helped move the city forward.

John T. Ward's life stretched across the great divide between bondage and power—between the chains of enslavement and the chambers of civic authority. From the hidden routes of the Underground Railroad to the public stone steps of Columbus City Hall, from the quiet resistance of Bluff Farms to the echoing halls of municipal decision-making, John T. moved with unshakable dignity—even when burdened by unspeakable loss.

His story wasn't one about titles; it was about transformation. History may remember him as a janitor, but that barely scratches the surface. John T. was a pioneer, a man who carved a path where none had existed, leaving his imprint on a city still trying to define what freedom truly meant. His life became a bridge—between enslavement and agency, silence and voice, invisibility and presence.

Long before emancipation was written into law—long before America celebrated freedom as if it were a finished product—Black men like John T. Ward had already learned how to wear the social mask, not as a disguise, but as a shield. It wasn't cowardice; it was strategy. A centuries-old survival mechanism passed down like an heirloom. It meant moving with grace and restraint in a country that refused to reckon with their full humanity. And even behind that mask, John T. built. He served. He loved. He endured.

John T.'s journey—from guiding fugitives in the shadows of the Underground Railroad to standing tall within the walls of Columbus City Hall—wasn't just a personal evolution. It was a blueprint. He went from sanctuary to structure, from safe house to city government. He became more than a janitor; he was a builder, a messenger, a sentinel of Black progress. His life was a living testament to what it means to hold dignity in a world that constantly tries to strip it away.

And he paid the cost.

See, the North was no promised land. It may not have had plantations, but it still had chains. Segregation ran deep in the so-called free states. Freedmen, though technically no longer enslaved, were still shackled by law, fear, and unspoken codes. To survive, they had to move carefully through a society designed to reject them. They had to wear what we've come to call the "social mask."

This mask wasn't fabric; it was behavioral. It was a performance, a script, a balancing act. It meant crafting a version of yourself that made white folks feel safe. You couldn't speak too boldly, couldn't laugh too loud, couldn't dress too fine or walk too proud. Black ambition had to be muted. Black excellence had to be dimmed. Every gesture, every word, every glance had to be measured.

Smile—but not too wide. Speak—but don't speak up. Dress sharp—but not too sharp, or it might be taken as arrogance. Don't show anger. Don't show fear. And for God's sake, don't look them in the eye too long.

Freedmen had to shrink themselves just to exist. Any sign of pride could be mistaken for a threat. Any dignity shown could cost you your job—or your life.

Wearing that mask wasn't weakness; it was brilliance. It was tactical—strategic. It was a means of keeping your head while holding onto your soul. But make no mistakes, it was heavy.

For men like John T. Ward—who dared to live with dignity and visibility during slavery and into Reconstruction—the mask was both armor and trap. He had to move like a ghost and a gentleman at the same time. He worked in spaces that weren't built for him, among people who weren't ready to see him. His work on the Underground Railroad, his advocacy for Black male suffrage, his civil service—all of it placed him in the crosshairs of a society that both feared and needed Black leadership.

And when a system feels fear, it always strikes back.

The mask wasn't just a daily act; it was a performance under pressure. It was survival theater, a costume stitched from fear, genius, and resilience. For freedmen navigating post-slavery America, every encounter with white society was a negotiation. The stakes were high. So, they learned to quiet their speech, soften their steps, and make their light just dim enough to pass.

But behind closed doors—in churches, kitchens, barbershops, and living rooms—they removed the mask. They were loud. They were brilliant. They were free. They built spaces where they could breathe, speak, celebrate, and mourn. But even in those spaces, the mask had left its mark.

And the truth is, the mask didn't vanish with Reconstruction. It followed Black folks into the twentieth century—and it's still here in the twenty-first.

Now it shows up in boardrooms, interviews, traffic stops, classrooms, even online. It's in the code-switching, the self-correction, the practiced smile, the silence in the face of micro-aggressions. It's the pressure to be twice as good just to be seen as enough. It's the legacy of a country that still, in too many places, values politeness over protest, and presence without power.

But still—we endure.

Because behind the mask lives a truth that no institution could ever erase, we've always known who we are. We've always fought to protect that truth. We've carried it, generation after generation, through fire and silence, through resistance and love.

The mask may cover the face.

But it can't silence the soul.

When I conduct research—especially on historical injustice—I always build a timeline. That's how you work a case. And once I began to lay out the events leading up to what happened with John Ward Jr., John T.'s son, certain patterns started to snap into focus.

One key detail stood out early: John T. Ward had just been reappointed as city hall janitor. On the surface, it might seem insignificant—just another civic job. But it wasn't. His reappointment came with opposition—resistance. Whispers that he didn't belong. And shortly after reclaiming that post, he was tasked with delivering notices to local property owners, informing them that their homes would be assessed for street improvements.

Now ask yourself: how would that have been received?

A Black man—not just walking into white neighborhoods but issuing legal warnings. Official documentation. Government authority. Even a decade after emancipation, the illusion of Black progress was fragile—paper-thin, really. And here was John T. Ward, a respected name, a visible Black patriarch with land, legacy, and power—reminding white homeowners that the system could touch *them* too.

That kind of power, especially from a Black man in post-Reconstruction Ohio, did not go unnoticed. It didn't go unchallenged.

Then I found something that made my stomach turn; it was just one year before John T. Ward and his son, William S. Ward, officially registered the Ward Moving and Transfer Company with the state. I assume business was lucrative and created a jealous buzz. The timing? Suspicious. The placement? Strategic. It wasn't just journalism; it was a prelude, an omen. The piece didn't name names, but it may as well have. It practically painted a target on the Ward family's back before the ink on their business license had even dried.

That's when my suspicion deepened.

This wasn't just about John Ward Jr. being in the wrong place at the wrong time. This wasn't about teenage rebellion or coincidence. No—this felt calculated. Like resentment that had been simmering beneath the surface for years in a town that shook your hand while quietly setting your legacy on fire.

The Ward name was rising—landowners, businessmen, respected voices in Columbus—and not everyone liked what they saw. Power like that, in Black hands, has always made some people nervous. And when they can't come for the man with the title?

They come for the son.

Because in America, power doesn't just fear your presence; it fears your permanence. And the fastest way to cripple a legacy … is to make sure it doesn't reach the next generation.

Disguised in the language of "law and order," a so-called report described a supposed crime wave in Truro Township—alleged "depredations" that the community supposedly needed to "clean up." But beneath the surface, the message was clear. This wasn't about crime. It was about control. It was about using fear and fiction to justify a targeted expulsion, a calculated effort to uproot Black families from their homes.

In the early era of Jim Crow, these tactics were common. Accusations were inflated, records manipulated, and headlines weaponized. What truly threatened the township wasn't violence; it was Black success. Families like the Wards, who dared to own land, start businesses, and build legacy. That was the real crime in their eyes.

These accusations—likely exaggerated or completely fabricated—were designed to push Black residents off their land, out of their homes, and away from opportunity. It was displacement disguised as justice—a tactic as old as the nation itself.

John T. Ward, a man who had once built sanctuaries beneath moonlight and council chambers under stone ceilings, now faced a different kind of assault: the slow, deliberate erasure of Black progress.

A father who had helped enslaved people cross into freedom now watched his own legacy come under attack. His son, John Ward Jr., born into that fragile post-slavery hope, was later accused of crimes that echoed the town's worst fears. They called him an outlaw, a threat, a member of the so-called Jesse James Gang of Ohio. But it wasn't just an accusation. It was a metaphor. A symbol of the kind of story white society loved to believe: that when Black men succeed, danger is not far behind.

And still, the mask remained.

By the time John Ward Jr. turned seventeen in the 1880s, he was no longer just a boy with a legacy, he was an accused outlaw.

It sounds absurd now. Almost darkly comedic—like Jesse James in Blackface. The very idea that a group of young Black men could co-opt the legend of Jesse James—the Confederate folk hero lionized in dime novels—and ride through Truro Township like some Wild West novella come to life? For the white residents, it was hysteria. For the accused, maybe it was something else.

Maybe it wasn't crime. Maybe it was performance, a rebellion in costume, an act of defiance wearing a mask shaped by myth.

Because if the system already sees you as an outlaw, what happens when you lean into the part?

The truth is murky.

Was John Ward Jr. guilty of the crimes? I don't believe it. But the conditions that made him vulnerable to the accusation were real. He may not have been following in his father's footsteps—but that doesn't mean he was trying to burn the path down either. Maybe he was just running—with no map, no refuge, and no real freedom.

To the townspeople, they were a menace. But to themselves, perhaps they were more than just a gang; they were a warning: "You've taken everything from us. Now watch what we become."

That's what would've broken John T. Ward.

He spent his life fighting for Black dignity, for order, for legacy. And now his son—his namesake—was being dragged into the caricature of lawlessness. The kind of caricature the justice system didn't try to correct. It amplified it, spotlighted it, made an example out of it.

And maybe John T. Sr. didn't know what to believe. Maybe he thought his son was innocent. Maybe he feared he'd been misled. Or maybe, like any father watching the world devour his child, he understood the truth but couldn't say it out loud:

That in a system built to crush Black boys, innocence never mattered much anyway.

Their story was tragic—surreal, almost cinematic. But beneath the frontier drama, there was no romance, only a father facing an impossible choice, a community teetering on the edge of madness, and a legacy nearly lost to legend.

Before we dive into the alleged crimes, let's step back and look at the legacy behind the curtain. Because this ain't just a story about crime, it's also a story about performance, spectacle, and a traveling empire born right in the heart of Columbus, Ohio.

The Sells Brothers Circus wasn't some ragtag sideshow; it was a major force in American entertainment. Founded in Columbus by brothers Ephraim, Lewis, Peter, and Allen Sells, the circus quickly became one of the biggest traveling shows of the late nineteenth century. It was known for its elaborate Wild West themes, grand parades, exotic animals, and daring stunts—feeding America's growing hunger for fantasy, rebellion, and frontier myth.

Eventually, the Sells Brothers Circus was sold to James A. Bailey, who later merged it into what would become the biggest show of them all: the Ringling Brothers and Barnum & Bailey Circus. Even after the sale, the Sells name kept touring under its own brand well into the early 1900s, leaving its mark on American entertainment.

But by then, John Ward Jr.'s name was no longer traveling with the circus.

It was stamped into the criminal records of Truro Township.

Whatever role he once played, the horse trainer, performer, and laborer got overshadowed. He wouldn't be remembered as a showman, a cowboy, or a young man shaped by the myths of the Wild West.

Instead, his name lived on in a darker archive. Not on circus posters, but in court records. Not in lights, but in ink—black, permanent, and damning.

And now, we turn to the accusations.

To the moment where fantasy and fear collided.

To the moment the curtain dropped—and the illusion gave way to something much heavier, much harder to carry.

What was reported in the article:

The winter of 1880 was cold and cruel in Truro Township, Ohio. Snow-covered roads stretched like white veins through the countryside, winding past darkened saloons, weathered barns, and scattered farmhouses where families huddled around their stoves for warmth. But on these frozen roads, lawlessness lurked—not from the notorious Jesse James and his gang, but from an unlikely crew of young, Black men who dared to declare themselves the outlaws of the Midwest.

The first major crime hit on February 2, 1880.

A young German farmer named William Neff had been to town selling hay, his pockets full of hard-earned money. As he steered his sled down the snowy roads, three men stepped out from Wahlenmaier's Saloon—John Ward Jr., Joe Johnson, and Will Johnson. They asked for a ride, and trusting them, Neff agreed.

A quarter mile later, the ambush began.

Blows rained down on Neff's head, the sled tipped, and his body hit the snow. Stunned and bloodied, he watched his attackers vanish into the night. His money was gone. The cold crept into his bones. By morning, his empty wallet was found tossed in a nearby field.

The second attack came weeks later, on February 27, when two young men—William Sandusky and Seymour Gillespie—were riding in a sleigh after a "society meeting" at the local schoolhouse. As their horse trotted along that same cursed road, three shadows leapt from the darkness.

One man grabbed the bridle, while another swung a fence board like a club, striking Gillespie over the head. But fate took a wild turn. Sandusky said he recognized the man holding the reins. "John Ward, what do you want? Let go there!" he shouted.

That moment of recognition was all it took. The gang, maybe spooked by being identified, fled into the night—leaving their victims shaken, but alive.

But the worst was yet to come.

Before the attacks on Neff and Sandusky, there had been another—far more brutal.

On a bitter night, a fifty-year-old man named George Yearling was walking alone when three men jumped him. They knocked him to the ground, fists and boots landing hard. As he lay there, one of the attackers made a bold declaration:

"We're the Jesse James Gang of Ohio!"

So, for a whole month, these attacks went down—and then suddenly, Yearling, with no witnesses, makes this claim? Suspicious, right?

But to the folks of Truro Township, they weren't asking too many questions. To them, these men were a menace. Period.

Tensions had already been brewing between the town's German immigrants and its Black residents. Truro Township—what we now know as Whitehall, Ohio—was a hard place with hard people and even harder prejudices. Even after emancipation, Black families were often treated like second-class citizens. Could this wave of violence have been a form of "get back"? A strike against a community that had mistreated them?

Either way, the town had had enough.

Led by Prosecutor Noah H. Garner, the townspeople banded together to bring down the so-called gang.

A month later …

The arrests came, one by one. John Ward Jr., Joseph, Will, and Charles Johnson, along with Joe Brown, were all taken into custody.

The most elusive of them all—Jesse Johnson—disappeared like smoke in the wind, never seen again.

But John Jr.? He was released. Twice.

For John T. Ward, the arrest of his son was a nightmare. A betrayal of everything he'd worked, fought, and sacrificed for.

He had spent his life fighting for Black dignity, for honor, for justice. And now, his own flesh and blood was being branded a thief, a highwayman, an outlaw. Everything he had stood against—now written into his bloodline.

And still, he paid his son's bail. Not once. Twice.

The first time, the court set bail at one hundred dollars—a steep but manageable amount. But then the whispers turned to headlines. The "Jesse James Gang of Ohio" became the town's obsession. White fear turned into full-blown fury.

That's when Prosecutor Noah H. Garner made his move.

John Ward Jr. was re-arrested. The charges stacked up. The bail was raised to three hundred dollars.

That jump from one hundred to three hundred dollars? That wasn't just inflation. That was a message, a setup. A warning shot dressed up in legal paperwork.

This wasn't justice. This was strategy.

The first bond was bait. Just enough to test how deep the Ward family's pockets, patience, and pride really went. The second bond? That was punishment. A three hundred dollars bond in the 1880s is nearly ten thousand dollars in today's money. And this wasn't about safety. This was about spectacle.

This wasn't a courtroom. It was a stage.

And John T. Ward—landowner, community leader, man of the Underground Railroad—wasn't just attending. He was the main act, not as a hero, but as a warning.

His son's freedom dangled like a carrot while the state built its story—fear, control, punishment. All wrapped up in one family name.

Twice, John T. Ward reached deep—into his savings, into his reputation, into the marrow of his manhood—and paid bail for a son who may have been guilty of nothing more than being young, Black, brilliant, and misunderstood.

Because he understood what many still refuse to see.

In an all-white courtroom, Black boys don't get justice. They get judgment. They get spectacle.

And that courtroom?

It didn't need a verdict. It already had one.

Guilty of upsetting the order. *Guilty* of carrying a name that meant something. *Guilty* of daring to inherit a legacy.

The wooden benches groaned beneath the weight of white curiosity. All eyes fixed on John T. Ward—not just a janitor, not just a messenger, but a man who dared to be something more: a Black patriarch.

Dressed in his Sunday best, he sat in the front row, holding that bond receipt like a battle flag. The paper shook slightly in his hand—not from fear, but from the weight of what it meant.

These bonds weren't just transactions. They were attempts at humiliation.

The first meant to detain. The second, to disgrace.

Both meant to break the Wards.

But John T. Ward paid it anyway.

Because when the law tried to shame him, he answered with defiance. When the system tried to silence him, he responded with sacrifice. And when the world told him his son wasn't worth saving, he saved him anyway.

"There are half a dozen charges against each of the quartet. Ward was an attaché of Sells' circus, and it is supposed gathered his mania for imitating Jesse James while in the West."

That line wasn't just a sentence in a newspaper; it was a public execution in print, a loaded verdict. A character assassination dressed up as journalism. And it deserves to be ripped apart for what it truly was:

A hit piece on a Black legacy.

This wasn't just about John Ward Jr. getting into trouble. It was about marking him, branding him, declaring him to the world not as a boy, not as a young man who made a mistake—but as a Black danger. A copycat outlaw—a threat.

And they made sure to say where he got it from: the Sells Brothers Circus, from time spent "in the West," and from what they called a *mania* for imitating Jesse James.

Mania.

Let that word sit in your mouth like a blade.

It wasn't enough to accuse him; they needed him to sound deranged, obsessed, like he had caught some sickness from idolizing white outlaws. Jesse James—a Confederate terrorist turned American folk hero—was glorified in dime novels and Wild West shows.

But when a Black boy started imitating that same fantasy? Suddenly it was madness.

Here's the truth: Jesse James stood for lawlessness. He robbed banks, stole land, and symbolized rebellion. White America made him a legend. Black boys were left to survive in the ruins Jesse James left behind.

So, why did some identify with him? Because Jesse James was lawless and still loved. He was feared but respected. He took what he wanted. He made white America blink. And for Black youth raised in a system that offered them nothing but labor, limits, and lies, that kind of myth looked a whole lot like power.

But the article didn't want to explore that complexity. It wanted blood.

"There are half-dozen charges against each of the quartette."

Six charges. Each. Not based on verdicts. Not on hard evidence. But on theatrics. Legal volume. This wasn't due process. It was stacked ammunition.

You don't pile on charges like that unless your goal is to bury someone—not convict them.

That's not justice. That's Jim Crow in a three-piece suit.

Because back then, the courtroom didn't need a lynch mob—just a judge with a pen. And today?

Same script. New cast.

Young Black boys are still overcharged, still over-policed, still punished for the idea of danger rather than any actual harm. A white teen joyrides and gets a slap on the wrist. A Black teen does the same and walks away with felony weight strapped to his name for life.

This isn't the past echoing. It's the present still screaming.

And why was John Ward Jr. the name dragged through the mud more than the others? Why him, when another boy vanished completely and no one even chased him down?

Simple.

Because of who his father was.

John T. Ward wasn't just a Black man with a job. He was a landowner, a city hall employee—a man with a voice, a reputation, and a past steeped in freedom work. He ran Bluff Farms, once a stop on the Underground Railroad. He was connected, respected, and outspoken.

And that made his family a target.

Because a free Black man is inconvenient. But a powerful Black man? A landowning, legacy-building, truth-speaking Black man?

That's a threat.

And the fastest way to kill a legacy is to ruin the next generation.

That's why the spotlight landed on his son. Not because he was guiltier. But because he was useful.

An example.

A warning to other Black families: don't climb too high. Don't speak too loud. Don't pass your name to your children with pride.

Because we will take it. We will stain it. We will throw your son into a myth—then crucify him for believing it.

This wasn't about crime. This was about control.

The press didn't just report the news. They helped write the verdict.

By tying John Ward Jr. to the myth of Jesse James—a white outlaw immortalized in dime novels and circus acts—they didn't just tell a story. They dehumanized a Black teenager.

They reduced a young man with a father, a future, and a name, into a footnote in someone else's fantasy. A dangerous trope. A walking headline. A myth made flesh, meant to be feared.

And in the process, they didn't just criminalize him; they smeared his father, too.

John T. Ward—landowner, civic servant, Underground Railroad conductor—wasn't treated like a pillar of the community.

Not in that moment.

He was framed by association, his legacy tainted by proximity. The message was clear. No matter your dignity, your service, or your sacrifice, your bloodline could be turned against you.

That's not justice. That's generational sabotage.

Choke the roots before they bear fruit. Cut the story short before it becomes too powerful to erase.

And make no mistake, it's still happening.

We just call it by new names now: character assassination, overcharging, gang enhancements, RICO cases.

The tools have changed, but the aim is the same ...

Cripple the future by vilifying the present. Make the Black boy a villain before he becomes a man. Turn trauma into spectacle. Strip away complexity. Reduce his life to a cautionary tale—for white consumption.

Back then, the press wasn't a bystander. It was the RINGMASTER.

It controlled the spotlight, choreographed the spectacle, and fed the frenzy.

And once the crowd was worked into a lather? It didn't matter what the facts were.

The trial was over before it began. The curtain had already closed.

And now?

The circus continues.

In modern media, the hoodie is the new mask. The mugshot becomes the story. The arrest becomes the conviction.

Black grief becomes clicks. Black resistance becomes threat.

And just like in 1880, the narrative wins before the truth ever gets a word in.

Let's stop pretending this is journalism.

It's performance.

It's theater dressed in fear, fueled by folklore, and propped up by a public that still needs a villain more than it wants the truth.

Let's call it what it is:

Weaponized white fragility—packaged as news, sold as justice.

Because Jesse James didn't burn Black towns. But the system that made him a legend?

Still does. Every. Damn. Day.

When the 1880 article casually mentions a "society meeting at the schoolhouse," don't be fooled by the politeness of the phrase.

That wasn't a PTA potluck or a quilting circle. That was a coded council of white power in action.

In places like Truro Township, schoolhouses weren't just for children; they were ground zero for preserving the social order. The phrase "society meeting" was code for status, segregation, and strategy. It meant white men gathering to decide what kind of town they were going to keep—and who wasn't going to be part of it.

By 1880, schools in Ohio were legally integrating, but in practice? Segregation was still gospel. And white communities were furious. So, what did they do?

They turned schools—our battleground for freedom—into their planning rooms for resistance.

These *society meetings* were where policies were whispered before they were enforced, where vigilance was plotted, where fear turned into action.

They didn't have to say the word "race." They just had to say "society."

The schoolhouse wasn't just a place of learning. It became a war room.

If young Black men like John Ward Jr. were being criminalized in the streets, then these meetings were where the blueprint was drawn—in neat, civil, bureaucratic handwriting.

A meeting here. A motion there. And suddenly an entire community is under surveillance.

So, let's be clear: a "society meeting at the schoolhouse" wasn't innocent.

It was power protecting itself. It was whiteness in strategy mode. And it was just polite enough to pass as normal.

This story, while tragic and deeply personal, also carries an irony I can't ignore.

It reminds me of my father, James E. Ward, and his deep love for old Westerns. He would've laughed at the absurdity of it all—young Black men, raised in the shadow of slavery and segregation, choosing to role-play as the infamous Jesse James. What's eerie is how closely the story mirrors his own.

At nearly the same age as John Ward Jr., my father found himself accused—not of something he did, but as retaliation by race soldiers still seething from Dr. Martin Luther King Jr.'s assassination. At the time, his father—my grandfather, Harold E. Ward—was running the family moving business with the same kind of determination and integrity that John T. Ward had shown decades earlier. And just like John T. Ward, my grandfather fought to protect his son. He got my father off on a technicality, navigating a system rigged to break young Black men before they ever had a chance to build anything.

And the town? The town was no different, gullible and eager to believe that these Black boys were some kind of criminal syndicate—a modern-day Jesse James gang. When in reality, they were just reckless kids swept up in the fantasy America sold them. Cowboys, outlaws, freedom, those myths weren't made for us. But we still chased them, hoping to write ourselves into a story that never truly had us in mind.

What happened in Truro Township wasn't about petty crime or youthful rebellion.

It was a coordinated purge.

A surgical strike meant to sever Black families from their property, their peace, and their future. The accusations, whether imagined, inflated, or outright fabricated, did what they were designed to do: justify racial cleansing under the banner of justice.

So, the question lingers, begging for an honest answer. Will history remember this as law and order?

Or will we finally name it for what it was—a community weaponizing the legal system against those it never intended to include?

Because this was never just about robbery.

It was about erasure.

And unless we speak its name, history will keep repeating the lie. Not justice. Not order.

A purge. Plain and simple.

The record shows no conviction. No trial. No sentencing. Just bail posted, headlines faded, and a family forced to hold its dignity in silence. No official statement from the Ward family has ever been found. And maybe that silence wasn't avoidance—but strategy. Survival.

Just within a year of his release from jail, John Ward Jr. did something unexpected.

He got married.

Maybe it was the nearness of ruin that shook him. Or maybe it was the quiet weight of his father's unwavering support that reminded him who he was. Whatever it was, he turned a page, walked away from the myth, and stepped out of the shadow.

Not with fanfare. Not with a fight.

But with vows.

Because even in the face of falsehood, John Ward Jr. did what every stolen headline tried to deny him.

He kept living.

He chose legacy over legend, dignity over drama.

And in that quiet act of defiance, he did something far more radical than run.

He stayed.

In the quiet halls of city hall, something happened in 1893 that, while it might seem minor on the surface, carried weight far beyond its words. A note, found on the desk of the Director of Law, read:

"June 30, 1893. J.T. Ward will not never clean this room again, but not with tears."

At first glance, it might've come off like an odd little message, maybe a cryptic resignation from a janitor. The office staff joked about it: "Did he clean the office with tears before?" But under that casual mockery was something they missed—or maybe chose not to see.

Because that note wasn't just a farewell. It was a statement. A layered message packed with pride, frustration, and purpose. And when you know who John T. Ward was, it all hits different.

John T. was no ordinary janitor. He was a Black abolitionist, a conductor on the Underground Railroad, and a key figure in Columbus history. A man who had risked everything to help enslaved people escape to freedom. But even with that legacy, by the end of the nineteenth century, the system had pushed him into the shadows—confined to cleaning offices and running errands in government buildings that didn't reflect his true stature. The same halls he once helped free others to walk, he was now expected to mop in silence.

That double negative—"will not never clean this room again"— wasn't just bad grammar. It was intentional, poetic even: a declaration. He was done. Done letting the world pretend his work was invisible. Done being overlooked while carrying a legacy on his back. And that last line— "but not with tears"—was the real message. This wasn't sadness. It wasn't surrender.

It was strength.

John T. Ward was walking away, but he wasn't broken. He was standing tall, even as he stepped down. The work may have gone unseen, but the man behind it refused to fade quietly.

So, was it a resignation? Most likely. Whether it was age, politics, or just plain protest, John T. made his choice with care. After decades of sacrifice and silent service, he walked away from a system that had failed to honor his full worth. He'd held elected positions as a city messenger and janitor, but those titles never defined him. His real title had always been something greater:

Freedom fighter. Legacy bearer. Elder of resistance.

June 30, 1883.
J. T. Ward wil
not never clean
this room again,
but not with tears.

However, as much as this resignation marked a quiet protest, it also symbolized a new chapter in John T.'s life. With one door closing, he set his sights on something more personal. He was ready to slow down, to breathe, and to fully enjoy the love and joy he found in his marriage to Catherine, his devoted wife. Together, they had raised nine children, and now, John T. looked forward to time spent with his growing flock of grandchildren. He had earned that right—the right to step back and savor the legacy he built, both in history books and at the family dinner table.

As he walked away from city hall's marble floors, it wasn't a retreat born of defeat. It was a transition into peace, into purpose, into the warmth of home. That final note—humble, poetic, defiant—was more than a farewell. It was a declaration that, while the public battles may have ended, the fight for dignity had never been more personal. He wasn't disappearing; he was finally showing up for the life he'd fought to build.

This moment, small as it might seem in the broader sweep of history, stands as a quiet reminder of the unsung battles waged by those pushed to the margins. Folks like John T., whose names might not sit in bold print on government plaques, but who poured sweat, heart, and soul into the foundation of those same institutions. When city hall underwent its so-called modernization, John T.'s resignation wasn't just about stepping down; it was a silent stand against being erased. A declaration that invisible labor still matters, and history doesn't only live in headlines.

The following year, John T. Ward carved out the time—and the budget—to honor the love of his life. John and Catherine Ward, his rock and backbone, had been married since March 21, 1844. And fifty years later, they celebrated that bond in grand fashion. Their golden anniversary was held at Columbus City Hall—yes, the same place he had just left behind—and it was nothing short of magnificent. The event brought together the top echelon of Black Columbus, alongside dozens of friends and well-wishers. More than forty of their children and grandchildren were in attendance, filling the room with legacy and love. John T. and Catherine stood tall on a platform, side by side. Even some of their white friends were present—an uncommon sight, and a quiet nod to the respect John T. commanded across lines that usually didn't bend.

It wasn't just a party. It was a statement. A Black man, once hunted by slave catchers, once silenced in the back offices of power, now stood in the spotlight, surrounded by his people and his pride. A full circle moment—not just for him, but for everyone who came after.

Longtime friend and revered confidant, Rev. James Poindexter, stood at the center of the room, his presence commanding and profound. His voice—steady, yet rich with raw emotion—filled the space as he officiated the vow renewal of John T. Ward and his beloved wife, Catherine. This was no ordinary ceremony. It was the culmination of a lifetime's journey—one marked by the weight of struggle, the light of perseverance, and the unshakable foundation of love. For John T. and Catherine, this moment was more than a renewal of vows; it was a living testament to the trials they had survived and the victories they had claimed together.

From the crushing horrors of enslavement to the hard-won sweetness of freedom, their journey had been anything but easy. Every step they had taken was shadowed by loss, marked by violence, and defined by sacrifice. Yet through it all, Catherine had stood resolutely by John T.'s side—his anchor, his strength, and his greatest source of grace. She had been there, unflinching, through every battle, every heartbreak, and every fleeting victory. In her, John T. found not just a partner, but a beacon of hope—a light that never dimmed, no matter the darkness around them.

As they stood there, hands clasped tightly together, time seemed to pause. The painful memories of their past—the chains, the fear, the endless fight for justice—faded into the background. In that moment, there was only the present. Only the quiet beauty of a love that had weathered every storm. The lines etched into their faces weren't just marks of age, but of battles fought and survived, of a life lived with purpose and dignity. In John T.'s eyes, you could see the depth of his gratitude for Catherine—the woman who had been with him through it all, the woman who had helped him build a life from nothing. This vow was not just an obligation; it was an offering of honor, of respect, and of unwavering admiration for the woman who had stood with him through every battle—both external and internal. She had been his refuge when the world was cruel, his strength when he had none, and his greatest blessing.

As the ceremony drew to a close, there was a sense of reverence in the room—but also joy. A joy that radiated from the Wards and spilled out to everyone present. Mr. Galloway, a representative from Columbus City Hall, approached with a gift—a symbol of respect for all that John T. had accomplished, for the legacy he had built. In his hands was a gold piece, worth over three thousand dollars, its weight symbolizing the depth of John T.'s triumphs over the brutal reality of slavery. Alongside it, a black walking cane with a gold-capped handle was presented—a keepsake of the day, a token of his enduring dignity. That cane, which would later rest proudly beside the poker on the Ward family's fireplace, would serve as a silent reminder of the road they had traveled together, a symbol of their strength and resilience.

The celebration that followed was filled with music that seemed to echo the joy in their hearts, with laughter that rang through the room like the melody of a life well-lived. The sweet, intoxicating scent of cake filled the air, mingling with the sounds of joyful dancing and the warmth of love shared. Each guest, each family member, showered the Wards with gifts—tokens of respect, admiration, and appreciation for the unwavering love they had demonstrated over fifty years. Every carefully chosen gift—from a simple bouquet to a lovingly wrapped treasure—spoke volumes about the community that had stood witness to their struggles and now celebrated their victories. This was not just a celebration of time passed, but a recognition of all they had overcome and the legacy they had built.

For the Wards, their golden anniversary was more than a milestone; it was a radiant, shining beacon in their shared story. A testament to the unyielding power of their love. A love that had not only survived the brutal realities of enslavement but had triumphed over them. It was a reminder that, despite the darkest days of their lives, love had been the constant that carried them through. And in that room, surrounded by the generations they had raised and the friends they had made along the way, they celebrated not just the past, but the enduring strength of their bond—a bond that had withstood every trial life had thrown their way.

Fifty years of teamwork, love, sorrow, joy, and struggle—of land gained and justice claimed and a relentless desire for freedom and liberty.

That night, Columbus City Hall was transformed. It didn't feel like a government building anymore, it felt like a sacred Black sanctuary. Their children and grandchildren stood proudly beside them, living proof of a legacy built on hardship and hope. My great-great-grandfather, William S. Ward, and his wife were there too—dignified, grounded—carrying the weight of a last name that now *meant* something in this city. A name forged in struggle, sacrifice, and unwavering perseverance.

But just three years after that golden celebration, life struck a cruel blow.

John T. Ward—a veteran janitor and trusted messenger for the Columbus City Council Chamber and City Clerk's office—was more than a public servant. His greatest duty had always been family. By 1877, his daughter, Catherine "Kate" Ward Wilkerson, had been abandoned by her husband, left alone to raise two children. The grief overwhelmed her. With nowhere else to turn, she was admitted to an insane asylum.

And like he always did, John T. stepped in, strong, steady. He took in both her daughters. He raised Jessie, right alongside Effie, as his own.

The Ward family's strength was tested in ways few could imagine. But even through all the trials, that golden anniversary stayed with them—a rare, bright joy in a world that often gave none. A beacon of what love, faith, and grit could build.

John T. stood tall. His Black cane resting beside him like punctuation. Not a crutch. A legacy. Not a sign of weakness—but a symbol of the path he'd walked. Sometimes alone. Always forward. And maybe that's why that night mattered so much.

Because not long after the music faded, after the gold keepsake was placed gently on the mantel, and the laughter became memory— another kind of knock came.

A telegram.

A message no grandfather should ever have to read. Jessie was gone. Burned in a fire. Far from home. Alone.

And just like that, the memory of that perfect night—cake, music, generations gathered—shifted from celebration to elegy.

Jessie Ward, bright and restless, left home at seventeen— searching for freedom, or maybe just escape. But what she found was tragedy. Two years later, in a rundown Pittsburgh boarding house, her life ended in flames. The newspapers called it suicide. The report was brutal: early Friday morning, she allegedly soaked her bed—

and herself—in coal oil and struck a match. Her companion, a man named Rhodes Highwarden, escaped without a scratch. Jessie didn't.

But the story never sat right.

The facts didn't line up. A cousin had visited her just the day before—begged her to come home. Jessie's answer was chilling: "I would rather go to my death than go back."

What pain was she holding? What fear? And who was this man—Rhodes Highwarden—who disappeared the second she died?

Pittsburgh authorities reached out to Columbus. Chief Kelly summoned John T. Ward to his office. There, under the cold weight of civic protocol, he received the kind of news that breaks something inside a man.

Jessie—his nineteen-year-old granddaughter—was gone. Dead in a fire. The Pittsburgh report called her "an unknown-colored woman from Columbus," claiming she set herself ablaze. With no family nearby to claim her, the city planned to bury her in a pauper's grave—anonymous, unmarked, forgotten.

But she wasn't unknown. She was John T.'s granddaughter. And nothing about her death made sense.

John T. wasn't with family when he found out. He wasn't in church or at home with loved ones. He was in a sterile government office. They told him Jessie would be buried in a pauper's grave. No headstone. No service. As if her life—and her *lineage*—meant nothing.

John T. tried. He tried to bring her home. But by the time the telegram arrived, it was already too late. The county had buried her. No name. No witness. Just dirt. Just silence.

And that silence? It haunted him.

John T. Ward—who helped *hundreds* find freedom—couldn't save his own granddaughter. He couldn't answer the questions her death left behind. Did she light the match? Or was she lit—like a wick in someone else's plan?

Was she running from danger? From shame? From something too private and painful to name?

The mystery of Jessie's death never left John T. It clung to him like the scent of scorched flesh—impossible to wash away. Did she really strike that match herself? Or did someone else pour the coal oil, set the fire, and walk away while she burned?

Her last words still echoed: "I would rather go to my death before I go back home."

What did she endure to say that out loud?

That was the tragedy. Not just the fire. But the *inferno* that came before it.

The emotional blaze that raged inside Jessie long before the flames touched her skin. And when they did, they didn't kill her right away.

She didn't die from burns.

She died from shock.

And that one word? It changes everything.

Shock ain't quiet. It's the body's final scream. It means she *felt* the fire. She was conscious. Aware. Trapped.

The flames didn't take her instantly—they *finished* her.

Whatever broke her started long before the match was struck.

In 1897, transporting a body across state lines took permits, fees, and coordination with coroners and train companies. But Pittsburgh authorities moved fast—*too* fast. They buried Jessie in a pauper's grave. No warning. No headstone. No funeral. Likely within forty-eight hours—maybe even before her grandfather had time to respond to the telegram.

They stamped the death certificate with one word: **Suicide.**

That word did more than condemn her—it erased her. **Suicide** meant no church bells. No cemetery plot. No prayers. No mourning. Just moral failure. In the eyes of both the state and the public, Jessie wasn't a victim; she was a cautionary tale. A girl who fell from grace and lit her own match.

And in a world already built to erase Black girls, that label made her death *convenient.* Quiet. Disposable.

But Jessie's story would not stay buried.

She had been living with a man: Rhodes Highwarden. The papers made sure to highlight that. A young Black woman. A man not her husband. A fire. A body. It was nineteenth-century tabloid gold—the perfect storm of race, scandal, and sex. They didn't just report her death; they turned it into a parable.

To white readers: *This is what happens when they stray.* To Black readers: *Step out of line and burn.*

Jessie became a symbol—but not the kind her grandfather had spent his life building. Not a symbol of hope or dignity. She became a warning. A freak show in print. A shameful morality tale designed to fuel fear and control.

And what about Rhodes Highwarden? He vanished. No trial. No testimony. No interrogation. He disappeared—into the smoke, into the night. His absence wasn't just suspicious. It was a final insult.

Jessie spoke to another relative at the hospital the morning after the fire. She was in pain. She spoke of regret. But not once did she mention suicide.

And yet, that's how they buried her.

A young Black woman, possibly murdered, reduced to ashes in a potter's field. Unmarked. Unmourned. Forgotten by everyone—except her grandfather. The man who had fought for dignity his whole life was forced to watch it be denied to his own blood.

The silence around her death wasn't justice. It was a cover-up.

And the questions that haunted John T. Ward—Who lit the fire? Why did she say she'd rather die than come home? What was she running from?—still linger like smoke, refusing to fade.

Unanswered. Unfinished. Unforgiven.

Three months later, John T. Ward died November 3, 1897, a man worn down not just by age, but by grief. A man whose daughter

Mary died in silence, whose granddaughter perished in fire, whose daughter Catherine unraveled into madness.

And still, through every devastation, he showed up—for his city, for his people, for his family.

Jessie's death was more than a tragedy. It was erasure. A brutal reminder that even the most dignified among us can't always shield our children from the burn of injustice. Her story didn't echo through the generations as a celebration; it lingered like a warning, wrapped in flames.

And maybe that's why Chicken Man clucked.

Maybe he dragged his pain in a cart because he had nowhere else to put it. Because when the world buries your people in unnamed graves and tells you to move on, sometimes the only way to survive is to make *somebody* hear your grief.

John T. Ward didn't cluck. But he carried his loss in other ways—in the quiet between his words, in the way he held his Black cane, in the way he stood tall when everything else had fallen.

I understand that silence now.

Because I, too, lost my mother while writing this book. And no amount of history, research, or righteous anger can dull the ache of that absence. But if this chapter means anything, it's about love. *Fierce, defiant love.* The kind that builds legacies even while the flames try to consume them. The kind that carries us through madness, through injustice, through unspeakable loss—and still dares to stand tall.

To every person who's ever fought to protect their family, their name, their block—this story is yours too.

We don't run from the fire. We walk through it—staff in hand, ancestors at our back. Because what matters most ain't just what we survive.

It's what we carry forward.

CHAPTER 18

"Let Ward Do It"

"In Columbus, Ohio, when someone said, 'Let Ward Do It,' it wasn't just about hiring a man— it was about trusting a legacy. It was about letting someone who had carried people to freedom carry your community forward. In a time when Black businesses were rare and Black leadership was resisted, Ward built a name that became a motto. His name meant dependability. His work meant dignity. His legacy? Generational."

-The Black Community of Columbus, Ohio

The genesis of my journey with Bequest traces back several years, but the catalyst for writing this story emerged in 2019 when I contemplated launching a T-shirt business to honor

John T. Ward. During my research, I unearthed the original business name: E.E. Ward Transfer and Storage Company. A quick online search revealed that my Uncle Eldon Ward had allowed the name to lapse after his retirement in 1996.

Inspired, I reviewed the Secretary of State of Ohio's requirements and confirmed with a representative that the business name was available. This discovery filled me with excitement and profound sentimental value. Rather than immediately launching a business, I held onto the name for over a year, cherishing its connection to my family's legacy.

In 2021, I received an unexpected email from a prominent Black-American attorney who represented the current owners of E.E. Ward Moving and Storage Company, a man my uncle allegedly had familial ties to. This man, who passed as my uncle's godson, claimed no knowledge of me or my family. The email included a cease-and-desist letter, demanding that I release the name registration with the state of Ohio. Failure to comply, they warned, would result in a federal lawsuit and I would be held accountable for their legal fees, estimated at twenty-five thousand dollars.

The mounting legal and financial pressure was overwhelming. I sought legal advice but couldn't afford to retain an attorney. When I requested additional time to launch a GoFundMe campaign for community support, their response was disheartening. I was reminded of the attorney's significant influence and told that my connection to the Ward family was unrecognized by the current owner, Brian. My father later recounted that he had been approached by a third party seeking to feature him in a media piece about the company, an invitation he declined.

Despite presenting evidence of my lineage—memories of growing up in the office owned by my grandfather, Harold E. Ward,

before it transitioned to his brother, Eldon Ward—my claims were dismissed. Their insistence that I had no connection to the Ward family was both deeply unsettling and hurtful, instilling in me a fear for my family's legacy.

In my search for guidance, I discovered a parallel story: Mary Trump's legal battle with her uncle, Donald Trump. Inspired, I contacted her attorney, who listened to my predicament with compassion. While unable to practice law in Ohio, she assured me that what I experienced was unjust and encouraged me to report it to the Columbus Bar Association.

Ultimately, I relinquished the registered name but resolved to share this story. They may own the business, but they cannot claim our history.

When I shared the outcome with my parents, my mother sympathized with how important this was to me. My father, however, felt a sense of deep disrespect. For him, it reopened old wounds— memories of how he and his brother Ascari had been cheated out of their birthrights and inheritance, denied the opportunity to claim what generations of the Ward family had built. Once again, we were left fighting for what had been bequeathed to us.

This journey has reinforced the importance of preserving our family's legacy, not just for ourselves but for future generations. The story of John T. Ward, our ancestors, and their contributions to history cannot and will not be forgotten.

In 1881, right in the heart of Columbus, Ohio, my great-great-great-grandfather John T. Ward stepped out with a vision that couldn't be shaken and a passion for excellence that ran deep. He came from humble beginnings—a manumitted freedman, farmer, husband, father, abolitionist, conductor, delegate, government contractor, and businessman. Through sheer determination, he built a legacy that reached far beyond his personal accomplishments.

John T. Ward's legacy lives on, not just through the continued success of E.E. Ward Moving & Storage, but in the lives, he touched and the community he helped mold. His drive for excellence, his focus on customer care, and his heart for service laid the foundation for the values E.E. Ward still stands on today. That's why folks came to know us by the slogan: "Let Ward Do It." It wasn't just some slick tagline. It rang through our neighborhoods like church bells on Sunday morning—a call to action that folks understood deep in their bones.

"Let Ward Do It" meant something. It called for strength, for resilience. It pushed people to chase their dreams even when the world told them not to. Like Nike's "Just Do It," our motto wasn't just about getting the job done. It was about breaking through barriers and achieving more than what this country ever thought we could.

Our family's mission was (and still is) to spark that same fire in others—teaching folks to find unity, build community, and encourage each other to reach higher. "Let Ward Do It" is more than a family saying—it's a challenge. A charge to take risks, grab every opportunity, and claim what's owed to us in honor of those who came before and paved the way.

The Ward family has always stood for more than just business. We've been a symbol of resistance and resilience, committed to justice no matter the odds. Every year, we handed out calendars—not just for promotion, but as bold reminders. Those calendars showed the faces and names of Black American heroes—people who fought for freedom, dignity, and the rights we're still fighting for today.

I remember walking through the neighborhood, seeing those calendars hanging in homes, Black-owned stores, and kitchens filled with love and legacy. They weren't just marking the months—they were telling our story. Every page was a tribute, a nod to the freedom fighters whose spirit still lived among us.

Inside our office, the energy was always alive. You could smell fresh coffee mixing with the scent of worn leather chairs. Laughter bounced off the walls, and the hustle never stopped. But everything changed when my brother Sharif walked in. He had that presence, commanding, sharp, all business. One day, when offered a quarter, he didn't hesitate. "I want a dollar," he said. The room went silent— and then nodded in respect. "A true businessman," someone said. And just like that, Sharif was on his path, stepping into the legacy with confidence and ambition.

Watching Sharif, I felt the weight of our family's history settle on my shoulders. The Ward name ain't just a name, it's a legacy built on struggle, survival, and success. Our roots go all the way back to 1827. We're one of the oldest Black families in Ohio. Continuing that legacy meant more than just keeping a business afloat—it meant holding the line for our people's future.

When John T. Ward founded E.E. Ward Transfer and Storage Company, he wasn't just thinking about his own success. He built a vehicle for Black self-sufficiency and economic independence at a time when the world was designed to keep us down. The business created wealth, provided jobs, and planted seeds of opportunity—not just for us, but for the entire community.

His dream was about more than making money. It was about creating a space where Black folks could thrive. His business became a platform to empower others, to show what was possible even in the face of deep systemic injustice.

John T.'s legacy didn't stop at the business door. He was all in—supporting education, fighting for civil rights, and leading by example. He showed that business could be a vehicle for change, a way to lift up the next generation and push the community forward. It wasn't just about profits. It was about purpose.

My father taught me that early. He told me success wasn't just about what you earned, it was about what you gave back. A real business lifts others. It creates jobs, supports causes, builds bridges. That's the Ward family philosophy: success is shared.

I'll never forget one moment that stuck with me. I was walking with my grandfather Harold, one of the family's solid rocks. We passed by businesses our family helped start. He turned to me and said, "Our success ain't just for us—it's for everybody. We carry this legacy, and we have to pass it on."

That right there? That's what we stand for. It ain't just business, it's responsibility.

That same spirit runs deep through every generation. My Uncle Eldon, for example, wasn't just building a name—he supported the Elsie and Eldon YMCA, making sure Black kids had access to swimming lessons at a time when those doors were closed to us.

My Uncle James took his knowledge of antiques and started a business that doubled as a mentorship space. He knew that lifting up our youth meant nurturing their creativity, their minds, and their confidence—because wealth ain't just money. It's knowledge, pride, and community.

Throughout every era, the Ward family has lived by one truth: business success and community service go hand in hand. From the Underground Railroad to boardrooms and beyond, we've used our platforms to uplift others.

For us, wealth has never been just dollars—it's been about power, purpose, and passing the torch. And we're still running that race. Still building. Still believing. Because what John T. Ward started wasn't just a business. It was a movement. And we're the ones carrying it forward.

The Ward family legacy is one of bold action, strategic community-building, and unwavering commitment to justice. We learned from John T. Ward that true leadership means lifting others as you climb—making sure your success benefits not just you, but your people. We stay rooted in his values: business, service, empowerment, and above all, the relentless pursuit of justice and equality. Just like John T. before us, we push forward with purpose, making sure the Ward name continues to thrive for generations to come.

John T. Ward, alongside his son William, founded the Ward Transfer Line—a company that would go on to leave a powerful mark on the moving industry. But long before the business earned national recognition, Ward and his close friends had already committed themselves to something greater than profit. They were part of an informal yet deeply committed network—a brotherhood of men determined to serve, protect, and uplift their community in every way they could. Through mutual support, resource-sharing, and organizing, they laid the foundation for a future where Black businesses could grow, and Black families could dream beyond survival.

The very fact that Ward once helped transport fugitive slaves and freedmen to safety is symbolic of the legacy he built—a legacy rooted in freedom, empowerment, and responsibility.

John T. Ward was more than a businessman—he was a man of vision, grit, and purpose. He understood that moving a person's most valuable possessions wasn't just a job; it was a matter of trust. Whether he was transporting goods, furniture, or whole families, John T. made sure his work reflected integrity and excellence. His reputation grew quickly, and by 1889, the company rebranded as E.E. Ward Transfer and Storage under the leadership of his grandson, Edgar Earl Ward.

Under Edgar Ward's guidance, the company became one of the most respected relocation companies in the country. E.E. Ward provided moving services for businesses, libraries, museums, and even institutions like The Ohio State University—all while maintaining the highest standard of care and professionalism.

As the company transitioned to motorized vehicles in the early 1900s, it expanded its reach and influence, landing contracts like delivering a million pianos for Steinway & Sons. Over time, E.E. Ward became a household name in the Midwest, known for its quality and reliability.

In 2003, the U.S. Department of Commerce and the Congressional Black Caucus officially recognized E.E. Ward Moving & Storage as the oldest Black-owned business in America—a powerful recognition of a family's unwavering commitment and enduring success.

But what truly set E.E. Ward apart wasn't just its business acumen; it was its heart. John T.'s great-grandson, Eldon E. Ward, believed deeply that a business wasn't successful unless it was also giving back. He built partnerships with local charities, invested in youth programs, and championed causes that mattered to the people. That spirit of community uplift didn't die with him; it lives on in every initiative the company supports today.

The Ward way has always been about more than just profit. It's about people. John T. Ward believed in creating spaces where his employees felt respected, valued, and empowered. Many stayed with the company for decades, growing alongside the business and carrying his values forward.

One of my clearest memories is of the calendars we passed out every year—free of charge. They weren't just about dates or appointments. They were tools of remembrance. Each one featured Black heroes—leaders, fighters, change-makers—whose faces reminded us daily of the power of resilience and vision. You'd walk into homes, churches, barber shops, and see those calendars hanging proudly. They weren't advertisements, they were affirmations. They said: we've come a long way, and we're still going.

Those calendars carried more weight than most people realized. They were reminders of where we came from, what we'd been through, and what still needed to be done. Just like the company itself, they were rooted in our truth and served as tools for empowerment and pride.

I can see it now, clear as day. The Ward family, one of the oldest Black families in Ohio, stretching back to 1827, had endured so much and built even more. With every step we take today, I can feel the weight of that history. The legacy we carry isn't just about the business, the land, or even the calendar. It runs deeper. It's about justice. It's about dignity. It's about reclaiming what was rightfully ours.

For generations, our family was denied land that belonged to us by right. Land that was stolen, manipulated, and buried under layers of lies and legal loopholes. There was a piece of land in Virginia—once Ward family land. A place that should have been our home. But that right was torn away, hidden behind fraudulent deeds and outright denial. Samuel Ward's name was forged on a deed while he was living miles away in Ohio, and yet officials in Virginia had the nerve to claim the land didn't even exist.

This wasn't some mistake. This was deliberate. Systematic. A clear attempt to erase our presence and strip us of what was rightfully ours. But in all those contradictions, in the inconsistencies buried deep in public records, lies the very proof we need. That evidence can be used to build a powerful case—not just one to reclaim land, but one that demands recognition, respect, and restitution for all that was stolen.

This wasn't just about property. It was about our freedom. Our identity. Our future. What happened to the Ward family was more than legal fraud; it was a direct attack on who we were and who we were trying to become. But the story doesn't end there. We have the power to rewrite it. We might not be able to get that land back outright, but that doesn't mean we can't act. We can fight to preserve the truth, correct the historical record, and make sure Samuel Ward's legacy still shines.

Our story—our ancestors' struggle and perseverance—is a living testimony. A call to action. It pushes us to speak up, to keep demanding what was taken, and to never let silence win. Through legal action, public pressure, and the unity of our people, we can turn this loss into fuel. We can demand accountability. We can fight back.

They may have stolen the land, but they will never steal our future.

The fight for land in Black communities has always been about more than acreage. It's about power. About independence. About dignity. Owning land means stability. It means generational wealth. It means a legacy that outlives you. For freed families like the Wards, land wasn't just property, it was a promise. A promise that we could shape our own destiny.

But that promise was stolen—over and over again. Through fraud. Through backroom deals. Through a system that preyed on people who were once enslaved—people who didn't have access to education, legal counsel, or even basic knowledge of how property laws worked. It was intentional. It was cruel. But it wasn't the end.

That fight—that legacy—is ours now. And we carry it with pride. Through remembering the truth, advocating for justice, and standing united, the descendants of the Ward family can turn this pain into purpose. We're not just fighting for what was taken; we're fighting to honor the ones who came before us.

We fight so that our children, and their children, will know the truth. We fight so that the names of our ancestors live on in the light, not in the shadows of stolen land. This struggle for justice, for recognition, and for the preservation of our family's story—that's the work we'll continue, until the legacy of the Ward family is honored the way it always should have been.

For strength. For resilience. For greatness.

John T. Ward's life was extraordinary—a living thread woven through some of the harshest chapters in Black American history. He didn't just witness slavery, the Civil War, Reconstruction, and Jim Crow; he *endured* them, *survived* them, and built a legacy that stands as a living testament to Black resilience and resistance. His journey is more than just history; it's a roadmap. A guide for survival, dignity, and the relentless fight for justice.

To live through slavery meant carrying the weight of a system built to erase your name, your lineage, and your humanity. John T. Ward bore that weight. He watched a nation rip itself apart in a war that—at its core—was about whether men like him had the right to be free. But freedom, as John T. understood, was never a promise. It was a fight. It meant carving out space where none was given. It meant building a future in a world that refused to see you.

During Reconstruction, there was a flicker of possibility. Black men were voting, holding office, buying land, starting businesses. John T. seized that moment—not just for himself, but for generations to come. He built a business that would go on to become the oldest Black-owned business in America. But even that beacon of progress wasn't safe. In America, Black success has always been seen as a threat.

From Tulsa to Wilmington to Rosewood—Black prosperity has been met with rage. Our businesses have been targeted by economic sabotage, racist zoning laws, denial of access to capital, violence, and outright destruction. E.E. Ward didn't survive because the system made space for it. It survived because John T. Ward refused to let it die. He kept it alive with grit, faith, and an unshakable devotion to his people.

His life and his work are not just a legacy—they are a reminder of the brutal paradox of Black American history: trying to build permanence on land designed to erase you. John T. Ward's bequest is a blueprint. A map drawn in sweat, sacrifice, and strategy. A guide for those who carry on the fight for dignity and self-determination.

That legacy has lived on, passed from generation to generation, each family member adding their own chapter to the story. My great-great-great-grandmother, Catherine Moss—the daughter of Littleberry Moss—walked that same line between fear and freedom. Together, John T. Ward and Littleberry turned Bluff Farms into more than land; they turned it into a sanctuary, a place of refuge in the long shadow of the Fugitive Slave Act. Their courage turned property into promise.

My great-great-great-grandfather John T. Ward served the city as a messenger for fifty years. My great-great-grandfather, William Shelton Ward, contributed to the Underground Railroad, hauled bread for Union soldiers during the Civil War, and later threw himself into the transfer business—never giving up his role as an activist, all the way until his passing.

My grandfather, Harold E. Ward, was a conductor in every sense of the word. A leader. A builder. He helped establish the first all-Black fire station in Columbus, Ohio, and founded the *Merry Makers Club*—a space for Black men to gather, grow, and build each other up. It still exists today.

Uncle Eldon kept our history alive with faith and storytelling. Uncle James, always fly and full of flair, brought style and a love of antiques that added richness to our legacy. Uncle Edgar's brilliance and strength were deeply admired, and Aunt Marie—full of grace and pride—left a mark on us all through her unwavering commitment to our family's story.

My father, James Eldon Ward, stood tall in the movements of his time. He played a significant role in the Black Panther Party and the Black Nationalist movement. And his brother, Ascari—formerly known as Harold E. Ward—brought a more philosophical and artistic approach to the struggle. His creation of the Earth Shoe became an icon of counterculture and a bold symbol of forward thinking.

Each of them, in their own way, upheld the bequest of John T. Ward—not just in name, but in spirit. Through business, activism, family, and faith, they preserved the fire that still burns today.

When my grandfather Harold passed away, I was only ten years old. That's when my Uncle Eldon stepped up and took over the family business. But he didn't just keep things running, he turned it into something bigger. He used it as a tool for change. One of his proudest moves was sponsoring the Eldon and Elsie Ward YMCA, breaking the lie that Black kids couldn't swim. He gave a generation the chance to learn skills we'd been denied for far too long.

But this wasn't just about business. It was about justice.

We had to claim what was ours—the land, the legacy, the respect. It was time for the Ward family to be seen and honored—for the sacrifices we made, for the work we put in, and for our deep commitment to pushing our people forward. We weren't just asking. We were *demanding* recognition.

And so, the quest continues.

This fight? It ain't over. It's just getting started.

My bequest is more than a name—it's a call to action. It's a promise to those who came before and a pledge to those yet to come. It's time for us to rise up, to stand tall, and to take what we are owed. To honor John T. Ward and every ancestor who laid bricks on this road to freedom. This is our story—and it's far from finished.

The Ward name, the Ward legacy, the fight for justice, this isn't history in a textbook. It's alive. It breathes through us. And we are its keepers now. This is the bequest of John T. Ward—and we carry it forward, proud and unyielding, until justice is no longer a dream, but a reality.

In the small city of Bexley, Ohio—right between the Black upper-class neighborhoods of Eldon and Eastgate—stands the Eldon and Elsie Ward YMCA. That building represents more than brick and mortar. It represents a new chapter in our story. A space where

Black children could learn to swim, stand tall, and feel seen. A place of empowerment. A place where community rises.

Today, E.E. Ward Moving & Storage continues to thrive, still guided by the principles John T. Ward set down generations ago. But his legacy isn't just about a business. It's about the *movement* he was part of.

John T. Ward was a founding member and delegate for the National Colored Men's Association—a pivotal group that shaped Black political voice and demanded rights in an era defined by violence and oppression. John T. didn't just move people physically through the Underground Railroad—he moved us politically, spiritually, and socially.

His commitment to our dignity didn't stop at life. He extended that care into death.

He was instrumental in helping create Greenlawn Cemetery, a space where Black people could be buried with dignity and respect—something often denied to them in life. That act alone was revolutionary. In a time when even our deaths were marginalized, John T. carved out space for honor. For peace. For final rest.

John T. Ward is buried at Greenlawn himself. His presence there is more than symbolic; it's a final, unyielding testament to everything he fought for. Even in death, he made space for us. When the world tried to erase us, he insisted: we belong.

John T. didn't just leave behind a business. He left behind a blueprint—for resistance, for dignity, for radical self-determination. His life reminds us that freedom ain't free; it comes with cost. And it demands courage.

The phrase "Let Ward Do It" isn't just a slogan. It's a cultural emblem. A legacy in five words. A community handshake passed from hand to hand, generation to generation. It means trust. It means tradition. It means … *We've got this.*

This is the bequest of John T. Ward: To rise. To claim our space. To speak our names with pride. To demand justice—not just for ourselves, but for our children's children.

The struggle lives in us. The victory will too.

The legacy of John T. Ward doesn't live in the past. It lives right here—in every act of resistance, every business built, every community uplifted, and every ancestor honored. We carry it now. Standing tall. Standing proud. Standing *unshakable.*

Until justice is no longer an idea but a *living reality.*

IN MEMORIAM.

The resolutions upon the death of John T. Ward, were reported by Messrs. King, Keenan and Evans, and adopted by a rising vote. They were:

Whereas, Death has taken from our midst our esteemed friend and public servant, John T. Ward, who for many years had well and faithfully discharged the duties of janitor of this council chamber, and who, by his integrity and sagacity won the respect and confidence of those whom he served and whom he met; now, therefore, be it

Resolved, by the city council of the city of Columbus, That, meekly bowing our heads to the inexorable hand of death, we deeply regret the loss of the good citizen, honest servant, affectionate and provident parent, John T. Ward, and to the bereaved kin extend our sincere condolence, while we commend his life to them as a noble example.

Although I never had the honor of meeting him, I am part of him—forged from the same fire that shaped his struggle and survival. In uncovering his life, what I've learned, what I carry, and what I've grown to love about my great-great-great-grandfather, John T. Ward, mirrors the very sentiment the City of Columbus once rang from its chambers in a powerful memorial after his passing.

In a time when Black men were being pushed out of public life—exiled, erased, terrorized—John T. Ward stood unbroken.

Not just surviving. Thriving. Leading. Bequeathing.

John T. Ward was a giant—a living testimony that Black excellence could not be erased, even when every system tried to bury it.

He carried the weight of his people's suffering and still walked with dignity, never folding under burdens designed to break him.

He transformed spaces built to exclude Black people into places where his name, his labor, and his legacy could not be denied.

Where others were written out of history, he wrote himself in.

During an era when survival alone was revolutionary, John T. Ward became something even rarer: a man respected across racial lines, a Black figure admired in halls that once conspired to erase men like him. That kind of reverence was almost unthinkable in his time—and it remains an extraordinary lesson in ours.

John T. was more than a survivor of slavery. He was a builder of standards. A quiet revolutionary who didn't just "make do"—he made way.

He built bridges where none existed. He set expectations so high they couldn't be ignored. He didn't wait for recognition; he demanded it.

When John T. Ward died, Columbus didn't just lose a worker. It lost a heartbeat.

The city council—the very seat of power that once rendered Black dignity invisible—stood on their feet to honor him.

They didn't just mention his name. They memorialized it.

Not merely as a public servant, but as a man of unmatched integrity, wisdom, and perseverance. They bowed their heads not out of habit, but because something larger than them demanded it: the undeniable force of his life.

They called him a "good citizen," an "honest servant," an "affectionate and provident parent." And in doing so, they offered his family—and all of us—the highest tribute they could:

Look to his life as a noble example.

When they adopted his memorial by a rising vote—standing shoulder to shoulder to affirm his memory—it wasn't empty ceremony.

It was reluctant admiration.

It was the uncomfortable acknowledgment that even in a country built to forget men like him, John T. Ward forced remembrance. Through dignity. Through duty. Through legacy.

He didn't just work for Columbus. He helped shape its moral backbone.

And now, his story—our story—demands to be told. Not as a footnote buried in someone else's history, but as a monument carved into the soul of a nation still struggling to understand the price of its survival.

CONCLUSION

"We are all bound up together in one great bundle of humanity, and society cannot trample on the weakest and feeblest of its members without receiving the curse in its own soul."

-Frances Ellen Watkins Harper

In 2018, I took my son to Chicago—not just to witness a moment in history, but to be part of something bigger than ourselves. It wasn't merely about attending a graduation for Power omics Certification; it was about stepping into a movement that would shape not just my views, but his as well. We were there for the first graduating class of a program dedicated to empowering Black communities, a program carrying the weight of our collective struggle.

The fiery, impassioned historical presentation delivered by Dr. Claud Anderson shook me to my core. His words didn't just land— they hit like a tidal wave, crashing through every mental barrier I hadn't even realized I'd built.

His voice filled the room with authority. Each sentence cut through the air—sharp, deliberate, and impossible to ignore. He spoke of political leverage, of the urgent need for Black Americans to negotiate from a position of power, not desperation. I was locked in—transfixed—not just by his knowledge, but by the clarity and conviction with which he demanded truth, dignity, and ownership.

But it wasn't just what he said; it was who was there to hear it. I looked around the room and, for the first time in a long time, felt like I was among my tribe. These were people who got it. Who understood the weight of generational struggle. Who weren't afraid to speak the uncomfortable truths. There was no need to code-switch, no need to explain why the fire inside me burned so hot.

There, in that space, I didn't feel isolated in my thinking; I felt seen. Understood. Empowered. It was more than a lecture; it was a homecoming of the mind and spirit.

"We have no allies," he said. And that line? It echoed in my head long after he left the stage. It wasn't just some political catchphrase; it was a gut punch. A wake-up call. A challenge.

As I stood there, I felt the weight of history pressing on my shoulders—the weight of my ancestors' struggles. Struggles that paved the road to this very moment. Dr. Anderson wasn't just talking politics; he was daring us to do more. To hold our leaders accountable. To stop begging. To take our place at the table without apology. To never trade power for proximity.

I turned to my son, standing right beside me, his eyes wide with a quiet kind of knowing. I could see him piecing it together. The gears turning. The magnitude of it all settling into his chest.

"Do you get it?" I asked, my voice low but fierce with urgency. "What he's saying—it's not just about voting. It's about leverage.

It's about knowing our worth and using that knowledge to demand what's already ours."

He nodded slowly. "Yeah, Mom. I hear it," he said, his voice soft but sure. That moment hit me. He heard it. He *felt* it.

That night, in the stillness of the hotel room, I sat with everything I had just witnessed. Dr. Anderson's words had stirred something deep, but it was the connection to John T. Ward's legacy that struck my soul. John T.—who fought for his people, his community, and future generations—had already done what Dr. Anderson was preaching. The fight wasn't just about surviving. It was about strategizing. About leverage. About demanding what was rightfully ours and building a future out of nothing but will.

After the event, I got a chance to talk to Dr. Anderson. I shared my family's story, my desire to serve my city, my need to do more. He listened. Encouraged me to keep going. Follow up. Stay the course. Then he signed my copy of *PowerNomics*, the blueprint for everything I was already beginning to build. His parting words were simple—but heavy:

"Seek truth."

Later that night, I zoomed in on the inscription he'd written in my book. And that's when it hit me—like lightning in my chest.

Without the knowledge of our history—without understanding the fight from the Headright System to Black Codes, Jim Crow, and manumission, I couldn't truly grasp the magnitude of what we were up against. My family's story was laced through those same struggles. It shaped the way I saw the world. This wasn't just a conference, it was preparation. It was a call. Without that understanding, I wouldn't know how to begin—or how to properly honor the legacy of my ancestors, especially John T. Ward. He didn't just fight for freedom, he fought to break the chains of economic bondage, laying the groundwork for generations.

That night, I called my father. I needed to hear his voice, needed to process. His wisdom always grounded me, and this moment demanded it.

"Dad," I said, leaning back in my chair, the day still rolling through my mind. "I was just at this event in Chicago. Dr. Anderson was speaking about political leverage—how we got to hold politicians accountable, not just out of loyalty, but so our interests get served. And it hit me—this is what John T. Ward did. He didn't just hope for change—he planned for it. He demanded it."

There was a pause, then my father spoke, his voice calm, reflective—rooted.

"You're right," he said. "John T. understood leverage long before we even had the language for it. He wasn't just asking for freedom, he was securing it. He wasn't just trying to survive—he was building something that would outlive him. He moved with strategy. With purpose. He didn't wait for change. He became it."

His words settled in, but I wasn't done. The fire inside me burned brighter. "But how do we do this today, Dad? How do we make sure we're doing it right? How do we keep fighting like John T. Ward did?"

My father's voice grew firm, a quiet authority threading through his words. "You build alliances, but you never lose sight of your agenda. John T. didn't just follow any party—he followed what benefited his people. You can't walk into a room with demands unless you know exactly what's in it for them to back your agenda. That's politics. That's power."

My chest tightened, and my voice rose with a new urgency. "But we've been patient for too long. John T. wasn't patient. He organized.

He pushed for unity. He made them listen. If we don't press forward now, then when?"

I could almost hear my father smile through the phone—that familiar sound I'd known all my life. "Boldness without strategy is just noise," he said, his words grounding me like roots. "That's what John T. taught us. It's not just about being loud, it's about being effective. His loyalty wasn't to a party—it was to the cause. If we want our voices to matter, we've got to make them matter—on our terms."

And just like that, it all clicked. John T. Ward wasn't just a freedom fighter—he was a tactician. A master of negotiation. A visionary who understood that real power comes from strategic alliances and unwavering demands. His approach wasn't just political, it was philosophical. And now, that philosophy belonged to me.

As our call ended, I felt a surge of energy that couldn't be quenched. Dr. Anderson's truth, my father's wisdom, and the legacy of John T. Ward had sparked something deep in my spirit. The fight for justice, for reparations, for economic power, it was no longer just about survival. It was about reclaiming what was already ours, about demanding it. And making sure we were never again denied our rightful place at the table.

Back in that moment in Chicago, 2018, I had only just begun to understand the path I was walking. This wasn't just my journey; it was a continuation of the one my ancestors started. From the Headright System that commodified Black bodies, to the Black Codes that criminalized their freedom, to the Jim Crow laws that denied their humanity—those who survived didn't fight in vain. Their struggle lit a fire in me that will never go out.

It wasn't just a speech—it was a revolution in my soul. And with my son standing beside me, I knew this was just the beginning. The legacy of John T. Ward, the teachings of Dr. Anderson, and the fire in my father's voice had all come together to light the way.

The fight for justice, for reparations, for true equality, that's our mission now. And we won't rest until the truth is brought to light, until the sacrifices of our ancestors are honored, and until we, as a people, are finally and fully free.

John T. Ward never hesitated to challenge himself, perhaps the ones he deeply respected—if he felt they weren't fully committed to the cause of abolition. At the Columbus Colored Conventions, his debates with James Poindexter weren't just heated back-and-forths, they were urgent calls to action, reminders that the fight to end slavery couldn't wait. John T.'s boldness in calling out hypocrisy, especially from those who failed to take real steps toward freedom, spoke volumes about his moral backbone. These gatherings weren't just about talking; they were strategy sessions, spaces where Black men sharpened their political skills, exchanged powerful ideas, and laid down blueprints for a future built on liberation and self-determination.

The Colored Conventions were more than meetings; they were movement-building. They brought structure, unity, and resolve to the fight. In these rooms, brothers learned how to organize, plan, and lead. By studying tools like *Cushing's Manual of Parliamentary Practice*, they weren't just participating in democracy, they were showing they knew how to run it. Understanding the rules gave their movements legitimacy, helped them manage complicated agendas, and allowed them to move tactically in political spaces that weren't made for them.

John T.'s moral code didn't just shape his politics; it shaped how he dealt with people close to him, too. He called out church leaders— men he prayed with—if they preached about justice but still enslaved people or sold them instead of setting them free. To John T., faith without action meant nothing. If your beliefs weren't backed up by your deeds, especially in the fight for freedom, they didn't count.

The bonds formed in those days were built on risk, trust, and purpose. Whether in church basements or behind closed doors at home, abolitionists came together like family. Many were deeply connected to the Underground Railroad, but you'd never know it from their records. Their silence wasn't fear—it was strategy. They knew what they were doing had to stay hidden until the time was right.

And they didn't stop at fighting for freedom; they fought for *full* citizenship. They pushed Presidents Grant and Hayes for access to education and voting rights. They demanded that if they were being taxed, they deserved representation. They knew real liberty wasn't just about breaking physical chains; it was about being seen, heard, and respected as full citizens in every part of society.

David Jenkins, editor of *The Palladium of Liberty*—Ohio's first Black-owned newspaper—was one of John T.'s closest allies. Jenkins used his pen to expose injustice and elevate the voices of abolitionists across the state. His work made sure the movement had a platform, a record, and a way to connect freedom fighters from all corners.

James Poindexter was another giant in the fight. He didn't just speak on freedom; he helped make it real. As an Underground Railroad conductor, he provided safe passage, resources, and real protection to those fleeing slavery. After the war, he and his wife founded the Colored Soldiers Relief Society to support Black Union veterans who were denied help by the government. Poindexter didn't stop there; he became Columbus's first Black city councilman, helped Black children gain access to education, and served on the boards of Wilberforce University and the State Forestry Bureau.

These actions—along with the work of figures like Charles Langston—weren't isolated efforts. They were part of a larger movement rooted in Black empowerment, built on a foundation of economic independence, political representation, and cultural dignity. Langston's fearless advocacy, whether in courtrooms or public forums, showed the kind of courage it took to speak truth to power when the risks were real. His commitment to education, walking the same path his brother Mercer Langston helped blaze, emphasized the necessity of creating real opportunities for the next generation.

The work of Ward, Jenkins, Poindexter, and Langston wasn't just about resisting injustice; it was about building a future where Black people didn't just survive but thrived. They weren't waiting to be included in someone else's vision of America; they were shaping one of their own. Their legacy isn't just some history book mention; it's a blueprint, a guidepost for us still fighting for justice, still fighting to be seen, heard, and respected. By standing on their principles and carrying forward their victories, we inch closer to the society they dreamed of—one where Black freedom is not up for debate.

John T.'s 1871 speech on political strategy still hits hard today. He made it plain: we must hold our leaders accountable and refuse to blindly pledge loyalty to any party that doesn't put our interests first. Just like he questioned party loyalty back then, we've got to ask the hard questions now—like who really benefits from mass incarceration? Who profits when Black survival is criminalized?

"I think these are the most sensible resolutions I have heard tonight. They express what we, as colored people, ought always to carry in our hearts. They speak of the Republican Party, because the Democratic Party has not done what the Republican Party has done for us. As long as the Republican Party continues to uphold those principles, we ought to stick to them, united and unwavering.

We have the Democratic Party, the Republican Party, and the so-called Conservative Party—which claims to be a great friend of the colored people. However, we must be vigilant, as it may lead many of our brethren astray, particularly in the North. The Republican Party has done for us all that a downtrodden people could hope for—and more than any other party has done.

Now, as the resolutions state, I believe we should stand by the Republican Party until such a time as they deviate from their own principles. Only then would it be appropriate for us to come together and consider turning to the Democratic or Conservative Party."

John T. Ward once said:

"We should stand by them until such a time as they deviate from their own principles."

For decades, Black Americans have been the most loyal voting bloc in the country, yet neither major political party has taken reparations seriously. Why? Because there has been no consequence for their inaction.

John T. Ward understood that freedom was more than escaping physical bondage; it was about securing political, social, and economic independence. He fought for Black businesses, Black political representation, and Black self-sufficiency.

Sadly, if he were alive today, he would see the same patterns:

Across the United States, Black individuals are stopped, searched, arrested, and incarcerated at rates far exceeding their share of the population. For example, Black drivers are more likely to be pulled over for routine traffic stops and subjected to vehicle searches—even though studies show they're no more likely than white drivers to carry contraband. In many cities, predominantly Black neighborhoods bear the brunt of aggressive "zero-tolerance" policing strategies; minor infractions like loitering, public drinking, or panhandling can quickly escalate into fines, warrants, and jail time. This cycle of surveillance and punishment doesn't just fill prison cells; it disrupts families, undermines community stability, and leaves lasting criminal records that hinder access to housing, employment, and education.

Targeting of Collective Black Resistance

When Black communities organize—whether in protests against police violence, tenant unions fighting discriminatory housing policies, or mutual-aid networks providing food and medical care—those collective efforts often face legal pushback. Lawsuits, injunctions, and policing tactics are deployed to break up protests and silence leaders. For instance, peaceful marches may be met with riot charges, organizers may face felony conspiracy counts, and community centers can lose their nonprofit status for alleged regulatory violations. This isn't merely enforcement of neutral statutes; it's a strategic use of the legal system to stifle movements that challenge entrenched power structures. By criminalizing protest tactics and penalizing solidarity networks, authorities aim to fracture social cohesion and deter sustained resistance.

The Centrality of Economic Autonomy

True liberation extends beyond voting rights or desegregation; it demands control over the means to build and sustain wealth. For Black communities, economic autonomy means owning businesses in neighborhoods long starved of investment, securing land and property free from predatory lending practices, and accessing capital on fair terms. The legacy of redlining, job discrimination, and the racial wealth gap makes entrepreneurship and homeownership uphill battles. Without economic power, political gains can be rolled back; when communities lack independent sources of revenue, they remain vulnerable to budget cuts, gentrification, and corporate exploitation. Thus, establishing robust Black-owned enterprises, community land trusts, cooperative ventures, and equitable lending programs is not just an economic imperative—it is the linchpin of a truly resilient and self-determined future.

Reparations isn't just about slavery—it's about generations of stolen wealth, stolen land, and stolen opportunities that have kept Black Americans at an economic disadvantage.

Slavery ended, but wealth was never redistributed.

Black Wall Streets were burned, but no reparations were given. Homeownership was blocked, businesses were sabotaged, and generational wealth was denied. Now, just as before, politicians give empty promises and expect blind loyalty.

If John T. Ward were here today, he would remind us:

"Support must be earned."

In the decades after the Civil War, the brutal reality of racial oppression didn't fade—it deepened. Freed Black men and women trying to claim basic rights—especially the right to vote—were met with violence, threats, and death. Many were beaten, jailed, or lynched just for trying to register. Jim Crow laws and white supremacist groups like the Ku Klux Klan rose up to lock Black folks out of the democratic process altogether. What came to be known as the Betrayal of the Freedmen wasn't just symbolic, it was systematic. Promises of freedom and equality were quickly replaced by new chains: political suppression, economic exploitation, and social terror.

Rutherford B. Hayes, the nineteenth president of the United States—the man who pulled the plug on Reconstruction—retired to Ohio in 1881 and chose not to run for re-election. His decision marked a turning point, one that made it clear: the federal government was washing its hands of Black folks' struggle for justice. The country had moved on, even if the wounds it left behind were still wide open.

Now, some folks might say that drawing a line between the abolitionists of the 1800s and people today facing RICO charges is a stretch—maybe even disrespectful. How could we possibly compare folks who fought to end slavery with those the government now accuses of running criminal enterprises? And yes, the context is different. Abolitionists were fighting to destroy an immoral system built on human bondage. RICO laws are used to target things like organized crime, gangs, and the Mafia.

But look a little closer. What connects them is how the law was used—and who it was used against. Both abolitionists and some modern-day activists got hit not just for what they did individually, but for how they moved together. The law came down hard on collective action—on unity that challenged the power structure. Whether it was helping someone escape slavery or building resistance against state-sanctioned violence, both groups were labeled criminals for pushing back against injustice.

Back then, abolitionists weren't seen as heroes, they were seen as lawbreakers. The Fugitive Slave Act of 1850 made it illegal to help a runaway slave. Folks caught doing so could face steep fines, prison time, or worse. That meant if you opened your home to a fugitive, gave them a ride, offered food or water—you were a criminal in the eyes of the law.

But they did it anyway.

They formed networks like the Underground Railroad— tight-knit, disciplined, and deeply committed. They used secret codes, trusted couriers, and support that crossed state lines. It was coordinated. It was intentional. It was dangerous. And that made them targets. Law enforcement didn't just see isolated good deeds, they saw a movement. A threat. An organized resistance.

Now, consider the RICO Act (Racketeer Influenced and Corrupt Organizations Act) of 1970. It was created to dismantle organized crime syndicates like the Mafia—but in recent decades, it's been used disproportionately to target Black communities, especially young Black men from low-income neighborhoods. Under RICO, prosecutors can charge entire groups as criminal enterprises—even when only a few members are accused of breaking the law.

Just like the Fugitive Slave Act criminalized entire abolitionist networks, RICO gives law enforcement the power to go after whole communities, social circles, and organizations—regardless of whether everyone in them actually committed a crime. The law doesn't require proof that an individual did something illegal; just being affiliated with a group is often enough to get charged.

This modern use of the RICO Act echoes the same old strategy: criminalize collective resistance, punish Black unity. After slavery, freed people were denied land, education, and economic opportunity. Today, Black youth face those same systemic barriers—still boxed out, still written off, still targeted.

The structural problems that crushed newly freed Black folks after the Civil War haven't gone away—they just wear different clothes now. Take education, for example. Black and low-income students are far more likely to attend underfunded schools with outdated textbooks, overworked teachers, and not enough resources. On top of that, "zero-tolerance" policies hit Black students hardest—kids getting suspended or expelled for things that should've been handled with a conversation. That kind of discipline doesn't teach; it funnels students straight into the school-to-prison pipeline.

Then there's the over-policing in Black neighborhoods and schools. Instead of counselors, kids get cops in their hallways. A fight doesn't lead to a talking-to; it leads to handcuffs. That's how young Black kids get branded as criminals before they're even old enough to vote, setting them up for a lifelong battle with the justice system.

Lack of economic opportunity only adds to the pressure. When doors to steady work, generational wealth, or entrepreneurship stay locked, many young Black men turn to whatever means they can to survive. And when they form groups—whether it's for music, business, or just brotherhood—they suddenly become targets for RICO. Just like the abolitionists were punished for organizing against slavery, these young people are punished for organizing at all.

There's an old saying that still hits home: "Crime is the child of poverty, but the mother of survival." When the system blocks every legal path to stability—when it keeps people from owning homes, building wealth, or protecting their families—folks are going to do what they have to do to survive. That was true after slavery, when Black men were criminalized for being unemployed and forced into convict leasing. And it's still true today, when systemic joblessness, underfunded schools, and racial profiling keep feeding the prison system.

For generations, this country has denied Black folks the right to thrive. After the Civil War, there was hope that freedom might finally mean something. But Black Codes, vagrancy laws, and Jim Crow snatched that hope away. Today, the justice system still targets us—just with new language and different laws. RICO is just one more tool in a long line used to label Black collectives as threats.

But here's what they can't erase: the legacy of resistance.

Just like John T. Ward, David Jenkins, James Poindexter, and Charles Langston pushed back in their time, we're pushing back now.

The fight for justice, the call for reparations, the demand to be seen and valued, that's not new. It's part of an unbroken line. And if we're wise enough to learn from those who came before us, we've already got the blueprint.

The struggle continues. But so does the strength.

None of this is coincidence. These systems weren't built to uplift—they were built to contain. To maintain a social order that's always treated Black life as second-class and disposable. That's why, when someone breaks out of that mold—when they take a life, even in desperation—the punishment is swift and severe. Because deep down, this country's legal foundation still values property over people.

This mentality isn't new. It goes back to when Black people were considered property. Back then, our worth was tied to our labor, not our humanity. We were policed, controlled, and bought and sold. And that mindset—treating Black life as something to manage, own, or discard—still lingers. The law might've changed on paper, but its purpose? Still the same.

The Power of Property: The 13th Amendment and Its Loopholes

Look at the 13th Amendment. Yeah, it abolished slavery—but with a catch: "except as a punishment for crime whereof the party shall have been duly convicted." That one line became the loophole that brought slavery back under a new name. All it took was a conviction. Black folks were arrested in droves, then leased out to work for corporations or the state. That wasn't justice; it was exploitation, wrapped in legality.

The Paradox of the 14th Amendment

Then there's the 14th Amendment—supposedly created to ensure equal protection under the law. But in reality, it's been used more to protect property rights than to defend marginalized communities. Sure, it granted citizenship. But legal decisions like *Plessy v. Ferguson* turned around and said, "Separate but equal," making segregation the law of the land. Black folks were still seen as second-class citizens on paper, but expendable in practice.

Laws like the Black Codes and Jim Crow weren't about giving us freedom. They were about keeping control. They protected the interests of the powerful—those who owned land, businesses, and formerly enslaved people. And they made sure Black folks stayed at the bottom of the economic and social ladder.

Even after slavery ended, the mindset that treated Black people as property never really died. It just evolved. Policies were put in place that criminalized poverty, survival, and Black existence itself.

The Enduring Impact: From Property to Punishment

Today, slavery is technically abolished—but the prison system still disproportionately targets Black communities. It criminalizes poverty and survival, just like it always has. Black people are still denied access to the tools of freedom: education, employment, land ownership, and safety. And when we're boxed into corners and forced to act out of desperation, the system doesn't look at the conditions that created the crisis. It only sees a criminal.

The punishment stays harsh. The cycle stays spinning. But the truth stays standing too: this system was never about protecting us. It was about protecting what they own.

This is where the phrase "Crime is the child of poverty, but the mother of survival" still hits hard. Even now, the law continues to prioritize protecting property, wealth, and capital over basic human dignity and survival. The criminal justice system upholds that same hierarchy—punishing people simply for trying to survive, because their struggle threatens the status quo. Our legal system wasn't built to value life—it was built to protect ownership. And that mindset? It was born from a time when human beings were owned.

A Reflection on the Property of Life: Bob vs. Lucy

To really understand how the law has historically treated Black life, look at the case of Bob—an enslaved man who killed his enslaver, Dr. Lynch. No matter the reason, no matter the circumstances, the courts never acknowledged Bob's humanity. There was no talk of self-defense. The system saw it as one piece of "property" damaging another. The focus wasn't on justice—it was on compensation. Dr. Lynch's family wanted their "loss" restored. So, what happened to Bob? He was forced back into slavery. Just like that. His life, his pain, his reason—none of it mattered. The law wasn't concerned with justice. It was about reclaiming "damaged goods."

Now, let's flip it. Think about Lucy—a Free Black woman who was murdered. Her status was different. She wasn't considered property, so her death was treated like an act of violence against a person. But that distinction is key: it shows how the law picks and chooses who gets to be seen as fully human. One Black life was seen as property: the other as a person. That difference reveals the deep cracks in a system that's always devalued Black lives—depending on our status, our freedom, and our place in society.

The Core of the System: Property Over People

What these two stories make clear is this: the legal system was designed to protect property—not people. From Bob's case to today's headlines, that same mentality still runs the game. The laws may look different now, but the power structure hasn't shifted much. It still punishes Black folks for simply trying to live and survive in a world rigged against us.

Back then, we were forced into a system that defined us as property. Now, we're locked into a system that treats us as disposable. Whether it was convict leasing, vagrancy laws, or mass incarceration today, it's the same playbook. And the message hasn't changed: capital is king—Black life is expendable.

Dismantling the Legacy

That's why the fight for reparations, equality, and justice isn't just about righting a few wrongs—it's about tearing down a whole system that's been rooted in injustice from the start. Until we confront and correct that foundation—the one that's always valued property over people—the cycle will continue. We'll keep being criminalized, dehumanized, and pushed aside.

But Black people have never stopped fighting. We've always resisted. We're still here—still demanding the world see us not as threats or statistics, but as human beings with value, dignity, and the right to live free.

The final question is not whether we've suffered. That's been documented in blood, in chains, in every whispered story and shattered lineage.

The question is, are we ready to fight for what is owed?

The abolitionists did not beg for mercy. They risked their lives— ran through forests, swam through rivers, forged freedom out of a nation built to deny it. They dared to believe that a different future was possible.

So, what will we do with their bequest?

Today, Black Americans stand at another crossroads. Not asking for justice, but demanding it. Not with empty slogans—but with strategy, unity, and unflinching truth.

Reparations are not a favor. They are unpaid debt.

Economic justice must be our nonnegotiable. It must be the litmus test for every ballot cast, every politician endorsed, every system we choose to engage with—or walk away from.

Because if we don't demand what is ours—who will?

And if not now—when?

Our ancestors dreamed us into existence. And our children are watching—waiting to inherit either our silence or our courage.

Let this not be the end of a book.

Let this be the beginning of a movement.

"We will not continue to support systems, politicians, or policies that fail to address or correct the economic harm done to our people. This is not a request. It is a demand. And we will not back down from it."

It's a call for power, not pity. Empowerment, not empty promises.

EPILOGUE

Chris Saunders never intended to become the heartbeat of a hidden history. Nearly thirty years ago, what started as a casual curiosity—tracking down names linked to the Underground Railroad in Lawrence County, Ohio—evolved into a relentless obsession. "I thought it would last a few weeks," he told me, eyes distant with memory, "maybe a month." That was twenty years ago.

Today, Chris has meticulously uncovered more than fifty combined Underground Railroad conductors and historical sites within that single county, and he continues digging relentlessly. He breathes life into forgotten names, resurrects maps lost to time, and reverently handles faded ink that bridges centuries. He's the type of man who treats court records like sacred texts and abandoned cemeteries like holy ground. Had this been 1827, townsfolk surely would have called him The Timekeeper.

When PBS produced a segment on John Legend's ancestry, they turned to Chris. He didn't merely provide facts—he guided the crew through history itself, pointing out the courthouse and the precise records that secured freedom for John Legend's ancestors. That infamous 1849 court case—the tragic ordeal where the Polley children were ripped from their family and sold south—became the longest freedom trial in American history. Chris was the key figure who unearthed the evidence, finally delivering justice after 162 years. Freedom granted, *nunc pro tunc*—now for then.

I was captivated by this powerful concept and began researching. *Nunc pro tunc* is a Latin legal term meaning "now for then," signifying the correction or formalization of an earlier action retroactively—as if that action had always been acknowledged correctly from the very beginning. In courtrooms, it corrects official errors retroactively. But here, I borrow it not as a legal motion—but as a moral metaphor. Because history itself has made clerical errors far greater than any docket misfiled. This isn't about paperwork; it's about people.

Let us apply *nunc pro tunc* to the land stolen from my family. The land from Cook's estate in Virginia was promised, legally granted, and then unjustly stripped away. Today, we demand restoration—justice *nunc pro tunc*—officially recognizing and restoring, now for then, what was always rightfully ours. This isn't a request for something new; it is a rightful claim for the acknowledgment and restitution of what has been unjustly withheld for generations.

Let us also apply *nunc pro tunc* to reparations—justice now for then. Reparations rectify wrongs that should have been addressed generations ago, settling debts that have accumulated through centuries of injustice, unpaid labor, stolen land, and broken promises. Reparations represent the court of history finally correcting its record—not as a new act of generosity today, but as delayed justice, delivered as if it had been granted at the rightful moment in history.

When I asked Chris how he'd like to be acknowledged in this book, he humbly replied. "I don't really have a title. I do all this for fun. I love it. It makes my soul happy."

The documents were sealed. The testimonies archived. The laws repealed or forgotten.

Yet history refuses to rest.

It breathes in the land, whispers in the silence, pulses through bloodlines.

And sometimes … it stares back at you from a screen.

Chris is undoubtedly a Guardian of Legacy. For me, he became something far deeper—a compass guiding me through layers of truth. He was the first to confirm the history behind Sulphur Spring Plantation, the Ward family, and the profound manumission that changed everything—136 souls freed in 1826, among them my ancestors. Once, I asked how close the Ohio River was to his home—the very river crossed by those newly freed Wards. "It's my backyard," he answered quietly. Chills ran down my spine. Without hesitation, I invited myself for a tour.

Then, a revelation struck I never anticipated.

Chris reached out one evening, his tone reverent yet tense. "I think I've found descendants of the European Ward family—the ones who owned your people."

My heart stopped.

I called everyone I knew, declaring passionately, "We ride out at dawn!" Yes—like some 1800s freedom fighter meets Angela Bassett in *Waiting to Exhale*. I was hyped. Emotional. Ready to storm the gates of history like it owed me money. This wasn't just a trip—it was a *mission*. A pilgrimage. A whole ancestral side quest. But the responses from my family and friends? Perplexed. Confused. Deeply concerned.

I got texts like: "Ride where exactly?"

"Do we need snacks?"

"Wait—are you visiting the people who *owned* us?"

And suddenly, I had to pause. Because yeah—how do you rationalize the desire to visit the *land* where your people were enslaved, and maybe even *shake hands* with the descendants of those who held the whip?

I had to sit with that.

Not because I wanted reconciliation or some feel-good ancestry. com moment—but because deep down, I needed to see the soil. To stand where they stood. To confront what was taken and name it out loud.

I wasn't chasing closure. I was chasing *truth*. And somehow, that realization—combined with the side-eyes from my loved ones—centered me.

We didn't ride out at dawn.

I was left to carry confusion, history, ancestors, and all with me.

Chris gave me details—yes, some descendants still lived on that land, still bore that surname. My breath hung suspended between the weight of history and raw horror. Eventually, I found her—a young woman's face on social media. My finger hovered over the "send friend request" button, trembling with uncertainty. I clicked. She accepted.

Then … silence.

Neither of us has spoken. I find myself staring at her image, searching for echoes of the past in her features. What floods me in these moments? Rage? Curiosity? Grief? A strange, unsettling kinship? I've filled pages with questions—my own personal arsenal.

Weeks passed, and I circled back to Chris, eager for more details about her family. When he casually mentioned an aunt's name, my breath caught sharply. It was the same blogger who had assisted me years before—my initial source on this very journey, a woman who unknowingly guided me toward a truth neither of us could have predicted.

The web tightened.

Now, I stand at the brink of revelation. The past murmurs through the trees. The land holds its memories. The river remembers. And now … so do I.

Yet the question looms, heavier than ever:

Do I reach out? Should I dare ask the questions no one wants to confront? Do I hold her family accountable—or do I create space for a conversation that might heal more than it wounds?

The river remembers. And now, undeniably, so do I.

But the current has brought me to the precipice of something deeper.

Do I reach out? Or allow silence to claim victory again?

What would you do?

Unlock the Legacy Behind the Pages

Thank you for reading *The Bequest of John T. Ward.* This book is rooted not only in oral tradition, but in documented truth.

Scan the QR code to explore authentic historical records that support the story, including:

- Tithables and tax documents dating back to the 1700s.
- The original will that manumitted the Ward family.
- Archival photographs and legal documents that provide visual and legal evidence of the legacy.

These materials offer a deeper look into the generations whose lives shaped the story you've just read.

If this book moved you, challenged you, or taught you something new, I kindly ask that you leave a review. Your feedback helps bring this history to light for others—and honors the legacy of those whose stories have gone untold for far too long.

Thank you for being part of this journey.

Scan me!

ABOUT THE AUTHOR

Shanna Ward

Shanna Ward is an author, family historian, Certified Freedmen Genealogist, and passionate advocate for preserving Black history and advancing economic empowerment. A fifth-generation descendant of abolitionist John T. Ward, she was born and raised in Columbus, Ohio, where she continues her research into Black land ownership, genealogy, and post-Reconstruction survival. Her personal and professional mission is grounded in historical reclamation, truth-telling, and legacy-building.

Her journey began not in archives, but in whispers—fragments of a legacy passed down at family gatherings, stories of an ancestor who risked everything for freedom. That spark ignited a relentless pursuit to reclaim a name nearly erased. Through years of archival research, oral history, and genealogical discovery, she unearthed the remarkable life of John T. Ward: a conductor on the Underground Railroad, a civil war military supplier, and the founder of America's oldest Black-owned business still in operation today.

But John T. was more than a freedom fighter, he was a strategist, organizer, and visionary in the fight for Black liberation. As a participant in the Colored Conventions Movement, he stood shoulder-to-shoulder with Black leaders who demanded civil rights, education, and economic justice during some of America's most volatile eras.

Shanna's debut book, *The Bequest of John T. Ward*, brings his story to life in a sweeping historical narrative rooted in family truth and national reckoning. She has also authored children's books including *Little John T. Ward and the Quilted Code* and *Little John T. Ward and the Underground Railroad Codes*, making history accessible to young readers and future legacy bearers.

What sets Shanna's work apart is the fusion of family lineage and national history—placing the reader in the crosscurrents of personal truth and public record. Her writing invites readers to question what was lost, what was stolen, and what can still be reclaimed.

What's in a Name?

"The name Ward has always carried weight in my family—not because of European lineage, but because of what it has come to mean through generations of survival, service, and self-determination."

Historically, the name *Ward* comes from the Old English "weard"—meaning *guardian* or *watchman*—and from the Irish "Mac an Bhaird," *son of the bard*, or storyteller. Shanna identifies with both meanings: as a guardian of truth and as a storyteller of the forgotten.

The Ward family traces its name to enslaved ancestors who inherited it from slaveholders. This name may not have been "theirs" by blood—but it is now theirs by truth, sacrifice, and reclamation. Shanna honors that history not only by keeping the name but by transforming it into a banner of survival, excellence, and legacy. In fact, some family members have legally changed their names to embrace that truth.

"I am taking a name once forced on my family and turning it into a symbol of strength. Not nobility by blood—but nobility by endurance."

She also reminds readers that Africa had rich symbolic traditions long before European heraldry existed. While European coats-of-arms were inherited through title, African identity was encoded in symbols of resilience, spirit, and memory—often tattooed on the soul more than the shield.

Family Motto & Reclaimed Crest

Motto: *Comme je fus* — *"As I was."*

"As I was, so I remain—unyielding, undiminished, and rooted in purpose."

Shanna reclaims her family crest through its deeper symbolic elements:

- Blue for truth and strength
- Gold for dignity and honor
- A knight as warden and protector

Her life and work are grounded in these principles. Like her ancestor John T. Ward, Shanna carries the name not for status—but for service.

"Let Ward Do It" isn't just a motto. It's a mission. A call to protect what matters, speak the truth, and move our people forward.

John T Ward

Catherine Moss Ward

Oliver Ward

Top: Wakeman Ward and Nellie Ward and their children
Bottom: James Ward, Marie Ward, Doris Ward,
Harold E Ward and Eldon Ward

William Ward & Mary Hodge Ward

Edgar Ward

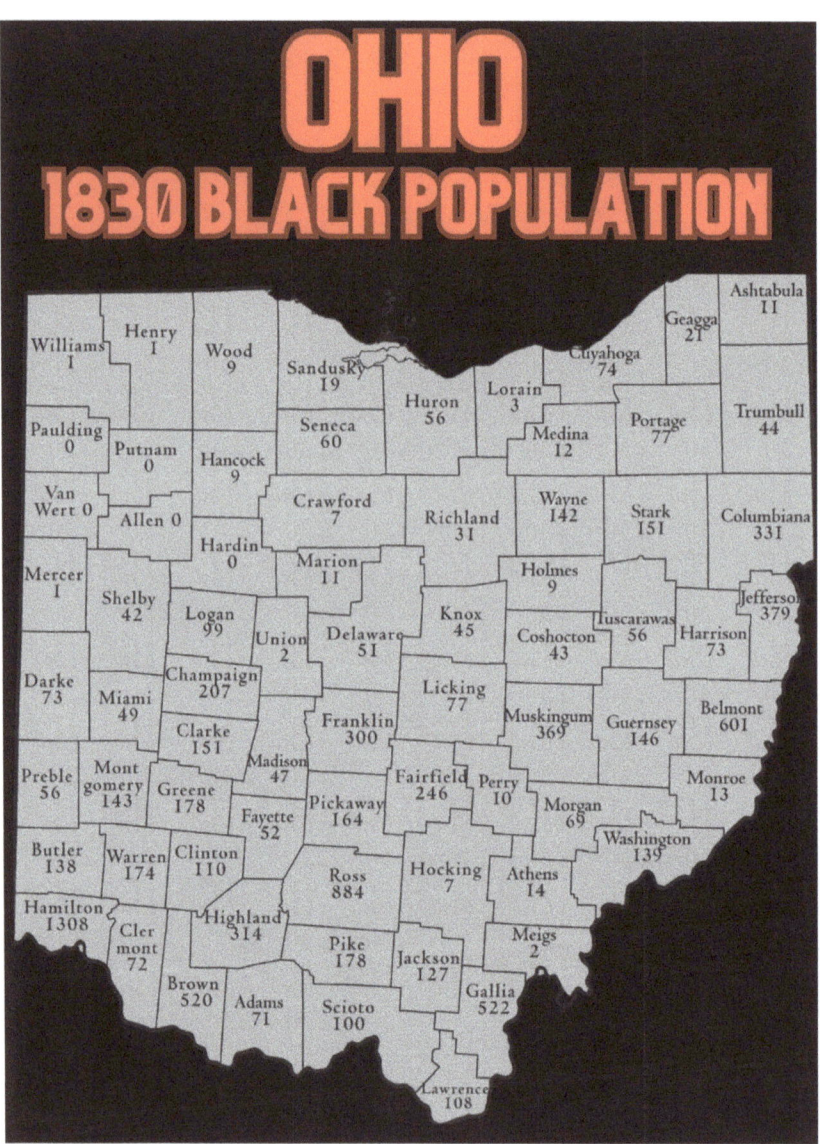

SECOND BAPTIST CHURCH-COLUMBUS' OLDEST BLACK BAPTIST CHURCH, 1836

HISTORIC
UNDERGROUND
RAILROAD SITE

Second Baptist Church cordially received its independence as a mission church from the First Baptist Church on January 7, 1836. Rev. Ezekiel Fields was chosen as pastor from 1836-1839. Formal Articles of Inc. were granted on March 12, 1844 by the 42nd General Assembly of the State of Ohio. Early church locations were 69 Mulberry, 105 E. Gay Street, and 90 E. Rich Street. In 1843, the Palladium of Liberty Newspaper began through meetings at the church. The Ohio Black Laws meant loss of livelihood causing many members to actively participate in the covert operations of the Underground Railroad. The Anti-Slavery Baptist Church in 1847 was led by Rev. James P. Poindexter, along with Rev. Isaiah Redman and member John T. Ward until the two churches merged again in 1858.

BLACK CONDUCTORS OF COLUMBUS

HISTORIC
UNDERGROUND
RAILROAD

Early legislators did not want slavery in Ohio, nor did they want Blacks to settle here. Declaring people of color a menace, they passed the Black Laws. Outside the Statehouse, Blacks went unnoticed. The turnover of black waiters and porters at the Buckeye House aroused no suspicion. White customers overlooked barbers James Poindexter and Andrew Redmond. No one saw John T. Ward, clerk at Zettler's. These men were invisible to all but the desperate faces secreted in attics, barns, smokehouses, and in wagons traveling northward at night to Clintonville. Teamsters Louis Washington and his son Thomas were drivers. "The UGRR was actually going on here in Columbus when I came in 1828," recounted James Poindexter. Conductors David Jenkins, NB Ferguson, and John Bookel were all members of Poindexter's Antislavery Baptist Church.

In 1842, John T. Ward began assisting Shepherd Alexander to convey runaway slaves through Columbus. William Washington, William Ferguson, Jeremiah Freeland, and others were involved as well. "Some one or the other of us was with Alexander on every trip," stated Ward.

CO-SPONSORSHIP OF ODOT AND FRIENDS OF FREEDOM SOCIETY

MELVIN T. JACKSON
Second Lieutenant

Lt Col. Lott Carter

Harold E. Ward

James Eldon Ward & Shanna Ward

Harold E. Ward (Ascari Tshaka)

JOHN T. HARNADAY
35 YEARS EXPERIENCE
AS PENSION AGENT
YELLOW SPRINGS, OHIO

January 26th 1922

Ennis Ward,

#812 East Main Street,

Xenia, Ohio.

Dear Cousin Ennis:--

For the very great kindness shown me by you and your
good wife, I am sending you copy of the John Ward WILL, about
which there is so much ado about. You will notice that I
have attempted to improve on the manner in which it was written
without changing it in any way. But simply made it plainer to
understand.

I had already arranged my business in the office to go with
you and the other folks to-day to Wilmington, but received word
yesterday from Mrs. Shoecraft that owing to Mr. Shoecraft's Machine going bad on them they had to postpone their the trip
The more I study over the action of the Atty. the more now I
believe that there is something in the case for all who are
entitled. Remember me kindly to Mrs. Ward and the children. I hope to be able to go with you all the next time you
go to Wilmington.

Sincerely yours
John T. Harnaday

Simon Ward Sr
1807–1880

LifeStory   Facts   Gallery

Show ⌄

When Simon Ward Sr was born in 1807 in Pittsylvania, Virginia, his father, Samuel, was 41 and his mother, Lucy, was 37. He married Chaney Chana Lynch on June 5, 1830, in Clinton, Ohio. They had 12 children in 31 years. He died on September 10, 1880, in Clarksville, Ohio, at the age of 73, and was buried in Clinton, Ohio.

Daisy D. Ward Bailey

Ward-37942	112	Samuel	Ward	60	1767
Ward-37943	113	Lucy	Ward	56	1771
Ward-37982	114	Aaron	Ward	34	1793
Ward-37989	115	Handy	Ward	20	1807
Ward-37991	116	Charles	Ward	12	1815
Ward-37988	117	Mary	Ward	22	1805
Ward-37990	118	Rachel	Ward	17	1810
	119	Patsy	Ward	10	1817
Ward-32788	120	Hannah	Ward	26	1801
Ward-32790	121	Charles	[Ward]	12 mos	1826
	122	John	Ward	11	1816
	123	Harrison	Ward	8	1819
	124	Lindy/Lindey	Ward	8	1819
Ward-32789	125	Simon	Ward	4	1823
Ward-37984	126	Jack	Ward	30	1797
	127	Christian	[Ward]	20	1807
	128	Lynch	Ward	2	1825
Ward-37986	129	James	Ward	25	1802

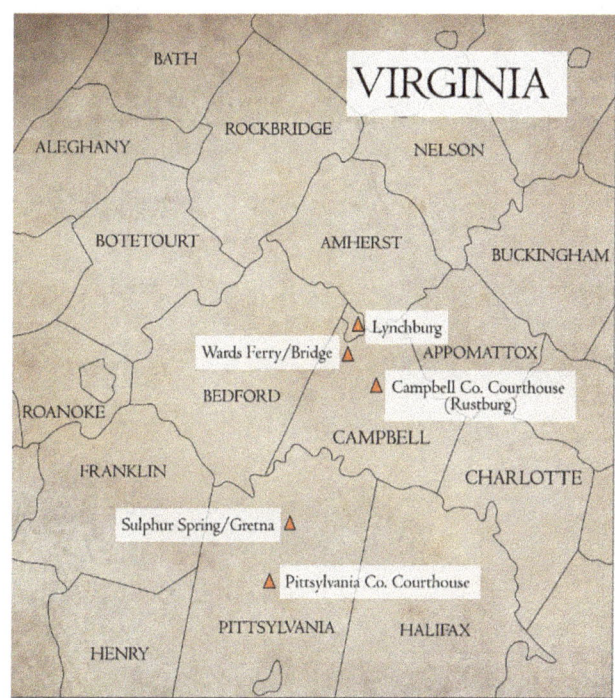

1814 MAP

△ Wards Ferry/Bridge

△ Lynchburg

△ Campbell Co. Court House (Rustburg)

Note: Map likely in error in that Wards Road never ran as far east as the Campbell County Court House at Rustburg.

△ Pittsylvania Co. Court House (Competition/Chatham)

△ Sulphur Spring - Could this be the future Gretna?

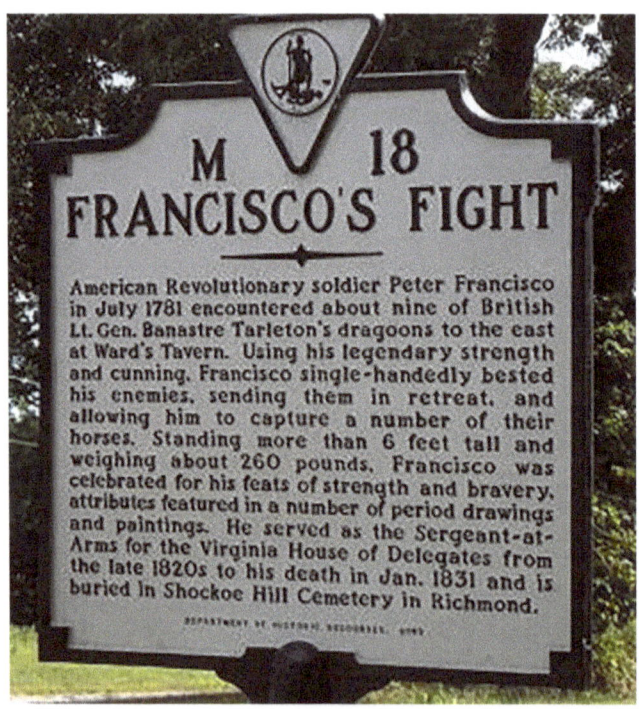

Enslaved Ward Family Gravesite in Virginia

Plantation Owners Gravesite in Virginia

Shanna,

This is a friendly reminder that the signed Agreement and Authorization are due no later than noon today, if you choose to go that route. Should you decide to litigate this matter in Federal court, our name partner and Managing Partner, Larry James will be handling this matter.

You mentioned that you are known in the community. With all due respect, Larry James IS well known in the community. There is no political, business, civic, cultural or arts leader that does not owe Larry anything. More importantly, he and his wife, Donna James, has helped countless of folks down on their luck. The only reason I am bringing this up is because you brought up your "community support." I would hazard a guess that very few people would like to go against Larry James after everything he and Donna has done and continue to do for this community.

Eileen

J. Kenneth Blackwell, Secretary of State
30 East Broad Street
Lower Level
Columbus, Ohio 43215

11/12/2002

RE: E. E. WARD TRANFER & STORAGE COMPANY
REGISTRATION NO: RN245940
ORIGINAL DATE: 3/11/1998

ELDON W WARD
1289 E MAIN ST
COLUMBUS, OH 43205-0110

Dear Sir or Madam:

Please be advised that pursuant to Ohio Revised Code Section 1329.04, the above referenced trade name registration is due to expire. Renewal of the registration for another five (5) year term is available. A renewal form has been enclosed for your convenience.

Please recognize that if not renewed, the registration will be cancelled from our records. If renewal is desired, please complete the enclosed renewal form, and forward the same, together with a filing fee of twenty-five dollars ($25.00) to the **Secretary of State's office, P.O. Box 670, Columbus, Ohio 43216.**

If you have questions regarding this notice, please contact our Customer Service Area at (614) 466-3910 or (toll free) 1-877-SOS-FILE. You may also email our Customer Service area at BusServ@sos.state.oh.us or visit our web site at www.state.oh.us/sos/ to contact us or review your corporate records.

If you have already submitted your renewal, please disregard this notice.

Sincerely,

J. Kenneth Blackwell
Secretary of State

Enclosures

MR. WARD (in buggy) AND VIEW OF WAGON SHEDS.

LARGEST CIRCULATION IN CENTRAL OHIO

THE OHIO STATE JOURNAL

EVERY MORNING IN THE YEAR

THE OHIO STATE JOURNAL CO.

COLUMBUS, OHIO.

ESTABLISHED 1811

BUSINESS
DEPARTMENT

Columbus, O. November 18th, 1911.

The E. E. Ward Transfer & Storage Co,
E. E. Ward, Pres.
171 S. Champion Ave,
City.

Dear Sir:-

We thank you for the display advertising contract, made with our
Mr. F. T. Hooley, and assure you the copy furnished us on this contract will
have our careful attention.

Yours very respectfully,
The Ohio State Journal Co,

Business Manager.

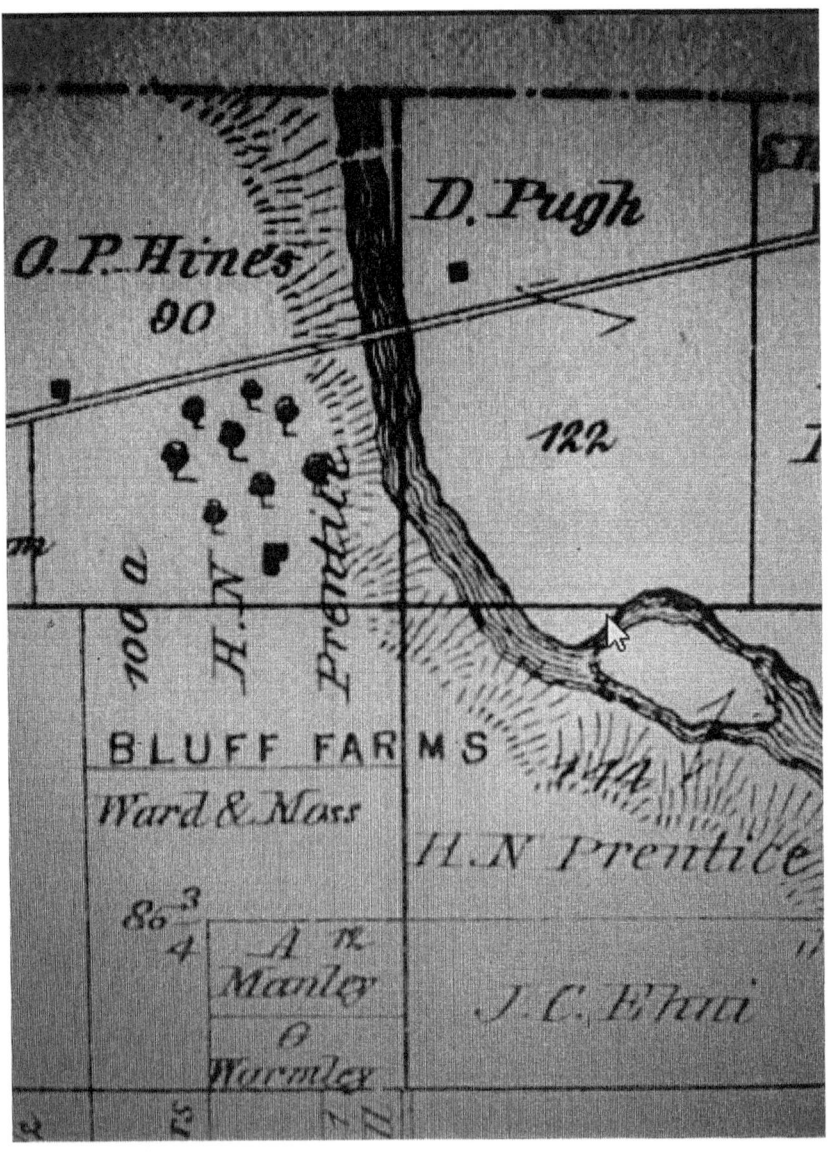